THE INDIAN MUTINY OF 1857

George Bruce Malleson (8 May 1825–1 March 1898) was an English officer born in Wimbledon.

Educated at Winchester, he obtained a cadetship in the Bengal infantry in 1842, and served through the second Burmese War. He was a prolific writer. He had written extensively on the Sepoy Mutiny. His important works include *History of the Indian Mutiny of 1857-58* (six volumes), *History of the French in India* and *The Decisive Battles of India*.

He authored the biographies of the Mughal Emperor Akbar, the French governor-general Dupleix and the British officer Robert Clive for the Rulers of India series.

He died in London on 1 March 1898.

The Indian Mutiny of 1857

G.B. Malleson

RUPA

Published by
Rupa Publications India Pvt. Ltd 1998
7/16, Ansari Road, Daryaganj
New Delhi 110002

Sales centres:
Allahabad Bengaluru Chennai
Hyderabad Jaipur Kathmandu
Kolkata Mumbai

Edition copyright © Rupa Publications India Pvt. Ltd. 1998

ISBN: 978-81-291-0790-9

Fifth impression 2016

10 9 8 7 6 5

Printed at Yash Printographics, Noida

Preface

In writing this short History of the Indian Mutiny of 1857 I have aimed at the compilation of a work which, complete in itself, should narrate the causes as well as the consequences of a movement unforeseen, undreamt of, sudden and swift in its action, and which taxed to the utmost the energies of the British people. Preceding writers on the same subject, whilst dealing very amply with the consequences, have, with one exception, but dimly shadowed forth the causes. The very actors in the Mutiny failed to detect them. Sir John Lawrence himself, writing with the fullest knowledge of events in which he played a very conspicuous part, mistook the instrument for the chief cause. He stopped at the greased cartridge. But the greased cartridge was never issued to the great body of the troops, if indeed to any. There must have been a latent motive power to make of an unissued cartridge a grievance so terrible as to rouse into revolt men whose fathers and whose fathers' fathers had contributed to the making of the British Empire in India. The greased cartridge, too, did not concern those landowners and cultivators of Oudh and the North-western Provinces, who rose almost to a man. What that latent motive power was I have described fully, and I believe truly, in this volume.

My belief in this respect is founded on personal knowledge and personal observation. Locally chief of the Commissariat Department at Kánhpur when, in January 1856, Sir James Outram crossed the Ganges to depose the King of Oudh, I had witnessed the indignation which the very rumour of his purpose caused among the sipáhís of my own guard. I reported their excited state to my superiors, and was laughed at for my pains. But, impressed with the accuracy of my forecast, viz., that the annexation of Oudh would rouse indignation and anger in the sipáhí army, I continued then, and after my transfer, two months later, to an appointment in the Military Audit Department in Calcutta, to keep a careful record of the several occurrences, all apparently of minor import, which supervened when the effects of the annexation of Oudh had been thoroughly realised by the sipáhís. My observations led to the conclusion that they were thoroughly angered, and, a little later, that their minds were being mysteriously worked upon. I kept copious notes of the matters I observed, and I discussed them with my brother officers, without, however, finding that my views were shared by any one of them. It would seem, however, that the officer who held the responsible post of Town Major, Major Orfeur Cavenagh, had, from his own observation, arrived at conclusions not dis-similar. He has narrated in his admirable work[1] the observations forced upon him by the changed demeanour of the natives of the North-western Provinces in 1856. But he, too, stood, amongst high-placed Europeans, almost alone in his convictions. The fact is that, up to the very outbreak of the Mutiny at Mírath, no one, from highest to lowest, believed in the possibility of a general combination. Those, and they could be counted on the fingers of one hand, who endeavoured to hint at an opposite conclusion were ridiculed as alarmists. So ingrained was the belief in the loyalty of the sipáhís, and so profound was the ignorance as to the manner in which their minds were affected, that neither the outbreak of Mírath nor the seizure of Delhí entirely removed it. The tone of the governing classes was displayed when the Home Secretary prated about 'a passing and groundless panic,' and when the acting Commander-in-Chief, an old officer of sipáhís, babbled, in June 1857, of reorganisation. But the fact, nevertheless, remained. Circumstances had proved to me that extraneous causes were at work to promote an ill-feeling, a hatred not personal but national, in the minds of men who for a century had been our truest and most loyal servants. When the Mutiny had been quelled I renewed my researches regarding the origin of this feeling, and, thanks to the confidences of my native friends in various parts of the country, I arrived at a very definite conclusion. That conclusion I placed on record, in 1880, when I published the then concluding volume of a History of the Mutiny, begun by Sir John Kaye, but left unfinished by that distinguished writer. After the publication of that volume I again visited India, and renewed my inquiries among those of my native friends best qualified to arrive at a sound opinion as to the real origin of the Mutiny. The lapse of time had removed any restraints which might have fettered their freedom of speech, and they no longer hesitated to declare that, whilst the action of the Government of India, in Oudh and elsewhere, had undermined the loyalty of the sipáhís, and prepared their minds for the conspirators, the conspirators themselves had used all

---

[1] *Reminiscences of an Indian Official.* By Sir Orfeur Cavenagh. On the subject of the services rendered by this officer, in 1857, I have entered fully in the sixth volume of my larger history.

the means in their power to foment the excitement. Those conspirators, they declared, were the Maulaví of Faizábád, the mouthpiece and agent of the discontented in Oudh; Náná Sáhib; one or two great personages in Lakhnao; the Ráni of Jhánsí; and Kunwar Singh. The action of the land system introduced into the North-west Provinces by Mr Thomason, had predisposed the population of those provinces to revolt. There remained only to the conspirators to find a grievance which should so touch the strong religious susceptibilities of the sipáhís as to incite them to overt action. Such a grievance they found in the greased cartridge. By the circulation of chapátís they then intimated to the rural population that the time for action was approaching. This version of the immediate causes of the Mutiny is known to be true by some at least who will read these pages; it is known to be true by all who have taken the trouble to dive below the surface. I have accordingly given it a prominent place in this volume.

The task of compressing within about four hundred pages the story of a Mutiny which abounded in scenes of action, so many, so varied, so distinct from each other; of a Mutiny in which every station occupied by English men and English women was either a camp or a battle-ground; in the outset of which our countrymen, in the several sub-divisions of India, were in the position of detached parties of a garrison, unable to communicate with headquarters or with one another, suddenly surprised and set upon by men whom they had implicitly trusted; has been one the difficulty of which I never realised until I had taken it in hand. When a writer has at his command unlimited space, his task is comparatively easy. He can then do justice to all the actors in the drama. But I have found it most difficult to mention the names of all who have deserved in a volume every page of which must be devoted to the relation of events. And although my publishers, with a generosity I cannot sufficiently acknowledge, permitted me to increase, by an additional fourth, the number of pages allotted to the series of which this volume is the second issue, I am conscious that I have not sufficiently dwelt upon the splendid individual achievements of many of those who contributed to the final victory. The fact is that there are so many of them. There never has been an event in History to which the principle of the Order of the Day, published by Napoleon on the morrow of Austerlitz, applies more thoroughly than to the Mutiny of 1857. ' "It will be enough for one of you to say," said the Emperor, in his famous bulletin, "I was at the Battle of Austerlitz," for all your fellow-citizens to exclaim, "There is a brave man!" ' Substitute the words 'Indian Mutiny' for the 'Battle of Austerlitz' and the phrase applies to that band of heroes whose constancy, whose courage, and whose devotion saved India in 1857.

One word as to the spelling I have adopted. It is similar to the spelling which appears in the cabinet edition of *Kaye's and Malleson's History*, to the spelling adopted by Captain Eastwick in Murray's admirable guide-books for India, and it is the correct spelling. Some critics have ignorantly remarked that the natives of India employ no definite spelling for their proper names. But this remark betrays the prejudice of the traveller who disdains to learn. The natives use not only a well-defined spelling for their proper names, but every name has a distinct meaning. The barbaric method adopted by our forefathers a century and a half since, when they were ignorant of the native languages, and wrote simply according to the sound which reached ears unaccustomed to the precise methods of an Oriental people, totally alters and disfigures that meaning. Take, for example, the word 'Kánhpur,' written, in accordance with barbaric custom, 'Cawnpore.' Now, 'Kánhpur' has a definite meaning. 'Kánh,' or 'husband,' is one of the favourite names of 'Krishńa.' 'Pur' means 'a city.' The combination of the two words signifies 'Krishńa's city.' But what is the meaning of 'Cawnpore'? It does not even correspond to the pronunciation as the name of the place is pronounced by the natives. It serves to remind us of a period of ignorance and indifference to native methods over which it is surely kind to draw the veil. The same reasoning applies to every proper name in India. It is true I have spelt 'Calcutta,' 'Bombay,' and the 'Ganges' according to the conventional method; but the two places and the river have a long European record, and their names thus spelt are so ingrafted in the connection between India and Europe that it would be pedantry to alter them. But Kánhpur and the places to the north-west and north of it were but little known before the Mutiny, and it seems becoming that the events which brought them into European prominence should introduce them under the names which properly belong to them, and which no European prejudice can permanently alter.

It remains for me now only to acknowledge gratefully the courteous manner in which Messrs W. H. Allen & Co. granted me permission to use, in a reduced form, the plans they had prepared for their larger history of the Indian Mutiny.

27 West Cromwell Road,   **G. B. Malleson**
October 10, 1890.

Contents

CHAPTER I

Introductory

In the history of the world there is no more wonderful story than that of the making of the British Empire in India. It was not the result of deliberate design. The early English settlers on the coasts of India thought only of protecting the small tracts of territory conceded to them against aggression from native princes and European rivals. For a long time they never dreamt even of questioning the sovereign rights of the native princes who exercised authority in the territories nearest to their possessions. The instructions which the agents on the spot received from the directors of the parent Company at home indicated, in the plainest language, that their business was to trade; that to trade advantageously, it was necessary to humour the native princes, to display courtesy and civility, to put away from them all thoughts of aggression. The object of the Company was to pay good dividends. Such a result could only be obtained by the development of peaceful enterprise.

Suddenly, there came a change in the action of the English agents on the Coromandel coast. The English had been the third European nation which had sought to open a profitable trade with India, and which, for that purpose, had secured lodgments on her coasts. Of the two nations which had preceded them, the Portuguese had declined; the Dutch were declining. The vigour and energy of the race which inhabits England was producing, in the rapid increase of the trade, the results which invariably follow the development of those qualities, when a fourth power France, the hereditary rival of England in Europe, began, under the influence of MM. Dumas and Dupleix, to develop, in an extraordinary manner, the resources of a settlement which one of her children, François Martin, had made, under very difficult circumstances, on the same coast. This settlement, called from the town of which Martin had obtained possession of Pondichery, had reached a high state of prosperity under the careful nursing of the immediate predecessor of Dupleix, M. Benoit Dumas. This able man had known how to conciliate the friendship of the native princes on the coast. In return for many civilities and good offices, he had been granted permission to enlist sipáhís and to erect fortifications. Between Pondichery and the English settlement of Madras there had been in his time no thought of hostility. Peace between the rival powers reigned in Europe, and no temptation arose in India to disturb the happy relations of friendship.

In October 1741, M. Dupleix succeeded Dumas at Pondichery. A man remarkably gifted, endowed with a genius which could conceive the largest schemes, he continued that system of ingratiating himself with the native princes, which had been attended with such favourable results in the time of his predecessor. The policy was soon to bear the most brilliant fruits. In 1743, the English and the French had taken opposite sides in the war of the Austrian succession. The battle of Dettingen had been fought (June 16, 1743) before war had actually been declared. But the declaration soon followed, and it was not long before war-like operations, begun in Europe, extended to India.

. Both nations despatched squadrons to the Indian seas. The English squadron, preceded by instructions from the directors of the East India Company to its agent at Madras, Mr Morse, to use it to destroy the French settlement at Pondichery, arrived first. But before Morse could carry out his instructions he was compelled to ask the sanction to the undertaking of the ruler of the country of which Madras formed a part, the Nuwáb of the Karnátik. But that prince was under the spell exercised by Dumas and Dupleix. He refused the permission, and Pondichery was saved.

Two years later the position of the two principal European powers on the Coromandel coast was inverted. The English squadron was absent: the French squadron was on the spot. Dupleix then prepared for his rivals the fate with which they had threatened him. In vain did the English appeal to the Nuwáb of the Karnátik. That prince, gained by Dupleix, declined to interfere in the quarrel between the settlers. The result was that, on September 21, 1746, Madras surrendered to the French, and was promptly occupied by a garrison composed of French troops and of sipáhís trained by French officers.

The capture of Madras by the French is an important event in the history of the connection of France and England with India; for it was indirectly the cause of the development of that sipáhí army, the great outbreak of which, against its masters, it is my object to describe in this volume. It would seem that Dupleix, when pleading to the Nuwáb for permission to attack Madras, had promised that prince that he would transfer it, after he had captured it, to the Nuwáb for disposal. But when the Nuwáb called upon him to fulfil his promise, he displayed great unwillingness to comply. He wished, at least, to level its fortifications, to dismantle it before making it over. The Nuwáb, however, had despatched his son with a force to take possession. To dismantle the place in the presence of that force was impossible. Dupleix determined then to use every diplomatic means at his disposal to persuade the Nuwáb to allow him to retain it. But the young prince who represented the Nuwáb was impatient, and precipitated a contest by cutting off the water supply of the town and fort. The French governor, Desprémesnil, despatched then 400 men and two guns to recover the water springs. It was the first contest on the Coromandel coast between the settlers of either nation and the indigenous population. Up to that time French and English had carefully refrained from all acts of hostility towards the children of the soil. In the princes of the coast they had recognised their landlords, their masters, to whose complaisance they owed the permission to maintain trading stations on the coast. They were to be courted, persuaded, won over, but never opposed. The sortie from Madras of the 2nd November 1746 was, then, a rude infringement of a custom till then religiously observed. Its consequences were momentous. The fire of the two French field-pieces, well directed and continuous, put to flight the cavalry of the Nuwáb. The water springs were regained without the loss by the French of a single man, whilst about seventy Mughal horsemen bit the dust.

The son of the Nuwáb, Máphuz Khán by name, was not present on this occasion. When he heard of it he attributed the result to accident, to bad leading, to any cause but the right one. He would show himself, he said, how these Europeans should be met. He had heard, the very day of the defeat of his cavalry, that a small force, composed of 230 Frenchmen and 700 trained sipáhís, was approaching Madras from Pondichery, and would attempt to cross the little river Adyár, near St Thomé, on the 4th (November). Máphuz Khán had at his disposal 10,000 men. He took at once a resolution worthy of a great commander. He marched with his whole army to St Thomé, occupied a position on the northern bank of the Adyár, so strong and so commanding that he could not fail, if the combatants were at all equal in military qualities, to crush the little force marching on Madras.

Máphuz Khán was on the chosen spot, eager for combat, when the small French force appeared in sight. Paradis, who commanded it, was an engineer, a man who knew not fear, and who was not easily moved from his purpose. He saw the serried masses in front of him, barring his way. To attack them he must wade through the river, exposed to their fire.

Had he hesitated an instant the story of the Europeans in India might have been different. But Paradis recognised, as many English commanders after him have recognised, that the one way for the European to pursue when combating Asiatics is to go forward. He did not hesitate a moment. Without waiting even to reconnoitre, he dashed into the river, scrambled up the bank, formed on it in line, delivered a volley, and charged. The effect was momentous. Never was there fought a more decisive battle, a battle more pregnant with consequences. The army of the Nuwáb was completely defeated. Vigorously pursued, it vanished, never again to appear in line against a European enemy, unless supported by the presence of that enemy's European rival.

It is impossible to over-estimate the effects on the minds of the native princes and native soldiers of Southern India of the victory gained by the French at St Thomé. The famous historian, Mr Orme, who was almost a contemporary, wrote of it that it broke the charm which had invested the Indian soldiers with the character of being 'a brave and formidable enemy.' Another writer[1] has recorded of it that, 'of all the decisive battles fought in India, there is not one more memorable than this. The action at St Thomé completely reversed the positions of the Nuwáb and the French governor. Not only that, but it inaugurated a new era, it introduced a fresh order of things, it was the first decided step to the conquest of Hindustán by a European power.'

There can be no doubt but that the result of the battle gave birth in the mind of Dupleix to ideas of conquest, of supremacy, even of empire, in Southern India. It is no part of this work to follow the course he adopted to secure the triumph of those ideas; but this at least has to be admitted, that the scheme of forming a regular force of trained native soldiers, if it did not actually date from the victory of St Thomé, acquired from it a tremendous impetus. Thereafter the spectacle was witnessed of the representatives of two European nations, longtime enemies in Europe, taking opposite sides in the quarrels of native princes in Southern India, and for that purpose employing not only their own countrymen but natives armed and drilled on the European system, led by European officers, vying with their European comrades in deeds of daring and devotion, and becoming by degrees the main supports of their European masters. After the lapse of a few years the European nation which inaugurated the new system was completely vanquished by its rival. But before that could be accomplished the system had taken a firm hold of that rival. When, in 1756, Clive set out from

---

[1] *The Decisive Battles of India, from 1746 to 1849 inclusive. New Edition. Page 16.*

Madras to recover Calcutta from the hands of Suráju-daulah, he took with him, in addition to his 900 Europeans, 1200 sipáhís, natives of Southern India, armed and drilled on the European system. These men formed the nucleus of that glorious native army which, led by European officers, helped their English masters to win Bengal and Bihár from the satraps of the Mughals; to wrest Banáras and the delta of the Ganges from the Nuwáb Wazir of Oudh; to expel the Maráthás from the North-west Provinces; to establish a frontier on the Satlaj; to invade Afghánistán; and, finally, to acquire the Panjáb.

In another work[2] I have told in detail the principal achievements of that army up to the time when Lord Dalhousie annexed the Panjáb (1849). During that period of a hundred years the organisation of the native army had been more than once altered, but the spirit of devotion to its European officers had been manifested throughout all the changes on many memorable occasions. In the time of Clive the sipáhís had stood firmly by their European masters (1766) when the European troops in India, officers and men, had mutinied. They had never shrunk from following their European officer whithersoever he would lead them. And if, on some rare occasions, some few of them had displayed momentary disaffection, that disaffection had been, up to 1857, the result of feelings in which there was not the smallest tinge of patriotism. Speaking broadly, the result in each instance was the consequence of an attempt, well meant but clumsily carried out, to graft western ideas upon an oriental people. The secret of the influence of the Englishman in India has lain in the fact that he had so conducted himself, in all his relations with the children of the soil, that his word had come to be regarded as equal to his bond. It was only when the sipáhí, at Vellor in 1806, at Barrackpur in 1824, and again in 1852, in the North-western Provinces in 1844, in the Panjáb in 1849–50, deemed that the promises made to him on his enlistment had been deliberately violated, that he displayed an obstinate determination to break with his master rather than to continue service on terms which, it seemed to him, could be disregarded at that master's pleasure.

Action of a different character, although based on the same principle, so dear to the untravelled Englishman, of forcing the ideas in which he has been nurtured upon the foreign people with whom he is brought into contact, assisted, especially after the first Afghán war, to loosen the bonds of discipline, which, up to that period, had bound the sipáhí to his officer. In the time of Clive the sipáhí army had been officered on the principle

---

[2] *The Decisive battles of India.* London: W. II. Allen & Co., 1888. New Edition.

which, in India, is known as the irregular system. The men were dressed in the oriental fashion, the companies were commanded by native officers; the European officers attached to each battalion, few in number, were picked men, selected entirely for their fitness to deal with and command native troops. The powers of the commanding officer were large. He was, to the sipáhí, the impersonification of the British power in India. His word was law. Beyond him the mind of the sipáhí did not care to travel. The sipáhí did not concern himself with regulations and appeals to the Commander-in-Chief. The system had answered admirably. It was in force throughout the reigns of Clive and Warren Hastings, and in no single respect had it failed.

But in course of time the idea came to the ruling authorities in India that great advantage would accrue if the sipáhí regiments were to be remodelled on the system then prevailing in the British army. Just before the great Marquess Wellesley, then Lord Mornington, arrived in India, such a scheme was carried into effect (1796). The dress of the sipáhí was assimilated to that of his European comrades. The native officers, though maintained, were relegated to an inferior position. The English system, with its list of captains, lieutenants, and ensigns, supervised by a colonel, a lieutenant-colonel, and a major, was introduced into the native army, and that army was brought more completely than it had ever been before into the European centralising system.

Fortunately for the tranquillity of British India it was only gradually, almost imperceptibly, that the great powers of the commanding officer were interfered with. Under the new system the sipáhís fought well against Típu Sáhib, against the Maráthás, against the Pindárís, and against the Peshwá. They conducted themselves with their accustomed courage and resolution in the first war with Burma, 1825–26. Then came a period of peace, to be broken only in 1838 by the first invasion of Afghánistán.

That the disasters of the first Afghán war had an effect on the feelings with which the sipáhí had until then regarded his English master is undeniable. During that war he had behaved with remarkable courage, self-denial, and devotion. A distinguished officer who served in it declared on a public occasion, after the return of the troops, that his personal experience had convinced him that, properly led, the sipáhí would follow his English officer anywhere, and would bear uncomplainingly any amount of hardships. But the imagination exercises upon the mind of an oriental an influence which is often not at all understood by the colder nature of the Englishman. Notwithstanding the triumphs of Nott and Pollock in the last phases of the war, the sipáhí recognised that for the first time the enterprise of his English master against a native power had failed. There was no disguising the fact that the English troops had suffered greatly, and had finally retreated; that the soldiers of the Punjáb, a territory which they had traversed on sufferance, had scoffed and jeered at them whenever they came in contact with them. They realised that a heavy blow had been dealt to British prestige. Possibly, with that tendency to exaggeration which characterises imaginative natures, they thought the blow greater than it actually had been.

But the retreat from Afghánistán was but the beginning of many evils. Within two years of the return of the army Lord Ellenborough annexed the province of Sind. The annexation was absolutely necessary, and had the Government of India been ruled by men of Indian experience, that is, by men possessing experience of the natives of India north-west of Bengal, the annexation might have been made a source of strength, instead of for a time weakening the relations of the Government with its native army, and in the end impairing its efficiency.

The first step taken by the Government shook the confidence of the sipáhís in its promises. Up to that time certain extra allowances for food had been granted to all sipáhí regiments serving beyond the then British frontier. Now, service in the hot and arid regions of Sind had always been distasteful to the sipáhí of the Bengal Presidency, but he was reconciled to the discomforts by the promise that, whilst employed in that province, he should receive a considerable addition to his pay. But the Government of India argued that the incorporation of Sind within the British territories had cancelled the prevailing regulations referring to service beyond the Indus, and they notified the fact to the several divisional commanders. The result was to create so great a revulsion in the minds of the sipáhís that the native regiments under orders for Sind refused to march thither.

Ultimately the difficulty was got over, but in a manner not very creditable to the Government. The Bengal troops were relieved of the necessity of · garrisoning Sind, and their place was taken by native troops from Bombay. One commanding officer was dismissed from the service because, to induce his men to march, he had guaranteed them the allowances to which they considered themselves entitled, as indeed, upon the principles of abstract justice, they were. One regiment was disbanded. Sipáhís in others were selected for punishment. The Government of India believed they had by these and kindred measures stayed the plague, when in reality they had shaken to the core the confidence of the sipáhís in their justice, and laid the foundation of the evils which followed thirteen years later.

Those evils were precipitated by the conduct of the Commanders-in-Chief sent out from England, often without the smallest experience of

India, to command, that is, to administer, an army of sipáhís outnumbering, in the proportion of five to one, the European garrison—men born under a different sky, bred in a religion and in the respect of customs regarding which the Commanders-in-Chief knew nothing and desired to know nothing, and animated by sentiments which prompted them either to be the most docile of followers or the most importunate of solicitors. These Commanders-in-Chief were, up to the close of the Mutiny, men trained in the traditions of the Horse Guards, and who, in their narrow view, regarded any deviation from those traditions as an evil to be at all cost eradicated. For a long time they had chafed at the largeness of the powers exercised by commanding officers of native regiments. They were eager to introduce into the guiding of those regiments the rule of red tape and routine. For some time the Adjutants-General, men trained in the native army, and placed at their elbow to prevent the too great exercise of a mischievous zeal, had restrained their action. But after the first Afghán war there arose a series of courtly Adjutants-General who, far from checking, even stimulated the narrow instincts of their chief. It gradually became the fashion at army Headquarters to quote the Horse Guards as the model for all that was practical and military. When it is recollected that in those days the military instincts of the Horse Guards had been displayed by devising a clothing for the European soldier so tight that if he were to drop his bayonet he could scarcely stoop to pick it up, that the weapon known as 'Brown Bess' was lauded up, from the Commander-in-Chief downwards, as the most perfect of weapons, that inventions tending to improve our military system were steadily discouraged, that the highest authorities of the British army—the great Duke himself—deliberately preferred to live in a fool's paradise, declaring that because the British army had been able to go anywhere and do anything in 1814, therefore, without taking advantage of the improvements developed in the course of thirty years of peace, it could accomplish the same results in 1844, it can easily be understood why the Commanders-in-Chief in India, the nominees and adulators of one great man, should do their utmost to bring the native army within the fold of red tape, the fold which they had been taught to regard as the most perfect in the world.

By degrees, then, after the first return from Afghánistán, and when the refusal of the sipáhís to march to Sind afforded an excuse for the contention that the discipline of the native army required to be looked to, the Commanders-in-Chief in India reduced that army to the Horse Guards' standard. They restricted the powers of the commanding officers; they encouraged appeals to army Headquarters; they insisted that promotion to the rank of native officer should be regulated, not by merit, but by seniority. They issued order after order the tendency of which was to impress upon the mind of the imaginative oriental the conviction that the Government desired to pet the sipáhís at the expense of his actual commandant. In this way they undermined the discipline of the army, and made their European regimental officers contemptible in the eyes of their men.

The sipáhís have always obeyed a master who knows how to command. But they will not obey a lay figure. Nor, equally, will they transfer their respect to an unseen authority residing in the lofty hill ranges which over-look the plains of Hindustán. They may use that unseen authority, indeed, to vex and annoy and baffle their own commandant. And that was the manner in which, for a few years immediately prior to the Mutiny, the sipáhís did use it. By petitions against the rulings of the officers appointed to command them, petitions examined and acted upon by the authority in the hills who did not know them, they in many cases rendered the enforcement of a rigid state of discipline impossible.

Whilst the determination of inexperienced Commanders-in-Chief, that is, of Commanders-in-Chief unacquainted with the oriental mind, but tied hand and foot to the traditions of the Horse Guards, was thus under-mining the discipline of native regiments, other causes were supervening to alarm them as to their personal interests. The sipáhís of the Bengal army were enlisted, with the exception of those of six regiments, for service in India only. They were never to be required to cross the sea. It happened, however, in 1852, whilst the second Burmese war was being waged, that the Governor-General, Lord Dalhousie, desired to send a native regiment to that country in addition to those then employed there. There were many ways of accomplishing this end without riding roughshod over the rights and engagements of the sipáhís. Lord Dalhousie might have despatched one of the six regiments pledged to service across the sea, or he might have called for volunteers. He did neither. He arbitrarily selected a regiment stationed at Barrackpur, the sipáhís of which had enlisted on the condi-tion that they were to serve in Hindustán, and in Hindustán only. The sipáhís, whose minds had been emancipated, by the process referred to in the preceding page, from all respect for their commanding officer, had none for a Governor-General who trod upon their privileges. They flatly refused to embark. Lord Dalhousie was placed by his own act in the invidious position of having to succumb. The story spread like wildfire all over India. The effect[3] of it was most disastrous to discipline. In the

---

[3] I am writing from my own personal experience.

lines and huts of the sipáhís the warmest sympathy was expressed for a regiment which could thus successfully defy a Governor-General.

Then followed the crowning act: the act which touched to the quick nine-tenths of the sipáhís in the Bengal army, and many of those serving in the Bombay Presidency. The sipáhís serving in Madras were not affected by it. When the storm came, in 1857, the Madras sipáhís then took no part in the revolt. The case may thus be stated. The majority of the sipáhís serving in the Bengal Presidency, and a proportion of those serving in the Bombay army, were recruited from the kingdom of Oudh. The sipáhís so recruited possessed the right of petitioning the British Resident at the Court of Lakhnao (Lucknow) on all matters affecting his own interests, and the interests of his family in the Oudh dominion. This right of petition was a privilege the value of which can be realised by those who have any knowledge of the working of courts of justice in a native state. The Resident of Lakhnao was, in the eyes of the native judge, the advocate of the petitioning sipáhí. The advantage of possessing so influential an advocate was so great that there was scarcely a family in Oudh which was not represented in the native army. Service in that army was consequently so popular that Oudh became the best recruiting ground in India. Events subsequent to the Mutiny have shown that the reason why it was so regarded lay in the enormous benefits accruing to the sipáhí from a system which made the British Resident his advocate.

All at once this privilege was swept away. The British Government decided to annex Oudh. Oudh was annexed. Sir James Outram was sent from Calcutta to take possession. I happened, at the time, to be the officer at Kánhpur (Cawnpore) upon whom devolved the duty of supplying carriage to the force which was to cross the Ganges and march upon Lakhnao. Never shall I forget the agitation which prevailed in the sipáhí guard over my official quarters when the object of the expedition oozed out. Most of those forming it were Oudh men, and I had to use all the influence I possessed to prevent an outbreak. My native subordinates in the Commissariat department assured me that a similar feeling was being manifested in the lines of the sipáhís. I reported the matter to the general, and I mentioned it to one of the highest of the new officials who passed through the station to take up his post in Oudh. My warnings were disregarded; but when the crisis at Kánhpur arose, and when those regiments displayed against British officers, their own included, a truculent hatred not surpassed, and scarcely equalled, at any other station, they were remembered.

The annexation of Oudh was felt as a personal blow by every sipáhí in the Bengal army, because it deprived him of an immemorial privilege exercised by himself and his forefathers for years, and which secured to him a position of influence and importance in his own country. With the annexation that importance and that influence disappeared, never to return. English officials succeeded the native judges. The right of petition was abolished. The great inducement to enlist disappeared.

Nor was the measure more palatable to the large landowners. The two officers to whom the Government of India confided the administration of the newly annexed province, Mr Coverley Jackson and Mr Gubbins, had been trained in the school the disciples of which, endeavouring to graft western ideas upon an eastern people, had done their best in the North-west Provinces to abolish landlordism in the sense in which landlordism had flourished in those provinces since the time of Akbar. The result of their revolutionary proceedings was shown, in 1857, by the complete sympathy displayed by the civil districts in the North-west Provinces with the revolted sipáhís. It was shown in Oudh by the rising of the landowners throughout the province.

The causes I have stated had brought the mind of the sipáhí, in 1856, to fever heat. He had lost faith in the Government he served. The action of army Headquarters had deprived him of all respect for his officers. He was ready to be practised upon by any schemer. His mind was in the perturbed condition which disposes a man to believe any assertion, however improbable in itself.

Conspirators to work upon so promising a soil were not wanting to the occasion. There was a large amount of seething discontent in many portions of India. In Oudh, recently annexed; in the territories under the rule of the Lieutenant-Governor of the North-west Provinces, revolutionised by the introduction of the land-tenure system of Mr Thomason; in the Southern Maráthá territory, the chiefs of which had been exasperated to the very verge of revolt by an inquiry, instituted under the auspices of a commission, called the Inám Commission, into the titles of estates which they and their forefathers had held without question since the beginning of the century, men's minds were excited and anxious. Suddenly, shortly after the annexation of Oudh, this seething discontent found expression. Who all the active conspirators were may probably never be known. One of them, there can be no question, was he who, during the progress of the Mutiny, was known as the Maulaví.[4] The Maulaví was a very remarkable man. His name was Ahmad-ullah, and his native place was Faizábád in Oudh. In person he was tall, lean, and muscular, with large deep-set eyes, beetle

---

[4] The word 'Maulaví' signifies 'a learned man,' also 'a doctor of law.'

brows, a high aquiline nose, and lantern jaws. Sir Thomas Seaton, who enjoyed, during the suppression of the revolt, the best means of judging him, described him 'as a man of great abilities, of undaunted courage, of stern determination, and by far the best soldier among the rebels.' Such was the man selected by the discontented in Oudh to sow throughout India the seeds which, on a given signal, should spring to active growth. Of the ascertained facts respecting his action this at least has been proved, that very soon after the annexation of Oudh he travelled over the North-west Provinces on a mission which was a mystery to the European authorities; that he stayed some time at Agra; that he visited Dehlí, Mírath, Patná, and Calcutta; that, in April 1857, shortly after his return, he circulated seditious papers throughout Oudh; that the police did not arrest him; that the executive at Lakhnao, alarmed at his progress, despatched a body of troops to seize him; that, taken prisoner, he was tried and condemned to death; that, before the sentence could be executed, the Mutiny broke out; that, escaping, he became the confidential friend of the Begum of Lakhnao, the trusted leader of the rebels.

That this man was the brain and the hand of the conspiracy there can, I think, be little doubt. During his travels he devised the scheme known as the chapátí scheme. Chapátís are cakes of unleavened bread, the circulation of which from hand to hand is easy, and causes no suspicion. The great hope of the Maulaví was to work upon the minds, already prone to discontent, of the sipáhís. When the means of influencing the armed men in the service of the British Government should have been so matured that, on a given signal, they would be prepared to rise simultaneously, the circulation of chapátís amongst the rural population of the North-west Provinces would notify to them that a great rising would take place on the first favourable opportunity.

It is probable that, whilst he was at Calcutta, the Maulaví, constantly in communication with the sipáhís stationed in the vicinity of that city, discovered the instrument which should act with certain effect on their already excited natures. It happened that, shortly before, the Government of India had authorised the introduction in the ranks of the native army of a new cartridge, the exterior of which was smeared with fat. These cartridges were prepared in the Government factory at Dam-Dam, one of the suburbs of Calcutta. The practice with the old paper cartridges, used with the old musket, the 'Brown Bess,' already referred to had been to bite off the paper at one end previous to ramming it down the barrel. When the conspirators suddenly lighted upon the new cartridge, not only smeared, but smeared with the fat of the hog or the cow, the one hateful to the Muhammadans, the other the sacred animal of the Hindus, they recognised that they had found a weapon potent enough to rouse to action the armed men of the races which professed those religions. What could be easier than to persuade the sipáhís that the greasing of the new cartridges was a well-thought-out scheme to deprive the Hindu of his caste, to degrade the Muhammadan?

If the minds of the sipáhís had not been excited and rendered suspicious of their foreign masters by the occurrences to which I have adverted, the tale told by the conspirators would have failed to affect them. For, after all, they, up to January 1857, had had no experience of the greased cartridges. A new musket had been partially issued, and a certain number of sipáhís from each regiment at Barrackpur were being instructed in its use at Dam-Dam. But up to that period no greased cartridges had been issued. The secret of their preparation was, however, disclosed in January, by a lascar employed in their manufacture to a sipáhí, and the story, once set rolling, spread with indescribable celerity. In the olden days, the days before the confidence between the sipáhí and his officer had been broken, the sipáhí would at once have asked his officer the reason for the change. But, in 1857, they sullenly accepted the story. They had been told that the object of their foreign masters was to make them all Christians. The first step in the course to Christianity was to deprive them of their caste. This end could be accomplished insidiously by the defilement to be produced by biting the greased cartridge. Existence without a religion was in their minds intolerable. Deprived of their own, having become outcasts by their own act, they must, in despair, accept the religion of their masters.

That such was the reasoning which influenced them subsequent events fully proved. In the times of the earlier invasions of India by the Muhammadan princes who preceded the Mughals the conqueror had employed compulsion and persecution as the one mode of converting the Hindus. The sipáhís, alarmed and suspicious, could conceive no other. It was in vain that, in the earlier stages of the Mutiny, General Hearsey, an accomplished linguist, addressing the sipáhís in their own language, told them that such ways were essentially foreign to the Christian's conception of Christianity; that the Christian's religion was the religion of the Book; and that conversion could only be founded on the conviction of the mind. They heard, but heeded not. What was this argument but a wile to entrap them? The conspirators had done their work too well. Before the hot season of 1857 had set in there were but few sipáhís in the Bengal Presidency who were not firmly convinced that the greased cartridge was the weapon by means of which their foreign masters had resolved to deprive them of their religion.

No sooner had it become certain that this idea had taken a firm root in their minds than chapátís passed from village to village in the rural districts of the North-west Provinces, announcing to the population that grave events were impending for which it became them to be prepared.

CHAPTER II

The Conspirators

On the 29th of February 1856, Charles John, Viscount Canning, succeeded Lord Dalhousie as Governor-General of India. Lord Canning possessed many qualities which fitted him for the onerous office. The second son of an illustrious statesman, he had himself received the education which trains a man to enter upon a Parliamentary career. He had sat in both Houses, had filled with credit some high offices, and had been a member of the Cabinet of Lord Palmerston which had decided to annex Oudh. To that annexation Lord Canning, as a member of the Cabinet, had given his assent. He was a large-minded man, possessing noble and generous instincts, a taking presence, was a thorough worker, conscientious, scrupulous, and resolute. The only objection which the most captious critic could have made to the appointment was an objection which would have equally applied to the great Marquess Wellesley, and to all the intermediate rulers of India—he possessed no practical knowledge of India and its people.

A statesman, however gifted, despatched from England to rule a country with a population of two hundred and fifty millions, must be for some time after his arrival dependent on the councillors bequeathed to him by his predecessor. Now, the predecessor of Lordx Canning had been a very masterful man: a born ruler of men; a man who required, not councillors with whom to consult, but servants to carry out his orders. In one sense it was a misfortune for Lord Canning that immediately after his arrival he had to depend upon those servants for advice.

Amongst them, doubtless, were some very able men. The ablest of all, Mr John Peter Grant, was a member of his Council. Mr Grant was, in every sense of the term, a statesman. His views were large and liberal. He saw at a glance the point of a question. He decided quickly; unravelled, with remarkable clearness, the most knotty questions, and spoke out with the fearlessness which becomes a real man. If Mr Grant had had a larger personal experience of the people, he would have been one of the greatest of the civil servants of India. But his service had been mainly spent in close connection with Calcutta, and he had no personal knowledge of the country to the north-west of Patná, or of its people.

The military member of Council, General Low, was likewise a man of ability; but he had passed the greater part of his service as Political Agent or as Resident of native Courts. His experience of the native army was, therefore, somewhat rusty.

The legal member of Council, Mr Barnes Peacock, was remarkable for his sound legal acquirements, but he had no experience outside Calcutta.

Of the others, and of all the principal secretaries, it must suffice to state that they were excellent clerks; but not having been accustomed to act on their own initiative, having been accustomed to take their orders from the imperious lips of Lord Dalhousie, they were little fitted to act as councillors to a newly arrived master at a moment when the country was about to pass through a crisis—a crisis the more terrible in that there was not one of them who would allow himself to regard it as possible; not one of them, with the exception of Mr Grant, who believed in its immensity even when it was upon them.

But, at the moment of Lord Canning's arrival, it seemed as though clerks would be as useful to him as councillors. The surface was calm and unbroken. There was not visible on the horizon even the little cloud no bigger than a man's hand. On his journey homewards Lord Dalhousie had written a minute, in which he had painted in roseate hues the condition of India, the contentment of the sipáhís, and the improbability of disturbance from any cause whatever. He had quitted India amid the applause, largely mingled with regret at his departure, of multitudes of sorrowing disciples. By these he was reverenced as the greatest of men. If some captious subaltern dared to insinuate that the discipline of the army had deteriorated, that the minds of the sipáhís were inflamed against their masters, he was silenced by the contemptuous remark that it was improbable that his knowledge could be more deep-reaching than was that of Lord Dalhousie.

On the 29th of February, then, and for the rest of the year 1856, all was calm and smiling on the surface, and Lord Canning was well content with his clerks.

Nor, during the remaining months of 1856, did there occur any overt act on the part of the many discontented throughout India to weaken the impression that the picture painted by Lord Dalhousie in his elaborate minute was absolutely correct. As far as appearances went, the prevailing impression made on the minds of those residing in the great centres of the several provinces was that it was a year of more than ordinary humdrum. It was argued that the strong impression made by Lord Dalhousie on the country and its diverse races remained active even after his departure. Lord Canning simply administered the country on the principles and by means of the men bequeathed to him by his predecessor. He had experienced, indeed, some difficulty with Oudh. Not, indeed, that the question, which was recurring with increasing intensity every day to the minds of the sipáhís,[1] as to the injurious effects which the annexation had produced on their prospects, ever presented itself to Lord Canning or his councillors. The difficulty was caused by the squabbles, amounting to a public scandal, between the two senior members of the Commission whose administration had supplanted that of the deposed king, Mr Coverley Jackson and Mr Martin Gubbins. The scandal lasted throughout the year, and was only terminated by the removal of Mr Jackson, in January of the year following, and the appointment in his place of one of the most illustrious of the men who have contributed to the securing on a firm foundation of the British rule in India—the wise and virtuous Sir Henry Lawrence. The task bequeathed to Sir Henry was no light one; for the principle which had sown discontent throughout the North-west Provinces, the principle of grafting western ideas on an eastern people—a principle which he had combated all his life—had made every landowner in Oudh a rebel at heart.

There was another event, outside India indeed, but connected with India, which occupied the attention of Lord Canning during the first year of his incumbency of office, and which temporarily somewhat diminished his power of grappling with any military difficulty which might arise. I refer to the war with Persia.

Up to the year 1856, certainly, it had been a cardinal principle of British policy that Persia was never to possess Herát. Herát and Kandahár were the two points in Western Afghánistán which commanded the lines always followed, from the time of Alexander to that of Ahmad Sháh, by the invaders of India, and which, therefore, it was necessary should be held by the friends of British India, if not by British India herself. During the first war waged by Great Britain with Afghánistán, Persia had posed as a pawn pushed forwards by Russia to gain a dominant position on the Indian frontier. But, in 1838, Russia was disinclined to support her pawn. She was more prepared for action when the Crimean war broke out. But when the Sháh of Persia realised the fact that the powerful nation which had filched from him some of his most fertile provinces was in deadly grip with England and France, he suspended his insidious action regarding Herát until he should be able to form a definite opinion as to

---

[1] Vide page 15.

the result of the struggle. He resumed that insidious action as soon as he recognised that the peace of Paris had given Russia a free hand to subdue the barrier of the Caucasus. Regarding Russia as fully occupied, and England as exhausted, he despatched an army to besiege Herát. The ruler of the province of which Herát was the capital, who occupied a position of semi-independence, at once hoisted British colours, and implored the assistance of the Amír Dost Muhammad. Various circumstances, into which it is not necessary to enter, gave indications that the Persians would be resisted to the last. However, it was not so, and before any steps could be taken Herát had fallen.

The clear mind of the then Prime Minister of Great Britain, the resolute Lord Palmerston, had already recognised the importance of the situation, and he resolved to compel Persia to retire. The means he adopted were those best calculated to obtain the result aimed at with the smallest expenditure of blood and money. He directed the formation of a mixed force of English and Indian troops, to be commanded by Sir James Outram, to attack Persia on the side of the Persian Gulf, and he authorised the Governor-General of India to come to a cordial understanding with the Amír of Afghánistán.

Before the army could land on the Persian coast, Herát, I have said, had fallen. But very soon afterwards the Commissioner of the Panjáb, Mr John Lawrence, held at Peshawar (January 1857) that interview with Dost Muhammad which resulted in a cordial understanding between that sagacious prince and the stern and resolute representative of the might of Great Britain. Later still, Outram, landing at Bushir, gained two victories, which had the effect of forcing the Sháh to sue for peace. The consequence was that, in May 1857, he resigned all claim to Herát, which he surrendered, and signed, by his agents, at Paris, a treaty of peace. The troops composing Outram's force were thus available in May for any service which Lord Canning might require at their hands.

During the year the circumstances attendant upon the refusal of the 38th Regiment N. I. to proceed by sea to Burma had caused Lord Canning to look up an Act, already drafted, having for its object the so altering of the terms of the enlistment of the sipáhí as to make, in the future, every regiment available for service across the seas. The Act did not touch the interests of sipáhís already enlisted. It referred simply to those who might enter the service thereafter. In July 1856 that Act became law. In itself the Act was a just and righteous Act. Issued at any other time, it would have caused no feeling whatever. The men of the six regiments already enlisting for general service were of as high a caste as were the men who engaged only to serve locally. But the minds of the sipáhís were excited. The annexation of Oudh had caused them to lose faith in their foreign masters. And it is quite possible that the alteration, which did not escape the watchful eyes of the men who were fomenting disorder, acted as an additional argument to prove that gradual steps were to be taken to deprive them of their caste.

I have already referred to the action of the Maulaví of Faizábád as being instrumental in creating and increasing the undercurrent of hostility to British rule through Bengal and the North-west Provinces. It is impossible, however, to leave this subject without mentioning the action of the son of the ex-Peshwá, Bájí Ráo, and his agent, Azím-ullah Khán. It is the more necessary that such mention should be made, because, whatever may be the opinion of Europeans saturated with the western ideas, and with the conceit those ideas often engender, there can be no doubt but that, during the Mutiny, on the morrow of the Mutiny, and at the present day, the cultivated natives of India attributed and attribute a great deal of the bitterness attendant on the uprising to the treatment meted out to Náná Sáhib by the Government of India. I know that it has been contended, and recently most ably contended,[2] that that treatment was absolutely just. It was just according to western ideas. But the oriental mind does not admit of the validity of an agreement which deprives a man of his kingdom and makes no provision for his family after his death. Such was the grievance of Náná Sáhib. He had no title in law. But the natives of India believed then, they believe still, that he had a moral claim superior to all law.

The case may thus be stated. The Peshwá had been, by virtue of his title, the lord of all the Maráthá princes. Of all the Peshwás, Bájí Ráo had been the most false to his own countrymen, and the worst. But for many years he had been loyal to the British. Tempted, however, in 1817, by the rising of Holkar and the war with the Pindárís, and hoping to recover the lost influence of his House, he had risen, had been beaten, and, in 1818, had thrown himself on the mercy of the British. He was deprived of his dominions, and granted a pension for life of eight lakhs of rupees. He took up his residence at Bithor, near the military station of Kánhpur, adopted a son, and lived a quiet life till his death in 1851.

The Government of India permitted his adopted son, whose name was Dhundu Pant, but who was generally known as Náná Sáhib, to inherit the savings of Bájí Ráo, and they presented to him the fee-simple of the property at Bithor. But Náná Sáhib had to provide for a very large body of followers, bequeathed to his care by Bájí Ráo; and the two British Commissioners who, in succession, superintended the administration of

[2] Sir William Hunter's *Dalhousie*, 162–63.

the estate supported the proposal made from Bithor that a portion of the late ex-Peshwá's allowance should be reserved for the support of the family. They had some reason for their suggestion, for when, some little time before his death, Bájí Ráo had petitioned the Home Government that his adopted son might succeed to the title and pension of Peshwá, whilst the grant of the title was refused absolutely, the question of the pension was refused for future consideration, that is, until the seat of the ex-Peshwá should be vacant.

It seems to me that high policy should have shown some consideration for the heir of one who had been the lord of Western India, and whose territories we had taken. A slight relaxation of the hard and fast policy characteristic of Lord Dalhousie's rule might have saved the British from many future troubles. When, in 1844, the House of Sindhiá, defeated in battle, was at the feet of Lord Ellenborough, that nobleman imposed upon it no penalty. His generosity bore splendid fruit in 1857–58. Far different was the result of the policy pursued towards Náná Sáhib. Lord Dalhousie declared the recommendation made by the two Commissioners in his favour to be 'uncalled for and unreasonable'. He directed that 'the determination of the Government of India may be explicitly declared to the family without delay'. The determination was consequently so declared. Ought we to wonder that, in 1857, the crab-tree did produce the crab-apple?

Náná Sáhib appealed to the Court of Directors against the decision of the Governor-General of India. His appeal was couched in logical, temperate, and convincing language. He asked why the heir to the Peshwá should be treated differently from other native princes who had fallen before the Company. He instanced the case of Dehlí and of Maisur; and with reference to the assumption made in argument against him that the savings of his father were sufficient to support him, he asked whether it was just that the economical foresight of the father should militate against the moral claims of the son. The argument, which would have been accepted in any native Court in India, which was convincing to the two hundred and fifty millions who inhabited that country, had no effect whatever on the minds of the western rulers who governed the country from Leadenhall Street. Their reply emulated in its curtness and its rudeness the answer given by Lord Dalhousie. They directed the Governor-General to inform the memorialist 'that the pension of his adoptive father was not hereditary, that he has no claim whatever to it, and that his application is wholly inadmissible.' The date of the reply was May 1853. It bore its fruit at Kánhpur in June 1857.

Náná Sáhib accepted it with apparent composure, but it rankled in his bosom. To prosecute his claims he had, early in the year, despatched to

England a young Muhammadan in his service, Azím-ullah Khán by name, of a pleasant presence and a taking address. Before Azím-ullah could reach England judgment had already been recorded. Being in the receipt of a sufficient allowance from his master, the young man stayed in England, and entered freely into the pleasures of English life. But he always had an eye to the interests of Náná Sáhib. Whilst he was yet in England the Crimean war broke out. Shortly afterwards there came from the seat of war those stories of suffering which, from his place in the House of Commons, the late Lord John Russell described as 'horrible and heartrending.' The imaginative mind of the young oriental came to the conclusion that some terrible disaster was about to befall the British army. Were such to occur, there might be some hope for Náná Sáhib. He proceeded, then, to the seat of war, entered into communication with foreigners of diverse nations, and from his conversations with them, and from his own personal inspection, came to the conclusion that England, the England which had asserted herself with so much haughtiness in India, was on the brink of destruction, that it would require but a united effort on the part of the princes and people of her great dependency to 'push her from her stool.' With these convictions fresh and strongly rooted in his mind he returned, in 1856, to the Náná at Bithor. Shortly after his return the Náná paid a somewhat mysterious visit to Lakhnao, accompanied by Azím-ullah and a considerable following. I have called his visit 'mysterious,' for it so impressed the English authorities in that city that Sir Henry Lawrence, who was then Chief Commissioner, wrote to Sir Hugh Wheeler, commanding at Kánhpur, to caution him not to depend upon the loyalty of Náná Sáhib. It is not to be doubted that Náná Sáhib took advantage of his visit to enter into negotiations with the discontented nobles of the province, and to concert with them the outlines, at least, of a general plan of action.

Whilst the province of Oudh and the district of Bithor were thus fast becoming hotbeds of conspiracy, a similar process was taking place through the length and breadth of the North-west Provinces. That the system known as 'the village system,' under which the heads of villages represented, before the law, the communities of which they were the hereditary chiefs, may not have been a system which recommended itself theoretically to a ruler nurtured in western ideas may be conceded. But that system was rooted in the soil. The great Akbar, when engaged in the task of consolidating and systematising the territories he had conquered, had attempted to introduce reforms which would have tended to greater centralisation. But, after a few months of experiment, he shrunk from a task which, he recognised, would rouse against him the feelings of his subjects. Where Akbar had feared to tread, the English, guided by the rash hand of Mr Thomason, had rushed in. The result was that throughout the districts over which he had ruled, in Juánpur and Azamgarh, in Agra, Kánhpur, and the adjoining districts, throughout Bundelkhand, there reigned a discontent which lent itself very readily to the schemes of the major conspirators. The advocates of Mr Thomason's reforms have endeavoured, under the shield of anonymous criticism, to controvert this assertion. But facts are stubborn things. I have had it from the mouths of many influential native gentlemen, and from English officials concerned, that the grievance which caused disaffection was the harsh introduction, and the still harsher enforcement, of the Thomasonian system. And there remains the fact, which cannot be controverted, that in India the disaffection was greatest, and the hatred against Europeans most pronounced, in the districts to which that system had been applied.

Not very far distant from Agra there was a powerful chieftain who, from causes similar to those which had influenced Náná Sáhib, regarded herself as having been grievously wronged, and who therefore hated the English with all the bitterness of a woman who had been contemned. This chieftain was the Rání of Jhánsí. She was largely gifted, possessed great energy, had borne, up to the period upon which I am entering, 'a high character,' being 'much respected by everyone at Jhánsí.[3] But the hand of the despoiler had lashed her into a fury which was not to be governed. Under Hindu law she possessed the right to adopt an heir to her husband when he died childless in 1854. Lord Dalhousie refused to her the exercise of that right, and declared that Jhánsí had lapsed to the paramount power. In vain did the Rání dwell upon the services which in olden days the rulers of Jhánsí had rendered to the British Government, and quote the warm acknowledgments made by that Government. Lord Dalhousie was not to be moved. He had faith in his legions. With a stroke of his pen he deprived this high-spirited woman of the rights which she believed, and which all the natives of India believed, to be hereditary. That stroke of the pen converted the lady, of so high a character and so much respected, into a veritable tigress so far as the English were concerned. For them, thereafter, she would have no mercy. There is reason to believe that she, too, had entered into negotiations with the Maulaví and Náná Sáhib before the explosion of 1857 took place.

Such, then, were the conspirators. The inhabitants of Oudh, directed mainly by the Maulaví and a lady of the royal House known as the Begum, the inhabitants of the North-west Provinces, goaded into bitter hostility

---

[3] Report of the Political Agent at Jhánsí.

by the action of the Thomasonian system, and the Rání of Jhánsí. The executive council of this conspiracy had arranged, in the beginning of 1857, to act upon the sipáhís by means of the greased cartridge, upon the inhabitants of the rural districts by the dissemination of chapátís. This dissemination was intended as a warning that the rising was imminent. It was further decided that the rising of the sipáhís should be simultaneous, and more than once the actual day was fixed. Providentially something always happened to prevent the explosion on that day. The splutterings which occurred on such occasions served to give timely warning to the Government. The delays which followed the warning were partially utilised. It was not, however, till the rising actually took place at Mírath that the Government realised the real nature, though not the full extent, of the danger. That they never realised it thoroughly until after the massacre of Kanhpúr we have the evidence of their own words and their own actions to prove. Indeed, I may go so far as to declare that many of the actors in the drama failed to realise to their dying day that the outbreak was not merely a mutiny which they had to combat, but a vast conspiracy, the threads of which were widely spread, and which owed its origin to the conviction that a Government which had, as the conspirators believed betrayed its trust was no longer entitled to respect or allegiance.

CHAPTER III

The First Mutterings of the Storm

The effects of the workings of the conspirators on the minds of the population of the North-west Provinces soon made themselves manifest by the change of their usually respectful demeanour. Major Orfeur Cavenagh, an officer of great shrewdness and perspicacity, who filled the important office of Town-Major of Fort William in Calcutta, visited, in October and November 1856, the districts just beyond Agra. He had been struck everywhere by the altered demeanour of the sipáhís, and loyal natives had reported to him the great change which had taken place in the feelings of the natives generally towards the English. Disaffection, he was assured, was now the rule in all classes. To the clear vision of this able officer it was evident that, unless precautions were taken, some great disaster would ensue. Feelings so evidenced as to become the common talk of the community could not longer be repressed. In the middle of January occurred that incident regarding the greasing of the cartridges to which I have referred in the first chapter. It happened in this wise. A lascar engaged in the factory at Dam-Dam asked a Brahman sipáhís to let him have a drink of water from his lotah, or brass pot. The sipáhí indignantly refused, on the ground that his caste would not permit him to use the lotah afterwards if it should be defiled by the drinking of a man of a lower position in the Hindu hierarchy. The lascar, in reply, laughed at him for talking of defilement, when he said, 'You will all soon be biting cartridges smeared with the fat of the cow and the pig.' He then told the sipáhí the method of the new cartridges. The incident occurred when the minds of the sipáhís had been inflamed, in the manner already recounted, to a high state of tension. The story spread like wildfire. Thence-forward the sipáhís were as soft clay in the hands of the chief conspirators.

Some of these, it cannot be doubted, were to be found amongst the numerous followers of the King of Oudh. The Government of India had permitted that prince, on his removal from the province of which he was still the titular king, to take up his residence in a suburb of Calcutta. He had arrived there in April 1856 with a numerous following. His quarters had already become notorious as the Alsatia of Calcutta. If, as is probable, he was no party to the intrigues carried on in his name, or on his behalf, there were yet many of those who adhered to him who were less scrupulous. These men were the fellow-countrymen of the majority of the men who served the British, and entirely sympathised with them. Subsequent events proved that communications between the sipáhís in Fort William and at Barrackpur and some of the King's adherents had been frequent. It was unfortunate that, at such a period, at a crisis so momentous, so large a number of exiles from Oudh, sharing the indignation generally felt among the natives at the annexation of that province, should have been located close to a populous city, dependent for its safety on one weak European regiment.

Important consequences speedily followed the discovery of the fact regarding the greased cartridges. On the 26th of January the telegraph house at Barrackpur was fired. The same day one of the sergeants attached to Fort William reported to Cavenagh a remarkable conversation, between two sipáhís, which he had overheard. It was to the effect that the Europeans forming the garrison were entirely in the power of the sipáhís; that it would be easy to master the arsenal and the magazines, to slay the Europeans as they slept, then to possess themselves of the fort. They added that the firing of the telegraph house was the first incident in the far-reaching plot.

Cavenagh, who, as Town-Major, was responsible to the Governor-General for the safety of Fort William, took at once measures to baffle the designs of which he had been informed, and then drove straight to Lord Canning to report the circumstance to him. Lord Canning listened to Cavenagh with the deepest interest, and sanctioned the measures he proposed. These were to transfer from Dam-Dam, where one wing of the regiment which was responsible for the safety of the Presidency, the 53rd foot, was located, one company to Fort William. For the moment the outbreak was deferred.

Many little circumstances came at this period to intimate to the few who preferred not to live in a fool's paradise that something strange was impending. At Barrackpur, on the left bank of the river Huglí, fifteen miles above Calcutta, were stationed four native regiments—the 2nd Grenadiers, the 34th N. I., the 43rd Light Infantry, and the 70th N. I. At Barhámpur, 120 miles above Calcutta and five below Murshídábád, the capital of the Nuwáb-Názims of Bengal, was one native regiment, the 19th N. I. Between Calcutta and Dánápur, in Bihár, 344 miles from the capital, there was but one English regiment, the 53rd, already referred to, and that was, as I have said, distributed between Dam-Dam and Calcutta. The space of 344 miles was thus without European guardianship. For, though there was one regiment, the 10th foot, at Dánápur, there were also stationed there three regiments of native infantry, the 7th, the 8th, and the 40th.

There is reason to suppose that communications had passed at least as early as February between the men of these several regiments, and even of those stationed further north-westward. Small commands, treasure parties, and the post afforded ample opportunities for such exchange of ideas. One of these communications gave to the Government the first intimation of the general feeling. On the 18th and 25th of February two small detachments of one of the regiments stationed at Barrackpur, the 34th, a regiment peculiarly tainted, arrived at Barhámpur. The men of the 19th N. I., there located, received their comrades of the 34th with effusion. The evening after the arrival of the second detachment the talk between the two parties was a talk of more than ordinary significance. The men of the 34th poured into the willing ears of their hosts all their grievances. They related the antecedent causes, of which I have spoken, which had led them to distrust their foreign masters. They then dwelt on the story of the cartridges, of the alleged mission of Lord Canning to force Christianity upon them, and added their determination, and that of their brethren at Barrackpur and elsewhere, to take the first opportunity to rise in revolt.

This tale, told with all the fervour of sincerity—for it cannot be too strongly insisted upon that throughout these proceedings, and those which followed, the sipáhís were but the dupes of the able men who had planned the conspiracy—produced a remarkable effect on the minds of the men of the 19th N. I. They brooded over the information all the day following. They had not received the new rifle, and the cartridges in their magazine were innocent of the slightest stain of grease. They were the common paper cartridges to which they had been accustomed for years, the only change being that the paper in which they were wrapped was of a different colour. Yet when, in the course of the day, their commanding officer, Colonel Mitchell, ordered a parade with blank cartridges for the following morning, a great perturbation was visible in the lines. The men seriously believed that they were about to be juggled out of their religion by means of cartridges. How, they could not at the moment say. But the suspicion which had fallen on their minds had bred a great fear. Their non-commissioned officers first refused to receive the cartridges. The threat that those who should continue to refuse would be brought to a court-martial had the effect of inducing them to take them. But that night the whole regiment sat in deliberation. They dreaded lest by the use of the cartridges they should commit themselves to an act which might deprive them of their caste. The reader may ask how that was possible, considering that the cartridges were similar to those they had used for a century. The answer is that fanaticism never reasons. The Hindus are fanatics for caste. They had been told that their religion was to be attempted by means of the cartridges, and their minds being, for the reasons already given, in an excited and suspicious condition, they accepted the tale without inquiry. They therefore rose in a tumult, resolved to defy their officers. That same evening the information that the sipáhís of his regiment were in a state of great excitement and perturbation, on account of the cartridges, was conveyed to Colonel Mitchell. The officers of the Bengal army, as a body, were distinguished by the trust they reposed in their men. In estimating their conduct, it should be remembered that most of them had been associated with the sipáhís all their lives; that they had done their duty by them; that in Afghánistán, in the Panjáb, in the wars in Central India, these men had followed wherever they had led; that they knew that in the matter of proselytism the sipáhís had no real reason for their fears. Oudh had been annexed but little more than a year, and the effect of that annexation on the minds of the sipáhís had not then been disclosed to them. Colonel Mitchell was an officer with a good reputation; he understood the sipáhís as the sipáhís had been up to 1857. But he was not more discerning than his fellows; not more prescient than the Government he served. The news that the sipáhís were in a state bordering on mutiny was revelation to him. He could not comprehend why they should rise, or why they should even be excited. The cartridges, which he was told formed the pretext for the sudden ebullition, were, he well knew, the cartridges which had been used without a murmur throughout the period of his service. But what was he to do? His men—the men of the regiment for the good conduct of which he was responsible to the Commander-in-Chief and the Government—were gesticulating in front of the lines, and were in a state of incipient mutiny. Mitchell did his duty like the good soldier that he was; he rode down to the lines, accompanied by his adjutant, and sending for the native officers to the quarterguard, there addressed them. He told them that there was no reason for the fears expressed by the men; that the cartridges were similar to those which had been served out and used from time immemorial; that there was no question of asking the sipáhís to bite them or to use them in any other way but in that to which they were accustomed. Having thus explained the groundlessness of the fears of the sipáhís, he added that they were by their conduct placing themselves in a position which the Government could not tolerate; that the men who, after his explanation, should persist in refusing to obey his orders would be brought to a court-martial, and suffer the consequences. He concluded by urging the native officers so to influence the men that the name of the regiment should not be blackened.

Colonel Mitchell might as well have spoken to the winds. He told his native officers what Sir John Hearsey at Barrackpur, and what commanding officers all over the country subsequently told theirs, but he told it in vain. There is no terror like a religious terror; and there can be no doubt that the astute fomentors of the revolt—the men of Oudh, of the North-west Provinces, and of the Bundelkhand—had so saturated the minds of the sipáhís at Barrackpur and elsewhere with a real terror, that not all the words of the most gifted men on earth would have sufficed to expel it. The Barrackpur sipáhís had in a moment communicated their fears to those of Barhámpur. The native officers listened silently, and promised to do all they could to calm the excitement. Mitchell returned to his quarters confident that he had done all he was capable of, but that 'all' was little indeed.

However, there was the parade to be held the following morning. To countermand that now would be an act of weakness of which Mitchell was incapable. But the thought never occurred to him. Scarcely had he reached his home when information reached him that the men had risen and were in open revolt.

It was too true. Whether the native officers had correctly interpreted Mitchell's words to their men; or whether, as is more probable, their minds were under the influence which swayed them, cannot be certainly known. The fact remains that before midnight the regiment rose as one man, the sipáhís loading their muskets, and shouting violently.

There were at Barhámpur a detachment of native cavalry and a battery of native artillery. It was presumable, at that early stage of the great revolt, that to these the contagion had not extended. Mitchell then, as soon as he reached his quarters, ordered these to turn out. The order had been given but a few moments, when information reached him that his men had risen. Resolved to stop the mischief, he gathered his officers around him, and proceeded, accompanied by the guns, to the parade ground. The cavalry had preceded him thither.

There he met his men, excited but not violent, and there he harangued them. He spoke well and to the point, and finally wrung from them a promise that they would return to their duty, provided the artillery and cavalry were first ordered back to their lines. Mitchell's hands were tied. With the 200 men behind him he could not, even if they had been loyal, have coerced his 800 sipáhís. After events proved that, had he resorted to force, the men behind him would have joined the revolted regiment, and a catastrophe would have been precipitated which might, for the moment, have reduced the English in India to the greatest extremities. With admirable prudence, then, Mitchell sent back the cavalry and artillery. The men of the 19th then submitted, and returned to their lines.

The following morning the excitement was apparently forgotten by the sipáhís. They fell in for parade, and obeyed the orders given as in their palmiest days. But their suspicions were not lulled. Every night they slept round the bells of arms[1] in which their muskets were lodged instead of in the huts which formed their lines. Mitchell, meanwhile, reported the matter to his superior authorities. A Court of Inquiry was ordered, and after an investigation which, under the circumstances, may be styled prolonged, the Government, missing the point, choosing to shut their eyes to the fact that the conduct of the 19th was a premature movement of a plot which had its roots all over the country, determined to treat it as a local incident, which had attained undue proportions owing to the violent measures taken by Colonel Mitchell.[2] The Governor-General in Council, therefore, resolved to disband the 19th, and to make a scapegoat of Colonel Mitchell. Meanwhile, events were occuring under the very eyes of the members of the Government which should have convinced them that the Mutiny they were about to punish was not confined to the 19th.

---

[1] The brick buildings in which the muskets of the sipáhís were stored after parade were called "bells of arms," they being built in the form of a bell.

[2] Mitchell had committed no violence, nor had he used violent language. But his words were misquoted in order to support the then fashionable theory that there was no general feeling of mistrust among the sipáhís.

CHAPTER IV

The Spread of the Epidemic

The conduct of the men of the 19th N. I. at Barhámpur was known to the authorities in Calcutta on the 4th of March. To them, I have said, it appeared to be rather the consequence of the blundering of the commanding officer than of a widespread feeling of discontent among the sipáhís. But, whatever might be the cause, it was a fact which they had to deal with, and to deal with promptly and with effect.

The Commander-in-Chief of the army, General Anson, was in the Upper Provinces; the Adjutant-General was at Mírath; but the Governor-General, Lord Canning, and all the Secretaries to Government, were in Calcutta. These had, then, all the administrative means at their disposal for dealing promptly and effectively with revolt.

Of the terror which the notion of the greased cartridge had spread throughout the minds of the sipáhís they had had evidence since the 22nd of January, the day on which the conversation of the lascar at the Dam-Dam factory with the Brahman sipáhís had been reported to them. The general commanding at Barrackpur, General Hearsey, an officer who had passed his career in the native army, and who understood the character of the sipáhís, their language, and their idiosyncracies, had, when reporting the circumstance, recommended that the difficulty might be met by allowing the sipáhís at the depôt to grease their own cartridges. The Government had caught at the idea, and on the 27th January the official sanction had been given to the suggestion. It was ascertained at the same time that, although many cartridges had been greased at Dam-Dam, not one had been issued. The Government then, whilst according their sanction to General Hearsey's suggestion, transmitted orders by telegraph to the Adjutant-General to issue to the several musketry-depôts only cartridges free from grease, and to permit the sipáhís to do the greasing themselves. But the concession of the Government of India had the effect of bringing into prominence the ignorance of the executive branch of the army. The Adjutant-General, a man who had served the greater part of his career with the sipáhís, wired back that the concessions of the Government would rouse the very suspicion they were intended to allay; that for years past the sipáhís had been using greased cartridges, the grease being mutton fat and wax; and that he begged that the system might be continued. The Government, the Military Secretary of which was likewise an officer who had served with sipáhís, raised no objection to this proposal, but replied that the greased cartridges might be issued, provided the materials were only those mentioned by the Adjutant-General.

How the Adjutant-General managed to mislead the Government, and how the Government permitted themselves to be misled on this occasion, seems extrordinary. The Government had the fact before them that up to that moment no greased cartridges had ever been issued to the native army. That army still used the old 'Brown Bess' musket, and for that weapon unsmeared paper cartridges were invariably employed. It is true that a few regiments had rifle companies, or one company armed with rifles, and that, for facilitating the driving home of the bullet used with these, patches smeared with wax had been served out. No suspicion had ever attacked to these patches. But for the Adjutant-General, the right-hand man of the Commander-in-Chief, seriously to argue that the issue of these patches warranted him in remonstrating with the Government against their order forbidding the issue of greased cartridges, and for the Government to accept his statement that for some years greased cartridges had been issued, argued an ignorance and an absence of commonsense sufficient to account for the many grave blunders which followed.

Such had been the condition of matters at the end of January. There had been sufficient displays of dissatisfaction to cause grave suspicions, and that was all. In those displays the Government had recognised no sign of wide-spread disaffection. There were but two men holding prominent positions in or near Calcutta who saw in the action of the sipáhís some-thing more than a passing wave of discontent, and one of these saw it but dimly. The more prescient of these two men was Major Cavenagh, the Town-Major of Fort William, and the representative in that fortress of the Governor-General. The other was the Commander of the Presidency Division, General Hearsey. I have already recorded the action of the former in January, and I shall have to write of his action in March and April. For the moment I must narrate the proceedings of General Hearsey at Barrackpur.

The revelations of the lascar at Dam-Dam, in January, had deeply impressed that officer. He recognised that the minds of the sipáhís were in a state of great excitement. The real cause, the basis of that excitement, was not apparent to him. His intelligence was limited to the matters which came under his eyes, and it was not in his nature to probe the situation more deeply. He really believed that the whole offence of the Government had been the greasing of the cartridges for use by the sipáhís, and that the latter were under the influence of terror lest their religion should be tampered with. He did not ask how it was that, before a single cartridge had been issued, before one sipáhí had been asked to defile himself by applying his teeth to the greased paper, the demeanour of the men of the four native regiments at Barrackpur had displayed unmistakable signs of the discontent which raged within their minds. Believing that the greased cartridge was the outward sign and inward cause of the evident discontent, he had, with the sanction of Lord Canning, on the 9th of February, paraded his brigade, and addressing the sipáhís of the four regiments in their own language, had endeavoured to dissipate their fears. He had told them that the English were Christians of the Book; that they admitted no proselytes except those whom the reading of that Book had convinced; that the notion that any other mode of conversion was possible was absurd; that baptism only followed conviction; and he implored them to dismiss from their minds the tale told them by designing men that the English had any design to convert them by a trick.

General Hearsey meant well, and he thought he had succeeded in convincing his men of their delusion. But he had missed the point. The conspirators, who had fomented the ill-feeling of the sipáhís all over India, had not told their victims that the English would make them Christians by force. They had rather impressed on their minds that the object of their masters was to deprive them, by the compulsory use of the cartridges, of the caste, to which they adhered with the passionate conviction that it was the one thing necessary for consideration in this life, and happiness in the life to come; and that then, scared and miserable by their degradation, they would seek for admission into the ranks of a religion which had established missions throughout the country for the very purpose of converting them. General Hearsey's argument that his religion was a religion of the Book was all very well when addressed to Brahmans and Rájputs, whose position was secure, whose caste was intact. But, when it should be applied to men whose caste had been broken who had become pariahs and outcasts, deprived of consideration in this world, and of all hope in the hereafter it would have a different signification. Then the men who had lost the religion of their forefathers would be glad to read the Book, and to gain renewed hope in the religion of their masters.

The answer to General Hearsey's declamation was given by the 19th N. I. at Barhámpur. The news from Barrackpur, carried to Barhámpur by the sipáhís of the 34th, had produced the fermentation and partial outbreak described in the last chapter. And this was the news which disturbed the Government of India on the 4th of March.

It found that Government in a state of some perplexity. Lord Canning was new to the country, and was perforce, on all matters pertaining to the native army, dependent on his military advisers. The capacity of his military advisers may be judged from the fact that they were the very men who had allowed him to be swayed by the shallow reasoning of the Adjutant-General regarding the issue of greased cartridges. However, many facts had spoken too loudly to be disregarded. There was the one fact that a native regiment in the Presidency Division had mutinied; another fact that the troops at Barrackpur had displayed a sullenness of demeanour diffcult to account for; a third fact in the revelations of Major Cavenagh, described in the last chapter; and a fourth in the fact that between Calcutta and Dánápur, a distance of 344 miles from Calcutta, there was but one weak English regiment. The disaffection at Barhámpur had, they knew, been produced by the commnications received by the sipáhís of that regiment from the men of a detachment which had marched thither from Barrackpur. Who was to guard the line of 344 miles if the sipáhís of Barrackpur should emulate the conduct of the men whom some of their comrades had perverted? These facts, and this consideration, produced the conviction that it was necessary to strengthen the central position. They resolved to strengthen it by ordering the 84th regiment to proceed with all speed from Rangoon to the Presidency. On the 20th of March that regiment arrived in the Huglí. Orders were then transmitted to Colonel Mitchell to march the 19th N. I. to Barrackpur.

But there had been many significant occurrence before the 84th reached the Huglí. Máhárájá Sindhiá had visited Calcutta early in March, and, as a return for the civilities showered upon him, had invited the *élite* of the society of the Presidency to a *fête* at the Botanical Gardens, situated on the opposite bank of the river Huglí, on the 10th of the month. There can be little doubt but that the leaders of the conspiracy had resolved to strike their blow on that day. During the absence of the official English across the river they had planned to seize the fort and to strike terror into the town. A circumstance, slight in itself, frustrated their combinations. Rain, most unusual at that time of the year in India, fell heavily the day before and on the morning of the 10th, and the Máhárájá, aware that an out-of-door *fête* could be successful only when the weather was propitious, sent out notices to postpone the entertainment. It happened accidentally that no notice of the postponement reached the Town-Major, Major Cavenagh. That ever vigilant officer had quitted the fort to cross the river; but, on arriving at the ghât, he learned for the first time that no *fête* would take place that day, so he retraced his steps. His sudden return, and the rumour to which that return gave weight, that the *fête* had been postponed, roused in the guilty minds of the conspirators the suspicion that their plot had been discovered. Some of them, outside the fort, had indeed begun the part assigned to them in the general programme, but, under the mysterious circumstances of the return of Cavenagh and the postponement of the garden party, the more astute members of the conspiracy declined to move. They even assisted in the capture of their misled comrades, who were brought at once to trial, and suffered fourteen years of penal servitude for their premature temerity.

A week later the 84th entered the Huglí, and landing on the 20th, marched to the quarters assigned them at Chinsurah, twenty miles north of Calcutta. The Government immediately transmitted orders to Colonel Mitchell to march his regiment, the 19th N. I., from Barhámpur to Barrackpur.

In the interval the Court of Inquiry, referred to in the last chapter, had, as already stated, taken evidence, and on its report the Governor-General in Council had resolved to punish the sipáhís by disbanding the regiment. Previous experience of that punishment had proved that it was at best but a clumsy device. It was especially ill-adapted to the actual circumstances, for it would distribute over areas already partially infected a thousand men who regarded themselves, and who would be regarded by others, as martyrs for their religion. But in the Council of Lord Canning there was not one man upon whom had been bestowed the divine gift of imagination. No other remedy presented itself to their matter-of-fact minds. So the order for disbandment was issued. It was hoped that the impressive ceremony of disbandment, carried out in the presence of four native regiments, and supervised by their English comrades, would produce a great effect. But, unhappily for the theories of those in high places, an event took place at Barrackpur, before the arrival of the 19th there, which proved conclusively that the evil, which the disbandment of the 19th was to cure, was far more widely spread and deeply rooted than any official had conceived.

CHAPTER V

Barrackpur, Calcutta, and the North-west to the 9th of May

Meanwhile, the excitement at Barrackpur was not diminishing. Isolated actions on the part of the sipáhís, indicating a very mutinous spirit, were reported to the Governor-General. The incident referred to in the last chapter, which had led to the trial and sentence to fourteen years' penal servitude of several sipáhís, had produced considerable perplexity in the minds of the authorities. But they still refused to believe that there was anything like a general plot. They preferred to think that the disaffection was confined to some men of one regiment only, or to a few men belonging to two regiments. The suspicions of the disaffected men were not, it was hoped, so deeply rooted as to be proof against argument. The Government was conscious of its own innocence. It harboured no evil designs against the sipáhís. It had no desire to move to the right or to the left out of the path it had undeviatingly followed for exactly a century. If this could be made clear to the men, all would assuredly go well. It was essentially a European argument, an argument which proved the most profound ignorance of the modes of thoughts of a race which was Asiatic, and for the most part Hindu. But it was the argument which naturally presented itself to the European mind. Lord Canning had authorised General Hearsey to try the experiment once, and General Hearsey believed, as was quite natural he should believe, that his arguments had produced some effect. He was anxious to try once again the powers of his oratory. He therefore persuaded Lord Canning to authorise him to address the men of the four regiments in language and in terms which he had talked over with the Governor-General.

The parade took place on the Barrackpur plain, on the 17th of March, three days before the actual arrival of the 84th from Rangoon. General Hearsey spoke eloquently and well. He pointed out to the men the childishness of their fears; he entered into full details regarding the necessity to use lubricated cartridges with the new muskets; he told them that the Government were resolved to maintain discipline, and that they would mete out stern justice to the 19th by disbanding that regiment. He concluded by assuring the sipáhís of the brigade that they had nothing to fear, that their caste and religious convictions were safe, and that their officers would listen patiently to any complaint they might make. In the abstract, nothing could be more to the point or more satisfactory than the General's speech.

But it failed to touch the inner minds of the sipáhís. These were inspired by men who had a great object in view—a political object of vast importance—the detaching of the sipáhí army from the foreign Government. But for these men the question of the greased cartridge would never have arisen. The waxed patches had been used without complaint for years, why should the very rumour regarding greased cartridges, which, be it always remembered, had not been issued, so excite the sipáhís? There could be but one reason. The emissaries of the Maulaví and his comrades had done their work thoroughly. The midnight conferences in the huts of the sipáhís, not at Barrackpur only but in all the principal stations of the North-western Provinces of India, had gone to but one point—the implanting of a conviction in the mind of the native soldiers that the foreign masters who had annexed Oudh would hesitate at nothing to complete their work of forcing them to become Christians. They had discounted beforehand the arguments of General Hearsey, for they had pointed out that a Government which, in defiance of treaties, had entered Oudh like 'a thief in the night,' and deposed the native sovereign at the point of the bayonet, would shrink from no means, however fraudulent, to complete the scheme of which the annexation had been the first move. It was not a logical argument, and the European mind would have found it full of flaws; but the emissaries knew the men they were addressing. Sentiment goes much further than logic with Asiatics, and they appealed to the sentiments which touched the sipáhís to the quick. It is not surprising, then, that the logical arguments of General Hearsey produced no effect whatever.

Evidence of this was very speedily given. On the 29th of March, a Sunday afternoon, it was reported to Lieutenant Baugh, Adjutant of the 34th N. I., that several men of his regiment were in a very excited condition; that one of them, Manghal Pándi by name, was striding up and down in front of the lines of his regiment, armed with a loaded musket, calling upon the men to rise, and threatening to shoot the first European he should see. Baugh at once buckled on his sword, and putting loaded pistols in his holsters, mounted his horse, and galloped down to the lines. Manghal Pándi heard the sound of the galloping horse, and taking post behind the station gun, which was in front of the quarter-guard of the 34th, took a deliberate aim at Baugh, and fired. He missed Baugh, but the bullet struck his horse in the flank, and horse and rider were brought to the ground. Baugh quickly disentangled himself, and, seizing one of his pistols, advanced towards the mutinous sipáhí and fired. He missed. Before he could draw his sword Manghal Pándi, armed with a talwár with which he had provided himself, closed with his adjutant, and, being the stronger man, brought him to the ground. He would probably have despatched him but for the timely intervention of a Muhammadan sipáhí, Shaikh Paltu by name.

The scene I have described had taken place in front of the quarter-guard of the 34th N. I., and but thirty paces from it. The sipáhís composing that guard had not made the smallest attempt to interfere between the combatants, although one of them was their own adjutant and the other a mutinous soldier. The sound of the firing had brought other men from the lines, but these, too, remained passive spectators of the scene. At the conjuncture I have described, just, that is, as Shaikh Paltu had warded from Baugh the fatal stroke of the talwár, and as Manghal Pándi, to make assurance doubly sure, was attempting to reload his musket, there arrived on the ground, breathless from running, the English serjeant-major, one of the two English non-commissioned officers attached in those days to each native regiment. The new arrival rushed at the mutineer, but he was, as I have said, breathless, whilst the sipáhí was fresh and on the alert. In the conflict between the two men Manghal Pándi had no difficulty in gaining the mastery, and in throwing his adversary. Still the sipáhís of the regiment looked on. Shaikh Paltu, faithful among the faithless, continued to defend the two officers, calling upon the other sipáhís to come to his aid. Then these, on the order of the Jámadár of guard, advanced. Instead, however, of endeavouring to seize Manghal Pándi, they struck at the two prostrate officers with the butt-ends of their muskets. They even threatened Shaikh Paltu, and ordered him to let go his hold on Manghal Pándi. That faithful sipáhí, however, continued to cling to him until Baugh and the sergeant-major had had time to rise.

Meanwhile rumour, as quick as lightning on such occasions, had brought to General Hearsey an account of the proceedings at the lines. That gallant officer, writing hurried notes to the officers commanding at Dam-Dam and Chinsurah, where were a wing of the 53rd foot and the newly arrived 84th, to be despatched should occasion demand it, galloped to the ground, accompanied by his two sons. The scene that met his gaze was unprecedented even in his long experience. He saw Manghal Pándi, musket in hand, striding up and down in front of the quarter-guard, calling upon his comrades to follow his example. He saw the sipáhís crowding about the guard, waiting apparently for a leader to respond to their comrade's call. He saw the wounded Baugh, and the bruised sergeant-major, the commanding officer of the 34th, who had arrived just before him, and other English officers who had hastened or were hastening to the spot. The moment was a critical one. It depended upon his action whether the Barrackpur sipáhí brigade would then and there break out in open mutiny. But Hearsey was equal to the critical conjuncture. Riding straight to the guard, he drew his pistol, and ordered them to do their duty by seizing Manghal Pándi, threatening to shoot the first man who should display the smallest symptom of disobedience. For a second only was there hesitation. But a glance at Hearsey's stern face, and at his two sons by his side, dissipated it. The men of the guard fell in, and followed Hearsey in the direction where Manghal Pándi was still upbraiding them for their cowardice in leaving him unsupported. Then the mutinous sipáhí recognised that with him the game was up. Turning then the muzzle of the musket to his breast, he discharged it by the pressure of his foot, and fell burned and bleeding to the ground.

Hearsey then addressed the men, and reproached them with their passive demeanour. The excuses they made, that Manghal Pándi was mad, that he was intoxicated, that he had a loaded musket, ought to have convinced Hearsey that the hearts of the men were no longer with their British officers. He felt, indeed, that the situation was becoming greatly strained. The 19th N. I. were actually marching from Barhámpur to be disbanded at Barrackpur, and now the sipáhís of the four regiments of the Barrackpur brigade had displayed an indiscipline at least equal to that for which the 19th were to be punished in their presence. Rumours of all kinds filled the air—the rumour that the outbreak of Manghal Pándi had been preconcerted, but had broken out too soon; another that the arrival of the 19th would be the signal for a general rising; a third, a day or two later, that a conference between emissaries from the 34th and the 19th had taken place, on the 30th, at Barsat, one march from Barrackpur. It is probable that these rumours were true. But the mutinous army had no leader at Barrackpur, and for want of a leader, and in the presence of divided counsels, action collapsed.

On the 30th of March the Government concentrated in Barrackpur the newly arrived 84th foot, a wing of the 53rd, two batteries of European artillery, and the Governor-General's Bodyguard, which, though composed of natives was then believed to be loyal. The next morning the 19th N. I. marched into Barrackpur. There, in presence of the English regiments and the English-manned guns, and of the native brigade, the order of the Governor-General, stating their crime, and declaring absurd their fears for their religion, was read out to them. They were then ordered to pile their arms, and to hang their belts upon the piled bayonets. They obeyed without a murmur. They were then marched to a distance from their arms, and the pay due to them was distributed. They were allowed, mistakenly as it turned out, to retain their uniforms, and the complaisance of the Government went so far as to provide them with carriage to convey them to their homes. The Government, despite all that had occurred, was still in a fog. They could not see an inch beyond their own hands.

One or two circumstances showed the temper of the Government at this conjuncture. The gallant conduct of Shaikh Paltu, on the morning of the 29th of March, had presented so great a contrast to that of his comrades that Hearsey, with a true soldier's instinct, had then and there promoted him to be a Háwaldár, or native sergeant. For this act, which, though '*ultra vires,*' was justified by the special circumstances of the case, he was reprimanded by the Government. The general impression prevailed that the disbandment of the 19th would produce so salutary an effect throughout India that it was announced to the whole army in terms which, to say the least, displayed an absolute ignorance of the real feelings of the sipáhís. The Government thought that that disbandment had closed the chapter of the Mutiny, when in reality it was only the first page of the preface.

The wound of the mutinous sipáhís Manghal Pándi had not proved mortal. He recovered, was brought to trial, and hanged. The Jámadár who had incited the sipáhís of the quarter-guard to refrain from assisting their officer met the same fate a little later (April 22). Meanwhile, the Government had made a searching inquiry into the conduct of the men of the 34th N. I. generally, and after much hesitation, moved also by events at Lakhnao, to be presently referred to, Lord Canning came to the determination to disband that regiment also (May 4). Two days later the seven companies of that regiment which were at Barrackpur[1] were paraded in the presence of the 84th foot, a wing of the 53rd, and two batteries of European artillery, and were disbanded. They were not allowed to keep their uniforms, but were marched out of the station with every show of disgrace. Thus five hundred conspirators, embittered against the Government, were turned loose on the country at a very critical period.

The Government had, towards the end of April, been so satisfied that the disturbances were purely local, and that the disaffection displayed in Bengal had not penetrated to the North-west, that they had resolved, as soon as the 34th N. I. should have been dealt with, to send back the 84th foot

---

[1] The remaining three companies were on duty in Eastern Bengal.

to Rangoon, and they had actually engaged transports for that purpose. Nor did the advices they received from Oudh and the upper provinces, just before the disbandment of the 34th, induce them to reconsider the position and to change their plans. It required the outbreak of the 10th of May at Mírath to impress upon them the reality of the danger.

The disbandment of the 19th N. I., on the 31st of March, had sent back to Oudh nearly a thousand men to preach disaffection and treason. The seeds of distrust had already been sown there by the chief conspirators. It wanted, then, but practical proof of the determination of the Government to carry out their designs at all costs to apply the spark to the material collected. The presence of the disbanded men of the 19th supplied that spark. No overt action had taken place in Oudh before their arrival in that province. After their advent, Oudh became the chief focus of the rebellion.

At Lakhnao, the capital of Oudh, ruled the chivalrous and capable Sir Henry Lawrence. No man more than he had lamented the tendencies of the time to introduce a western system of local government among an oriental people. No man had been more desirous to stand on the ancient ways, the ways familiarised to the natives of India by centuries of use: to employ the utmost care and discretion in introducing changes, however meritorious those changes might appear to men of western race and western training. Hence Sir Henry Lawrence was popular with all classes of natives. He possessed a greater influence over them than any man then living; and, could the rill, then breaking into a torrent, have been stemmed, he was the one man to stem it. But Sir Henry Lawrence had come to Oudh after the evil seeds sown by his immediate predecessor had begun to bear fruit—when the native landowners had been alienated, the supporters of the native rule had begun to conspire, and when the effects of the annexation were being realised by the numerous families which had sent a son or a brother into the sipáhís' army, in order that he might procure for them the support of the English Resident in their local Courts. When Sir Henry arrived, then, the mischief had been done, and he had had no power to repair it.

The events at Barhámpur and Barrackpur had been watched by Sir Henry Lawrence with the deepest interest. Naturally, he had taken particular pains to satisfy himself whether the causes which had produced the outbreaks I have recorded at those stations had affected the three regular native regiments, the 13th, the 48th, and the 71st N. I., which garrisoned Lakhnao. But it was not till the end of April, just about the time when the disbanded men of the 19th N. I. were stealing into the province, that he detected, or thought he detected, suspicious symptoms in the 48th N. I. He reported the circumstance to Lord Canning, and at once received permission to write to the Commander-in-Chief to have the regiment removed to Mírath. But to Sir Henry's mind the proposed remedy was no remedy at all. He wrote in that sense, on May 1st, to the Governor-General.

Two days later he discovered that treasonable communications were passing between the men of a local regiment and the 48th, that the men of the 7th Irregular Cavalry, stationed seven miles from Lakhnao, had proceeded to overt acts against their officers, and that the greased cartridges were in both cases the alleged cause of the ill-feeling. The act of the 7th Irregulars, in the opinion of Sir Henry, required prompt repression. Accordingly, he marched that night, with the three native regiments I have enumerated, the 32nd foot, and a battery of eight guns, against the peccant regiment. The men of that regiment, terrified by this demonstration, submitted without a blow. They laid down their arms at the given order, and allowed their ringleaders to be arrested, with every sign of penitence and submission.

On the 4th of May the electric wire flashed to Lord Canning an account of this mutiny and its repression. It was the receipt of this news which decided his vacillating council to disband the 34th, a measure which, we have seen, was carried out on the 6th. The effect which the simple disbanding of a mutinous regiment produced on the other native regiments of the same brigade was illustrated a few days later. A Jámadár of the 70th N. I. was arrested at Barrackpur in the act of urging his men to rise in revolt. Brought to trial before a court composed of native officers of his own caste, he was sentenced merely to dismissal. Unfortunately this lenient punishment for mutiny was approved and confirmed by the Commander-in-Chief. The publication of this approval produced the worst effects.

Unfortunately for Lord Canning, himself one of the noblest of men, there was no one about him to tell him that the punishment of disbandment in such times as he was entering upon was no punishment at all. There was not a native regiment in the Bengal Presidency which was not at this period not only ready to disband itself, but to turn with all the fury of men excited by fancied wrongs against the masters they had served. But the truth is there was not a man about him who had penetrated below the surface, who had the wit to see that this disaffection was no ephemeral feeling, to disappear at the bidding of a few hard words. In the language of the Home Secretary, employed when the discontent had become infinitely more pronounced than it was at the beginning of May, it was, in the eyes of his councillors, 'a passing and groundless panic' which required no exceptional action on the part of the Government. When, then, Lord Canning punished a mutinous regiment by disbanding it, when the Commander-in-Chief announced to the army that he considered simple dismissal as a fitting punishment for a native officer caught red-handed in preaching mutiny to his own men, and when, finally, the Governor-General, notifying to the army the doom of the 34th N. I., declared to the sipáhís that similar conduct on their part would subject them to punishment 'sharp and certain,' the plotters in high places must have smiled contemptuously at the conception of sharp and certain punishment entertained by their rulers.

Notwithstanding the belief of the Government that the discontent was local, almost every post brought information that it was not confined to Bengal, that it had shown itself in other places than Lakhnao, that regiments, widely separated from one another, were equally infected. In the important station of Mírath, situated nearly midway between the Ganges and the Jamnah, thirty-six miles from the imperial city of Dehlí, the sipáhís had become impregnated with the idea that the flour sold in the bazaars had been purposely mixed with the bones of bullocks, ground to a fine powder. The conspirators who had fabricated this story were the men who had invented the tale of the greased cartridges, and they had fabricated it with a like object. Nothing tended more to prove the proneness of the minds of the sipáhís to accept any story against the masters they had served for a century than the readiness with which they accepted this impossible rumour. They were not to be persuaded that it was untrue. They displayed more than ordinary care in the purchase of the meal for their daily consumption, and, still unsatisfied, vented their discontent by the burning of houses and by the omission of the ordinary salute to their officers. They soon took a very much more decided step in the path of mutiny. A parade of the 3rd Native Light Cavalry had been ordered for the morning of the 6th of May. When, on the preceding evening, the ordinary cartridges were issued to the men, eighty-five troopers of that regiment declined to receive them. In vain did their commanding officer expostulate; in vain did the Brigadier attempt to persuade them. Such a breach of discipline could not be passed over. The men were confined, were then brought with all speed to a court-martial, composed entirely of native officers, and were sentenced by the members of that court to periods of imprisonment, with hard labour, varying from six to ten years. Under the orders of the Commander-in-Chief, to whom the question had been specially referred, the General commanding the Mírath division, General Hewitt, prepared to put into execution the finding of the court-martial on the mutineers of the 3rd N.L.C. He ordered a general parade for the morning of the 9th. There were present at that parade at daybreak, a regiment of Carabineers, the 60th Rifles, the 3rd Light Cavalry (native), the 11th and 20th regiments N. I., a troop of horse-artillery, and a light field-battery. The condemned mutineers were marched to the ground, were stripped of their accoutrements, then every man was shackled and ironed, and they were all marched to the gaol, a building about two miles distant from the cantonment, and guarded solely by natives. There were sullen looks among the armed troopers of the 3rd, and an acute observer might have detected sympathetic glances from the sipáhís. But there was no open demonstration. Like Lord Canning and his advisers after the disarming of the 34th N.I., only three days earlier, General Hewitt and the officers at Mírath congratulated one another on the promptitude and sucess with which a sharp punishment had been dealt out to men who had defied the authority they had sworn to obey.

But the acts of the 19th N. I. at Barhámpur, of the 34th at Barrackpur, of the men whom Major Cavenagh was carefully watching in Fort William, of the deluded sipáhís near Lakhnao, and of the 7th N.L.C. at Mírath, were but the precursors to a more terrible tragedy. The great movement, of which those acts were only the premonitory symptoms, was, on that 9th day of May, on the eve of its outbreak.

CHAPTER VI

The Revolt at Mírath and the Seizure of Dehlí

The parade at Mírath, the particulars of which are told in the last chapter, took place on a Saturday morning. The sipáhís who assisted at it had then the remainder of that day, the following night, and the early part of Sunday, in which to mature the plans rising in their minds.

In their opinion the eighty-five men who had refused to take the cartridges, and of whose degradation they had been witnesses on that Saturday morning, were simply martyrs for their faith. They had been a little bolder than their comrades: that was all. The idea which had prompted their refusal was common to all the sipáhís at Mírath. They, too, had lost faith in their masters, and their minds had been equally ready to believe the stories regarding bone dust and greased cartridges which designing men were daily pouring into their ears. They had not been insensible to the reproaches which their ironed and shackled comrades had cast upon them as they marched off, prisoners, to the gaol. They felt that they should deserve these reproaches if they were to continue silent witnesses of their degradation. They knew, though the Government wilfully shut their eyes to the fact, that the feelings under which their comrades had acted were wide-spread among the sipáhís of the Bengal army. That night's post would convey to every station in India the story of the punishment of their comrades, and of their own passive acquiescence. Such a disgrace was not to be borne. They must, before the world was forty-eight hours older, atone for their apparent acquiescence in the punishment of the men whose views they shared by action which should rouse all India.

In the consultations of that Saturday afternoon and evening the sipáhís of the three regiments called to mind that it was the custom of the English to hold Church parade on Sunday, morning and evening, and that on such occasions the men wore only their side-arms. The evening seemed to them more suitable for their enterprise than the morning, for in India there is no twilight, and the darkness which would rapidly supervene on the setting of the sun would greatly increase the confusion which the surprise of the sudden rising would produce.

But little occurred in Mírath on that eventful Sunday to warn the English of the coming danger. It was recollected afterwards that the native servants, alike in the barracks and in private houses, had strangely absented themselves from their customary duties; but no suspicions were aroused. It was the very height of the blasting season which scorches up vegetation, and renders the outer air scarcely endurable until the time of sunset approaches. The Sunday, then, passed like other Sundays, and when the bells began to toll for the evening service nothing had occurred to give any warning of the storm which was ready to burst.

But as the residents and the troops marched to the sacred edifice it became evident that some great event was pending. The native nurse of the chaplain had warned him, as he was setting out with his wife, that they would have a fight with the sipáhís. On their way the churchgoers heard the unwonted sounds of bugling and musket firing. They saw bodies of armed men hurrying on their way as if to a rendezvous. Then there succeeded columns of smoke, as if many bungalows had been set on fire. In a moment more the whole truth burst upon them. The native troops at Mírath had revolted.

Far differently had that day been passed in the lines of the native troops. There the utmost excitement had prevailed. Conspiring makes conspirers suspicious. Conscious of their own meditated treason, the sipáhís attributed to their masters designs not dissimilar to their own. It is very doubtful whether there were at Mírath, at this crisis, any of those who were deep in the conspiracy: who had fostered the movement from its very birth; who were in the confidence of the Maulaví and his colleagues. Their place was occupied by the committees they had caused to be formed in each regiment. But the sipáhís, excited, suspicious, ready to believe the idlest tale as they were, required leading. On this occasion the men of the 11th N. I. seemed inclined to hang back. To bring them to the right pitch, and to confirm possible wavering on the part of any of the others, the regimental committees took care that the most telling rumours should be circulated. Nowhere in the world does rumour rise so easily or take such exaggerated forms as in India. It appeals to a people singularly simple, and yet singularly superstitious. The fables of their religion teach them to believe in the supernatural, and for them the improbable is an ever-living power. When, then, rumour told them that the European troops at the station were preparing for them the fate of their manacled comrades, they believed the rumour. Hence they determined to rise and rescue those comrades whilst the Europeans should be unarmed and unsuspicious.

They waited, then, impatiently, how impatiently only those can know who are waiting for a given signal to launch themselves on an enterprise which shall ensure glory or death, until the church bells should give intimation that the coast was comparatively clear. Then, when they heard the tolling, their impatience could not be restrained. Armed with sabre and pistol, the men of the 3rd Cavalry galloped to the gaol to rescue their imprisoned comrades, whilst the sipáhís of the 11th and 20th hurried from their lines in tumultuous disorder. The troopers, on reaching the gaol, loosened the gratings of the cells in which their comrades were confined, the native guard fraternising with and assisting them. It took but a short time to drag out the manacled prisoners. A smith was handy. In a few minutes the fetters were removed, and the eighty-five rode back, mounted behind their deliverers, to the regimental lines.

When they arrived there they found that matters had progressed to a point from which there was receding. Some of the European officers of the 20th N. I. had been shot, and Colonel Finnis of the 11th had been riddled to death by the sipáhís of the 20th whilst endeavouring to persuade the men of his own regiment to remain true to their salt. Not for the moment only, but throughout that long night, first the mutinous soldiery, then the scum of the population and the prisoners whom they had released, were absolute master of the situation. The English authorities, civil and military, taken by surprise, had apparently lost their heads. Those in the highest places, the General, the Brigadier, the officers of the staff, were paralysed by the suddenness and tremendous character of the shock. Colonel Custance, commanding the Carabineers, on the first sound of the tumult, had ordered out his men, and had sent to ask for instructions. After a long delay the General sent to order him to proceed, not to the parade grounds of the mutinous regiments, which were close by, but to a gaol at a distance of some miles. The services of this gallant regiment were thus rendered unavailable at the time and at the place when and where they were most required. The night had well set in when General Hewitt, Brigadier Wilson, the 60th Rifles, the artillery, and the officers of the mutinous regiments reached the general parade ground. Across that ground the troops deployed into line, and joined by the Carabineers, who fortunately had lost their way and had returned, marched in the full expectation of meeting the revolted sipáhís. But these had disappeared, and no one knew whither they had gone. Believing that they had moved round to attack the quarters of the Europeans, the Brigadier, Archdale Wilson, advised the General to return for the protection of the women, the children, and the barracks. The General assented, and gave the necessary orders. On their way back the soldiers had some evidence of the damage already done by the mutineers. Lurid shoots of flame showed that many of the European bungalows were blazing. Some unarmed plunderers were seen, but no sipáhís. Where were they? Captain Rosser of the Carabineers offered, if he were permitted, to lead a squadron of his regiment and some H. A. guns along the Dehlí road, to ascertain if they had taken that route. The suggestion was not accepted; and subsequently the authorities denied that it had ever been made. It would seem that the officers in high places were sadly wanting in that spirit of enterprise and audacity which constitute the essential element of a good soldier. They would hazard nothing, not even the lives of a reconnoitring party. Contenting himself with establishing a few pickets, the General bivouacked his force for the remainder of the night on the European parade ground.

For the residents at Mírath, for the women, the children the civil section of the Europeans and Eurasians, that night was full of horror. The scum of the native population and the unchained gaol-birds had the field to themselves. Most thoroughly did they do their congenial work. The Commissioner, Mr Greathed, warned first by an officer of the 3rd Native Cavalry, and afterwards by an Afghán pensioner, had, with his wife and other English women, taken refuge on the terraced roof of his house. Against a foe whose weapon was fire that terrace was no sure hiding-place. But for the fidelity—I am happy to add, the by no means rare fidelity—of his native servants he and those with him must have perished in the flames. One servant in particular distinguished himself. He persuaded the rabble to move off to search for his master in an outhouse some distance off, and during their sudden absence Greathed, his friends and family, had time to descend from their perilous position and crouch in the empty garden. Others were less fortunate. Wives, left without protection during the enforced absence of their husbands, were butchered without mercy, and children were slaughtered under the very eyes of their mothers. Many instances of the devotion and presence of mind of English women could be given if space permitted. Those who did escape owed their safety to the possession of these qualities, but the roll of those who suffered was a long one. When day at length dawned, it dawned over a dismantled Mírath. The English men and women who had been saved crept from their hiding-places to see, in the mangled corpses which lay by the wayside, in the blackened ruins of houses, in the furniture of European make thrown out of the dwelling-houses, smashed and destroyed, abundant evidence of the thoroughness with which the 'scum' and the gaol-birds had done their work.[1] But of those destroyers not one was to be seen. They had done their deeds in darkness, and had slunk away to their homes when light came. Nor was a single sipáhí visible. The quiet prevailing in the places so recently the scenes of terrible outrage and disorder was the quiet of the charnel house.

I left the English troops bivouacked on the European parade ground. On that parade ground they slept whilst the enormities, of which I have given an indication, were being perpetrated in the civil lines. Nor, when day broke, did the morning light give greater energy to the councils of their commander. The General, it is true, speedily recognised that the sipáhís had quitted Mírath. He presumed, also, that they had made for Dehlí, thirty-six miles distant. There was not now time for the most energetic soldier to have followed and caught them, for it was clear that, with a start of eight hours, the 3rd Cavalry, at all events, would be there before them. But the idea of pursuit never occurred to anyone. The prevailing idea was how to secure the unthreatened Mírath. There were some good men at Mírath, but on this morning of the 11th of May not one of those in high authority was in the full possession of his faculties. The brains of all were paralysed by the blow of the previous evening. The General contented himself, then, with making a reconnaisance to the right of the Dehlí road. It was deemed to be too late, and it was then certainly too late to send a warning to the Dehlí authorities of the danger awaiting them. But the strangest thing of all was that no effort was made to punish the marauders and murderers of the previous night. 'It is a marvellous thing,' wrote, some time later, the Commissioner, to whom the Government entrusted the drawing up of a report of the proceedings of that terrible night and of that shameful morning, 'that with the dreadful proof of the night's work in every direction, though groups of savages were actually seen gloating over the mangled and mutilated remains of the victims, the column did not take immediate vengeance on the Sadar bazaar and its environs, crowded as the whole place was with wretches hardly concealing their fiendish satisfaction.' But so it was. Inaction was the order of the day. The authorities contented themselves with collecting and placing in the theatre the bodies of the murdered men and women, and left their murderers, unpunished, to the full enjoyment of their ill-gotten gains. Civil and military authorities vied with one another to attain perfection in the art of 'how not to do it.'

---

[1] It deserves to be recorded that all the natives of Mírath did not join in the outrages, an outline of which I have given. For instance, a Muhammadan in the city sheltered two families at great danger to himself. The servants, as a rule, showed the greatest devotion to their foreign masters.

Meanwhile, the sipáhís, having released their imprisoned comrades, and set on the populace and the gaol-birds to keep their late masters well occupied during the night, had taken the road to Dehlí. It is due to some of them to state that they did not quit Mírath before they had seen to a place of safety those officers whom they most respected. This remark applies specially to the men of the 11th N. I., who had gone most reluctantly into the movement. Before they left, two sipáhís of that regiment had escorted two ladies with their children to the Carabineer barracks. They had then rejoined their comrades. Of these the troopers of the 3rd Cavalry took the lead, anxious to gain the bridge across the Jamnah before tidings of the outbreak should reach the English authorities. Knowing the English as they did, how, when engaged with them on service, they had ever displayed a daring and an energy which had inspired their native comrades, they listened for some time anxiously for the sound of the galloping of the horses of the Carabineers. But when hour succeeded hour, and silence still reigned on all sides, they lost all apprehension, and galloping on with a light heart, caught sight of the minarets of the Jamí Masjíd glittering in the morning sun. Spurring their horses, they reached the waters of the Jamnah, crossed by the bridge of boats which spanned it, cut down the toll-keeper on the other side, fired the toll-house, slew a solitary Englishman whom they met; then hastening to the palace of the King, clamoured for admittance, declaring that they had killed the English at Mírath, and had come to fight for the Faith. We must leave them there whilst we examine the relative positions of the English and the Mughal Court at the Imperial city.

The city of Dehlí had and has still a circumference of five and a half miles. That of the King's palace, within its walls, is nearly one and a half. The city itself I shall describe when I come to the operations undertaken by the handful of soldiers who laid siege to it. For the moment our attention must be riveted to the palace.

The palace, more correctly called the inner fort or citadel, was built by the Emperor Sháh Jahán (1638–58). It is a magnificent series of structures, reached by a flight of 113 steps, and covered on its eastern face by the Jamnah. It contained some magnificent buildings: the Diwáni Ám, or public Hall of Audience, built of red sandstone; the Diwáni Kháss, or Privy Council Chamber, of white marble ornamented with gold, and inlaid; the King's Baths, the Moti Masjíd, or Pearl Mosque, a real architectural gem. Above the entrance gate was a turret twenty feet high, commanding, to the left, a magnificent view of the Jamí Masjíd, of a white Jain temple, and of the town. Straight in front of the entrance gate was the Chandní Chauk, or Silver Market; to the right, outside the walls of the city, were the Jamnah, Hindu Ráo's house, and the ridge, so famous during the siege, at the moment indicating the direction of the lines of the native infantry regiments which constituted the British garrison. Within the fort were gardens laid out in the formal style of the east, and along the river front were a number of marble pavilions, generally octagonal, covered with gilded domes, some of them of great beauty.

The principal occupant of this inner citadel was Bahádur Sháh, titular King of Dehlí, the twentieth successor of the illustrious Akbar. He was King of Dehlí in name, and in name only. The empire had departed from the feeble hands of his predecessors before the English had become a power in India. The Khorásání adventurer Nádir Sháh had plundered the palace in 1739. Less than ten years later, the Afghán Ahmad Sháh Duráni had repeated the infliction. In 1788 the rebel Ghulám Kádir had blinded, within the palace, the reigning Emperor Sháh Alám. For fifteen years the city had, then, been occupied by the Maráthás. The English had made their first acquaintance with it in 1803, when Lord Lake rescued the blinded representative of the Mughals from the tyranny of the Central Indian conquerors. From that date the English had maintained the representative of the Mughal in splendour and comfort in the halls and palace of his ancestors. There, in the citadel within Dehlí, his will was supreme. It did not extend an inch beyond it. Wisely, then, the English—when, under the able guidance of Marquess Wellesley, they assumed the responsibilities of empire—did not restore to the Mughal the power which he had already lost. Less wisely, perhaps, they had permitted him to enjoy the shadow after he had lost the substance.

At the moment, and for some time previously, the feelings of the King and his family had been considerably excited against the English ruler, in consequence of correspondence which had taken place with reference to the succession. Bahádur Sháh was an old man. A rumour had reached him, so far back as 1849–50, that Lord Dalhousie had not been indisposed to deprive the House of Taimur of the shadow of splendour still remaining to it. Rumour had told the truth. The acknowledged heir to Bahádur Sháh, Prince Dárá Bakht, had died in 1849. The next in the strict line of succession, Prince Fakir-ud-dín, had been born a pensioner. Lord Dalhousie was inclined to admit his accession to the chiefship of the family upon less favourable conditions than those which had been recognised in the case of his father. In plain language, Lord Dalhousie believed that the natives of India, the princes as well as the people, had become 'entirely indifferent to the condition of the King of Dehlí or his position,' and, considering the danger of retaining an *imperium in imperio* in the very heart of the ancient capital of India, he had desired to take the opportunity of the death of the immediate representative of the House of Taimur to sweep away all the privileges and prerogatives which had kept alive a pretentious mock royalty in the heart of the empire.

The Court of Directors gave Lord Dalhousie full power to act according to the views he had imbibed on this subject, but there was much difference of opinion in the India House, and Lord Dalhousie wisely deferred action. Meanwhile, rumours of the impending change had reached the palace, and had roused the most furious opposition, especially on the part of the favourite wife of the old King. This lady, in the manner of favourite wives generally, desired to secure the succession, with all its privileges, for her son, Jawán Bakht, then (1850) a boy of eleven. There existed at that time a strange ignorance of native feeling and native habits of thought in the Council of the Governor-General, and, notwithstanding the passionate entreaties from Dehlí, Lord Dalhousie and his advisers wrote a despatch to the Home Government recommending them to acknowledge the succession of the eldest surviving son, Fakír-ud-dín; and urging that, on the death of Bahádur Sháh, the opportunity should be taken to utilise the claims of the youngest son by obtaining from the eldest the desired concessions. Prince Fakír-ud-dín was induced to consent to this ignoble arrangement, though he hated himself for his weakness. But his death, in 1856, threw back matters into the channel in which they were before his consent had been obtained.

Lord Canning was then Governor-General, and at that time Lord Canning could see only with the eyes of the Councillors whom I have described. In reply to the urgent solicitations of the Queen to nominate her son, he determined not only to refuse her request, but to recognise as heir-apparent the eldest surviving son of the King. He determined likewise to exhort terms less favourable to native ideas than those which had been wrung from his deceased brother, for, in addition to the renunciations to which that brother had agreed, he stipulated that the succeeding prince should renounce the title of King.

It is right that the reader should bear in mind these transactions when recollecting the conduct of the representatives of the House of Taimur when, on that eventful May morning (May 11, 1857) the troopers of the 3rd Cavalry stood under the windows of the King demanding admittance and support. The King was an old man, ruled to a great extent by a favourite wife, whose hopes had been dashed to the ground by the British Government. He himself, his courtiers, his sons, his dependents, knew that the *fiat* had gone forth from Calcutta which, on his death, would humble to the dust the House of Taimur. We cannot wonder that their feelings should have prompted them to seize any opportunity which might present itself. We cannot wonder that, with the shadow of the despoiler before them, his threats ringing in their ears, they should have decided to strike a blow for the restoration of the family honours: to court death rather than submit to disgrace. Neither in the past nor in the present has a single man of the two hundred and fifty millions of natives of India condemned them for their action on that memorable morning. The reverse was the case. The sympathy of India was with them, and it was the conviction that it would be so which decided them.

Attached to the citadel, and representing British interests at the palace, were the Commissioner of Dehlí, Mr Fraser, and the Commandant of the Palace Guards, Captain Douglas. No sooner did the aged King hear the voices of the troopers under his windows than he sent to summon Captain Douglas to inquire the meaning of their presence. Captain Douglas pleaded ignorance, but, confident in the magic of the appearance of a British officer, declared he would go down to speak to them, and send them away. The King, apparently ignorant of their purpose, and yet dreading the reason of their presence, begged the young Englishman not to expose his life. The King's physician added his entreaties to those of his master. Douglas contented himself, then, with entering the verandah and ordering the troopers to depart, as their presence was an annoyance to the King. The men scornfully defied him. It happened that the sipáhís on duty at the palace belonged to the 38th N. I., the regiment which had successfully defied Lord Dalhousie's order to proceed to Burma but five years before. They were disloyal to the core. When, therefore, the troopers of the 3rd Cavalry, maddened by the sight of Douglas, attempted to force an entrance into the palace, they admitted them as comrades.

The troopers, once admitted, made short work of every Englishman they found there. They cut down to the death Mr Fraser, Captain Douglas, the chaplain, Mr Jennings, his daughter, and a young lady staying with them, Miss Clifford. The collector, Mr Hutchinson, fell a victim also to their barbarity. They were not alone in their thirst for blood. Not only had the guards of the 38th N. I. fraternised with them, but the orderlies of the King and the rabble vied with them in their savage fury. There is no reason to believe that the King gave any sanction to their proceedings. For the moment the old man was absolutely without authority. The soldiery had forced their way into his splendid Diwání Ám, and had turned it into a barrack. At that crisis they were the masters.

Outside the palace, especially in the quarter inhabited by the European residents engaged in mercantile pursuits, the carnage was even greater. The Dehlí Bank, supposed to contain treasure, was one of the buildings first attacked. Defended with gallantry by the manager, Mr Beresford, and his family, it was stormed and gutted, and the defenders were slain. The *Dehlí Gazette* press and its inmates met the same fate. The English church was stormed and rifled. Every house, in fact, occupied by European or Eurasian was attacked, and every Christian upon whom hands could be laid was killed. There was no mercy and there was no quarter.

Meanwhile, in the cantonments, matters were not going much better. The cantonments for the native brigade at Dehlí was situated on the famous ridge, about two miles from the city. There were quartered the 38th, the 54th, and the 74th N. I., and a battery of native artillery. The commanding officer was Brigadier Graves. On that eventful morning Graves had ordered a parade of the native troops, to have read to them the proceedings of the court-martial on Isrí Pándí, the mutinous Jámadár of Barrackpur. Some of those who were present thought they detected in the manner of the sipáhís, whilst the proceedings were being read, signs of sympathy with the condemned man. But there was no overt act, and the sipáhís were dismissed to their lines in the usual manner. It subsequently transpired that sipáhís from Mírath had arrived in the lines the previous day, and had communicated to the regiments located there the intentions of the Mírath native brigade. But for the moment all was quiet. The officers had returned to their quarters, and had eaten their breakfasts, when they were suddenly startled by the intimation that the native troops at Mírath had mutinied, and that the advanced guard of them, the 3rd Cavalry, had galloped across the bridge. So great was the faith of the officers in their own men, and in British superiority, that those at Dehlí never for a moment believed that the outbreak was aught but an isolated mutiny, which would be speedily quelled. The European force at Mírath must be, they thought, on the heels of the mutinied sipáhís, and whilst their own native brigade would show them a bold front the Carabineers and 60th Rifles would assail them from behind. With a light heart, then, the officers of the 54th N. I., and of the battery of native artillery, accompanied their men, to whom the sacred duty of defence had been committed, towards the city gates.

Their dream of confidence was not of long duration. Some men of the 38th, at the main-guard, set the example of revolt. Ordered to fire on the approaching troopers, they replied with insult. The 54th then fired, some in the air, some on their own officers. Colonel Ripley was wounded; Smith, Burrowes, Edwards, and Waterfield were shot dead. The 74th N. I. was then ordered to the front. Their colonel addressed them, reminded them of their past good conduct, and called upon volunteers to accompany him to the Kashmír Gate, adding that now was the time for the regiment to prove its loyalty. The sipáhís stepped forward to a man, and with the same hope which had characterised the officers of the 54th, those of the 74th led on their men. At the main-guard they found some men of the 54th N. I. who had returned from the city. The din within the walls of the city was now overwhelming. The sipáhís themselves evidently dreaded lest the strong English force stationed at Mírath should have arrived. As deeply imbued as their comrades with the spirit of revolt, they resolved, then, before they cast their lot with those who had 'pronounced,' to wait the turn of events. They remained halted, silent and thoughtful, at the main-guard. They were still there when a terrible explosion within the city shook that building to its foundations.

In the heart of the city, at no great distance from the palace, was the great magazine, full of munitions of war. On that morning there were in the magazine Lieutenant George Willoughby, in charge of it, Lieutenants Forrest and Raynor, of the Ordnance Commissariat department, Conductors Buckley, Shaw, Scully, and Crow, and Sergeants Edwards and Stewart. It would seem that at about eight o'clock the magistrate of Dehlí, Sir Theophilus Metcalfe, came down to the magazine with the information that mutineers were crossing the river, and asking for two guns to defend the bridge. But it was soon realised that the bridge was already in possession of the mutineers. Metcalfe then proceeded with Willoughby to ascertain whether the city gate had been closed to the rebels. When it became known that not only had it not been closed, but that the mutineers had been admitted to the palace, Willoughby at once realised the situation. Confident that his turn would soon come, he set to work with his subordinates to render the magazine as defensible as possible. The gates were closed and barricaded, guns were placed at salient points, double charged with grape, and a central position was established, from which the guns could bear upon any point which might be forced. Then came the crucial point. All the subordinate workers in the magazine were natives. Willoughby and his comrades hoped for a short time that these men, associated with their officers for so many years, would be faithful, and directed that arms should be served out to them. The manner in which these were received revealed to the few Europeans the fact that they would have to depend solely on their own energies. The natives, wrote Lieutenant

Forrest,[2] accepted the arms most reluctantly, 'and appeared to be not only in a state of excitement, but also of insubordination, as they refused to obey any orders issued by the Europeans.' Knowing it to be quite impossible to resist for long a serious attack, and resolved that so much valuable munitions of war should not, if they could help it, fall into the hands of the Queen's enemies, these gallant Englishmen then caused a train to be laid, communicating with the powder magazine, to be fired only when every other resource should be exhausted.

These arrangements had just been made when sipáhís from the palace came to demand the surrender of the magazine in the name of the King of Dehlí. No answer having been returned to this summons, the King, or someone acting on his behalf, sent down scaling ladders. On these being erected against the wall, the whole of the native establishment, climbing to the top of the wall, deserted by means of them, and joined the rebels. These consisted chiefly of the sipáhís of the 11th and 20th N. I. from Mírath. Against these a fire was kept up as long as possible, but the superiority of numbers was overwhelming. Still, a gallant defence was maintained. Nor was it until Forrest and Buckley had been disabled, and defence had become hopeless, that Willoughby gave the order to fire the train. Not one of the garrison expected to escape with his life. But it was otherwise ordered. Scully, who fired the train, and four of his comrades, were never seen again. They certainly perished; but Willoughby and Forrest succeeded in reaching the Kashmír gate. Raynor and Buckley, too, escaped with their lives. The loss of the assailants was far more severe. It has never, I believe, been mathematically computed, but it may be reckoned by hundreds. Nor were the casualties caused by that explosion the most important consequence of it. It was the first reply to the general revolt; it was the first warning to the King and to the sipáhís of the nature of the men whose vengeance they had dared; the first intimation to the rebels of the stern and resolute character of the Englishman when thoroughly roused. It was the sound of this explosion, occurring about four o'clock in the afternoon, which startled the English officers and sipáhís assembled at the main-guard. It was the sign for action to the latter. To them it plainly indicated that the rebels had penetrated to the heart of the city; that, for the moment, mutiny had triumphed. So, at least thought the sipáhís of the company of the 38th N. I. which had moved up to the main-guard. Raising their muskets to the shoulder, the men of that company fired a volley into the group of officers near them. Gordon, the field-officer of the day, fell dead from his horse

---

[2] Lieutenant Forrest's Report, dated May 27, 1857.

without a groan. Smith and Reveley of the 74th N. I. shared the same fate. There was nothing for it for the survivors but to run. There was a way of escape, perilous indeed, but certain for the time. This was to dash through the embrasure in the bastion skirting the courtyard of the main-guard, to drop thirty feet into the ditch, and ascending the opposite scarp, to gain the glacis, and thence the jungle beyond it. In an instant the conviction took possession of the minds of the yet unwounded officers that this way of escape must be attempted. Suddenly, however, the despairing cries of the women in the upper room of the main-guard reminded them that the escape which was easy to men might be impossible for the other sex. However, there was no other, so, conducting the women to the embrasure, the officers fastened their belts together, and whilst some of them descended first, the others from above helped the women to slide down. The whizzing of a round-shot over their heads hastened their movements, and at last, in a shorter time than had seemed possible, the descent was accomplished. More difficult was the climbing to the glacis; but this came to a fortunate end. Then the fugitives pressed on into the jungle, thence some to the cantonments, others towards the Metcalfe House.

But in neither of these places was there safety. The sipáhís were by this time thoroughly roused. There was nothing for it but flight to some less threatened spot. So men, women, and children sallied forth: alike those who had remained and those but just arrived from the main-guard. Their sufferings were terrible. They had to undergo physical tortures, and the still less endurable tortures of the mind. Tearing from their persons everything in the shape of glitter or ornament, crouching in by-ways, wading rivers, carrying the children as best they could, hiding in hollows, enduring the maltreatment of villagers, and the abuse of stray parties of wanderers, hungry, thirsty, weary, at times hunted, they at length reached shelter. Some found their way to Mírath, some to Karnál, others to Ambálah. A few perished on the way; some giving up the struggle from fatigue, others succumbing to disease. The behaviour of the women of the party was such as to make the men proud of their companions. When Captain Wood sank exhausted, unable to proceed, it was his wife, and his wife's friend, Mrs Peile, who supported him to the haven of safety. Nor was this a solitary instance. When it was found, on arriving at the night's bivouac, that one or more were missing, the less fatigued of the party went back to search for and bring them in. Generally the search was fruitless, for the scum of the population, which would have shrunk from attacking a party, had no mercy for a solitary invalid. It is due, however, to the natives to add that they were not all imbued with the hatred which animated a section of them. There were instances of assistance given by some of them, men of high and low caste alike, to the suffering and the wounded. There are those alive now who owed their safety to the compassion felt for them in their terrible straits by the kind-hearted Hindu and the loyal Muhammadan.

Meanwhile, in and immediately around the Imperial city, rebellion was triumphant. And in those early days rebellion had absolutely no mercy. Some fifty Christians, Europeans and Eurasians, who lived in the Daryá-ganj, the English quarter of the Imperial city, had at the first sound of alarm taken refuge in one of the strongest houses of the quarter, and had there barricaded themselves. But a handful of men and women, ill-armed and without supplies, was powerless against the roused rabble of the revolted capital. The house was speedily stormed, and the defenders were dragged to the palace, and lodged there in an underground apartment, without windows, and with only one door. After a stay there of five days they were taken out, led to a courtyard, and there massacred. Their bodies were thrown into carts, and were transferred thence to the waters of the Jamnah. One woman, terrified more for her three children than for herself, escaped, with them, the fate of her companions by declaring herself a convert to the faith of Islám. After that 16th of May there remained not in Dehlí a single Christian.

The King of Dehlí, Bahádur Sháh, had, meanwhile, assumed the respon-sibilities of the position which had been forced upon him. It is more than probable that the old man, left to himself, would have shrunk from the position. Outside of the walls of his citadel he had never wielded power, nor, up to the morning of May 11th, had he ever conceived it possible that he should assert himself against the western people who had conquered Hindustán. Though such a question might have been mooted in his harem, he had regarded the conversation as the wild 'chatter of irresponsible frivolity.' Yet, on that memorable morning, the position had been forced upon him. The mutinied sipáhís, who had bivouacked in his Hall of Audience, who had expelled the English from the city, who boasted their determination to drive them into the sea, must have a leader. Who so fit for such a post as the representative of the Mughal, the descendant of that illustrious Akbar, who had accomplished the union of India? From such a position it was impossible that Bahádur Sháh should recoil. Had he desired ever so much to hang back, and there is reason to suppose he was by no means eager to assume the foremost post, with its dangers, its responsibilities, its humiliations, he had a family the members of which were resolved that he should bind round his head 'the golden round.' There was the ambitious Queen, whose projects two Governors-General had in succession thwarted; her son, young, handsome, and full of ambition; her step-sons, the eldest of whom knew that, though in a certain sense the English would allow him to succeed his father, he would be shorn of all that had made succession desirable, even of the royal title. In these, and in the ambitious nobles by whom they were surrounded, and in whose bosoms dwelt the traditions of a past which had not been without glory, the 'irresponsible frivolity' of which I have spoken loudly asserted its influence. Under the pressure of that influence Bahádur Sháh agreed to assume the responsible position forced upon him. The revolted soldiery throughout India were called upon to fight for the restoration of the Mughal. The 'cry' was not altogether a happy cry for the revolters. Though it might conciliate and bind together many Muhammadans, it could scarcely fail to alienate the Marátha princes who had contested empire with the Mughal family. The result proved that the princes of Central India preferred the safe position they held under British suzerainty to aiding mutinied soldiers to restore a dynasty which they had been the first to trample under foot. Such thoughts did not, in those early days, present themselves to the minds of the 'irresponsible chatterers.' They believed that the expulsion of the English from Dehlí, and the proclamation of Bahádur Sháh as sovereign of India, was the consummation of the movement prematurely set on foot at Mírath. Unfortunately for their hopes it was only the untimely beginning.

CHAPTER VII

The Effect, Throughout India, of the Seizure of Dehlí

The story of the events of the 10th of May at Mírath, and of the 11th at Dehlí, came as a surprise alike to the revolters all over India and to the Government. It came as a surprise to the former because the astute men who had fomented the ill-feeling against the British, which by this time had become pretty general, had laid down as a cardinal principle that there were to be no isolated outbreaks; that the explosion should take place on the same day all over the Bengal Presidency; and they had fixed upon Sunday, the 31st of May, as the day of the general rising. But the chief conspirators had to employ a large number of instruments. The rashness or premature action of a single instrument may destroy the best laid plot. The heads of the conspiracy had corrupted the 3rd Native Cavalry and the 20th Regiment N. I., and had formed their committees in these regiments. But, at a critical conjuncture, the latter had been unable to restrain the rank and file of the regiments from premature action. Excited to fever pitch, eighty-five men of the 3rd L. C. had, with the sympathy of their comrades, refused to receive the proffered cartridges. Brought to trial for the offence, they had been condemned, sentenced, and lodged in gaol. This sentence had been too great a stimulus to the passions of the troopers to allow them to await patiently the day fixed upon. They saw that the English were unsuspicious, and they believed that the plot, so far as Mírath was concerned, might, by a prompt rising, be brought to a successful issue. In that events proved them to be right. But they had lost sight of the fact that, by acting solely for their own hand, they were imperilling the great principle which had been impressed upon them by their committees, and, with it, the general success aimed at by their chiefs. This premature action proved ultimately as fortunate for the English as disastrous to the cause of revolt. A blow which, struck simultaneously all over India, might have been irresistible lost more than half its power when delivered piecemeal and at intervals.[1]

On the 12th of May a telegram from Agra conveyed to the Government, in Calcutta, the information that the native cavalry at Mírath had risen, had set fire to several officers' houses and to their own lines, and had killed or wounded all the English officers and soldiers they had come across. It is not too much to record that the attitude of the Government on receiving this telegram was one of blank dismay. It was so little expected. Only two days before, Lord Canning had written a minute strongly supporting disbandment as a severe punishment to a regiment which should mutiny. Mr Dorin, the senior of his colleagues, had recorded an opinion of the same character. The military member of Council, General Low, little realising the nature of the catastrophe he had to face, had suggested that, after all, the conduct of the sipáhís might be due rather to actual dread of injury to their caste than to disaffection. Yet, on the 12th, these rulers were told that disaffection had reached its highest point; that a whole regiment, far from fearing disbandment, had actually disbanded itself, after slaying its officers. Then, indeed, they must have realised that, in their dealings with the 19th, with the 34th, with the men whose conduct Cavenagh had brought to notice, they had been pitiably weak when they had thought they had been strong; that from the first they had misjudged and misunderstood the whole business; that the disaffection, far from being confined to Bengal proper, was probably general—in a word, that they had been living in a fool's paradise.

It is due to Lord Canning to state that, within a short time of his perusal of the terrible news, he had not only recognised the grave character of the crisis, but had taken measures to meet it. On the 12th he did not know

---

[1] This is not mere surmise. Mr Cracroft Wilson, of the Civil Service, who was selected by the Government of India, after the repression of the Mutiny, to ascertain who were the guilty and who deserving of reward among the natives of the North-west, has recorded his conviction, derived from oral information, that the 31st of May was the day fixed upon by the conspirators for a general rising. Committees had been formed in each regiment, and to these alone was entrusted the general scheme of the plot. The sipáhís were directed to obey only the orders of the regimental committees. It is probable that the very severe punishment dealt out to the eighty-five men of the 3rd L. C. so excited the men that they overrode the directions of their committee and insisted upon prompt action.

From information I have obtained, in conversation with natives of the Upper Provinces, I am convinced that the theory broached by Mr Cracroft Wilson is true. It is very difficult to induce the natives who lived and took a part in the great uprising of 1857 to open their minds regarding it. But I have heard from some of them sufficient to produce conviction in my mind that a day was fixed, and that the premature action of the 10th and 11th of May was considered to have greatly damaged the chances of success.

the worst. Then it was the mutiny of the 3rd Light Cavalry that he had to meet. But two days later he received fuller particulars. On the 14th he heard of the seizure of Dehlí. On the 15th and 16th particulars reached him of the massacre of the Europeans, of the flight of the officers, of the rallying round the resuscitated flag of the Mughal. Then he stood forward as the bold, resolute, daring Englishman he really was. He telegraphed to the Governor of Bombay, Lord Elphinstone, to hasten, as far as he could, the return of the troops due in Bombay from the completed campaign against Persia. He telegraphed to the Commander-in-Chief to 'make short work of Dehlí.' He transmitted to the Chief Commissioner of the Panjáb, Sir John Lawrence, full powers to act according to the best of his judgment. Not only did he countermand the return of the 84th to Rangoon, but he sent for a second regiment from that place and from Moulmein. He wrote to the Governor of Madras, Lord Harris, to send him two regiments. More than that, recollecting that a combined military and naval expedition was on its way from England to China, to support there, by force of arms, the pretensions of the British, he took upon himself the responsibility of despatching a message to Lord Elgin and General Ashburnham to intercept that expedition, and to beg them to despatch the troops under their orders with all possible speed to India.

Having summoned those reinforcements, Lord Canning took a searching glance at the actual situation. The sudden outbreak at Mírath must have brought to his mind the conviction that he might have to meet a general rising of the Bengal army. What resources had he in his hand, not counting the troops he had summoned to his aid, to meet such a general rising? A glance at those resources was not calculated to inspire confidence. Between Calcutta and Dánápur there were no English regiments. At Calcutta and in its vicinity were the 53rd and the 84th. At Dánápur was the 10th foot. Stretching north-westward from Dánápur, the eye rested on Banáras, with no English regiment, and but a few English gunners. At Allahábád, with its important fortress, the same state of things. The same likewise at Kánhpur, the next military station beyond it. At Lakhnao, indeed, there was one English regiment, but that regiment was wanted to defend the whole province of Oudh. At Agra there was but one English regiment. Beyond Agra and Kánhpur came Mírath and Dehlí. We know, and Lord Canning knew, the condition of both those places. Beyond them were the military stations of Ambálah, and the hill stations between it and Simla, and Fíruzpur, and beyond these again, the Panjáb, as the Panjáb was then computed. Here the bulk of the British troops was concentrated, but their numbers were none too many for the needs of the province.

If the reader, bearing in mind the allotment of British troops I have just given, will study a map of India, he will realise that the prospect immediately before Lord Canning was far from reassuring. He had, as a statesman versed in affairs, to regard the native garrisons in all the stations mentioned, and in the smaller stations in their neighbourhood, as at least untrustworthy. After the events of Mírath and Dehlí, he was bound even to class them in the list of probable enemies, and to provide for them accordingly. There were native troops at Barrackpur, in eastern Bengal, at Dánápur, at Banáras, at Allahábád, at Kánhpur, scattered all over the province of Oudh, at Agra, at Alígarh, at Barélí, at Murádábád, and at other minor stations south-east of Mírath and west of Agra. In the districts in which those native troops were located Lord Canning could at the moment dispose of but four English regiments—the 53rd and 84th at or near Calcutta, the 10th at Dánápur, the 32nd at Lakhnao, the 3rd Europeans at Agra. Every man of these regiments was required for the purposes of the city or cantonment in which he happened to be. Lord Canning could not fail to recognise, then, that between Calcutta and Mírath he was absolutely powerless for aggressive purposes; that it would be marvellous could he succeed in maintaining his position until reinforcements should arrive.

On the other hand, he had great faith, and I believe at the time every Englishman south-east of Mírath had great faith, in the power of the Commander-in-Chief to retake the Imperial city. Past history afforded good reason for that belief. In September 1803 the troops of Sindhiá had not offered the semblance of a resistance to the small army of General Lake. In the wars of the earlier Mughals with the representatives of the dynasties which they supplanted, Dehlí had never offered any but the slightest resistance to the army which had been victorious in the field. Even amongst soldiers who had been stationed at that city the idea that Dehlí could present a prolonged resistance was laughed at. The conviction prevalent at Calcutta,[2] especially in military circles, was that the mutineers had played the British game by rushing into a walled city, where they would be as rats in a trap. It can easily be understood, then, how it was that the hopes of Lord Canning that the Commander-in-Chief would very soon be able to deal a deadly blow to the mutineers, by capturing their stronghold, was shared by every Englishman, or by almost every Englishman, at Calcutta.

---

[2] I write from my own knowledge, having at the time been attached to the Government of India, in Calcutta, as Assistant Auditor-General.

As to the Panjáb, though Lord Canning naturally felt anxiety, it was an anxiety tempered by confidence in the resolute man who there represented him, and in that resolute man's subordinates. He had precisely the same feeling regarding Oudh. If Oudh at this crisis could be preserved to the British, Sir Henry Lawrence, who represented there the Government of India, was the man to preserve it. He had, and justly, an equal confidence in the Governors of the minor Presidencies—in Lord Elphinstone and Lord Harris—a confidence which their splendid conduct in all the phases of the rebellion more than justified.

Looking back at the conduct of Lord Canning at this period, I cannot withhold my conviction that in all that related to his exterior policy, that is, in the efforts he made to procure assistance from outside, it was admirable. There was only one little thing, suggested to him by Lord Elphinstone, which he might with advantage have done, but which he did not do. In those days telegraphic communication with England had not been established. With the view, then, to secure the prompt arrival of reinforcements from England by the overland route, Lord Elphinstone suggested to Lord Canning the despatch to England of a special steamer, ready to his hand, which, steaming at her highest speed, should anticipate the regular mail steamer by some days. For some reason with which I am not acquainted Lord Canning declined the suggestion.

Having thus, in the manner I have recorded, endeavoured to reassure his lieutenants beyond Mírath, and to procure assistance from beyond India, Lord Canning set to work to take the measures which might be necessary to maintain his position within the country until reinforcements should arrive. In this attempt he was not nearly so successful as he was in his measures of exterior policy.

It was unfortunate that, in his measures of internal policy, Lord Canning was compelled, from his previous inexperience of India, to depend for his information on men, for the most part, of the shallowest capacity: men who, although they had served in India during periods of from fifteen to thirty years, and longer, had served with their eyes shut, and with a coil of red tape round their minds. Calcutta and its suburbs contained, in 1857, a native population exceeding half a million. In one of the suburbs lived the deposed King of Oudh, with a large following of retainers, not one of whom was disposed to love the Government which had made them exiles. To guard this large population there was but one weak wing of an English regiment, occupying Fort William. But there was a large body of Englishmen in Calcutta—merchants, lawyers, traders, clerks in public offices—who, apprehending the nature of the crisis far more clearly than the Government had apprehended it, were ready and anxious to place their services at the disposal of the Governor-General for the repression of disorder. There were also others—Frenchmen, Germans, Americans,—who were inspired by a similar sentiment. The feeling which animated these men was as simple as it was disinterested. They said in so many words to the Government: 'The situation is full of peril; you are short of men, you have to control a large population in Calcutta, and you have within call but two English regiments; there are three armed native regiments at Barrackpur, ready to emulate the conduct of their comrades at Mírath, why not utilise our services? We can furnish a regiment of infantry, a regiment of cavalry, and a battery of artillery; our interests and your interests are identical: use us.'

There was not the smallest approach to panic among these men. They were sincerely anxious to help the Government in the terrible crisis. What panic there was was confined entirely to the higher official classes and the scum of the Eurasian population. It was in the exercise of the purest patriotism, then, that the merchants and traders of Calcutta, English and foreign, offered their services, between the 20th and the 25th of May, to the Government. A wise Government would have met these offers with sympathy. The Government of Calcutta met them with language which was tantamount to insult. Whilst the English merchants and traders were told that, if they wished to enrol themselves as special constables, they might apply to the Commissioner of Police, who, it transpired, had been instructed to furnish them with clubs, the French community received from the Home Secretary, Mr Cecil Beadon, a reply which betrayed either infatuation or a determined attempt to deceive: 'Everything is quiet within six hundred miles of the capital. The mischief caused by a passing and groundless panic has been already arrested; and there is every reason to hope that in the course of a few days tranquillity and confidence will be restored throughout the Presidency.' In point of fact, the mischief had not been arrested; everything was not quiet within 600 miles of the capital; and, far from there being reason to hope that in the course of a few days tranquillity and confidence would be restored throughout the Presidency, there was the absolute certainty that disorder and insurrection would enormously increase.

The reply of the Home Secretary, representing the views of the Government, was alike untrue and impolitic. At a critical moment it alienated the sympathies of the Europeans of Calcutta. And it speaks largely in favour of the patriotism and self-abnegation of the members of that community that, about three weeks later, when the boastings of the Home Secretary had vanished into thin air, and the Government saw almost as clearly as the community had seen, at the time of their first offer, the danger of the situation, they agreed to form volunteer corps of the three arms to aid the Government in their dire necessity.

For the Home Secretary's vaunt had scarcely been made public when the ineptitude, or the wish to deceive which had prompted it, became apparent. His reply, already quoted, had been written on the 25th of May. Between that date and the 30th the native troops at Fírúzpur, at Alígarh, at Bulandshahr, at Itáwah, and at Mainpurí rose in revolt. The news from Agra, from Lakhnao, from Kánhpur, from Banáras, was of a most discouraging character. It became evident, even to the Government, that not only had the mischief not been arrested, but that it was yet in its infancy. Under these circumstances, Lord Canning could not but feel very anxious regarding the movement of the Commander-in-Chief against Dehlí. The maintenance of the authority left to the English, between the Huglí and the Indus, depended, he felt, on the promptitude of the action of the gallant soldier who, on the first news of the revolt at Mírath, had hastened to Ambálah to organise a force to march against the rebels. It was in this view that, on the 31st of May, he despatched to that officer a telegram which clearly shows how, since the Home Secretary had triumphantly 'snubbed' the French inhabitants of Calcutta on the 25th, the views of the Government had changed.[3]

Nothing reveals more clearly than this telegram that, at the very end of May, Lord Canning had but feebly grasped the situation. He had, it is true, realised the intense danger of the position below Dehlí, but no soldier himself, and having at his elbow men who were soldiers only in name, he had realised neither the difficulties which General Anson had to overcome before he could march from Ambálah, the strength of Dehlí, nor the extent of the disaffection. A more correct forecast would have made it clear to him that he had nothing to hope for from the Commander-in-Chief, that he had to depend solely upon God and his own right arm.

There was this advantage in the faultiness of his forecast that it made him confident. Those about him assured him that Dehlí could not hold out, and that the capture of Dehlí would be the turning point of the

---

[3] 'I have heard to-day that you do not intend to be before Dehlí until the 9th. In the meantime Kánhpur and Lakhnao are severely pressed, and the country between Dehlí and Kánhpur is passing into the hands of the rebels. It is of the utmost importance to prevent this, and to relieve Kánhpur, but nothing but rapid action will do it. Your force of artillery will enable you to dispose of Dehlí with certainty. I therefore beg that you will detach one European infantry regiment, and a small force of European cavalry, to the south of Dehlí, without keeping them for operations there, so that Alígarh may be recovered and Kánhpur relieved immediately. It is impossible to overrate the importance of showing European troops between Dehlí and Kánhpur. Lakhnao and Allahábád depend upon it.'

disturbances; and he believed them. Could he maintain the weak middle part, the unguarded country between Banáras and Dehlí, until succour from the North-west, from Persia, from China, from Burma, should arrive, all must go well. He had done what he could with the small means at his disposal to strengthen that middle part. On the 20th of May he had begun, and on following days he continued to despatch the 84th by driblets, as many as could be accommodated in a series of post-carriages, to Banáras and Kánhpur. On the 23rd of May the Madras Fusiliers arrived from Madras, and were promptly despatched in the same direction. The first week of June increased his hopes that the danger might be yet averted. That week witnessed the arrival in Calcutta of the 64th foot and 78th Highlanders from Persia, of a wing of the 35th foot from Maulmein, of a wing of the 37th and a company of artillery from Ceylon. These were pushed forward with all possible celerity.

It is as certain as can be, judging from his after conduct, that if Lord Canning, at this crisis, had been left to act upon his own instincts, or even if he had trusted to the experienced advice of the one capable counsellor at his elbow, Mr J.P. Grant, many of the mishaps which occurred during this month and the following would not have happened. But at this period he was under the influence of men whose knowledge of the country in which they had passed their lives was absolutely superficial. It was in deference to the advice of these men that, at a period when a plain and straight-forward declaration, followed by plain and straightforward action, would have relieved the situation, he acted towards the sipáhís in a manner the reverse of both. Thus, whilst he had three native regiments at Barrackpur, in dangerous proximity to Calcutta, he preferred to maintain troops to guard them rather than to disarm them. The case of Dánápur was even worse. The garrison of Dánápur, consisting of one English and three native regiments, was the guardian of the rich and populous province of Bihár. It was certain that, should the three native regiments break away, as their comrades in other places had broken away, a great danger would be con-stituted for Bihár itself, and possibly for Calcutta. Commonsense urged that the first opportunity should be taken to disarm them. But common-sense was a quality conspicuous by its absence among the Hallidays, the Beadons, and the Birches, who had the ear of Lord Canning. These men invented the policy of feigning confidence when confidence had been lost, and of declining to disarm men whom they knew to be rebels, lest they should instigate a premature rising. The terrible dangers which persistence in this policy—persistence in spite of warnings and remonstrances—led to will be recorded in subsequent chapters.

CHAPTER VIII

The Progress of the Insurrection in the North-west in May and June

The news of the insurrection at Mírath reached the station of Fíruzpur on the 12th of May. Fíruzpur lies immediately south of the river Satlaj, on the direct road from Dehlí to Láhor. There were stationed the 61st foot, the 45th and 57th Regiments N. I., the 10th Native Light Cavalry, and about 150 European artillerymen. The Brigadier, Colonel Innes, had only arrived the day before, and had had no opportunity of testing the temper of the native troops. But on receiving, on the morning of the 12th, news of the Mírath catastrophe, he ordered a brigade parade, that he might judge for himself. The impression made by the demeanour of the infantry was not satisfactory, but the commandants of the three regiments reported favourably regarding the disposition of their men.

That same afternoon information reached the Brigadier of the startling events at Dehlí. He at once directed arrangements for relieving the sipáhís of the 57th N. I. of the charge they had held of the magazine and arsenal. But his orders were either misunderstood or carelessly carried out, for the sipáhís, though relieved by a company of the 61st and some European gunners, were allowed to remain in the intrenched position in which the magazine was located. At five o'clock of the same day the Brigadier paraded the native troops, with the intention of marching them outside the cantonment. But as they approached the intrenchment they halted, despite the orders and entreaties of their officers, and endeavoured to escalade it. The sipáhís who had been allowed to remain within threw to them scaling ladders, and about 300 of them succeeded in effecting an entrance. The company of the 61st held them at bay until two other companies of that regiment arrived. The mutinied sipáhís made a last desperate effort, and on the failure of that fled in confusion. The Brigadier, instead of pursuing them, allowed them to roam about for a time unmolested. Gaining courage from the supineness of the authorities, the sipáhís then burned the church, the Roman Catholic chapel, the 61st mess-house, two vacated hospitals, and several bungalows. The Brigadier, in sheer panic, then caused the regimental magazines of the two mutinous regiments to be blown up. Hardly had this been accomplished when information reached him that the men of the 45th were about to start for Dehlí. Then, for the first time, he acted with vigour. With one party he disarmed the 57th N. I., whilst with another he pursued the 45th, caught and dispersed them. The greater number of them, however, and some of the 57th, found their way to the revolted city. Few affairs were worse managed during the rebellion than the affair of Fíruzpur. It almost matched the blundering at Mírath.

At Alígarh the four companies of the native regiment stationed there, the 9th N. I., considered one of the best regiments of the Bengal army, mutinied on the 20th of May. The circumstances were somewhat peculiar. Alígarh lies on the grand trunk road eighty-two miles to the south-east of Dehlí. Apparently the events of the 10th and 12th of May, at Mírath and Dehlí, had not shaken the loyalty of the sipáhís. They continued respectful in their demeanour and assiduous in the performance of their duties. But, on the 20th, a parade had been ordered to witness the infliction of the punishment of death on a man caught in the act of endeavouring to seduce the men from their allegiance. The man had been awarded this sentence by a court-martial composed entirely of native officers. It was carried out in the presence of the sipáhís, on that eventful morning, without a murmur or sign of disapproval from them. But as they were marching from the ground there arrived a detachment of men of their own regiment, one of whom, on seeing the dangling corpse, exclaimed, pointing to it, 'Behold a martyr to our religion.' These few words were sufficient to light a flame which had lain repressed in the bosoms of the sipáhís. They broke into open insurrection, and though they inflicted no injury on their officers, they plundered the treasury, released the prisoners from the gaol, and went off bodily to Dehlí.

The detachments of the same regiment at Bulandshahr, forty miles from Alígarh; at Itáwah, in the Agra Division, seventy-three miles from the city of that name; at Mainpurí, seventy-one miles from the same place, followed the example of their comrades at headquarters. The outbreak at Bulandshahr was unaccompanied by violence, though the men plundered the treasury; that at Mainpurí was chiefly remarkable for the courage, coolness, and presence of mind displayed by the officer second in command of the sipáhís, Lieutenant De Kantzow.

Information of the revolt of the 20th at Alígarh had reached Mainpurí on the evening of the 22nd. The magistrate, Mr Power, at once held a consultation with Mr Arthur Cocks, the Commissioner, as to the course to be pursued. It was resolved to despatch the ladies and children into Agra, and to march the sipáhís to a village some miles from the station. Early the following morning the ladies and children were duly despatched on their journey, and reached Agra, unmolested, in due course.

Meanwhile, the two officers of the 9th N. I., Crawford and De Kantzow, were doing all they could to induce their men to march from the station. The sipáhís, however, steadily refused to budge one inch from the extreme end of the parade ground. Finally, they warned their officers that it was well for them to depart, and some of them even discharged their muskets. In the confusion that followed, the two officers got separated from one another. De Kantzow had dismounted, and Crawford, believing that he had been killed, rode back to warn the civilians of the mutiny of the men, and to announce his own intention to ride for Agra.

Crawford found assembled Mr Cocks, above referred to, the elder Power, Dr Watson, and a missionary named Kellner. The younger Power, just returned from escorting the ladies on their first stage, joined them. After a brief consultation, Cocks and Crawford decided to make for Agra. The two Powers, Watson, Kellner, three sergeants of the Road and Canal departments, Mitchell, Scott, and Montgomery, and a clerk, Mr Glone, determined to remain. The cousin of the Rájá of Mainpurí, Ráo Bhowání Singh, with a small following, expressed his intention of standing by them.

Meanwhile, De Kantzow, on foot, had been doing all he knew to stem the torrent of mutiny. He had, in turn, implored, upbraided, and menaced the turbulent sipáhís. In vain did they level at him their loaded muskets, threatening to kill him; still did he persevere. At length, casting off the last bonds of discipline, they rushed towards the treasury, carrying their officer with them. Just as they reached the building, De Kantzow dashed forward to its iron gates, and appealed to the civil guard on duty there, consisting of thirty men, to be true to their salt, and repel the unauthorised invasion. The men of the guard responded; they rallied round him. The gaol officials joined them, and, by their united resistance, the torrent of the attack was stemmed.

More than that, it was stopped. Forbidding the men of the gaol guard to fire, De Kantzow drew them up facing the sipáhís, and for three hours kept them at bay. At the end of that period Bhowání Singh, above referred to, arrived on the spot, and induced the mutineers to retire. The only condition made by the baffled men was that Bhowání Singh should accompany them. He complied.[1]

At Itáwah the scene was more tragic and more bloody. The force at this station, which lies nearly midway between Agra and Kánhpur, though somewhat nearer to the latter, was a company of the 9th N. I. The chief civil officers were Mr Allan Hume and Mr Daniell. On hearing of the events at Mírath these gentlemen sent patrolling parties to watch the roads, and to intercept, if possible, any stray mutineers. On the night of the 16th of May one of the patrolling parties brought in as prisoners, though without depriving them of their arms, seven troopers of the 3rd Native Cavalry, a regiment which had mutinied. The patrols brought the prisoners to the quarter-guard of the 9th N. I., in front of which was drawn up the company of that regiment, with its two officers at its head. Seeing the state of affairs, the seven troopers suddenly levelled their carbines and let fly at the two Englishmen. But the men of the 9th N. I. were staunch, and, replying vigorously, they killed five of the troopers. The two survivors escaped for the moment.

Three days later the patrols attempted to lay hands upon and to disarm a larger body of troopers of the same regiment well supplied with fighting material. But in the struggle the men of the patrol were worsted. The rebels, then, probably fearing an attack in force, took up a position in a small Hindu temple, strong in itself, and stronger still in the approaches, which rendered assault difficult and dangerous.

Information of this action having been brought to Messrs Hume and Daniell, they resolved, despite the fact that assault was almost impossible, and that the villagers had shown a disposition to aid the troopers, to venture on an attack with the men of their police. But in reply to the summons to follow them but one of that force obeyed. He was promptly killed; Daniell was shot through the face. Hume, who was then left alone, forthwith retired, supporting Daniell to his carriage, and returned with him to Itáwah. That night the troopers evacuated the temple. Four days later, the company of the 9th, which had remained quiet in the interval, suddenly mutinied, looted the treasury, released the prisoners from the gaol, and inaugurated a reign of terror. Fortunately timely warning had enabled the civilians to ensure the safety of the women and children. Two days later there was a

---

[1] On the news of this occurrence reaching Calcutta, Lord Canning wrote to De Kantzow an autograph letter, from which the following is an extract:—'Young in years, and at the outset of your career, you have given to your brother soldiers a noble example of courage, patience, good judgment, and temper, from which many might profit.'

change. A regiment of the Gwáliár contingent, the 1st Grenadiers, which was to mutiny in its turn, arrived, and for the moment restored order.

But these isolated mutinies, however deplorable in themselves. counted for comparatively little so long as British authority remained supreme in the great station of Agra. Agra was a very important place. Not only was it the seat of the Government of the North-west Provinces, but, as a royal residence in the times of the early Mughals, it had great traditions, whilst its position, almost touching the territories of Gwáliar and of Rájpútána, made it a gate the possession of which by the rebels would constitute an enormous peril to British interests. A great deal, then, depended on the *personnel* of the officials, civil and military.

The Lieutenant-Governor was Mr John Colvin, a civilian trained in Bengal proper, but who had been private secretary to Lord Auckland during the troublous times of the first Afghán war. It is possible that in quiet times Mr Colvin might have gained a great reputation. He had a cultivated mind, and large intellectual faculties. But to guide the State vessel through a storm, to sway the minds of others in dangerous times, there was wanted a man with iron nerves, complete self-confidence, one who could impress his will alike on his friends and his foes. The Great Revolt of 1857 did bring to the front some men of that stamp—Havelock, Strathnairn, Nicholson, Hodgson, Roberts, Napier, and some others—but amongst them cannot be reckoned the amiable John Colvin.

The troops stationed at Agra consisted of the 3rd European Regiment, a battery of artillery (D'Oyley's), and the 44th and 67th Regiments N. I. The officer commanding the brigade was Brigadier Polwhele. The station was very straggling. The troops were cantoned in the open ground between the fort and the civil lines. The fort is a handsome quadrangle of red sandstone, built by the illustrious Akbar. It was used as a magazine and general emporium.

To the indications of ill-feeling and discontent given by the 19th and 34th N. I. in Bengal Mr Colvin had been as blind as the Government of India. Nor had the circulation of the chapátís, which had taken place about the same time in Bundelkhand and elsewhere, caused him any serious apprehension. Amongst minds of a certain order there always is the conviction that, however disturbed the surface may be, matters, if only one remains quiet, will settle down of their own accord. That feeling strongly prevailed at Agra during the early months of 1857.

The news of the mutiny at Mírath, on the night of the 10th of May, followed by that of the easy occupation of Dehlí, came to give the first **shock to** those notions. Never had men received a greater surprise. **Nor** was the surprise unmingled with apprehension. Dehlí is but 115 miles from Agra, and the first impression, based on information actually received, was to the effect that the rebels, after sacking Dehlí, would march on Agra. Under the influence of this impression, it was resolved, at a meeting of the notables of the station summoned by Mr Colvin, to secure the fortress by a detachment of the 3rd Europeans, to raise volunteers, horse and foot, and to hold a brigade parade the following morning, when the Lieutenant-Governor would address the troops.

The parade was held on the morning of the 14th, and Mr Colvin did address the troops, English and natives. He told the former not to distrust their native comrades, but added: 'The rascals have killed a clergyman's daughter, and if you meet them in the field you will not forget this.' His address to the sipáhís might have been spoken by any of Lord Canning's councillors. It breathed the same tone; it expressed the confidence which was not felt. He told them that he trusted them. The demeanour of the sipáhís was eminently suggestive. 'Prompted by their officers to cheer,' wrote Judge Raikes, who was present 'the sipáhís set up a yell; they looked, however, with a devilish scowl at us all.'

Wisdom dictated the disarming then and there of the two sipáhí regiments, but, alike at Calcutta and at Agra, 'wisdom was crying in the streets.' In both places this policy was urged upon the Government by those who did not wield authority. In both places the Government, to the detriment of the country, and to the sacrifice of many valuable lives, preferred to act the farce of feigning a confidence which they did not feel. Noting the demeanour of the sipáhís on that 14th of May, the Chief Engineer of the Agra Division, Colonel Hugh Fraser, advised Mr Colvin to recognise the emergency, to distrust the native soldiery, and to move into the fort. But Mr Colvin had not at all realised the nature of the crisis. He believed he would be able to maintain order, and he reported to this effect to the Government in Calcutta.

Far more astute was the native prince whose capital lay but sixty-six miles from Agra. I have said that the city of Agra almost touched the plains of the territory known as the dominions of Sindhiá. The actual representative of that family, Mahárájá Jaiájí Ráo, possessed a vigorous intellect, and a thorough knowledge of his country-men. He had read much, conversed much, and thought much, and the conclusion at which he had arrived had satisfied him with the position which, as a protected prince, supreme in his own territories, he held under the overlordship of the British. Between him and them no discordant clash had arisen. During his career he never ceased to remember that it was to the statesmanlike moderation of a Governor-General of India, Lord Ellenborough, that he was indebted for the complete inheritance of his immediate predecessor. During the visit to Calcutta, of which I have written in a previous chapter, this sagacious prince had noticed, with an accuracy never at fault, the signs of the times. He had observed the strong undercurrent of native feeling working against the British. The impressions conceived in Calcutta were more than confirmed after his return to Gwáliár, and he had informed the Governor-General's Agent at his Court that, in his opinion, the situation was extremely perilous. The news of the events at Mírath and Dehlí had driven fast into his mind these convictions, and he was satisfied that a very evil time was approaching for his overlord.

Could his great predecessor, Mádhájí Ráo, have risen from his grave, it is possible that, holding these convictions, he might have used all the resources at his disposal to drive home the blow which had been dealt at Dehlí. But Jaiájí Ráo had had far more personal experience of the English than had been granted to the greatest representative of his house. He knew, from his own dealings with them, that they were to be trusted implicitly. Under their suzerainty he enjoyed all the internal authority his ancestors had wielded, whilst his suzerain bound himself to assure him against aggression from without. For what compensating advantage was he to renounce this position? To place himself and the resources of his State at the disposal of mutinous soldiers or a puppet king? Who, too, was that puppet king? He was no other than the descendant of the Mughal sovereigns who had in vain tried to sudue the Maráthás, and whom the Maráthás had instead subdued. No; there was no temptation to turn against those whom he had proved to support others whom he despised. Not for a moment did he hesitate. From the hour he heard of the events at Dehlí he threw himself heart and soul into the cause of the British.

Sindhiá had in this very month warned the British Agent at his Court not only that the sipáhís' army was undermined to the core, but that the men of his own regiments, officered by British officers were not more to be depended upon. When, therefore, after the famous parade at Agra, described in a previous page, Mr Colvin, believing that the mutiny was a Muhammadan movement, in the repression of which those not imbued with the faith of Islám would aid, applied to the Mahárájá Sindhiá and to the Bharatpur regency for material assistance, that assistance was indeed immediately afforded by the despatch of native troops, alike from Gwáliár and Bharatpur. But, whilst responding to the call, Sindhiá expressed to the British Agent his grave doubts as to the consequence of his compliance.

The parade at Agra had been held on the morning of the 14th of May. On the 21st Mr Colvin heard of the mutiny at Alígarh, and two days later of the events at Bulandshahr, at Mainpurí, and at Itáwah. They were serious events for Agra, as they severed direct communications with the North-west, but they brought to the mind of the Lieutenant-Governor no solid conviction as to the cause of the general uprising.

Still mistaking the signs of the times, still beating the air, still hoping that an appeal to the reasoning powers of the sipáhís might induce them to reflect, Mr Colvin, at this period, issued a proclamation which, though well meant, was, to say the least, injudicious. The proclamation was based upon the possibility that the majority of the sipáhís had been, and were being, misled by turbulent ringleaders. It therefore offered a frank and free pardon to all sipáhís, irrespective of their offences. Naturally enough the proclamation produced no effect whatever, that is, it did not bring back a single penitent into the fold. But it had the result of convincing the sipáhís and their leaders that they might continue their treasonable work with impunity.

It is due to Lord Canning and his colleagues to add that they disapproved of Mr Colvin's proclamation, and substituted another for it of their own composition. This, though dealing largely with offers of mercy, made exceptions against men whose hands had been imbrued in blood. But this proclamation was as ineffective as that which it was intended to supersede.

Mr Colvin's proclamation was issued on the 25th of May. Five days later three companies of sipáhís, constituting the garrison of Mathurá, thirty miles to the north-west of Agra, mutinied, shot down one of their officers, wounded another, plundered the treasury, fired the houses of the English, released the prisoners from the gaol, and started off for Dehlí. Their example was followed by the bulk of the troops sent to the aid of Mr Colvin from Bhartpur.

This outrage, known the same evening at Agra, roused Mr Colvin to striking point. He directed the Brigadier to hold a parade the following morning to disarm the native troops. The parade was held (May 31), and in the presence of a battery of European artillery and the 3rd European regiment, the sipáhís of the 44th and 67th N. I. were directed to pile their arms. There was a moment of hesitation followed by sullen obedience. On examining the muskets afterwards many were found loaded with ball. The disarming of these regiments was followed by a resolution, promptly carried out, to raise volunteers, horse and foot, from the planters, clerks, traders, merchants, and others in the district.

Still the situation, though less immediately dangerous, did not improve. The risings in the vicinity had left Agra isolated. The power of taking an initiative had passed from Mr Colvin. It was for him now to await the action of the rebels. This, too, when he was to a great extent ignorant of the events passing around him. Nor was this all. The reports from Major Charters Macpherson, the British Agent at Sindhiá's Court, left no doubt upon his mind that the sipáhís of the Gwáliár contingent might break out at any moment. Any insurrection in that quarter must be full of danger for Agra.

The Gwáliár contingent was composed of four field-batteries—one of which, under Captain Pearson, had been sent to Agra—a small siege-train, two regiments of cavalry, and seven of infantry, aggregating 8,318 men. Some of these were absent on command, but the bulk was at Gwáliár.

On the night of the 14th of June the whole of these men broke out into insurrection. They rushed from their lines in tumultuous disorder, murdering every European they met. Seven British officers, one lady, wife of one of the officers, an English nurse, the wife of a warrant officer, three children, and six sergeants and pensioners, fell victims to their fury. The remainder escaped to Agra. They reached that place in driblets, and were kindly received. Mr Colvin, however, still maintained his position in the plains; nor was it until quite the end of the month that the pressure of circumstances compelled him to give the order to take refuge within the fort. There we must leave him whilst we turn to notice the action of the Commander-in-Chief.

CHAPTER IX

The March to Dehlí

The Commander-in-Chief in India, General George Anson, though he had had but a slight experience of the Bengal sipáhí, possessed in an eminent degree the gift of commonsense. If he did not penetrate the mysteries which baffled men who had been trained in India, and who had spent their lives with the sipáhís, no blame can on that account attach to him. He was conscientious, painstaking, self-sacrificing, and gave to the work which had been entrusted to him all his time and all his capacity. In intellectual ability he towered above the men who surrounded him.

The summer headquarters of the army were at the pleasant hill-station of Simla. Thither General Anson was progressing in the third month of 1857, inspecting troops and stations as he marched. Early in that month he had reached Ambálah, fifty-five miles north of Karnál, and thirty-seven from Kálka, immediately at the foot of the Himaláyan range. At Ambálah was one of the depôts of instruction in the use of the new rifle. Now, although no greased cartridges had been served out to the men, the instructors in the new drill had noticed a general feeling of alarm and suspicion pervading their minds, not only as to the nature of the grease, but as to the materials of which the ungreased paper wrapped round the cartridges was composed. The matter came to the knowledge of General Anson. A circumstance, slight in itself, convinced him that the suspicions of the men, unless removed, might lead to great danger. Accordingly, on the 23rd of the month, he inspected the instruction depôt, and after the inspection he summoned round him the native officers, and, assisted by the instructor, Lieutenant Martineau, an officer of great intelligence, who spoke the language like a native, and who translated to the native officers each sentence of the Commander-in-Chief as it was uttered, addressed them frankly and sensibly on the subject of the new rifle. He told them that great improvements had been made of recent years in the manufacture of small-arms, and that it was with the view of placing in the hands of the sipáhí a superior weapon that detachments from several regiments had been sent to Ambálah for instruction; that the improved weapon required improved cartridges; that it was madness to suppose that the British Government, which had no designs whatever on the religion of the people, should take advantage of the improvement of the cartridge to endeavour to subvert their caste by a fraud; that the Government of India would never countenance any scheme which would coerce the Hindu or the Muhammadan in the matter of religion. In the case before him, neither caste nor religion was involved; but another thing was, and that was discipline. That discipline he was resolved to maintain, and he trusted that the native officers present would exert themselves to allay the fears of their men, would caution them not to give credit to the insinuations of designing persons, and would thus avert the shame which would overwhelm those who should prove false to their colours and faithless to the oaths they had taken to the Government.

It was a new thing in the history of the Bengal army to see the Commander-in-Chief condescending to explain the action of the Government, and the reasons for that action, to a large number of regimental native officers. That the native officers present were touched by General Anson's act cannot be doubted. They listened respectfully, and, when the meeting was over, they expressed to Martineau their high sense of the goodness of the Commander-in-Chief, and of the honour he had done them. 'But,' they added, 'it is not a mere question to us of obedience or disobedience. The story has been so generally circulated, and is so generally believed, not only by the sipáhís but by their relations and by villagers all over the country, that the sipáhís cannot use the cartridges without incurring the certainty of social degradation, the consequence of their loss of caste.' They begged Martineau to represent this fact to the Commander-in-Chief. Martineau did so, and General Anson, who recognised more plainly than anyone about him the dangers staring him in the face, suspended the issue of the new cartridges until a special report should have been prepared of the composition of the paper with which they were wrapped.

The secret agents of the vast conspiracy hatched by the Maulaví of Faizábád and his associates had by this time done their work so thoroughly, had roused, to a pitch of pent-up madness of which an oriental people are alone capable, the feelings of the sipáhís and the population of the North-western Provinces generally, that it is improbable that, if the Government had even gone the length of withdrawing absolutely the new musket, and the new cartridge with it, the plague would have been stayed. The attempt of General Anson in that direction was undoubtedly the best thing to be done. But, unhappily, his scheme was not given a chance. Lord Canning and his advisers wrote to say that they would regard any postponement of the target practice at the drill depôts as a concession to unreasonable fears. No violation of caste would be caused by the use of the cartridges, therefore the drill must be persisted in. The main offence of the 19th N. I. had been the refusal to take the cartridges. For that they had been punished, and it would be inconsistent with discipline to go back on the resolution then taken. Despite, then, the consequences clearly shadowed forth by the assembled native officers to Martineau, the drill instruction was continued.

In due time General Anson continued his journey to Simla. He was there when the report reached him of the behaviour of the eighty-five troopers of the 3rd N.L.C. at Mírath, already described. The Commander-in-Chief considered their offence so serious that he directed they should be brought to trial before a court composed of their own countrymen. How they were tried, how condemned, how lodged in confinement, has been already told. It has been told, also, how the vindication of discipline led immediately to the revolt of Mírath and the uprising of Dehlí.

The news of this double catastrophe reached General Anson in a bleared and imperfect form on the afternoon of the 12th. His clear and practical mind recognised that immediate action was necessary. He had three English regiments near him, on three different spurs of the Himaláyas. To that on the spur nearest to the plains, the 75th foot, at Kasáuli, he sent orders to march immediately for Ambálah. To the two others, the 1st Fusiliers and the 2nd Europeans, at Dagshai and Sabáthu respectively, he transmitted orders to hold themselves in readiness to march at a moment's notice. Simultaneously he sent expresses to desire that the fort at Fíruzpur should be secured by the 61st, and that at Govindgarh by the 81st, and to order two companies of the 8th foot, from Jálandhar, to secure Philáur on the Satlaj. Bethinking then of the other means available to him, he ordered a Gurkhá regiment, known as the Nasírí battalion, stationed close to Simla, to march, with a detachment of the 9th Irregular Cavalry, to that important point (Philáur), in order to escort thence the siege-train which, he recognised at a glance, would be necessary for the operations he contemplated against Dehlí. On the afternoon of the 14th he started for Ambálah himself, and reached it early the following morning. He, at least, had lost no time.

But it was there that his difficulties commenced. He found the sipáhís of the native regiments there ready to break out in revolt. With the English force at his disposal he could easily have disarmed them, and that course was pressed upon him by Sir John Lawrence. It seemed so natural that he should do so. He could not take mutinous regiments with him. Still less could he leave them at Ambálah, unwatched, to perpetrate untold mischief in his rear. But General Anson was conscious that his own local experience was limited whilst he was surrounded by men who professed to understand the natives amongst whom their lives had been spent. These men protested that the disbanding of the sipáhís would be regarded as a breach of faith. The argument was absurd, but it was accepted.

Another misfortune came at this moment to render the situation more involved. The Gurkhás of the Nasírí battalion, when ordered to march to Philáur, refused point-blank, and made as though they would plunder Simla. The residents there were terribly frightened, and some of those who should have given an example of courage and daring betrayed a strong capacity for leading the way in pusillanimous flight. The fears, fortunately, proved unfounded. The Gurkhás of the Nasírí battalion were quickly satisfied, returned to their duty, and marched gaily for Philáur.

Meanwhile, at Ambálah, General Anson began to realise every day more keenly that the means at his hand for the recapture of a strong fortress, garrisoned by a superior number of disciplined troops, were very insufficient. Not only were his European troops few in numbers, but the several war departments—the Commissariat, the Medical, the Transport, the Ordnance, and Ammunition—taken by surprise, were unprepared for a prompt movement. On the 18th of May the men had no tents, but twenty rounds apiece of ammunition, no artillery reserve ammunition, no transport.[1] Under these circumstances, General Anson doubted whether it would be prudent with his small means to risk an attack on Dehlí. He wrote in this sense to Sir John Lawrence, expressing not only his own opinion but that of the chief officers of his staff. The Commissary-General, he added, declared his inability to provide the wherewithal for such a march under from sixteen to twenty days. These views, backed as they were by the highest military authorities on the spot, found no acceptance either with Sir John Lawrence, with Lord Canning, or with the self-constituted critics in other parts of India. The idea widely prevailed that, because Dehlí had never, in the history of India, offered a serious resistance to an armed force, it would not and could not do so now. There was absolutely no reason for this argument beyond that suggested by the notion that that which had happened before must always happen again. There was, I have already mentioned, a very indistinct idea in military circles as to the defensive power of the Imperial city. Everyone knew that it was encompassed by walls. But, it was argued, with the superficiality which was one of the signs of the times, that siege-guns were cast in order that they might batter

---

[1] Letter from General Barnard, dated Ambálah, May 18, 1857.

down walls. The man would have been laughed at who should have asserted that Dehlí was as strong as Bharatpur had been. It was expected, alike in Calcutta and in the Panjáb, that General Anson had but to appear with his British force before Dehlí to induce the rebels to surrender the city.[2] I write with the most absolute certainty when I state that this was the main reason which incited alike Lord Canning and Sir John Lawrence to urge the advance with a force they knew to be insufficient for a great enterprise. I am confident that if the givers of that advice had realised the strength of Dehlí, and its splendid capabilities of resistance, they would have urged the advance, if they had urged it at all, in language betokening far less confidence. Undoubtedly they felt, and felt most keenly, the enormous issues at stake. Sir John Lawrence did not attempt to conceal his conviction that the maintenance of order in the Punjáb depended on the prompt reduction of Dehlí. Lord Canning knew that the safety of the long and weak middle piece between Alláhábád and Mírath would be enormously affected by the retention by the rebels of a place possessing such a history and such prestige. Yet, keenly anxious as they were to strike the decisive blow at the decisive point, I doubt much whether they would have employed the language, almost of remonstrance, which characterised their letters to General Anson if they had imbibed anything like a correct idea of his difficulties, and of the still greater resistance which was awaiting his troops at their destination.

Goaded by the tone and matter[3] of the letters he received, General Anson prepared to march. For the task before him his force was singularly inadequate. It consisted of the 9th Lancers, the 75th foot, the 1st and 2nd European Regiments, two troops of horse-artillery, and a native regiment, the 60th N. I. These troops were at Ambálah. At Bághpat, one march from Dehlí, they would be joined, if the General's orders were carried out,

---

[2] Sir John Lawrence wrote (May 21): 'My belief is that, with good management on the part of the civil officers, it' (Dehlí) 'would open its gates on the approach of our troops.'

[3] For instance, such words as these from Sir John Lawrence: 'Pray only reflect on the whole history of India. Where have we failed when we have acted vigorously? Where have we succeeded when guided by timid counsels?' Lord Canning wrote him that everything depended 'upon speedily disposing of Dehlí, and making a terrible example.' To the letter from which I have quoted he added a paragraph which showed how incompletely he and his advisers had, at this period, grasped the situation: 'Your force of artillery will enable you to dispose of Dehlí with certainty. I therefore beg that you will detach one European infantry regiment and a small force of European cavalry to the south of Dehlí, without keeping them for operations there, so that Alígarh may be recovered and Kánhpur relieved immediately.' This request to a Commander-in-Chief whose troops were already too few, and who had before him the hardest task ever allotted to a British commander in India!

by the Mírath brigade, composed of two squadrons of the Carabineers, a wing of the 60th Rifles, one light field-battery, one troop of H.A., and some sappers. At the same place, where he expected to arrive on the 5th of June, General Anson hoped to be joined by a small siege-train from Lodiáná. It was a great advantage to him that at this critical period the Cis-Satlaj chiefs and the Nuwáb of Karnál decided to cast in their lot with the British. The assistance they afforded in keeping open the communications and in influencing the populations of the several districts cannot be over-estimated.

Providence did not permit General Anson to witness the triumph of the measures he had organised with so much diligence, so much forethought, and so much ability. He waited at Ambálah until he had despatched all but the very last of his troops, and with these, on the 25th of May, he set out for Karnál. Shortly after his arrival there, on the 26th, he was attacked by cholera, and a little after midnight succumbed to that terrible disease. He was succeeded by Sir Henry Barnard, who arrived just in time to be recognised by his dying chief. General Anson's death was a great loss to the army. Those who least cared for him have admitted that 'he was a brave soldier and an honest gentleman.' He was that, and much more. Those who knew him best were convinced that had he lived through the Mutiny he would have gained a splendid reputation.

Sir Henry Barnard was a worthy successor in command of the advancing force to General Anson. He, like his late chief, had felt bitterly the criticisms and the carpings levelled against the military plans by ignorant and uninstructed outsiders. But, imbued with the conviction that if a thing is to be done at all it must be done thoroughly, Barnard threw all his energies into the work which had devolved upon him. 'So long as I exercise any power,' he wrote to Sir John Lawrence, on the 26th, 'you may rest assured that every energy shall be devoted to the objects I have now in view, viz., concentrating all the force I can collect at Dehlí, securing the bridge at Bághpat, and securing our communications with Mírath.' Determining not to wait for the siege-train, he set out from Karnál, on the morning of the 27th, and reached Alípur, twelve miles from Dehlí, on the 6th of June. There I must leave him for a moment to look after the force which was to join him from Mírath.

The authorities at Mírath had taken some time to recover from the effects of the horrors of the night of the 10th of May. The country seemed to be surging around them. The scum of the population had risen in the villages, the gaols had disgorged their prisoners, and, generally, except on the actual spot still occupied by Europeans in Mírath itself, order had everywhere disappeared. In the cantonment and the civil lines martial law had been proclaimed. But a deep despondency had crept over all minds—a despondency augmented by the news of the success of the rebels in Dehlí, and of outrages from outlying stations. There had been risings at Rurkí, sixty miles from Mírath, the headquarters of the engineering science of the country, at Sahâranpur, and at Muzaffarnagar. There were murmurings, to break a little later into open mutiny, in the several stations of Rohilkhand. It is true that the energy and firmness of Baird-Smith, a man whose name will for ever be connected with the fall of Dehlí, saved Rurkí; and that the strong character and devotion of Robert Spankie and Dundas Robertson maintained order in Sahâranpur. But the alarm created by the attempts at rising there and elsewhere tended greatly to depress those at Mírath, who apparently had been thoroughly unnerved by the terrible night of the 10th of May.

Nothing created so much surprise throughout India as the inaction of the troops at Mírath during the days which succeeded that night. Two splendid English regiments, supported by two batteries of artillery, might surely, it was argued, do something in the district. Those in authority elsewhere, who argued thus, waited in vain for the development of the action they were impatiently expecting. At last Mr Colvin, who, from his post at Agra, the importance of which I have pointed out, had the best reason in the world to dread the consequences of inaction, noting its continuance, addressed Brigadier Wilson, passing over his senior officer, General Hewitt, and begged him, at the very least, to keep open the main road, so as to prevent the combinations of revolted troops pushing for Dehlí. But not from Wilson even did Mr Colvin receive the answers he hoped for. 'The only plan,' replied that officer, 'is to concentrate our forces and attack Dehlí.'

That was all very well and very true. But, in his general contention, Mr Colvin was right and Brigadier Wilson was wrong. The force might have been kept concentrated to join General Anson and yet have shown itself in the district. Because it did not show itself, the idea began to prevail in the villages round about that all the English had perished on the night of the 10th of May. Much looting and much bloodshed occurred in consequence. It was in repressing one of the outbreaks caused by this belief that a promising civil officer, Mr Johnston, lost his life.

At length orders arrived from the Commander-in-Chief that the brigade should take the field and join the force marching from Ambálah at Bághpat. It set out on the 27th of May. It consisted of two squadrons of the Carabineers, a wing of the 60th Rifles, Tombs's troop of horse-artillery, Scott's light field battery, two eighteen-pounder guns, manned by Europeans, some sappers and irregular horse (natives). Three days' marching brought the force to the town of Ghazí-úd-dín Nagar, about a mile from the left bank of the little river Hindan. Partly on the opposite bank, and partly in the bed of that river, then a fordable rivulet, abounding in quicksands and spanned by a suspension bridge, they beheld a considerable body of the mutinied sipáhís, well equipped, their guns occupying a strong position to the right of the bridge, commanding the advance. The English had to march along a causeway exposed to the enemy's fire. This opened at once, but it was almost immediately replied to by the eighteen-pounders and by Scott's field-battery. Under cover of this fire the rifles advanced, and soon came in contact with the enemy in the bed of the rivulet. The sipáhís fought well, and the contest was fiercely contested, when the Carabineers, making their way across the stream, turned the enemy's left. This was the decisive moment. Pressed in front by the 60th, and mauled in their left flank by the carabineers, the rebels gave way, and fell back on a walled village. The 60th, however, followed them close, and expelling them from this position, forced them to flight along the Dehlí road. The sipáhís lost many men, and left in the hands of the victors five of their guns. The British loss, though small in itself, was large in proportion to the numbers engaged. The intense heat prevented the following up of the victory.

Never was more clearly illustrated the truth of the axiom that a victory not followed up is but half a victory. Undaunted by their defeat, and possibly stimulated by the taunts of their comrades, the sipáhís returned the next day to the battle ground. Taking up about midday a position on a ridge to the right of the Hindan, they opened fire from their guns on Wilson's force. The English guns replied, and for two hours ensued a fierce artillery combat. At the end of that period, Wilson, noticing that the fire of the rebels was slackening, ordered a general advance. The sipáhís did not await it. Discharging into the advancing columns of the English a shower of grape-shot, they limbered up and fell back in orderly array. The intense heat, and the parching thirst suffered by the English, prevented any pursuit. The English were much exhausted, and there were some cases of sunstroke. But great satisfaction prevailed in the camp from the fact that the Mírath brigade, which had been the first to suffer from the treachery of the sipáhís, had been the first to retaliate.

The next day (June 1) the camp was cheered by the arrival of the 2nd Gurkhás, 500 strong, commanded by an officer who was to occupy a prominent position during the siege, Major Charles Reid. The brigade, after its two engagements, had halted for orders. These were received on the 4th. In pursuance of these, Wilson marched, on the 6th, to Bághpat. The day following he effected the desired junction at Alípur. There also had arrived the siege-train from Philáur, after having undergone some dangers from the contemplated treachery of the mutinous sipáhís of the 3rd and 5th N. I.

The junction of all the then available forces had been effected on the morning of the 7th of June. There was now, therefore, no excuse for delaying to carry out the policy insisted upon by Lord Canning and of Sir John Lawrence, that of marching straight into Dehlí. The one had expressed his opinion that the artillery with the force was sufficient to deal with the place; the other that, on the approach of the English troops, the city would open its gates. These theories were now put to the test. Early on the morning of the 8th of June (one o'clock) General Barnard gave the order to advance from Alípur. The scouts had reported that the rebels had taken a strong position at Badlí-kí-Sarái, six miles to the north of Dehlí, a place where groups of old houses and walled gardens, once the country residences of nobles of the Imperial Court, supplied positions capable of prolonged defence. Day was just dawning when Barnard came in sight of this position. As far as he was able to judge, the salient points were strongly armed with guns. To test their strength he sent to the front four heavy guns, a troop of horse-artillery, part of a battery of field-artillery, and directed them to open fire. A few rounds disclosed the fact that the enemy's guns, which had promptly returned the fire, were of heavier calibre than those Barnard had sent to the front. The British gunners began to drop, and it seemed doubtful whether they would be able to hold their own. There was but one remedy for this—a remedy which has never failed against Asiatics. Barnard tried it. He sent the 75th deployed, and supported by the 2nd Europeans, to charge the rebels' guns. The charge was splendid, but the rebels displayed a stern resolution, clinging to their guns and giving back thrust for thrust. There was no flinching, and there was no cry for quarter.

Whilst the 75th and the 2nd Europeans were struggling bravely for the guns, the second brigade, led by Brigadier Graves, attacked the enemy's left, whilst, a minute later, Hope Grant, with the cavalry and the horse-artillery, appeared on their rear. The movement of Hope Grant was decisive. The front defence collapsed almost immediately, and the rebels fell back. At first it seemed as though their retreat would be orderly, but the lancers and the horse-artillery took care that this should not be so. Making charge after charge, despite of water-courses and other obstacles, and firing round after round, they compelled the beaten enemy to loose his hold on his guns and his camp equipage, and to retire, baffled and humiliated, within the walls of the city. Barnard, with consummate judgment, pushed on; then having completed the rout of the enemy, he turned to the ridge overlooking Dehlí, drove thence the rebels posted there, and encamped in the position whence he could best direct his attacks on the proud city, which, in spite of his appearance before it, still defied his arms. He and his men had done good work on that eventful day. He had driven the enemy within the walls, with a loss to them of about 350 men, twenty-six guns, and some serviceable ammunition. He had gained and firmly occupied the finest base of operations against the city, a position open in the rear to the reinforcements which he hoped to receive, whilst commanding the plain right up to the walls. What was, perhaps, of scarcely less importance, he had distinctly announced to the rebels throughout India, avowed and concealed, the plain issue between themselves and the British. From this time forth there was no possibility of doubt. The fate of Dehlí would decide the fate of India.

Barnard had not accomplished his end without loss. The killed and wounded amounted to 137. Amongst the former was the Adjutant-General of the army, Colonel Chester, shot down at the commencement of the action. His death was a loss to the gallant soldier, who, fresh from his service in the Crimea, had, without much Indian experience, assumed the command of the besieging army at a moment's notice.

The day following the Corps of Guides, a regiment composed of cavalry and infantry, stationed normally at Hotí-Mardán, on the Panjáb frontier, arrived in camp, led by its commandant, Colonel Henry Daly. Soon after its arrival it was despatched to the front to drive back parties of horse and foot which had sallied from Dehlí to attack the advanced posts of the British. In the engagement which followed the Guides carried all before them. They had, however, the misfortune to lose their acting second-in-command, Lieutenant Quintin Battye, an officer of great promise and of far-reaching popularity. Mortally wounded by a bullet through the body, he murmured to the chaplain who tended him, and who had warned him that but a very brief span of life yet remained to him: '*Duice et decorum est pro patriâ mori.*' A few minutes later he died.

Leaving the besiegers on the ridge they had so gallantly won, I propose, before returning to Calcutta, to take a glance at Kánhpur and Lakhnao. I shall then visit Jhansí and Bundelkhand, and then devote separate chapters to the complete story of the places which bore the brunt of the early conflict. These, in the Bengal Presidency, were Bihár, Kánhpur, Oudh, Agra, and Dehlí. Western, Southern, and Central India will likewise demand a large share of the attention of the reader.

CHAPTER X

Kánhpur, Lakhnao, and Allahábád

Kánhpur was the centre station in that weak middle piece of which I have written as causing so much anxiety to Lord Canning. It lies on the right bank of the river Ganges, 270 miles south-east from Dehlí, and 120 above the confluence of the Jamnah and Ganges at Allahábád. From Calcutta it is distant by rail 684 miles, somewhat more by the river route. The station is long and straggling, the houses having been erected more with the view to secure pleasant and healthy situations than for military defence.

In 1857 the garrison of Kánhpur consisted of the 1st, the 53rd, and the 56th Regiments N. I., the 2nd Native Light Cavalry, and sixty-one English artillerymen, with six guns—five nine-pounders, and a twenty-four-pounder howitzer. The station also sheltered the families of the 32nd foot, then stationed at Lakhnao. Kánhpur was the headquarters of a division. The general commanding was Sir Hugh Massey Wheeler, an officer of the highest character as a soldier. He had spent fifty-four years in India, had served with the sipáhís, under Lord Lake, in the Marátháwars, in Afghánistán, and in the wars against the Sikhs. He was very much esteemed, and it was thought that if any man could unravel the mysteries which shrouded the early events of 1857 that man would be Sir Hugh Wheeler.

Sir Hugh had watched, with the deepest anxiety, the early development of the action of the sipáhís. It is due to his memory to record that he had taken a far more serious view of it than that which had commended itself to the advisers of Lord Canning. In his eyes it was 'no passing and groundless panic,' but a deliberate scheme for the overthrow of the British power. He did not know, he had no reason to suspect, that the principal conspirator was within a few miles of him. The outward demeanour of the Náná Sáhib was never more suave than it was just before the outbreak. He was the adviser, and the trusted adviser, of the civil authorities.

Confident that the native army was infected from the crown of its head to the soles of its feet, Sir Hugh, looking round at the straggling station in which he commanded, recognising the utter impossibility of organising a plan of general defence, resolved to select, partially to fortify and store with provisions, one spot in the station, which should be a rallying point, when the danger signal should sound, for all the English and Eurasians, men, women, and children, and which he might be able to defend until succour should arrive. The idea showed prescience and courage. It was the same idea which at the same time occurred to, and was acted upon, by the sagacious Mr Boyle at Árah, by Sir Henry Lawrence at Lakhnao.

His great difficulty was to select a suitable position. The station, I have said, was straggling, covering, as far as the magazine at its further end, that is, the end nearer to Dehlí, a length of seven miles. The cantonment was open, and possessed no kind of fortification. It was separated by the Ganges from Oudh, and Sir Hugh Wheeler was too experienced in the modes of thought of the natives not to be absolutely certain that in the men of Oudh the English would find their most persistent enemy. He had to choose a spot the situation of which should lend itself easily to succour from the side of Allahábád. From that direction alone was succour to be expected. In a military sense, then, it was doubly advisable to select a locality the approaches to which from the Allahábád side should be easy. Such a locality seemed to be at hand. In the centre of a large plain, with a tolerably clear space all round them, were two barracks, formerly used as the hospitals of the European regiment, but at the moment unoccupied. The locality was about the best he could have chosen. He has been blamed since alike for not choosing the magazine and for not choosing a place of refuge immediately on the river. But the magazine was an impossible locality. It was seven miles distant, and to reach it one had to traverse the lines of sipáhís and the native town. A barrack or large house on the river bank would undoubtedly have been the best place of refuge had any such of sufficient size existed, but there was none. The position chosen fulfilled some necessary conditions. It lent itself to aid from Allahábád. The space around it was tolerably clear, the only drawback being that on its left front, at a distance of about 400 yards, was a row of unfinished barracks then in course of construction. These might be used either by the defenders as an outwork, or by the rebels as a substantial place of cover, for their attacking parties.

It is further due to the memory of Sir Hugh Wheeler to add that no one then anticipated that the sipáhís, if they should mutiny, would endeavour to slaughter the Europeans. After the events of the 10th and 12th of May, at Mírath and Dehlí, the cry amongst the sipáhís had been to march to the centre point, to the ancient capital of the Mughals. By attacking the position on the plain they could gain neither loot nor glory. Such an attack, by chaining them to the spot, might ultimately involve their own destruction. I shall have to relate that, so far as the sipáhís were concerned, this reasoning was justified to the letter. No one dreamt at that time that the smiling and obsequious prince, who was wont to drive in from Bithor to aid the civil authorities with his advice, would possess the influence and the inclination to turn the fury of the revolted sipáhís against the wives and children of the officers they had followed in many a hard-fought field.

Sir Hugh Wheeler made the selection I have spoken of the very day that the sad story of the revolt at Mírath reached him. From that date there reigned in his mind the conviction that a rising at Kánhpur might take place at any moment. He pushed on, therefore, the fortifying and victualling of the two barracks with as much speed as possible. The fortifications were to consist of earthworks. But the rains had not fallen; the soil of the plain was baked almost to the consistency of iron, and the progress was consequently slow. Whilst pushing on these works, Sir Hugh communicated freely with the civil authorities at the station, with Sir Henry Lawrence at Lakhnao, and with the Government at Calcutta.

The Collector of Revenue at Kánhpur was Mr Hillersdon. Between this gentleman and Náná Sáhib there had been considerable official intercourse, and the Englishman had been pleased by the friendly and courteous manner and conversation of the Asiatic. When the news of the Mírath outbreak reached Kánhpur, the Asiatic showed his further friendliness by advising Hillersdon to send his wife and family to Bíthor, where, he assured him, they would be safe against any possible outburst on the part of the sipáhís. Hillersdon declined for the moment, but when, a little later, the Náná offered to organise 1,500 men to act against the sipáhís if they should rise, Hillersdon considered that the proposal was one to be accepted. To a certain extent it was acted upon.

I have said that Wheeler, feeling that the storm might burst any moment, pushed on with all his energy the preparation of the barracks. His spies told him that every night meetings of an insurrectionary character were taking place in the lines of the 2nd N.L.C. and of the 1st N. I. In ordinary times these meetings would have been stopped with a high hand; but the example of Mírath had shown that, even with a strong force at the disposal of the General, high-handed dealing was sure to precipitate mutinous action, and Wheeler had but sixty-one men to depend upon. On the 21st he received information that the 2nd N.L.C. would rise that night. He accordingly moved all the women and children into the entrenchment, and attempted to have the contents of the treasury conveyed thither; but the sipáhís would not part with the money. Then it was that the General, much against the grain, availed himself of the offer made by the Náná to Mr Hillersdon, and agreed that 200 of the Bíthor chief's men should be posted at Nuwábganj, guarding the treasury and the magazine.

The next day, Wheeler was cheered by the arrival of eighty-four men and two officers of the 32nd, sent to him in his dire strait by Sir Henry Lawrence. The week that followed was a particularly trying one. The officers of the native regiments, to show their sipáhís that they still trusted them, slept every night in the lines of their men. The non-combatants meanwhile, that is, the trading Europeans, the Eurasians, and their families, had removed, on the 22nd, to the entrenchment. Towards the end of the month the General had pitched his tent within the position. Still, time went on and no move was made by the sipáhís, and when, on the mornings of the 31st May and the 1st and 2nd of June, the first relays of the 1st Madras Fusiliers and the 84th, despatched by Lord Canning from Calcutta, reached Kánhpur, Wheeler considered that the crisis was past, that is, that the sipáhís, noting, from the arrival of English troops, that the country to the south-east was open, would feel that mutiny was too hazardous to be attempted. So great, indeed, was his confidence that he passed on fifty of the 84th to Lakhnao.

It is possible, indeed, that, could the line between Calcutta and Kánhpur have been maintained intact, this result might, to a certain extent, have been obtained. The sipáhís, that is to say, might have been content to march on Dehlí without attempting to molest the English at Kánhpur; but early in June that line was broken, in the manner to be described, at Allahábád; it was menaced at Banáras; and, later still, it was rent in twain at Dánápur. The consequences of the breaking of the line at the place first named, and of the example set by the sipáhís there and elsewhere in the vicinity, were seen when, on the night of the 4th of June, the men of the 2nd Cavalry mutinied. I must ask the reader to permit me to defer the story of the events which followed that uprising until I shall have cleared the ground by narrating the contemporaneous events at Lakhnao, at Allahábád, and at Calcutta.

In a previous chapter I have narrated how Sir Henry Lawrence met and suppressed the first attempts at mutiny at Lakhnao (May 3rd and 4th). Knowing the impressionable character of the natives of India, and having at the moment no means of judging the extent to which the ill-feeling had been nurtured, or the depth to which it had taken root, Sir Henry resolved to emphasise the first repression of disloyal action by the holding of a grand

Darbár, to be attended by all the English residents, by the officers and men of the native regiments, and by all the native officials. The announced reason for the holding of the Darbár was the presentation to the native officer and non-commissioned officers and men, who had behaved with distinguished loyalty on the 3rd of May, of honours to mark the sense entertained by the Government of their conduct.

The Darbár was held on the evening of the 12th of May. Sir Henry seized the occasion to make to the assembled natives, in their own language, an address which, if it had then been possible for words to affect the question, could scarcely have failed to produce great results. He began by alluding to the fears which had been expressed by the Hindus for their religion. Turning to them, he pointed out how, under the Muhammadan rule prior to Akbar, that religion had never been respected; how Hindus had been forcibly converted, and cruelly persecuted; how the third prince in succession to Akbar had reverted to a similar system. Turning then to the Muhammadans, he reminded them how the great sovereign who had founded the Sikh kingdom would never tolerate the exercise of the faith of Islám at Láhor. Speaking then to both sections, he asked them to contrast with such actions the action of the British rulers. He referred to the principle of toleration, acted upon for a century; to the manner in which Europeans and natives had worked together with a common purpose, sharing the same toils and the same dangers, and mutually congratulating one another when reaching the goal at which each had aimed. He then implored them not to allow themselves to be led away by the devices of men who were trying to entrap them, with the view of leading them, for their own selfish purposes, to assured destruction. Calling then to the front the native officer and the men who had signalised themselves by their loyalty on the 3rd, he bestowed upon them, in the name of the Government, substantial tokens of its appreciation of their conduct.

The solemn occasion, the character of the speaker, the truth of the language he employed, combined to produce a considerable effect. Those present were much moved; but the conspirators had done their work too well to allow their dupes to be baffled by a few eloquent and impressive sentences. Whatever was the effect produced by the speech of the 12th of May, that effect was entirely obliterated when, on the 16th, the events of the 10th and 11th of the same month, at Mírath and Dehlí, became common property. No one then recognised more clearly than Sir Henry Lawrence that the days of parleying had gone by, and that the differences between the sipáhís and the Government had entered upon a phase in which victory would be to the strongest. Much, in Oudh, he realised, would depend upon the action of those in whose hands should be concentrated the supreme civil and military authority. He possessed the first, but not the second. Representing the case to Lord Canning, he received, on the 19th, a notification of his appointment as Brigadier-General, in supreme command in Oudh. Then he set to work to prepare for the crisis which he knew might be upon him at any moment.

The city of Lakhnao, built on the west bank of the river Gúmtí, but having suburbs on the east bank, lies forty-two miles to the east of Kánhpur, and 610 miles from Calcutta. All the principal buildings lie between the city and the river bank. Here also are the Residency and its dependencies, covering a space 2,150 feet long from north-west to south-east, and 1,200 feet broad from east to west. A thousand yards to the west of it was the Machchí Bhawan, a turreted building used for the storage of supplies. Close to it, and in the present day incorporated with it, is the Imámbárah, a mosque, 303 feet by 160. The other palaces will be spoken of when it shall be my task to describe the 'leaguer' of this famous place. It must suffice to state now that a canal·which intersects the town falls into the Gúmtí about three miles to the south-east of the Residency, close to the Martiniére; that about three-quarters of a mile to the south-south-east of this is the Dilkushá, a villa in the midst of an extensive deer park. To the north-east of the Residency lay the cantonment, on the left bank of the Gúmtí, communicating with the right bank by means of two bridges, one of stone, near to the Machchí Bhawan, the other of iron, 200 yards from the Residency. Recrossing by this to the right bank the traveller comes to the palaces, to be hereafter mentioned, between the Residency and the Martiniére. To the south-west of the town, about four miles from the Residency, is a walled enclosure of 500 square yards called the Álambágh, commanding the road to Kánhpur. In May 1857, the troops at Lakhnao consisted of the greater part of the 32nd foot, about 570 strong, fifty-six European artillerymen, a battery of native artillery, the 13th, 48th, and 71st Regiments N. I., and the 7th Native Light Cavalry. Up to the time of the receipt by Sir Henry Lawrence of the patent of Brigadier-General these troops had been employed in the way then common in India, that is, the sipáhís had been entrusted with the care of important buildings, the Europeans being sheltered as much as possible from the heat of the sun.

Sir Henry at once changed this order. He reduced the number of posts to be guarded from eight to four, three of which he greatly strengthened. All the magazine stores he removed into the Machchí Bhawan, to be guarded by a company of the 32nd and thirty guns. At the treasury, within the Residency compound, he stationed 130 Europeans, 200 natives, and six guns. At the third post, between the Residency and the Machchí Bhawan, commanding the two bridges, he located 400 men, Europeans and natives, with twenty guns, some of them eighteen-pounders. The fourth post was the travellers' bungalow, between the Residency and the cantonment. Here he posted two squadrons of the 2nd Oudh Native Cavalry, with six guns.

In the cantonment, on the left bank of the Gúmtí, there still remained 340 men of the 32nd foot, fifty English gunners, six guns, and a complete battery of native artillery. The 32nd were, towards the end of May, reduced by eighty-four men, despatched to the aid of Wheeler at Kánhpur. The 7th Native Cavalry remained at Múdkípur, seven miles distant from the Lakhnao cantonment.

As soon as these arrangements had been completed, Sir Henry, on the 24th of May, caused to be moved into the Residency enclosure the ladies, the families, and sick men of the 32nd, and the European and Eurasian clerks. These last he armed and drilled, and had them told off into parties for night duty. On the 27th he wrote to Lord Canning that the Residency and the Machchí Bhawan 'were safe against all probable comers.' That very day, however, he had evidence that the country districts were surging around him, and he had to despatch one of the ablest of his assistants, Gould Weston, to Maliábád, fifteen miles from Lakhnao, to restore order. Further, also on the 27th, he despatched Captain Hutchinson, with 200 sowárs and 200 sipáhís, to the northern frontier of the province, there to be under the orders of the civil officer who had asked for them. The measure certainly ridded Lakhnao of the presence of 400 disaffected soldiers, but it resulted in the murder by them of all their officers save one. Hutchinson was able to return safely to his post.

Before this mutiny occurred (7th and 8th June) the catastrophe at Lakhnao had come upon Sir Henry. On the night of the 30th of May the greater number of the sipáhís of the 71st N. I. rose in revolt, fired the bungalows, murdered Brigadier Handscomb and Lieutenant Grant, wounded Lieutenant Hardinge, and attempted further mischief. The attitude of the European troops, vigilant at the posts assigned them by the Brigadier-General, completely baffled them, and they retired in the night to Múdkípur, murdering Lieutenant Raleigh on their way. Thither, at daylight, Sir Henry followed them, and though deserted by the troopers of the 7th N. L. C., who joined the mutinied 71st N. I., and by some men of the 48th N. I., drove them from their position, and pursued them for some miles. Their action had, in fact, proved advantageous to Sir Henry Lawrence. It had rid him of pretended friends, and had shown him upon whom he could rely. The great bulk of the 13th N. I. had proved loyal; but the whole of the 7th Cavalry, more than two-thirds of the 71st N. I., a very large proportion of the 48th N. I., and a few of the 13th N. I. had shown their hands. Their departure enabled Sir Henry still further to concentrate his resources.

Every day brought intelligence from the outlying districts of the seriousness of the crisis. At Sítápur, fifty-one miles from Lakhnao, there had been incendiarisms at the end of May. On the 2nd of June the sipáhís of the 10th Oudh Irregulars, there stationed, had thrown into the river the flour sent from the town for their consumption, on the pretext that it had been adulterated with the view of destroying their caste. On the 3rd the 41st N. I. and the 9th Irregular Cavalry broke out in mutiny, and murdered many of their officers and of the residents, under circumstances of peculiar atrocity. The number of men, women, and children so murdered amounted to twenty-four.

At Maláun, forty-four miles to the north of Sítápur, the natives rose as soon as they heard of the events at the latter place. At Muhamdí, on the Rohilkhand frontier, the work of butchery on disarmed men, women, and children, on the 4th of June, was not exceeded in atrocity by any similar event during the outbreak. At Faizábád, at Sikrorá, at Gondah, at Báhráich, at Malapur, at Sultánpur, at Saloní, at Daryábad, at Purwá, in fact at all the centres of administration in the province there were, during the first and second weeks of June, mutinies of the sipáhís, risings of the people, and conduct generally on the part of the large landowners which proved that their sympathy was with the revolters. By the 12th of June Sir Henry Lawrence had realised that the only spot in Oudh in which British authority was still respected was the Residency of Lakhnao.

We left Sir Henry chasing, on the morning of the 31st of May, the mutinied sipáhís from the station of Múdkípur. Between that time and the 11th June his health, undermined by long service in India, had given way. But the measures of Mr Gubbins, the officer who acted for him during his illness, and which were in direct opposition to the principles which he had inculcated, had the effect of rousing him from his bed of sickness. One of his strong points was to maintain at Lakhnao as many sipáhís as would serve loyally and faithfully. Without the aid of sipáhís the Residency, he felt, could not be defended against the masses which a province in insurrection could bring against it. Mr Gubbins, during his illness, had despatched to their homes all the sipáhís belonging to the province of Oudh. Sir Henry promptly recalled them. What was more. Believing he might successfully appeal to the memories of an imaginative people, especially to that class which had in former years enjoyed the benefits of British service, and in later had not been subjected to the manœuvres of the conspirators, he despatched circulars to all the pensioned sipáhís in the province inviting them to come to Lakhnao to defend the masters to whom they owed their pensions, and whose interests were bound up with theirs. The response to these circulars was remarkable. More than 500 grey-headed soldiers came to Lakhnao. Sir Henry gave them a cordial welcome, and selecting about 170 of them for active employment, placed them under a separate command. With these and the loyal sipáhís he had now nearly 800 able-bodied men fit for any work they might be called upon to perform.

But many disloyal sipáhís still remained in his vicinity. Of these the cavalry and infantry of the native police broke out on the night of the 11th and the morning of the 12th. Vainly did their commandant, the Gould Weston of whom I have spoken, endeavour to recall them to their duty. He owed his own life to his remarkable daring. The 32nd, sent in pursuit, followed up the mutinied policemen and inflicted some damage, but the ground was broken, the heat was great, and the mutineers had a considerable start. It was in many respects an advantage to be rid of them.

In view of the great crisis now so near as almost to be touched by the hand, Sir Henry had continued to strengthen the slight defences of the Residency enclosure, and to make the Machchí Bhawan as defensible as possible. He had originally resolved to hold both places. But as soon as he had realised the fact that the small number of his troops would permit only of his retaining one portion against the surging masses of the city and the provinces, he had decided to concentrate all his forces within the Residency. He still, however, for the moment held the Machchí Bhawan, believing that the report of his preparations there would have some effect on the rebels.

He was not quite certain, at this time, that he would be besieged at all. Everything depended on Kánhpur.[1] If British reinforcements could reach that place whilst Wheeler should still be holding it, then, he argued, the people of Oudh, in face of an English force within forty-two miles, would not dare to attempt the siege. He feared very much, however, for Kánhpur. He would have marched to succour the place if it had been possible, but, in the face of the masses of the enemy holding the Ganges, he could not have reached Wheeler's entrenchment, whilst he would have certainly been destroyed himself. At length, on the 28th, he heard that Kánhpur

---

[1] 'If Kánhpur holds out, I doubt if we shall be besieged at all.' Sir H. Lawrence to Lord Canning.

had fallen, and that the rebels of his own province, emboldened by the news, had advanced in force to the village of Chinhat, on the Faizábád road, eight miles from the Residency.

Sir Henry promptly decided to move out and attack the rebels. He held, and I am confident he held rightly, that nothing would tend so much to maintain the prestige of the British at this critical conjuncture as the dealing of a heavy blow at their advanced forces. Accordingly, he moved his troops from the cantonment to the Residency, and at half-past six o'clock, on the morning of the 30th of June, set out in the direction of Chinhat, with a force composed as follows: 300 men of the 32nd foot, 230 loyal sipáhís, a troop of volunteer cavalry, thirty-six in number, 120 native troopers, ten guns, and an eight-inch howitzer. Of the ten guns four were manned by Englishmen and six by natives. The howitzer was on a limber drawn by an elephant driven by a native.

After marching three miles along the metalled road the force reached the bridge spanning the rivulet Kukrail. Here Sir Henry halted his men, whilst he rode to the front to reconnoitre. Reining in his horse on the summit of a rising ground, he gazed long and anxiously in the direction of Chinhat. Not a movement was to be seen. Nor when he turned his glass in other directions did he meet with better fortune. There was no enemy. He sent back, then, his assistant Adjutant-General to order the column to retrace its steps. The column had begun to act on the order when suddenly there was descried in the distance a mass of men moving forwards. Instantly revoking his first order, Sir Henry sent fresh instructions that the column should advance. It advanced accordingly, and after proceding a mile and a half plainly saw the rebels drawn up at a distance of about 1,200 yards, their right covered by a small hamlet, their left by a village and tank, whilst their centre rested, uncovered, on the road. Just as the English sighted them the rebels opened fire.

Sir Henry at once deployed his men, and bidding them lie down, returned the fire. The cannonade lasted more than an hour, when suddenly it ceased on both sides. Shortly after the rebels were descried, in two masses, advancing against both flanks of the English. The ground lent itself to such a movement, made by vastly superior numbers. For, parallel to the line formed by the men of the 32nd, was the village of Ishmáilganj, and into it the rebels were now pouring. The seizure of this village by one-half of the rebel force was a very masterly manœuvre, for it enabled the rebels to pour a concentrated flanking fire on the English line, whilst the other wing was threatened from the opposite side. Conspicuous success attended the movement. In an incredibly short space of time the 32nd had lost nearly half its numbers, and it became clear that the English force would be destroyed unless it could reach the bridge over the Kukrail before the enemy could get there. The retreat was at once ordered, and the British force, though pounded with grape and harassed by cavalry all the way, pushed on vigorously. Just, however, as the retreating troops approached the bridge they noticed that bodies of the enemy's cavalry had worked round and were heading them in that direction. The commander of the thirty-six volunteers observing the movement, and realising on the instant its importance, dashed, at the head of his men, against the rebel cavalry. The latter did not wait to receive the impetuous onslaught, but giving way at the sight of the English, sought safety in flight. Still the rebel infantry pressed on, and what was worse, the gun ammunition of the British was exhausted. In this crisis Sir Henry had recourse to one of those heroic remedies of which only men are capable who have the faculty of maintaining undaunted presence of mind in dangerous circumstances. He pushed his men across the bridge; then placed the guns on it, and ordered the gunners to stand beside them with the port-fires lighted. The ruse produced the desired effect. The rebels shrunk back from attacking a narrow bridge defended, as they supposed, by loaded guns. The British force then succeeded in gaining the shelter of the city, and in retiring in some sort of order on the Machchí Bhawan and the Residency. But their losses had been severe, and they had left behind them the howitzer and two field-pieces.

Sir Henry Lawrence, crossing the Kukrail bridge, and disposing his guns in the manner related, had galloped off, leaving Colonel Inglis to bring home the force, unattended by anyone save his assistant Adjutant-General, Captain Wilson, to the Residency. Arrived there he despatched fifty of the 32nd, under Lieutenant Edmonstone, to defend the iron bridge against the rebels. This, despite the efforts of the elated enemy, they succeeded in doing, though with some loss. The rebels, however, had penetrated within the city, and, aided by the mass of the population, began to loophole many of the houses in the vicinity of the Residency and the Machchí Bhawan. They went so far as to attack one of the posts of the Residency, afterwards known, from the officer who ultimately commanded there, as 'Anderson's post.' The house which constituted the salient point of the post was the residence of Mr Capper. That gentleman was standing in the verandah when a shot from the rebels brought it down and buried him in the ruins. He would have been lost but for the determination to save him at all cost expressed by Anderson. Working with a will, under the concentrated fire of the rebels, this officer, aided by Corporal Oxenham, 32nd foot, M. Geoffroi, a Frenchman, Signor Barsotelli, an Italian, and two Englishmen, Lincoln and Chick, succeeded, by incredible exertions, in rescuing him.[2] It was a very gallant deed.

The following evening Sir Henry, threatened at both points by the enemy, caused the defences of the Machchí Bhawan to be blown up, and concentrated his forces within the Residency enclosure. From that date, the 1st of July, began that famous 'leaguer,' to the story of which I shall, in its proper place, devote a separate chapter.

Following the plan I have laid down or narrating in as close order as possible the contemporaneous events in the stations whose proximity rendered the action in one more or less dependent upon the action in the others, I propose to turn, for a short space, to Allahábád. That place, situated at the junction of the Ganges and the Jamnah, constituted the armed gate through which alone succours from Calcutta could reach Kánhpur and Lakhnao. Should that gate be closed, or should it be occupied, the fate of both the places mentioned would have depended entirely on the result of the operations before Dehlí.

The fort of Allahábád, founded by Akbar in 1575, lies on a tongue of land formed by the confluence of the two great rivers above mentioned. It is 120 miles distant from Kánhpur, seventy-seven from Banáras, 564 by the railway route, and somewhat more by water from Calcutta. It touched the southern frontier of Oudh, and was in close proximity to the districts of Juánpur, Ázamgarh, and Gorákhpur, the landowners in which had been completely alienated from their British masters by the action of the land and revenue system introduced by Mr Thomason.

The news of the disasters at Mírath and Dehlí reached Allahábád on the 12th of May. The force there was entirely native, the garrison consisting of the 6th Regiment N. I. and a battery of native artillery. Additions to this purely native force were made early in the month of May. On the 9th a wing of the 'Regiment of Fíruzpur,' a Sikh regiment which had been raised on the morrow of the campaign of 1846, and on the 19th a squadron of the 3rd Oudh Irregular Horse, also natives, reached the place. The bulk of these troops occupied a cantonment about two and a half miles from the fort, to which they furnished weekly guards. The commanding officer was the Colonel of the 6th N. I., Colonel Simpson, a polished gentleman, but scarcely a born leader of men. The chief civil officers were Mr Chester and

---

[2] Oxenham received the Victoria Cross; but Capper always felt that he owed his life primarily to Anderson, who was left unrewarded. It was Anderson who suggested the attempt to rescue, who summoned the others to assist him, and who took the chief part in the operation. That operation lasted three-quarters of an hour, during every second of which Anderson, acting against the advice of his superior officer, exposed himself voluntarily to imminent danger.

Mr Court, both men of ability—the last named, who was magistrate, one of the most energetic, daring, warm-hearted, and enterprising men in India.

These gentlemen had pointed out to the authorities in Calcutta the great danger of leaving a place so important as Allahábád entirely in the hands of natives, and they received permission, in May, to procure from Chanár, a fortress on the Ganges, seventy-six miles distant, some of the European invalided soldiers permanently stationed there. Sixty-five of these arrived on the 23rd of May, and a few more later. They were at once placed within the fort.

One of the most remarkable features of the great rebellion was the supreme confidence which officers of the native army reposed to the very last in their own men. This confidence was not shaken when the regiments around them would rise in revolt. Every officer argued, and sincerely believed that, whatever other sipáhís might do, the men of his regiment would remain true. This remark applied specially to the officers of the 6th N.I. I had shortly before been serving at the same station with that regiment, and in no other had I noticed such complete sympathy as existed in it between officers and men. To make their men comfortable, to see that all their wants were attended to, had been the one thought of those officers. I am bound to add that the men, by their behaviour, seemed to reciprocate the kindly feelings of their superiors.

When, then, regiments were rising all over India, the officers of the 6th boasted that, whatever might happen elsewhere, the 6th N. I. would remain staunch and true. So strong was this conviction among them that when, on the 22nd of May, a council was held of the chief civil and military authorities, Colonel Simpson deliberately proposed that the whole of his regiment should be moved into the fort to hold it. Mr Court most strenuously, and ultimately successfully, opposed this proposal. The day following the invalids arrived from Chanár, and then all the non-combatants of the station, those in the civil service excepted, moved into the fort with their property.

A circumstance occurred towards the end of May which seemed to justify the confidence of the officers of the 6th N. I. The sipáhís of the regiment, professing the greatest indignation at the conduct of their brethren in the north-west, formally volunteered to march against Dehlí. Their offer was telegraphed to Calcutta, and afforded ground to the councillors of Lord Canning to insist upon their contention that the mutinous spirit was confined to but few stations.

About a week after the sipáhís of the 6th had volunteered to march against the capital of the Mughals they rose in revolt, and murdered many of their own trusting officers, and some young boys, newly-appointed ensigns, who happened to be dining at the regimental mess. It happened in this wise. In reply to the offer to volunteer, the Governor-General had thanked the regiment for its loyalty. A parade was ordered for the morning of the 6th of June to read the Vice-regal thanks to the sipáhís. Colonel Simpson read the words of Lord Canning, and then, on his own behalf, spoke feelingly to the men in their own language, telling them that their reputation would be enhanced throughout India. The sipáhís seemed in the highest spirits, and sent up a ringing cheer. But that evening, whilst the officers and the new arrivals from England were dining at the regimental mess, they rose in revolt, and whilst one detachment attempted to secure the guns of the native battery, the bulk of the men gathered in front of their lines and received their officers as they rode to the spot with murderous volleys. Amongst those who fell were Captain Plunkett, an officer who loved his men, and who only that morning had expressed to them his admiration of their loyalty, the Adjutant, Lieutenant Steward, the Quarter-Master, Lieutenant Hawes, and Ensigns Pringle and Munro. Of officers not belonging to the regiment, the Fort Adjutant, Major Birch, Lieutenant Innes of the engineers, and eight of the unposted boys but just arrived from England, were mercilessly slaughtered. Nor was the attempt to capture the guns less successful. Despite the exertions of Lieutenant Hardward, commanding the battery, who narrowly escaped with his life, and of Lieutenant Alexander of the Oudh Irregulars, who was killed, the guns were dragged into the lines of the mutineers. The native gunners, in fact, and the troopers of the Oudh Irregulars had fraternised with the rebellious sipáhís. The other officers of the 6th succeeded in securing refuge within the fort..

But was the fort a sure refuge for them? At the moment it seemed very doubtful. And if the fort were to go, the sacrifice of the lives of those behind its ramparts would be the least part of the evil. The strongest and most important link between Calcutta and Kánhpur would in that case be severed. The bulk of the troops garrisoning the fort were Asiatics. There was one company of the 6th N. I., and there was the wing of the Sikh regiment of Fíruzpur. On the other side were sixty-five European invalided soldiers, the officers, the clerks, the women, and the children. The temper of the Sikhs was known to be doubtful. News had arrived that, at Banáras, their countrymen had been fired upon by English gunners. Much, if not everything, depended upon the control possessed over them by their officers.

Fortunately their senior officer on the spot was a man of great daring, of strong character, and absolutely fearless. This was Lieutenant Brasyer, an officer who had been promoted from the ranks for his splendid conduct during the Satlaj campaigns of 1846, and who had risen to a high position in the regiment of Fíruzpur. Brasyer's keen instinct detected on the instant the necessity of taking a quick and bold initiative. Bringing up, then, his Sikhs, supported by the guns on the rampart manned by the sixty-five invalids from Chanár, and on his flank by the hastily armed Europeans and Eurasians, to a point commanding the main gate, at which was posted the company of the 6th N. I., he ordered the sipáhís to pile their arms. There was a moment of hesitation, but then, sullenly and unwillingly, the mutinous soldiers obeyed the order. The muskets were secured, and the sipáhís were expelled from the fort.

The fort was secured, but the town, the civil station, and the cantonments were for the moment in the power of the rebels. Most cruelly did they abuse that power. The gaols were broken open, and then the released scum of the population perpetrated atrocities at which the human mind revolts. Not only were the European shops pillaged, the railway works destroyed, the telegraphic wires torn down, but the Europeans and Eurasians, wherever they could be found, were cruelly mutilated and tortured. The death that followed their indescribable torments was hailed by the sufferers as a blessed relief. It need scarcely be added that the treasury was sacked. Then the sipáhís, glutted with blood and gold, abandoning the intention they had previously announced of marching to Dehlí, formally disbanded themselves and made their way, in small parties of twos and threes, each to his native village.

Their departure did not for the moment affect the state of affairs in the city and the station. The land-owners, influenced mainly by their dislike of the system known as the Thomasonian system, had risen about the city and in the neighbourhood. A day or two later there came to lead them a man who styled himself the 'Maulavi,'[3] and who possessed considerable organising powers. There we must leave them, whilst we return to Calcutta to note the impression which the events I have recorded in this chapter made upon Lord Canning and his advisers.

---

[3] This man is not to be confounded with the Maulaví of Faizábád, of whom I have spoken as having been one of the chief organisers of the rebellion. The Allahábád 'Maulaví,' whose name was Laiákat Alí, had been a schoolmaster, with a great reputation for sanctity.

CHAPTER XI

Calcutta in June and July

I left Lord Canning and his councillors, at the end of May, endeavouring, by the despatch of troops by driblets from the capital to the North-west, to strengthen that weak middle piece upon the security of which, until reinforcements should arrive in sufficient strength, or until Dehlí should fall, the safety of the Empire seemed to depend. For a moment the opinion prevailed that the second of these contingencies would happen first. For, as I have had occasion more than once to mention, the strength of Dehlí was greatly underrated, and the majority of British residents, military as well as civil, believed that the appearance of General Anson before the gates of the city would suffice to induce the rebels to surrender it. That was certainly the opinion of Lord Canning and his councillors. It was under the influence of this conviction that the Home Secretary had disdained the offers of the Englishmen and foreigners who had volunteered to enrol themselves, telling them that 'the mischief caused by a passing and groundless panic had been already arrested.'

But the first week of June saw the hopes of the Government rudely shattered. Thick as hail, post by post, came tidings of disaster. Accounts of the mutinies at Kánhpur, at Allahábád, at Lakhnao, of the defection of Oudh, related in the last chapter, of revolts and murders at Ázamgarh, at Juánpur, at Banáras, at Jhánsí, to be yet related, followed one another in quick succession. To counter-balance these misfortunes came the news of Brigadier Wilson's victory at Ghazí-úd-dín Nagar on the 31st of May. But the information, which reached Calcutta about the same time, that General Anson had succumbed to cholera at Karnál, on the 27th, seemed at the moment a misfortune great enough to outweigh even this victory.

Lord Canning and his councillors, however, made a great attempt to repair it. They telegraphed to Madras for Sir Patrick Grant, Commanding-in-Chief at that Presidency, to come up to Calcutta to replace Anson. Grant was an officer in the Bengal army who had filled the office of Adjutant-General, and it was supposed that, in the existing terrible crisis, one who had been able to rise to such a position would possess experience from which the Government might profit. The mistake was a natural one, but it was not the less a mistake. A clerk promoted to the headship of the department in which he has served is rarely able to lift his mind above routine. So it was with Sir Patrick Grant. Sent for in the crisis of a mutiny, whilst the entire country was surging with revolt, he arrived with his mind full of reconstruction and reorganisation, and he was unable to the last to apply it to any other consideration. For all the good he effected he might as well have remained at Madras.

Before he arrived the news from the revolted districts became daily more alarming. To the list already given might be added Rohilkhand, Bundelkhand, and a part of Central India. The Government was indeed to be pitied. Little more than a fortnight had elapsed since they had refused the offers of the British and foreign residents of Calcutta to volunteer, on the ground that all difficulties had been arrested, and now insurrection was approaching daily nearer to their doors.

For the state of the three armed native regiments, within fifteen miles of Calcutta, was such as to cause great alarm. The followers of the ex-King of Oudh, considerable in number and hostile in feeling, swarmed in a very near suburb of the capital. Lord Canning could not but feel, under these circumstances, that he had been somewhat hasty in rudely repulsing the offers made to volunteer on the 25th of May. On the 11th of June, then, he sent for the Town-Major, Major Cavenagh, a man possessing a singularly practical mind and quick perceptions, and consulted with him as to the advisability of conceding the prayer which he had previously rejected. The advice of Cavenagh was in entire accordance with his character. On the following day, then, the necessary orders were issued. The enrolment began immediately, and in an incredibly short space of time the Government had at its disposal a serviceable body of gentlemen, horse, foot, and artillery—men devoted, unselfish, desirous only to serve their country, and serving it with all their might, and whose enrolment permitted Lord Canning to despatch to the threatened districts the croops which, but for the volunteers, he would have been forced to retain at the capital.

The order for the enrolment of the volunteers had been issued on the 12th of June. On the 13th the Governor-General and his councillors passed an Act to gag the press. That some restraint was requisite for the native press may be admitted, for it was preaching sedition all over the country. But to include in the gagging measure the loyal English press, which, whilst it had supported the English interests, had not shrunk from indicating, in no measured language, the mistakes and shortcomings of the Government, was considered as but a poor return to the independent classes of Calcutta for the services which the Government had but the day before accepted. The feeling engendered by the inclusion of the English press in this otherwise necessary Act was, then, very bitter, and remained so to the very last.

The Act was read three times on one day, and passed. The day was a Saturday. At a late hour that night Sir John Hearsey, commanding at Barrackpur, sent an express to Lord Canning telling him that he had certain information that the sipáhís of his brigade would rise the following day; that he had therefore ordered down from Chinsurah the 78th Highlanders, and that, with their aid and that of the 35th foot and a battery of guns, he proposed to disarm the sipáhís the following day. Lord Canning gave him the required permission.

It is perhaps as well that I should state what I witnessed in the capital on that eventful day, known in history as 'Panic Sunday.' The morning was clear and bright. There was nothing at the time to indicate that a crisis was at hand. At eleven o'clock I proceeded, as was my wont, to the church within Fort William. As the service there proceeded I was struck by the continuous sound of the trampling of horses and the rolling of gun-carriages, evidently quitting the fort. On the conclusion of the service I drove to the house of the Home Secretary, Mr Beadon, then residing with two other gentlemen in Chauringhí. Mr David Money, of the civil service, a relation of my wife, was staying with him. Mr Beadon was in his shirt sleeves, engaged in writing, and apparently much occupied. I told him and his friends what I had heard in the fort, but my remarks elicited no reply. I returned home to luncheon, and remained in my house the rest of the day. About four o'clock I was roused by a sound of the movement of horses and carriages, and almost immediately afterwards a note was placed in my hand. It was from Mr David Money. It ran as follows: 'Come over with M. at once; the regiments at Barrackpur have mutinied, and are marching on Calcutta. There is no time to be lost. We have a stone staircase, five good rifles, and plenty of ammunition. Come without delay.' Proceeding to the gate of my house, which was in Chauringhí, and commanded the plain as far as the glacis of the fort, I saw that plain covered with fugitives, some riding, some in carriages of sorts, some in palanquins, some running, some walking—men, women, and children all making for the nearest fort gate. It was a sight, once seen, never to be forgotten. Deeming that at such a crisis it was the duty of every Englishman to stay at his post, I declined the kind offer made me, and stood there for some time watching the extraordinary scene. I noticed, as I drove out that evening, that many of the houses near me were deserted, and that a terrible panic had taken hold of the Eurasians. I ascertained, too, that many high-placed officials had sent their families on board ship, that some of them had proceeded thither themselves, whilst others had been content to barricade their houses, to await, without undressing, the events of the night.

There was just this reason for the alarm. The native regiments at Barrackpur had contemplated rising on that day. The admirable foresight and energy of General Hearsey defeated their plans. That night, Saturday, he summoned, by express, the 78th Highlanders from Chinsurah. One wing of the regiment started at once, and though misled by a guide, reached Barrackpur at daybreak. The other wing came in about three hours later. At four o'clock in the afternoon Hearsey paraded the brigade—the three native regiments, a wing of the 35th foot, and the 78th, the two latter having their muskets loaded with ball, and a battery of artillery, the guns of which were also ready for action. The sipáhís obeyed without a murmur the orders given to them to pile their arms, and the danger was over. It was the dread of what might have happened which had led so many in Calcutta to believe that it had happened.

Early the following morning the Foreign Secretary, Mr Edmonstone, escorted by a party of English soldiers, proceeded to the residence of the ex-King of Oudh at Garden Reach, and, at the interview which followed with that prince, informed him that the exigencies of the time required that he should change his quarters to Fort William. The ex-King behaved with dignity and propriety, protesting in the most solemn manner that neither by word nor deed had he encouraged the mutineers. He declared himself ready to proceed whithersoever the Governor-General might direct. Taken to the fort, accompanied by his late prime minister and a few other nobles, he was lodged in the Governor-General's own house. There his comforts were thoroughly attended to, and as, even when he was residing at Garden Reach, he had never quitted the domain allotted to him, it may be said truly that never was captivity less felt.

The day after this event Sir Patrick Grant arrived in Calcutta and took up the nominal command of the army. He did not quit the city during his six weeks' tenure of office. His presence there may then be passed over as an incident not affecting the progress of affairs.

The next day, the 17th, the news of the action fought by General Barnard before Dehlí reached the capital. It was even rumoured that the success was greater than that which had been achieved, and that Dehlí had fallen.

Everyone expected that it would be so. In the exultation caused by the impression, Lord Canning, four days later, despatched a request to Barnard to send down a column to clear the weak middle part of the Duáb. But the truth soon became known. Before many days had passed the Government and the public alike realised that General Barnard's task was only beginning, and that assistance for the weak middle piece would be available only from Calcutta.

Meanwhile, darkness was closing round them. At the close of the third week of June, whilst they had heard of further mutinies at Jhánsí, at Náogang, at Nímach, and at Juánpur, they had no news from Kánhpur and Lakhnao later than the 4th. Agra was safe, they knew, on the 10th. They knew likewise that Banáras and Allahábád had been made secure in the manner yet to be described.

During the next fortnight, up to the 4th of July, the accounts became worse and worse. On the 2nd of July the Government heard of the mutiny of the native regiments at Kánhpur, and that, joined by Náná Sáhib and his followers, they were besieging Wheeler in his entrenchment; that Sir Henry Lawrence was about to be besieged in the Resideney at Lakhnao, but that all was well there to the 30th of June; that Agra was safe up to the 15th, but that Bandah had gone; that the troops of the Gwáliár contingent had mutinied on the 15th; and that an uneasy feeling prevailed at Haidarábád. The next day Lord Canning received a letter from Sir Henry Lawrence, dated the 28th of June. The letter simply stated that the writer had every reason to believe that the English at Kánhpur had been destroyed by treachery. Certain details, which eventually proved to be correct, were added as native reports, but these reports, it was said, were not believed at Allahábád or Banáras.

The Government had up to that moment hoped that Wheeler would be able to hold out until they could relieve him. One regiment had been despatched in May, under Colonel Neill, and that officer had already secured Banáras and Allahábád. It was even hoped that he would be able to leave Allahábád for Kánhpur, somewhere about the 25th of June, with the four regiments which had been gradually collected at that station. Sir Henry Havelock, fresh from his Persian campaign, having come up with Sir Patrick Grant on the 16th, had on the 24th been directed to proceed to Allahábád to assume command of that force. He had started the very next day. But if the news received from Sir Henry Lawrence were true, he must inevitably be too late to relieve Wheeler. The situation was alarming in the extreme. If Kánhpur were indeed gone, the weak middle piece was broken in twain. With rebellious Oudh on the one side, and the mutinied Gwáliár contingent on the other, what hope was there that even Havelock, with his four English infantry regiments, his scanty artillery, and his volunteer horsemen could possibly prevail?

In this state of terrible supense I must leave the Government at Calcutta whilst I tell the sad story of the 'leaguer of Kánhpur.'

CHAPTER XII

The Leaguer of Kánhpur

In the tenth chapter I have described how, towards the close of the month of May, a rising of the native troops at Kánhpur seemed inevitable; how the officer commanding there, Sir Hugh Wheeler, had fortified, as a place of refuge for the Europeans and Eurasians, two barracks in the centre of a vast plain; how he had stored in those barracks supplies of all sorts; how, on the 22nd of May, the non-combatant portion of the residents had crowded to those barracks for refuge; how, a day or two later, the General himself, with his family, had repaired thither; how, on the 22nd likewise, he and they had been cheered by the arrival from Lakhnao of eighty-four men of the 32nd foot; how, on the 31st of May and the two following days, the arrival from Allahábád of fifteen men of the Madras Fusiliers, and a hundred of the 84th, bearing with them the information that they were but the forerunners of several regiments, for that troops were pouring into Calcutta, had so influenced General Wheeler that, believing his position now to be secure, and feeling very anxious regarding Lakhnao, he had forwarded on to that station fifty men of the 84th; how that, on the night of the 4th of June, the native troops broke into open and violent mutiny; and how, from that date, the 'leaguer' of Kánhpur may be said to have begun.

The fifty men of the 84th had left for Lakhnao on the morning of the 3rd of June. On the evening of the same day half of the 3rd Oudh field-battery, under Lieutenant Ashe, which had been sent from Oudh to Fathgárh to keep open the road between Kánhpur and Agra, but which had been compelled to retreat on account of the mutiny of the native troopers accompanying it, marched into Kánhpur. Their guns, two nine-pounders and a twenty-four-pound howitzer, were at once placed in the entrenchment. The native gunners had behaved so well on the march that it was hoped that they would continue their good service. But the result showed that the defection was almost universal.

On the following morning, the 4th, Wheeler received certain information that the 2nd Cavalry and the 1st and 56th Regiments N. I. had resolved to rise within the next four-and-twenty hours and murder their officers. This information caused the issue of an order to the officers of those regiments to discontinue the practice of sleeping in the lines of their regiments. Wheeler saw, too, that the guns in the entrenchment were placed in position, and that arrangements were made to render a surprise impossible.

On the night of the 4th the troopers of the 2nd Cavalry rose, with a great shout, and setting fire to the sergeants' bungalows, mounted their horses, and rode to the cattle-yard of the Commissariat department. Taking thence thirty-six elephants, they marched to the treasury, guarded by the soldiers of Náná Sáhib. The two bodies fraternised, and helped each other in packing the contents of the treasury on the elephants and on carts. They were still engaged in this congenial occupation when they were joined by the sipáhís of the 1st N. I., who, refusing to join their comrades at the first bidding, had been unable to resist when they heard of the proceedings at the treasury. Vainly had their English officers tried to restrain them. But, whilst deaf to the call of duty, they were not at the moment bloody-minded. They had begged their officers to return to the entrenchment, adding that they wished them no harm, but that their own course had been decided upon.

But the mutineers were not content with the looting of the treasury. They first secured the magazine, with its priceless wealth of heavy guns and ammunition. General Wheeler had placed there a warrant-officer with instructions to blow it up as soon as the sipáhís should break out. But the guard over it was a sipáhí guard, and the warrant-officer, though he did his best, was prevented by the men from carrying out his orders. The sipáhís then broke open the gates of the gaol and turned loose on the abandoned station hundreds of miscreants of the worst description. These made the night a night of horror. The burning of bungalows, and the excited cries of looting parties, gave to the Europeans in the entrenchment a clear idea of the storm which had burst upon them.

Through all this turmoil the sipáhís of the two other regiments, the 53rd and 56th, remained apparently quiescent. About seven o'clock in the morning Wheeler despatched four officers to reconnoitre. They had proceeded two miles when they were fired upon, and one of the number was hit. Wheeler then ordered to their support a company of Europeans and Ashe's half-battery, but these had not moved far when the native officers of the 53rd and 56th arrived to report that their men could no longer be depended upon. The troops, having picked up the officers first sent out, then returned to the entrenchment.

It was now nine o'clock. The sipáhís of the 53rd and 59th, in response to a bugle call, turned out at this moment, and ranging themselves in columns, made as though they would march on the entrenchment. To prevent this, Wheeler brought a gun to bear upon them. At the third discharge the bulk of them dispersed to join their brethren of the 1st N. I. at Nuwábganj, the suburb in which were located the treasury, the magazine, and the gaol. But a few sipáhís, true to their salt, made their way by a circuitous route to the entrenchment, and served there loyally to the very end.

The station was now clear of insurgents. These, at Nuwábganj, barred the road to Dehlí. To the eastward, the Allahábád road was open. It was from that quarter alone that help could come. Wheeler, then, had no alternative. He must remain where he was. He still cherished the hope that the sipáhís, satiated with loot, and knowing that but little in that respect could be gained by an attack on the entrenchment, would march to swell the national movement at Dehlí. There were some, too, in the entrenchment who, not remembering the bitterness engendered in the mind of Náná Sáhib by the refusal of Lord Dalhousie and the Court of Directors to continue to him the pension of the prince of whom he was the adopted son, hoped much from his loyalty to the foreign overlord.

Meanwhile, the assembled sipáhís of the four regiments, now united, had elected Náná Sáhib as their leader, and had tumultuously demanded to be led to Dehlí. The sipáhís had no desire to kill their officers. Against them they had no grudge. They had shaken off the bonds of discipline, they were free, they had looted to their hearts' content, and now they would join those comrades who had resuscitated the rule of the Mughal. They were not to be thwarted. With loud shouts, then, they set out that same afternoon and marched seven miles to Kaliánpur.

Náná Sáhib had been powerless to prevent this march. A too great insistance on his part would have shaken to pieces his newly assumed authority. He had, then, apparently acquiesced in the propriety of the policy. But recognising that, if the movement were to continue, his labour had been in vain; that at Dehlí he, a Marátha, would be a cypher, whereas at Bithor it might be possible for him to play the part of a sovereign prince; that the first essential to the success of his plans was to root out the hated English, to infuse his own hatred of them into the minds of the sipáhís, so that with them also it should be a race hatred; that to leave the English masters at Kánhpur was to leave open a gate upon the closing of which depended the success of his schemes, he and his agents employed all that night in endeavouring to persuade the sipáhís that their work was but half done so long as one English person remained alive at Kánhpur. Not that he and they were so unwise as openly to oppose the march to Dehlí. 'By all means,' they said in so many words, 'let us march to Dehlí; but let us first exterminate the

English now at Kánhpur. If you do not exterminate them, they will soon receive reinforcements and march on your track. At present they are few in number; they have women and children with them; the position they occupy cannot be long defended. In a few days you will be able to wreak your vengeance upon them. Then we will march to Dehlí—I first of all at your head. If you decide to march thither now, you can never be sure how quickly they may recover, and then you will all be marked men. But dead men tell no tales.' Whether the precise arguments used were in these words cannot be affirmed, but that they were in this sense is certain. They were effectual, for on the morning of the 6th the rebelled sipáhís marched back from Kaliánpur to Kánhpur. On arriving there the Náná pitched his camp in the centre of the station, hoisted two standards—one to propitiate the Hindus, the other to humour the Muhammadans. He then sent out fifty troopers to kill any Christians who might be found, and directed the looting of the houses of those native gentlemen whom he suspected of being favourable to the English. Within his position he threw up works and mounted heavy guns.

General Wheeler had hoped, when he heard of the march to Kaliánpur, that his difficulties were practically over. But in the return of the sipáhís he recognised the hand of the Marátha chief. Even if he had had any doubts on the subject, such doubts would have been no longer possible on the 7th. On the morning of that day he received a letter from Náná Sáhib intimating his intention to attack the garrison. It was soon recognised that this was no idle threat, for two guns began at once to play upon the entrenchment. On the 8th three more guns opened fire, and on the 11th the rebels had in position, playing upon the garrison night and day, three mortars, two twenty-four-pounders, three eighteen-pounders, two twelve-pounders, the same number of nine-pounders, and one six-pounder. Their numbers had, meanwhile, considerably increased. From Allahábád, from Oudh, from the districts evil-disposed men had flocked in. Náná Sáhib assumed, during these operations, the position of, and received the honours due to, a sovereign prince. In this capacity he appointed Subahdár Tíká Singh of the 2nd Cavalry to be general of that arm, and Subahdár Gangá Dín and Jámadár Dalganjan Singh of the native infantry to be colonels of the infantry brigades.

The garrison which had to sustain the attacks directed by these men was composed of 210 English soldiers, and nearly a hundred officers and civilians. The railway engineers, traders, and clerks were another hundred, and there were some forty Christians besides, including the drummers. They had six guns of different calibres. Had the 450 men above enumerated been alone, they could have fought their way to Allahábád. But they had with them 330 women and children, many of them reared tenderly, and some unable to travel. Their lot, indeed, in the terrible contest was the hardest of all.

The defences which, since the 14th of May, Wheeler had been able to throw up were far from formidable. The earthworks were little more than four feet high, and were not bullet proof at the crest. The apertures for the artillery exposed alike the guns and the gunners, whilst in the unfinished barracks on the left front an enterprising enemy could easily find cover for attack. The scantiness of the earthworks was mainly due to the iron-like hardness of the ground, baked by a sun which had shone uninterruptedly for seven months, and unmoistened during that period by a drop of rain. Within the entrenchment supplies calculated to last four weeks had been stored. But these, like everything else behind the feeble earthworks, were subject to destruction from the various causes incidental to war.

From the very first the sufferings of the garrison were intense. The heat was great, the space was scanty, the fire of the guns of the rebels was incessant, the absolutely necessary exposure of the officers and men to that fire was deadly. From the first day the casualties were considerable. Then rose the question how to dispose of the dead. There was a well, outside the entrenchment, not far from the unfinished barracks. This was appointed to be the cemetery. The bodies of those killed during the day were placed at once outside the verandah, among the *débris*, until the fall of night should afford the required opportunity to the fatigue party. Then they were carried to the well and let down.

Prominent among the officers who distinguished themselves in the defence of the entrenchment may be mentioned Captain Moore of the 32nd, a soldier of the highest class and the most undaunted courage; Captain Jenkins of the 2nd L. C., one of the bravest and best of the party; Lieutenant Daniell of the same regiment, full of pluck and fire; Captain Whiting of the engineers, gifted with a clear brain and coolness unsurpassable; Major Vibart of the 2nd L. C., determined, unyielding, and ever watchful at the post assigned him, one of the most exposed and difficult of the defences; Mowbray Thomson of the 56th N. I., daring even to rashness, ever longing to be where the fight was the thickest; Delafosse of the 53rd N. I., cool and calm in danger, ready to sacrifice his own life if that sacrifice could benefit his comrades; Glanville of the 2nd Europeans; Ashe of the artillery, as daring as devoted; Jervis of the engineers, proud of his race, and maintaining to his last gasp its glorious prestige; Sterling, whose splendid feats with his rifle were the terror of the rebels. Worthy to be classed with these and others like them, soldiers by profession, were the civilian Mackillop, one of the noblest of men, and throughout the siege a hero; Heberden the railway engineer, Moncrieff the chaplain, and others whose names have not survived their deeds. The women of the garrison, too, displayed, under all circumstances, the pride and endurance of their race. Where all behaved nobly it is difficult to distinguish. But conspicuous amongst them all was the wife of the leader of the sallying parties, Mrs Moore. Her splendid courage and fortitude endeared her to every man, woman, and child within the entrenchment. Nor must I omit to record the stalwart courage of Bridget Widdowson, wife of a private of the 32nd, who stood sentry, sword in hand, for some time over a batch of prisoners, bound only by a rope, and took care that not one of them escaped.

It would serve no purpose to enter into the details of a siege of three weeks, the circumstances of every day of which differed only in minor details from the circumstances of its predecessor. The sufferings of the defenders throughout that period were terrible. On the second day of the attack the garrison realised that the supply of water would present great difficulties. There was but one well, in the middle of the entrenchment, and its locality was known to the rebels. Upon that spot they kept so continuous a fire that to attempt to draw water exposed the daring volunteer to almost certain death. So great was the danger that, after the second day, it was resolved that every man should draw water for himself and his belongings. There was generally a cessation of fire about dusk, and then the space round the well became crowded with men, who endeavoured to utilise the fleeting moments by filling their buckets.

After the fire of the first few days the barracks became so riddled with shot as to afford little or no shelter. To secure some sort of refuge a great many made holes under the walls of the entrenchment, and covered them with deal boxes, cots, or the first suitable article they could lay hands on. The heat in these was, however, very oppressive, and many died from apoplexy. At night every person in turn was required to take watch. The women and children belonging to them then slept under the walls of the entrenchment, near to their relatives. Here the bombshells kept them in perpetual dread, for during nearly the entire night these were seen flying through the air and bursting, often doing mischief. Another source of misery was caused by the stench arising from the dead horses, and, what was even worse, by the myriads of flies they collected. Still the garrison bore up without a murmur. There was not a man who was not a hero. Hillersden, the Collector, who had negotiated the treaty with Náná Sáhib, fell dead at the feet of his wife, killed by a round-shot. She survived him but a few days. A round-shot likewise carried off the head of the General's son, Lieutenant Wheeler, as he lay wounded in the room occupied by his mother and the members of his family. Another round-shot mortally wounded Major Lindsay. He, too, was soon followed to the grave by his wife. Colonel Williams of the 56th was carried off by apoplexy, whilst his wife died from the effect of a wound which had completely disfigured her. Colonel Ewart of the 1st was disabled early in the siege. Captain Halliday was shot dead, whilst carrying some horse-soup for his famishing wife, midway between the entrenchments and the barracks. Mackillop, of whom I have spoken, and who, in his unselfish anxiety to contribute to the necessities of the suffering, had in the last week constituted himself captain of the well, was mortally wounded at his post. Death was very near him, yet in his last moments he begged a bystander to carry the water he had drawn to the lady to whom it had been promised. Nobly, indeed, did the sons of the island-heart of the British Empire do their duty.

In not one single respect did they fail. They succeeded to the very last in holding the outposts formed of the unfinished barracks, which, if the position of besieger and besieged had been reversed, they would not have permitted their enemy to retain for a single day. The officers who com-manded the small detachments which held those outposts were Jenkins and Glanville of the 2nd Europeans. The latter, after holding number two barrack, with sixteen men, for almost as many days, was incapaci-tated by a severe wound. Mowbray Thomson succeeded him. Needless to add that the defence did not lose from being entrusted to his capable hands.

All this time the rebels were receiving reinforcements. Revolted sipáhís from Oudh, from Ázamgarh, from various stations in the vicinity, swarmed in constantly. Every day, on the other hand, saw a diminution of the resources of the besieged. Towards the end of the third week the supply of food had become very short.

Meanwhile, the Náná, puffed up with his brief authority, was venting on stray captives his hatred of the British race. In the early days of the attack his myrmidons had dragged from hiding, in a house near the dák-bungalow, an old gentleman, supposed to be a merchant, his wife, and two children, both in their teens. He caused them to be shot on the spot. A like fate was meted out to four clerks found in a house on the bank of a canal. Another European, whose name could not be traced, was similarly treated. Later on, on the 10th of June, an English lady, travelling with her four children from the North-west Provinces to Calcutta, and arriving, unsuspicious of evil, at Kánhpur, was taken before Náná Sáhib. They were all shot. The same fate was dealt out to another lady who arrived there under similar circumstances the day following.

On the 12th information reached the Nán̄á that a party of Europeans was approaching by water from the North-west. He at once despatched cavalry and infantry to reconnoitre. These returned to report that they were European fugitives from Fathgarh, mostly women and children. These, likewise, numbering 126, were murdered. Flushed with his easy conquest over unarmed women and children, Nán̄á Sáhib urged on his generals to push their attack on the entrenchment with vigour. For some time past his gunners had been firing shells in the hope of setting fire to the barracks. On the evening of the 13th their labours were to a certain extent crowned with success, for at five o'clock on that day they succeeded in kindling the roof of the hospital barrack. As this barrack sheltered not only the sick but the families of the English soldiers, the advantage to the Nán̄á was considerable, for the fire spread so rapidly that some forty of the inmates were burned to death, and nearly all the medicines and surgical instruments were destroyed. The sipáhís took advantage of the evident confusion to advance, 4,000 in number, to deliver an assault which should be final. But what were 4,000 Asiatics against one-tenth of their number of Englishmen? Afraid to try the hand-to-hand encounter which the latter invited, and daunted by the fire of the six guns, they slunk back, without daring an assault, discomfited, to their lines.

Between the 13th and the 21st the rebels tried attacks or rather advances of the same character, and invariably with the same result. But on the 23rd, the anniversary of Plassey, having received large reinforcements from Oudh and the districts, they made the most serious attack in force they had ever tried. They gained possession of three of the empty barracks, and attempted to dislodge Moore from the remainder, but that gallant officer was quite equal to the occasion. With twenty-five men he advanced, under cover of a discharge of grape, and after a desperate contest expelled the rebels from the barracks they had seized. Meanwhile, under cover of some bales of cotton which they had appropriated, the rebels advanced to within 150 yards of the entrenchment, which they then attempted to carry with a rush. But the steady discharge of canister, and rounds of file-firing from the infantry, speedily induced them to change their minds. They fell back, leaving about 200, including their leader, dead or dying, on the field.

The next day Lieutenant Delafosse particularly distinguished himself by an act of combined coolness and courage. About midday one of the English ammunition waggons had been ignited by the enemy's fire. Whilst the waggon was still burning, and endangering by its proximity the other waggons, the fire of the rebels, who had noticed the catastrophe, was concentrated on that one spot. The situation was critical, for unless the fire should be extinguished it could not fail to cause immense damage. In this crisis Delafosse crept up, and lying at full length under the burning waggon, pulled away from it all the loose splinters he could reach, at the same time throwing earth on the flames. Two soldiers, animated by his example, joined him with buckets of water, and by their united efforts the flames were extinguished.

From the 21st to the 24th of June the defenders were subjected to an incessant bombardment. The time for the commencement of the rainy season had arrived, and it was evident to them that the initial storm, generally a fall of great severity, would bring down with a run the walls and roofs of the riddled barracks. They had already been for some time on half rations, and their supplies were now so attenuated as to threaten famine at a very early date. It was clear to all that, if the lives of the garrison were to be preserved, there must be a new departure. Had there been a single sign of relief from the direction of Allahábád they might have decided to fight on as they had fought, hoping that any day might bring relief. But since the arrival of the men of the 84th, on the 31st of May, a dead calmness, significant of disaster, had fallen on the district around them. They felt it must have gone hard with their countrymen in Oudh, to the east and to the west, since they were left unaided to perish. The bolder spirits talked, at times, of a sortie in force, but in their cooler moments even they rejected a measure which would have entailed the destruction of the women and the children, and which did not offer one chance in a thousand of success.

I have spoken of the splendid repulse of the rebels on the 23rd. This blow, severe as it was, seemed to the garrison almost the last they would be able to strike. Their guns were fast becoming unserviceable, ammunition was failing them, starvation was staring them in the face. They were in this position when, on the 24th, a slip of paper was brought them by Mrs Greenway, wife of one of the merchants of Kánhpur, who had been made prisoner, on which the following words, written by Azímullah, were traced: 'All those who are in no way connected with the acts of Lord Dalhousie, and are willing to lay down their arms, shall receive a safe passage to Allahábád.'

The idea of capitulation was revolting to every soldier of the garrison. Sir Hugh Wheeler, the first to speak, protested strongly against it, and he was supported by the younger combatants. The Náná, they felt, was not to be trusted. To him they owed their actual position. But Moore and Whiting, who had borne the brunt of the defence, thought otherwise. It would be impossible, they knew, to prolong the defence. Their ammunition and their food supplies were alike all but exhausted. The one chance of saving the women and children was to capitulate. For themselves they cared not. They would have preferred to die sword in hand, but in that case the women and children would perish too. If there were but one chance in a thousand of saving these, that chance, they thought, should be taken. They did not know how the Nána had dealt with the stray travellers from the north-west, or with the fugitives from Fathgarh, and they believed that, faithless as he might be in other respects, he was not the man to war with women and children. A message was therefore sent to the Maráthá chieftain to the effect that a reply would be given on the morrow.

An armistice was then proclaimed for the 26th, and on that day Azímullah and Jawála Parshád, a Hindu high in his master's confidence, met Moore, Whiting, and the postmaster, Roche, outside the entrenchment. An arrangement was easily arrived at. The Nána agreed to allow the British to march out with their arms and sixty rounds of ammunition; to escort them safely to the river side, where, at the Satí-Chaurá Ghaut, boats stored with provisions should be ready to take them to Allahábád. The Nána wished to carry out the arrangement that very night, and for a time strongly insisted on the point, but he ultimately gave way. Mr Todd, who had been his tutor, was sent to his headquarters to obtain his signature to the agreement, now fixed to take effect on the morning of the 27th. He found him courteous in manner, and full of pretended compassion for the sufferings of the English ladies and children.

On the morning of the 27th the members of the garrison set out, escorted by numbers of the rebel force. The distance to the ghaut was but a mile, but to the women and children the time to traverse it seemed an eternity. When, at length, about eight o'clock, they reached the ghaut, their hearts bounded with joy. The forty boats were there, and to them the boats promised safety. The river was very low, as the periodical rains, though overdue, had not begun to fall, and our countrywomen had to wade ankle-deep in the water before they could be pulled on board. The embarkation lasted about an hour; then some of the Englishmen began to push off. Two or three boats only had just moved, when suddenly, from the platform of a Hindu temple from which the ghaut takes its name, on which sat enthroned Tantiá Topi, the military adviser of the Nána, there issued a bugle note. Instantly the boatmen hurried from the boats, climbing over their sides, whilst upon the European passengers the assembled sipáhís opened a concentrated fire of grape and musketry. Vainly did the men on board exert themselves to push off. Some, whose boats were under weigh, managed to reach the opposite bank, only to find there the mutinied sipáhís of the 17th N. I. and the rebel cavalry of Oudh. The sipáhís on the Kánhpur side, meanwhile, were running along the bank and pouring in shot after shot. There was no escape; defence was impossible. In many cases the fire kindled the thatch which formed a covering to the boats. Then all was over. Those who took to the water were shot. All the males, in fact, were massacred. The women, reserved for a worse fate, were dragged on shore and lodged in a brick building near the bungalow which for many years had served as the residence and office of the commissariat officer of the division.

Of the forty boats so treacherously provided thirty-nine were now in the hands of the rebels. One, however, had managed to run the gauntlet. On board of this were Moore, Vibart, Whiting, Mowbray Thomson, Ashe, Delafosse, Bolton, and others. The thatch of this boat had fortunately escaped ignition, and, vigorously propelled by its English crew, it for a short time escaped the notice of the murderers, busily intent upon the other thirty-nine. Not for long, however. Soon sipáhís were discerned running along the bank in pursuit, whilst others, embarking on two boats, followed the fugitives. Their aim was but too deadly. Moore, Ashe, and Bolton were shot dead as they were propelling the boat with the only implement available, a long pole, for the oars had been taken away. During the first day and the first night the pursuit continued, varied occasionally by the launch of a blazing fire-boat of smaller tonnage. One pursuing boat, armed with fifty natives, was rapidly approaching when it grounded, to the joy of the pursued, on a sandbank. For them this was an opportunity. Disembarking, they attacked the rebels on the sandbank so vigorously that but few were left to tell the tale. They then seized their boat, which they found well provided with ammunition; then casting it on the stream, they slept whilst it drifted down stream.

They woke soon after midnight to find the wind had risen, and that the boat was still drifting, whither they knew not. The hope that it might have descended beyond the enemy's range was dissipated as soon as the day broke. They found to their despair that the boat had been carried out of the main channel into a small creek, on the banks of which the enemy were huddled, with muskets loaded. In such an extremity there was but one chance—the English charge, which has never failed. The few able-bodied survivors tried it. There were but two officers unwounded capable of such a service, Mowbray Thomson and Delafosse; but they had with them a few stalwart men of the 32nd and 84th. Wading through the water, they dashed at the astonished sipáhís, rushed through them, then back again to the place where they had left the boat. But the boat was no longer there. They saw her in the distance, drifting down the stream.

The two officers and their companions pushed at once down the river-bank in the direction taken by the boat, but seeing no chance of overtaking her, and still followed by the sipáhís, they made for a Hindu temple which seemed to offer a position of vantage. The door of this temple they defended so fiercely against the advancing enemy, with their bayonets, that there was soon formed in front of it a barrier of corpses, which served to them as a rampart. Within the temple they obtained a little putrid water, which refreshed them. Meanwhile, the assailants, despairing of other methods, heaped up beneath the walls of the temple leaves, faggots, and other combustible materials, with the intent to smoke out the little garrison. But the wind was on the side of the English. It blew the smoke strongly in the eyes of the assailants. Under cover of it, the besieged made a sudden spring forward, and firing a volley, charged them. In the hand-to-hand fight seven of the English were struck down. The remaining seven, unhurt, dashed into the stream, the sipáhís following along the bank, and firing as they ran. Presently two of the swimmers were shot through the head; a third was caught on a sandbank and killed, but the remaining four, Mowbray Thomson, Delafosse, and privates Murphy and Sullivan, struck vigorously down the stream, and, aided by the current, succeeded in evading their pursuers. They pushed on till, panting and exhausted, they reached, on the Oudh side, the territories of a rájá friendly to the British, who befriended them until they could rejoin the army in the field.

It is a sad supplement to this story to add that the boat from which they had issued to charge the sipáhís on the bank was captured, and its living cargo taken back to Kánhpur. The number of the survivors of the massacre at the ghaut and in the boats amounted to eighty-four. Four of these, as we have seen, escaped. The remaining eighty were carried before the Náná. That chieftain now regarding himself as reigning by divine right, had the men shot, and the women and children confined in the little house of which I have spoken.

Thus sadly terminated the 'Leaguer of Kánhpur.' On the 1st of July the Náná proceeded to Bithor and there, with great pomp and circumstance proclaimed himself Peshwá. There, for the moment, I must leave him, whilst I relate the circumstances which prevented the timely arrival of relief to the devoted garrison, and which ultimately led to the chastisement of the men who had treacherously worked its destruction.

CHAPTER XIII

Neill at Banáras and Allahábád— Havelock's Recovery of Kánhpur

I have told in a previous chapter how, on the 23rd of May, the 1st Madras Fusiliers, commanded by Colonel Neill, an officer of great decision of character, reached Calcutta, and how the regiment was despatched with all the expedition possible to the north-west. Neill reached Banáras, the morning of the 4th of June, at a very critical moment. To understand the crisis it will be necessary to explain the state of affairs in that important centre.

The city of Banáras lies nearly midway between Calcutta and Dehlí, being 469 miles north-west of the former and 485 south-east of the latter. The normal population is about a quarter of a million, but the number ebbs and flows with the arrival and departure of pilgrims. The city lies picturesquely on the left bank of the Ganges, which, in 1857, was crossed by a bridge of boats. The district of which the city is the capital has an area of 998 square miles, and a population of, in round numbers, 900,000. It is bounded to the north by Gházípur and Juánpur, to the west and south by Mírzápur, and to the east by the Sháhábád district of Western Bihár.

At the time of which I am writing the garrison of Banáras consisted of half a company of European artillery—some thirty men—of the Sikh regiment of Lodiáná, and of the 13th Regiment of Irregular Cavalry. The cantonment for the infantry was at Sikrol, three miles from the city, that of the cavalry was some five miles distant. The force was commanded by Brigadier George Ponsonby, a man who had rendered excellent service in his day; but he had only just assumed command, and was suffering from ill-health and increasing years.

The citizens of Banáras had always had the character of being a turbulent people. They required a master who would be obeyed. Fortunately, in 1857, they had such a master in the person of Mr Frederick Gubbins, of the Civil Service, then District Judge. Some years before, when that gentleman filled the office of Magistrate of Banáras, he had inaugurated sanitary and other improvements within the city. The inhabitants showed their appreciation of these improvements by receiving Mr Gubbins, on the occasion of his next visit to the city, with a shower of stones, and by compelling him to run for his life. But Mr Gubbins was not the man to be baffled. He persisted in carrying out his reforms. The people, on their side, seemed equally determined. They closed their shops, and declined to sell grain or other wares. But Mr Gubbins was firm. He procured supplies from Mírzápur, and when, three days later, he heard that the leaders of the movement were about to hold a meeting in the city, he proceeded to the spot with two companies of sipáhís, arrested them, and lodged them in gaol. The next morning he rode through the city and opened all the shops. From that moment Mr Gubbins was lord of Banáras.

In 1857 Mr Henry Carre Tucker was the Commissioner of Banáras. But, from the moment affairs there assumed a threatening attitude, the strong character of Mr Gubbins asserted itself, and he became practically supreme. Well supported by the Magistrate, Mr Lind, by the assistants, Mr Archibald Pollock and Mr Jenkinson, by a loyal native nobleman, Ráo Devnáráin Singh, by a brave and resolute Sikh gentleman, detained in Banáras for complicity in some of the troubles in the Panjáb, Surat Singh, and to a considerable though lesser extent by the Rájá of Banáras, and by an influential Brahman, Pandit Gokal Chand, he maintained order in the populous city until the arrival and action of Neill and his troops removed the pressing danger.

For very soon after the information of the events at Mírath and Dehlí reached Banáras it became clear that the sipáhís of the 37th N. I. were infected, and would break out on the first convenient opportunity. They were somewhat restrained by the presence of the Sikhs, who were believed to be loyal to the core. Of the probable behaviour of the 13th Irregulars few except the officers of that regiment entertained the smallest doubt. The position, then, was critical, and it was recognised to be so specially by those civilians upon whom it devolved to maintain peace and order within the city.

One resolution Mr Gubbins and his friends stood by in the darkest hour of the crisis, and that was to remain at their post. In the early days proposals were made to abandon the position and retreat to the fortress of Chanár. But Messrs Gubbins and Lind, Gordon, who commanded the Sikhs, Dodgson the Brigade-Major, and one or two others opposed this plan so resolutely that it was abandoned. Nor when the districts round and near to Banáras broke out into rebellion did they swerve a hair's-breadth from that determination. The one precaution which, in concert with the military authorities, they did take was to fix upon a strong central post to serve as a place of refuge for the ladies and children. The mint, a large, oblong, fire-proof brick building, capable of holding out against men unprovided with guns, was selected for this purpose.

Towards the end of May the English at Banáras were cheered by the arrival of 150 men of the 10th foot from Dánápur, and on the 3rd and 4th of June, Colonel Neill, with some sixty men of the 1st Madras Fusiliers, followed. On the morning of the 4th news reached the place of the mutiny of the 17th N. I. at Ázamgarh. A council was then called of the chief civil and military authorities to consider the advisability of disarming the 37th N. I. Gubbins, Gordon, Dodgson, and all the bolder spirits were in favour of carrying out that necessary measure at once. They were listening to the strong recommendations of Mr Gubbins on this point when Neill himself entered the room, and in his plain, blunt way insisted that delay would be fraught with imminent danger. Orders then were issued for a parade of the troops of the garrison at five o'clock that afternoon.

The lines of the 37th N. I. were in the centre of the general parade ground, about midway between those occupied by the Sikhs and by the artillery. The question was how, with the 250 Europeans, to disarm a native regiment, nearly a thousand strong, in the presence of three or four hundred cavalry, suspected of sympathy with them, and of a Sikh regiment, believed to be loyal, but whose loyalty must remain unproven until it had been tried. It was a difficult question, and I am bound to add that it was solved in a very clumsy fashion. Before the men of the 37th had formed up in front of their lines, the artillery and the few men of the 10th and the Madras Fusiliers had taken up a position on their right, the Sikhs and irregular cavalry on their left. Colonel Spottiswoode and the English officers of the 37th then walked down the lines of their regiment, and directed the men to lodge their muskets in the bells of arms attached to each company. Some of them quietly obeyed, but others, calling out that the Europeans were coming to shoot them down unarmed, incited the rest to resist. Their appeal was responded to, for suddenly the sipáhís grasped their muskets, and noticing the Europeans approaching from the right, faced towards them and opened a brisk fire. At the first fire some eight men of the 10th foot were shot down. This was more than could be borne. The English infantry returned the fire, still moving on, whilst the guns, unlimbering, poured in a volley of grape. Meanwhile, a shot from a sipáhí of the 37th had killed Captain Guise, commandant of the 13th Irregulars. Dodgson, the Brigade Major, as brave a man as ever lived, and as modest as he was brave, rode up to the men, and taking command, ordered them to advance. Instead of obeying, one trooper drew his pistol and fired at Dodgson. Another attempted to cut him down. At this crisis one of the Sikhs fired upon his colonel, Gordon. The rest of them, not knowing apparently what to make of the position, began shouting and firing indiscriminately, their muskets levelled in the direction in which the guns were posted. The guns were unsupported, for the English infantry was following the 37th N. I., and it seemed as though the Sikhs and the irregulars were about to charge them. But the commandant of the artillery, William Olpherts,[1] was quite equal to the occasion. He turned the fire of his battery upon the Sikhs. These then wildly charged, only, however, to be broken and to flee in disorder. The troopers of the 13th accompanied them. The men of the 37 N. I. were already dispersing in wild disorder.

But the danger was not yet over. So clumsy had been the programme that the sipáhís had been allowed to escape, with arms in their hands, in close vicinity to a populous city, the inhabitants of which were renowned for their turbulent character. In this crisis Frederick Gubbins, Súrat Singh, Devnáráin Singh, and other loyal men were able to render splendid service. The Sikhs on guard over the assembled non-combative Europeans were pacified by Súrat Singh, himself a Sikh. Gubbins, entering the city, exerted the supreme influence which his character as a resolute but just man had gained for him. The citizens preferred to trust him rather than cast in their lot with rebellious sipáhís. His vigorous action, that of Súrat Singh, supported by Devnáráin Singh, by the Rájá of Banáras, and by Pandit Gokal Chand, preserved the great city of Banáras to the British.[2]

Meanwhile, Neill was not idle. In the midst of the contest he had assumed command. Some of the 13th Irregulars had remained faithful. The Sikhs, recovering from their mad escapade, returned to their duty. The indigo planters of the district, prominently Mr F. C. Chapman, volunteered their services. In a few days order was restored in the immediate vicinity of the holy city. The presence of Mr Gubbins and his companions was a voucher that that order would not be again disturbed. Other European troops were coming up from below. On the 9th of June, then, Neill, full of resolution to save Allahábád and to recover Kánhpur, set out for the former place.

---

[1] It was of this officer that the late Lord Napier of Magdala said to me, that 'William Olpherts never went into action without entitling himself to the Victoria Cross.'

[2] For their conduct during these trying times Mr Gubbins was made a Companion of the Bath; Rao Devnáráin Singh and Súrat Singh received titles and rewards. The Rájá, too, received the thanks of the Government.

While he is hastening to it, I must ask the reader to glance at the districts which, with Banáras, face the south-east frontier of Oudh—the districts of Juánpur, of Ázamgarh, and of Gorákhpur. I will not detain him long.

The landowners of those districts had been made hostile to British rule by the introduction of that land system with which Mr Thomason, forcing European ideas upon an oriental people, had superseded the time-honoured methods which not even Akbar had dared to repeal. Ázamgarh was the first to display disaffection. The bulk of the 17th Regiment N. I. stationed there rose on the 3rd of June, and though the place, abandoned by the civilians, was afterwards recovered by two men cast in the heroic type, Messrs Venables and Dunn, it continued for a very long time to be a festering sore in the British side. At Juánpur, nearly midway between Banáras and Ázamgarh, the Sikhs stationed there, excited by the story of the manner in which their countrymen had been mowed down at Banáras, rose on the 5th of June. That place, though constantly reoccupied, continued to give trouble until the autumn of the following year. Gorákhpur, on the Nipál side of Ázamgarh, saved for a long time by the splendid daring and cool judgment of its Judge, Mr William Wynyard, gave way in July. Few districts gave more trouble during the revolt, or afforded more scope for the display of the noblest qualities of the British race, than did those three districts—bounded to the north-west by Oudh, to the north by Nipál, to the south by the city of Banáras, and to the south-east by the inflammable division of Western Bihar—represented by Juánpur, Ázamgarh, and Gorákhpur.

Meanwhile, Neill, accompanied by forty-three men of his splendid regiment, had left Banáras by post, on the night of the 9th of June, to assume command at Allahábád. His journey was a difficult one, for the road was deserted, the post-horses had been carried off, and the district was full of marauders. It was not, then, till the afternoon of the 11th that he and his party reached Jhúsí, a village on the high bank overlooking the junction of the Jamnah and the Ganges, and the point where the road from Banáras passed over the bridge of boats then maintained across the former river. But Neill found the bridge partially destroyed, and the further end of it occupied by the rebels. He noticed that Daryáganj, a suburb of Allahábád, which commanded that further end, was also in their possession. He knew, too, that his men were worn out by fatigue. But the great aim of Neill's life was to conquer difficulties. Descending the Ganges, he espied and hailed a fisherman pursuing his craft in a solitary boat. He bought the man, and was about to trust 'Cæsar and his fortunes' to the frail canoe when the

English guard on duty on the ramparts of the fort of Allahábád recognised his men. Boats were then sent over in sufficient numbers.

Neill entered the fort. He was aware that the task before him was a heavy one: that to restore order the means at his disposal were scanty. In his journey from Banáras he had noticed that the entire country along the Ganges was in a state of anarchy. He now found the fort invested: the troops who mainly formed the garrison—the Sikhs of the same regiment he had laid his hand upon at Banáras—coaxed into the appearance of subordination: confusion and disorder in every department: an unchecked enemy without, vacillation ruling within.

He immediately assumed command. Notwithstanding his fatigue, and the exhaustion consequent upon it, he did not sleep until he had arranged his plans for the morrow. The day of the 12th had scarcely dawned when he opened fire from the fort on the suburb of Daryáganj, held by a large body of insurgent rabble. When he had cleared the outskirts with a few rounds he despatched the forty-three men of his own regiment, three companies of Sikhs, and forty native horsemen to expel the rebels from the suburb and secure the bridge of boats. This they accomplished without loss. He then repaired the bridge, and placed a company of Sikhs to guard it. A company of the fusiliers from Banáras crossed it that same afternoon to enter the fort.

The next day and the day following he continued his reorganising measures. With great tact he moved the Sikhs to a position outside the fort. He bought up all the liquor, and lodged it in the Government stores. On the 15th he despatched by steamer to Calcutta the numerous women and children, and then cleared of the enemy the villages in immediate vicinity to the fort. The effect of these strong measures was quickly visible. On the 17th the Magistrate, Mr Court, proceeded to the city, and reinstalled his own officials at the Kotwálí. Not only was there no resistance, but the whole place seemed deserted. The Maulaví himself had fled to Kánhpur. Neill improved the occasion by marching the following day, with his whole force, to the cantonment, the scene of the massacre of their own officers by the men of the 6th N. I. He found that a complete reaction had set in, that terror had taken the place of insolence, that the desire to escape punishment had succeeded to the love of killing.

Leaving to the authorities appointed under the martial law, which had been proclaimed, to deal with rebels and murderers, Neill proceeded to develop the plan he had arranged in his own mind, viz., a march, as soon as possible, to the relief of Kánhpur. On the 18th his force amounted to 360 English soldiers. The same day 150 more arrived. He had placed on a serviceable footing the Commissariat and Transport departments. These had procured carts and camels, and more were coming in. His executive officers, Captain Russell, in the Ordnance department, Captain Davidson of the Commissariat, Captain Brown of the artillery, were working with a will. The natives, too, were now displaying untiring energy on behalf of the British cause. Messrs Chester and Court, of the Civil Service, were rendering invaluable aid. Cholera, though it came, did not stop the efforts of a single man of that heroic band. On the 24th the force had attained somewhat larger proportions, so much so that Neill could talk of the advance on Kánhpur as a matter of a few days. That same day he heard that the Government had decided to entrust the command of the relieving force to Havelock. Bitterly as he felt the supersession, he did not in the least relax his efforts. On the afternoon of the 30th of June he despatched an advance force of 400 Europeans, 300 Sikhs, and 120 troopers, under one of his best officers, Major Renaud, on the road to Kánhpur. He arranged, also, to embark a hundred men and two guns, under Captain Spurgin, on a river steamer, under orders for the same destination. This intention was carried out—but by Havelock.

Havelock, in fact, reached Allahábád on the 30th of June, the day on which Renaud started. A very capable soldier, possessing large experience, and gifted with the power of leadership to a rare degree, Havelock was the very man for the situation. One may sympathise with Neill in his disappointment, and yet recognise that Henry Havelock was the fittest soldier in all India for the occasion. He at once took up the thread of Neill's preparations, despatched Spurgin and his steamer on the 3rd of July, and at four o'clock of the evening of the 7th started at the head of his small brigade for Kánhpur.

Rumours of disaster at that place had reached Allahábád on the 2nd. Neill disbelieved them. Even Havelock doubted. But not many hours elapsed after he set out ere the state of the districts gave to his mind the fullest confirmation of the worst reports.

The force led by Havelock from Allahábád, on the afternoon of the 7th of July, consisted of seventy-six artillerymen, 979 English infantry, taken from the 64th, the 78th, and the 84th foot, eighteen volunteer cavalry, Englishmen, 150 Sikhs, and thirty irregular cavalry. He was preceded by Renaud's small detachment, already noted, and by Spurgin's 100 men on board the steamer. He left behind him Neill and the remainder of the 1st Madras Fusiliers, with instructions to follow as soon as another column should be organised and he should be able to consign the fort to proper hands.

In the selection of his staff Havelock had been particularly happy. From the 10th foot he had taken his son, a daring soldier, full of resources, and eager for opportunities, as his Aide-de-Camp. Stuart Beatson, a man instructed, able, and devoted was his assistant Adjutant-General. Fraser Tytler, an excellent cavalry officer, was his assistant Quartermaster-General.

Assured that Kánhpur had fallen, and advised that the station of Fathpur, seventy-one miles from Allahábád and forty-nine from Kánhpur, had fallen into the hands of the rebels, Havelock transmitted orders to Renaud to halt where he was, fourteen miles to the east of Fathpur. Pushing on as rapidly as possible, Havelock reached Khágah, nineteen miles from that place, on the 11th. There he received information from Renaud, then only five miles in advance of him, to the effect that the mutinied regiments of Kánhpur, reinforced by other rebels, were marching on Fathpur, with the apparent intention of holding that place against the advancing British. Havelock then broke up his camp at midnight, joined Renaud an hour and a half later, and pushed on to Balindah, four miles to the east of Fathpur.

The story of the mutiny at Fathpur may be told in a few words. The native troops stationed there, consisting of fifty men of the 6th N. I., had, after a show of loyalty, joined other rebels and mutineers in a general outbreak on the 9th of June. The Europeans, who for more than a fortnight had been daily expecting a rising, escaped, with one exception, to Bandah. That exception was Mr Robert Tucker, the Judge. He, after defending himself with great gallantry, and, if the testimony of a native Christian is to be believed, slaying sixteen men with his own hand, was captured, subjected to the forms of trial, and executed on the spot. The natives of Fathpur and of the districts around it, under the guidance of one Hikmat-ullah, a Deputy Magistrate under British rule, rose in revolt, and declared their readiness to submit to the authority then paramount at Kánhpur. It was to secure this place that Náná Sáhib now despatched a force composed of 1,400 trained sipáhís, 1,500 local levies, 500 trained cavalry, and 100 artillerymen, with twelve guns, to bar the road to the English. It was commanded by Tíká Singh, a Subáhdár of the 2nd L. C., who had taken a prominent part in the leaguer of Kánhpur.

On reaching Balindah Havelock sent Tytler to the front to reconnoitre. Tytler came upon the rebels as they were marching, having passed through Fathpur, towards the British position. Their infantry, in column of route, held the high road, with three guns in front of the column, the remainder in the rear, and the cavalry on both flanks. These latter, noticing Tytler almost as soon as he saw them, dashed at him. Tytler had to ride hard to give timely information to Havelock. The latter, who was resting his troops after their early march, at once formed them in order of battle. He placed the guns, eight in number, commanded by Captain Maude, R.A., in front; in the same line with them a body of skirmishers, in loose order, armed with the Enfield rifle, then new in India, ready to open fire on the enemy as soon as he should appear. Behind the guns he disposed the several detachments of infantry, forming a line of quarter-distance columns ready to deploy. The eighteen volunteer-horse guarded the right flank; the bulk of the irregulars the left.

These dispositions had not quite been completed when the enemy's guns, now well within distance, opened fire, whilst their cavalry, galloping round, threatened the flanks of the English. For a few seconds their fire was unanswered. Only, however, for a few seconds. Then Maude, moving his battery to the front, opened fire, and in a second it became a species of duello at a distance of 400 yards between the rival guns, those of the British being backed up by the fire of the Enfield rifles. Very soon this double fire silenced that of the rebels, and Maude, pushing on to within 200 yards of the rebel infantry, poured upon them the fire which had silenced the guns. The English infantry advanced at the same time, and although the rebels seemed as though they would stand to protect their heavy guns, their resolution faded away in the presence of the advancing British, and they turned and fled.

During this time the rebel cavalry had been steadily manœuvring on both flanks. Their efforts on the British left were checked by the handful of volunteers; but on the right, where the horsemen were, with the exception of the officers, entirely natives, a disaster threatened. Some eighteen or twenty of the rebel cavalry, advancing at a trot, called out to the men serving under Havelock to turn and join them. They seemed to hesitate, when Palliser, who commanded them, sounded the charge. He was followed by Simpson, the Adjutant, but by only three or four of the men. Noticing this, the rebels charged in their turn. In the scrimmage which followed Palliser was unhorsed, and it would have gone hard with him but that some of the men who had refused to follow him rallied round him and brought him off. The irregulars then fled, followed by the rebel cavalry.

Meanwhile, the main body of the infantry had pushed into Fathpur. Just as the right column entered it, Beatson, who was with it, noticed the handful of irregulars dashing towards it, followed by the mutinied 2nd Cavalry. To halt, to allow the fugitives to pass through, then to pour upon the enemy a volley which sent them reeling back, was the work of a few moments. Whilst he was engaged in this, the centre and left had pushed through the one narrow street of the town, attacked the rear-guard of the rebels, driven it into flight, and captured all the baggage. Amongst the latter were two new six-pounders, large quantities of ammunition, and two tumbrils laden with specie. It was past midday when a final parting shot was sent after the retreating foe. The heat was intense. The sun, in fact, proved more deadly than the fire of the rebels. For though the casualties amounted to twelve, these had all been caused by sunstroke. It was one o'clock before the men of the little force, which had marched nineteen miles, and fought a pitched battle on an empty stomach, reached the encamping ground. They had captured twelve guns, and had given the perpetrators of the Kánhpur massacre a first lesson of retaliation. There was but one drawback to complete success. A victory, not followed up, can never be reckoned as complete. Havelock had no cavalry to follow up his victory. Eighteen volunteers—and he could then trust only Englishmen—were all insufficient to pursue thousands.

On the 13th Havelock gave his men a rest. The day following he resumed his advance, and as he marched received abundant ocular demonstrations of the precipitancy of the rebels' flight. The road was strewed with properties hurriedly cast away. The only event of importance which marked the day was the disarming of the native irregular cavalry. To mark his sense of the behaviour of these men in the Fathpur fight, Havelock had placed them on duty as baggage guards. It happened that as the force was marching, on the 14th, a report was made that the enemy were occupying a village in front. The guns were therefore brought up, and opened fire. The report turned out to be unfounded, but the native troopers took advantage of the firing of the guns to plunder the baggage. They were caught in the act, and promptly disarmed and dismounted. Havelock utilised their horses for the public service.

As the force was encamping that evening, information was brought to its leader that the rebels were in force at Aoung, a village some six miles distant. He marched, then, early the following morning, confident that he would have to fight them. The volunteers commanded by Captain Barrow, who formed the advance, descried them about daybreak, their position covered by an entrenchment thrown up across the road, and ready for the contest. Barrow galloped back with the information, followed by round-shot, and by a body of 700 sipáhís, who promptly took possession of a hamlet, several hundred yards in front of their position, and opened from it a smart musketry fire. Havelock at once made his dispositions. Remaining with the rearguard himself, he sent Tytler to the front with about a third of the force. Tytler ordered two companies of the Madras Fusiliers, under Renaud, to dislodge the rebels from the hamlet they had seized. Renaud started on this errand with his habitual gallantry, and carried it out thoroughly, though at the cost of his own life. He was struck in the thigh by a bullet, and died two days afterwards. Meanwhile, Maude's battery had come to the front and had begun to play on the entrenchment. The issue of his fire was not long doubtful. After a few rounds the rebels gave way. In the interval their cavalry had made a wide détour, in order to come round and plunder the baggage of the advancing force. A sergeant of the Highlanders, who had charge of it, saw them coming, and collecting his men, received them with so sharp a fire that they were glad to make off. Again did the enemy's guns fall into the hands of the victors. But they had fought better, and their fire had inflicted more damage, than had been the case at Fathpur.

But the work of the day was not yet over. The fight had lasted fully two hours. As the soldiers were resting after it, in the position whence they had dislodged the rebels, reports were brought to Havelock that the latter had retired to a very strong position, covered by a rivulet, swollen by the rains, known as Pándu Nadí. As the rivulet was unfordable at the season, Havelock recognised the importance of securing the stone bridge which crossed it ere it should be destroyed by the rebels. He therefore pushed on without delay, and after marching three miles came in sight of the rivulet, the stone bridge intact, and the rebels in force, covered by earthworks, on the opposite side. Another second and a puff of smoke, followed by the pounding shot, revealed the fact that the bridge was guarded by a twenty-four-pound gun and a twenty-five pound carronade. Again was the order given to bring the guns to the front. Whilst a detachment of men, armed with the Enfield, moved down the lateral ravines and opened a steady musketry fire, Maude, moving forward under the fire of the enemy, held his reply until he had placed his guns in positions whence they could envelop the entrenchment in a concentric fire. No sooner had these opened than the fire of the rebels ceased as if by magic. It transpired that the very first discharge from Maude's guns had smashed their sponge staffs, and having none in reserve they could no longer load their pieces. They made one desperate effort to blow up the bridge—an effort which failed—and then gave way. Simultaneously the Madras Fusiliers advanced, followed by the Highlanders, and rapidly crossing the bridge, caught the rebel gunners ere they could escape, and bayoneted them as they stood or ran. Maude followed with his guns, and pounded the enemy as they fled. Havelock pushed on for a mile beyond the bridge, and then halted for the night. The British loss in the two actions was about thirty men killed and wounded. The most regretable of these was that of Major Renaud, an excellent officer, always to be depended upon.

The soldiers bivouacked that night on the spot whence the last gun was fired at the retreating enemy. That evening Havelock received information that Náná Sáhib, at the head, it was said, of 7,000 men of all arms, would oppose his entry into Kánhpur on the morrow. But other information, to the effect that there were still alive in that station some 200 women and children of British blood, who had escaped the massacre of the 27th of June, cheered him and his men. 'With God's help, men,' he exclaimed, 'we shall save them, or every man of us die in the attempt.' Such was his spirit, such, also, the spirit of the men he commanded.

Kánhpur was twenty-two miles distant from the spot on which the handful of British troops was encamped. For them there was but little sleep that night. The knowledge that some of their countrywomen were alive, and that it might be theirs to rescue them, had excited them to feverish impatience. Very early the following morning they were ranged in marching order. A tramp of sixteen miles brought them to the village of Máhárájpúr. The sun was well up in the heavens, and the heat was fearful—greater than on any previous day. Halting there, Havelock despatched Barrow to the front for information. Barrow had not proceeded far when he met two loyal sipáhís on their way, at the risk of their lives, to convey to the leader of the avenging force the particulars they had carefully noted regarding the dispositions of Náná Sáhib. The information they gave was of the last importance. Náná Sáhib, they said, was in front, occupying, with about 5,000 men and eight guns, a position about 800 yards in rear of the point where the branch road into Kánhpur leaves the grand trunk road. His left rested on an entrenched village, standing among trees on high ground, within a mile of the Ganges, and was defended by three twenty-four-pounders. His centre was covered by swampy ground, and by a low-lying hamlet, on the edge of which, commanding the trunk road, were a twenty-four-pound howitzer and a nine-pounder, covered by mud earthworks. His right was covered by a village in a mango grove, surrounded by a mud wall, through the embrasures of which two nine-pounders pointed their muzzles towards the fork. The sipáhís further reported that the rebels, certain that Havelock would advance towards the fork, had taken the measurements from their positions to that point very carefully, and had laid their guns with the view of meeting him with a concentrated fire.

This timely information decided Havelock to attempt a turning movement. He halted long enough to allow his men to have their dinners, then 'remembering,' as he said, 'old Frederic at Leuthen,' he advanced, covered by his cavalry, until he reached a point where a line of groves, on his right, promised to cover a flanking movement in that direction. This point was within half-a-mile of the forking of the roads. Directing Barrow to move straight on, accompanied, to deceive the rebels, by a company of the Madras Fusiliers, in skirmishing order, on either side of the road, he marched with the bulk of the force to his right, covered by the groves spoken of. The enemy, meanwhile, believing that in the horse and foot in front of them they beheld the heads of the British columns, opened a concentrated fire on the fork. This lasted the time it took the main body to march half-a-mile. Havelock's leafy screen then failed him, and the rebels discovered to their surprise that their left flank had been all but turned, and they at once changed, as best they could, the direction of their fire. The English general, however, recognising that the turning movement was not completed, withheld all reply to the shot and shell, which soon came whizzing about him, until he had reached a point at a right angle to the enemy's position. He then wheeled into line and advanced against it.

The occasion was one which permitted a general to defy the rules which chain down pedants. Havelock had abandoned his baggage, his communication with Allahábád, and he had placed his army between his enemy and the mighty Ganges, at the full swell of her power. In taking each of these steps he deliberately broke the rules of war. But never was there a clearer proof given that such rules are not made to bind; and never will bind, a man of genius. And certainly, on that 16th of July, Havelock amply vindicated his claim to that title.

The time which had elapsed since the enemy caught sight of Havelock's turing movement and his completion of it, short as it was, had yet been sufficiently long to enable them to change their alignment, and to bring their guns to bear in the new direction. They had no longer, however, the exact knowledge of the distance, which they had hoped to utilise in the first position. But as Havelock advanced their superiority in weight of metal became perceptible, and Havelock recognised that there was nothing for it but the bayonet. When within eighty yards of the rebel batteries, then, he gave the order to charge. Like an eager pack of hounds racing to the kill the Highlanders dashed forward. In a few seconds they were over the mound covering the rebel position and into the village which they had held. They did not fire a shot or utter a shout, so fierce was their anger; but they did the work with the bayonet. It need scarcely be added that the slaughter was proportionate. But the great gun in the enemy's centre was now turned against the victorious soldiers. Havelock, noticing this, galloped up to the Highlanders, and with a few cheery words incited them to make one more charge. Then, indeed, they cheered, and scarcely waiting to make a regular formation, dashed on against the gun, led by the General in person. They carried it, completely smashing the rebel centre as they had smashed his left. Then they halted, impatient to direct their prowess in a new direction.

Nor had success been less pronounced on the right. There the 64th and the 84th, the Sikhs and Barrow's handful of volunteers, had forced back the rebels, and compelled them to concentrate in a village about a mile in the rear of their first position. To drive them from this position, a very strong one, was now the work before the undaunted infantry. The 64th. approached it from the left, the Highlanders from the centre, whilst on the extreme right the Madras Fusiliers were carrying all before them. When the soldiers, tired and panting, arrived within charging distance, Havelock, appealing to the regimental spirit of rivalry, called out: 'Who is to take that village, the Highlanders or the 64th?' Instantly the two regiments raced for the village, and carried it without a check.

The battle now seemed won. After the storm of the village Havelock halted to reorganise his line, and then advanced up the low rise which covers the entrance into Kánhpur. But scarcely had he crowned the summit when a fierce fire opened upon him, and he beheld, drawn up at a distance of half-a-mile, straight in front of him, the reunited masses of rebel infantry. From their centre a twenty-four-pounder gun belched forth its fire, whilst two smaller pieces on either side of it followed its example. Conspicuously seated on an elephant was Náná Sáhib, moving about amongst the troops, encouraging them with sounds of native music and appeals to their fanaticism. The sight was as unexpected as it was formidable, for Havelock had fain hoped that the serious part of the business was over.

He had, indeed, need of all his coolness and self-possession. His men, who had marched twenty miles, and fought one fierce battle, were worn out. His guns were a mile in the rear, and the horses which had drawn them were knocked up. It was asking a great deal of the infantry soldier to require him to charge those masses and those guns. But Havelock recognised that there was nothing else to be done. He recognised, moreover, that if to be done at all it must be done at once, for the spirits of the soldiers were still high, and the sight was one calculated to discourage men not on the move. Realising the situation on the moment, he rode to the front on his pony—for his horse had been shot under him—and turning round to the men, sitting between them and the enemy's fire, he said in a high-pitched voice: 'The longer you look at it, men, the less you will like it. Rise up. The brigade will advance, left battalion leading.'

The left battalion was the 64th. I shall follow the example of the last of the biographers[3] of Havelock, to whose vivid and picturesque account of the battle I am much indebted, and describe the action that followed

---

[3] *Havelock*. By Archibald Forbes. Macmillan, 1890.

in the words of the General himself: 'The enemy sent roundshot into our ranks until we were within 300 yards, and then poured in grape with such precision and determination as I have seldom witnessed. But the 64th, led by Major Sterling and by my Aide-de-Camp'—his son, the present Sir Henry Havelock-Allan—'who had placed himself in their front, were not to be denied. Their rear showed the ground strewed with wounded; but on they steadily and silently came, then with a cheer charged and captured the unwieldy trophy of their valour. The enemy lost all heart, and, after a hurried fire of musketry, gave way in total rout. Four of my guns came up, and completed their discomfiture by a heavy cannonade; and as it grew dark the roofless barracks of our artillery were dimly descried in advance, and it was evident that Kánhpur was once more in our possession.' The little force bivouacked for the night on the edge of the plain which marks the entry into the station, about two miles from the town. They had neither food nor tents; they had marched twenty miles, and had defeated an enemy, stronger in all arms, outnumbering them by nearly five to one, and occupying a carefully prepared position, but they lay down happy because conscious of deserving. Well might Havelock tell them, as he did in the order he issued on the occasion, that 'he was satisfied and more than satisfied with them.' The troops and the general were alike worthy of one another. The loss sustained by the victors in this fierce contest was about 100 killed and wounded. Amongst those who passed away was Stuart Beatson, the Adjutant-General of the force, a daring and most accomplished officer, who fell a victim to cholera. Knowing his end approaching, he had yet insisted in following, on a tumbril, Barrow's cavalry into action. So keen was his soldierly perception that, despite his agony, he had pointed out to Barrow, at a critical phase of the action, an opportunity for a cavalry charge. That officer had promptly availed himself of the hint. In the very presence of the destroyer, whose clutch he knew to be upon him, Beatson could yet devote all his energies to the interests of his country. Such men are priceless. But the campaigns of the Crimea and Indian Mutiny proved that Great Britain had a store of them.

Meanwhile, Náná Sáhib had by a foul and barbarous massacre deprived the troops who had defeated him in the field of the most ardently desired fruits of their victory. When he saw, on the 15th, that the British soldiers were not to be withstood, when they had forced his position on the Pándu Nadí, and when he recognised that they would assail him in Kánhpur, he gave orders for the massacre of the women and children still confined in the little house I have described. These, with some fugitives from Fathgarh, numbered nearly 200. They were all, without one exception, brutally murdered by the myrmidons of the Náná, and their bodies were cast into a deep well adjacent to the house. The massacre was accompanied by circumstances of peculiar barbarity. It was a massacre which the Náná and those about him must have known was absolutely without excuse, even the excuse, which some crocheteers, eager to excuse the enemies of England, have urged, of self-preservation. For those who were acquainted with the English character knew well that such an outrage, far from inducing Havelock to retire 'because there remained no one to be rescued,' would only stimulate his determination to exterminate the perpetrators.

So, in fact, it was. The next morning Tytler, who had been sent forward to reconnoitre, returned to report that the rebels had evacuated the city and its environs. Shortly before a concussion which shook the plain had conveyed the information that the magazine had been blown up. It was the last parting shot of the rebels. They retired, then, on Bithor.

After breakfast the troops marched into the station to witness the horrible and heart-rending sight I have spoken of. It was sufficient to stir up the mildest among them to revenge. But before that vengeance could be wreaked many things required to be accomplished. Havelock stood, indeed, victorious at Kánhpur. But it was a position, so to speak, in the air. Close to him, at Bithor, was, he was informed, the army of Náná Sáhib, still largely outnumbering his own. The Ganges alone separated him from the revolted province of Oudh, one spot in the capital of which, still held by Englishmen, was besieged and in imminent danger. At Kalpí, to the south-west, forty-five miles from Kánhpur the mutinied Gwáliár contingent was gradually concentrating, and their presence there was a menace to his left rear. He had but 1,100 men all told. On the 15th, presaging his early reoccupation of Kánhpur, he had directed Neill to bring him all the reinforcements he could. Neill brought him 227 men on the 20th, a mere handful. The position was difficult in the extreme. To hold Kánhpur at all with such a force as his, with an enemy in front, an enemy on his right flank, and an enemy making for his left rear, was against all rules. But Havelock, we have seen, knew when to discard rules. With a noble courage he resolved, then, first to storm the position of the rebel chieftain who had ordered the massacre of his countrymen, and then to make a desperate effort to ward from the English, nobly defending the Lakhnao Residency, the fate which had overtaken Wheeler and his party at Kánhpur. He had the right to hope that the troops which he knew were daily reaching Calcutta would be sent on to strengthen him.

Before describing his action it is necessary to bestow a glance on the position of affairs within the Lakhnao Residency.

CHAPTER XIV

The Residency at Lakhnao after Chinhat—Havelock's First Attempts to Relieve It

I left Sir Henry Lawrence, on the 1st and 2nd of July, concentrating his troops within the Residency of Lakhnao. He had, on the evening of the 1st, caused the Machchí Bhawan to be blown up, and its garrison, guns and treasure to be withdrawn to the enclosure which he had fixed upon as the place most capable of offering resïstance to the rebels. Within that enclosure he had, on the morning of the 2nd of July, 535 men of the 32nd foot, fifty of the 84th, eighty-nine artillerymen, 100 English officers attached to the loyal sipáhís, or unattached, 153 civilians, covenanted and uncovenanted servants of the State, and 765 natives. The place these held was, from a military point of view, not defensible. The slight fortifications, in the shape of earthworks, which had been contemplated, were still incomplete, whilst distant from these less than the width of the Strand were houses capable of being occupied in force by the rebels. The west and south faces of the enclosure were practically undefended, the bastion commenced at the angle of the two faces having been left unfinished. The position may, in a few words, be roughly described as comprising a number of houses built for ordinary domestic purposes, separated originally from one another by small plots of ground, but now roughly united by mud walls and trenches. These houses were contained in a space called, from the chief house within it, the Residency, 2,150 feet long from north-west to south-east, and 1,200 broad from east to west. The defences, as they were gradually constituted, beginning from the Baillic guard at the easternmost point, and continuing northward, were (1) Alexander's battery, (2) the water-gate battery, (3) the Redan battery, (4) a palisade. From that point southward there followed (1) Innes's garrison, (2) the bhúsá guard, (3) Gubbins's garrison and Gubbins's battery, (4) the Sikh square. Thence eastward (1) the Kánhpur battery, (2) Thomas's battery, (3) Anderson's garrison, (4) the post-office garrison,

(5) the judicial garrison, (6) Sago's guard, (7) the financial garrison. The defences were not, I have said, complete when the blockade began. They were, at the best, very rough, run up under great difficulties, and never in their finished state deserving the character of regular fortifications. It was only gradually that the several houses and their occupants came to be distinguished by the names I have appended to each.

From the day when Lawrence concentrated his troops within the enclosure the fire of the rebels upon it had been continuous. The mutinous sipáhís, the old aristocracy, the dispossessed landowners, the discontented middlemen in the districts, all contributed their quota to the memorable leaguer. In the cause to the triumph of which they devoted their energies they displayed a persistence, a perseverance, and a resolution which gave evidence of the strength of their convictions. Night and day, from the tops of the houses in close vicinity to the entrenchment, from every point where cover was available, they poured in an unremitting fire of round-shot, of musketry, of matchlock balls. From the howitzers they had filched from the British they sent shells hissing into the Residency itself. One of these, the very first day of the siege, caused to the assailed a calamity which was mourned wherever the English language is spoken.

Sir Henry Lawrence had occupied in the Residency a room convenient for noticing the movements of the enemy, but much exposed to their fire. Seated in this room, the day after the fight at Chinhat, conversing with his Secretary, Mr Couper, he was startled by the bursting within the room of an eight-inch shell. No harm followed the explosion, but the danger to the most precious life in the garrison made a deep impression on his staff, and Sir Henry at length agreed to remove to a less exposed room on the morrow. The following morning, the 2nd, he went out early to arrange the disposition of the force which had come in from the Máchchí Bhawan. He returned, tired, about eight o'clock, and lay on his bed whilst he transacted business with his Adjutant-General, Captain Wilson. Lying near him was his nephew, George Lawrence. Suddenly there came a sheet of flame, a terrific report and a shock, followed by intense darkness. It was a shell from the howitzer which had been fired in the morning. It left George Lawrence, as it burst, unscathed, it tore off the shirt from the back of Captain Wilson, and it mortally wounded Sir Henry Lawrence. He lingered in extreme agony to the morning of the 4th, and then died.

The death of this great man was felt by the garrison as a loss only not irreparable, because they inherited the splendid courage which had animated him from the first hour of the insurrection to the moment when he was called away. They felt, one and all, that they could best testify their respect for his memory by carrying out their stern defence on the lines he had laid down. He was succeeded, as chief commissioner, by Major Banks, an officer of rare merit, who had been his friend and confidant. The command of the troops, however, devolved upon Brigadier Inglis of the 32nd.

Whilst Havelock was fighting his way from Allahábád to Kánhpur, in the manner described in the preceding chapter, the garrison of the Residency was exposed to the unremitting attacks of an enemy vastly superior to it in numbers and strength of position. The compass of this volume will not permit me to give in full detail a history of the several assaults. It must suffice to refer to those of the greatest importance. From the very outset the damage done to life and material were great. Sir Henry Lawrence died, as I have told, on the 4th of July. Mrs Dorin and Mr Ommanney, the latter one of the prominent members of the Civil Service, were killed or mortally wounded the same day. Major Francis, of the 13th N. I., a very gallant officer, who had successfully brought in the garrison of the Machchí Bhawan, and Mr Polehampton, the Chaplain, succumbed to the rebels' fire on the 7th. Before the dawn of the 20th of the month the casualties had been increased by Mr Bryson, at one time Sergeant-Major 16th Lancers, shot through the head on the 9th; by Lieutenant Dashwood, 48th N. I., who succumbed the same day to cholera; by Lieutenant Charlton, 32nd foot, shot through the head on the 13th; by Lieutenant Lester, mortally wounded on the 14th; by Lieutenants Bryce and O'Brien, wounded on the 16th; by Lieutenant Harmer, wounded, and Lieutenant Arthur, killed, on the 19th.

Nor was the damage less to the materials which formed the component parts of the defences. On the 15th Anderson's house was entirely destroyed by round-shot. The garrison, however, still continued to hold the ground on which it had stood. On the 18th many round-shots were fired into the post-office, Fayrer's house, commanded by Gould Weston, Gubbins's house, and the brigade mess-house. At one time the rebels nearly succeeded in setting fire to the Residency house by means of carcasses.[1]

The difficulties the garrison had to contend with were enormous. They had, in addition to the work of active defence, to dig out and carry stores, to shift the guns, to dig trenches, to sink shafts for mines, to bury the dead, especially the dead animals, whose putrifying carcasses contaminated the air, to repair damages. In all these duties the officers shared equally the labours with the men, and all exerted themselves to the utmost.

---

[1] A carcass is a hollow vessel, filled with combustibles.

Sometimes they made a sortie. They attempted the first on the 7th. The sallying party succeeded in driving out the enemy from a position they held commanding the defences. Lieutenant Lawrence, who led it, obtained for his cool daring the coveted Victoria Cross.

I have given the casualties of the officers and others up to the 20th, because on that day the rebels made their first grand assault. Their movement began at half past eight in the morning, was sustained vigorously for several hours, and was finally beaten back at four o'clock. Several officers and men covered themselves with glory. Conspicuous amongst them was Ensign Loughnan of the 13th N. I., against whose post, Innes's house, the weight of the attack was directed. The garrison here consisted of twelve men of the 32nd foot, twelve of the 13th N. I., and some clerks. They repulsed an enemy vastly superior in numbers. Another attack, made simultaneously against the Redan, was repelled with equal courage and equal determination.

Of this general attack, the first grand assault against the garrison, it has been remarked that it was a triumph of British coolness and pluck over Asiatic numbers and swagger; of the mind over matter. The writer[2] adds that, in another sense, it was still more important. It proved to the mutineers that they had miscalculated their chances; that, unless famine should come to aid them, they and their countrymen would never triumph over that handful of Europeans.

The result of that day's action, doubtless, greatly encouraged the garrison. Their losses, four killed and twelve wounded, had been small, whilst the casualties of the rebels had been severe. The day following however, they suffered a bereavement second only to that which they had experienced when Sir Henry Lawrence died. His successor, Major Banks, whilst reconnoitring from the top of an outhouse, was shot dead through the head. He had been an invaluable colleague to Brigadier Inglis, and it was felt there was no one left who could replace him. The office he had held was accordingly left vacant until the Government of India could be communicated with.

The garrison had no certain knowledge of the events passing at Kánhpur. They had despatched many letters by native messengers believed to be faithful, but up to the 25th of July no reply had been received. Three days previously, however, on the 22nd, their most trusted messenger, a pensioned sipáhí named Aṅgad, arrived to state that he had seen the victorious English regiments at Kánhpur; but it was not till the 25th that

---

[2] Kaye's and Malleson's *History of the Indian Mutiny.* Cabinet edition. vol. iii., page 303.

the same messenger, who had been sent out again, returned with a letter from Tytler stating that 'Havelock was advancing with a force sufficient to bear down all opposition, and would arrive in five or six days.' Inglis replied by despatching, by Angad, to Havelock a plan of his position and of the roads by which it could be approached. This reply reached Havelock at Mangalwár, a village five miles from the Ganges, in the province of Oudh. To reach Lakhnao there still remained forty miles to traverse. Before describing the further progress of the leaguer of the Residency it is necessary that I should return to Kánhpur, and narrate how it was that Havelock had been able to push on so far, and yet failed to accomplish the entire journey.

Neill, I have said, had joined Havelock, with a few troops, on the 20th of July. Five days later Havelock crossed the Ganges with the intention of endeavouring to relieve the Residency. In the interval between the two dates he had despatched Major Stephenson to destroy Bithor, evacuated by Náná Sáhib and his troops. Stephenson burned down the palace, blew up the magazine, and brought back to Kánhpur twenty cannon abandoned by the Náná. Simultaneously Havelock had designed, armed, and nearly finished at Kánhpur a fortified work commanding the river, large enough to accommodate the 300 men, all he could spare to hold the place in his absence. The command of these he entrusted to Neill. He had begun, on the 21st, his preparations for crossing the river; had sent over his guns on that day, the infantry on the succeeding days. On the 25th he crossed himself, and moved that day to Mangalwár, five miles. There he halted to complete his arrangements for the carriage of his ammunition and supplies. These were completed by the 28th, and he made his first move forward the following morning.

For the purpose which he had in view his force was small indeed. It was composed of less than 1,500 men, of whom barely 1,200 were Europeans. His cavalry consisted of sixty volunteers and mounted soldiers, his artillery of ten small field-pieces, his infantry of portions of the 64th, the 84th, the 78th, the Madras Fusiliers, and Brasyer's Sikhs.

At five o'clock, on the 29th, this little force began its forward movement. After a march of three miles Havelock discerned the rebels occupying a strong position in front of and in the village of Unáo. From this position he dislodged them after a fierce conflict, in which they lost fifteen guns and about 500 men. He then pushed on to Bashíratganj, six miles distant. Bashíratganj was a walled town, intersected by the high road, its entrance protected by a turreted gateway, with lateral defences, and a wet ditch in front. Still more to the front of it was a large jhíl, or shallow pond, whilst another, still larger, lay behind the town, on the road to Lakhnao, traversed by a narrow causeway. Havelock conceived the idea of sending round the 64th to cut off the enemy from the causeway, whilst he should assail it in front. Unfortunately the turning movement took longer than was expected, and the troops with Havelock made their front assault before the 64th had completed it. The result was that, though the rebels suffered severely, the bulk of them escaped across the causeway.

The British loss in the two actions had been severe also. Eighty-eight men had been placed *hors-de combat*, and eighty-eight men represented nearly a twelth of his European fighting strength. A nearly equal number of sick reduced that strength still further. Havelock had used up, too, one-third of his gun ammunition, whilst he had accomplished but fifteen miles out of the forty-five necessary to traverse. In front of him were positions which would be held against him still more steadfastly, and by a greater number of troops. Then, too, the question forced itself upon him, how could he carry his sick and wounded? He could not leave them, because he could spare no troops to guard them. Just at the moment moreover, he had received information of that fatal mutiny at Dánápur, the consequence of the imbecility of the Calcutta Government, which came at the moment to add terribly to the existing complications. There were, also, rebel troops in the districts, any number of whom combining might, if he were to advance further, cut him off from the Ganges. Feeling that these difficulties were too great to be encountered with the force at his disposal, he fell back, on the 31st, to Mangalwár, and despatched thence his sick and wounded into Kánhpur, with a letter to Neill informing him of the reason of his retreat, and adding that, to enable him to reach Lakhnao, it was necessary he should receive a reinforcement of 1,000 men and another field-battery.

To this letter Neill wrote a most intemperate, even an insulting reply. Havelock was very angry. He contented himself, however, for the moment with warning Neill that considerations of the public service alone prevented him from placing him under arrest. But it is the opinion of Havelock's latest biographer[3] that Neill's letter may so have operated on a high-strung temperament, made sensitive by disappointment following on an inspiriting sequence of brilliant successes, as to induce Havelock to attempt another advance without adequate reinforcements. At all events Havelock did attempt a second forward movement. Setting out on the 4th of August, he found himself the following morning in front of Bashíratganj; occupied it, but could not prevent the rebels from carrying off all their guns, and taking

---

[3] Archibald Forbes.

a strong position a little further on. He then recognised that to advance further would probably involve the loss of his whole force. Fortified by the opinion of the three officers of his staff whom he consulted, Tytler, Crommelin, and young Henry Havelock, he determined then to fall back. He had once again reached Mangalwár, on the 10th, when he heard that the rebels were making a great show at Bashíratganj. Glad to seize the chance of inflicting upon them a severe blow before he should cross, he promptly marched on that place, caught his enemy, killed 200 of them, and captured two guns; then turning again, he recrossed the Ganges into Kánhpur on the 13th. There he read the details of that insane action of the Government of India by which the much desired and needful reinforcements had been withheld from him at the most critical period of his command.

To understand how this happened I must ask the reader to return with me to Calcutta, and to accompany me thence to Dánápur and Patná.

CHAPTER XV

Calcutta and Western Bihár in July and August

Reports of the terrible fate of the English men and English women who had been besieged by the rebels at Kánhpur had reached Calcutta early in July, but it was not until Havelock telegraphed, on the 17th of the month, the account of his victory, and of their murder, that all hope of their survival disappeared. Then, for a moment, the crushing blight of despair succeeded to the agony of suspense. Only, however, for a moment. Almost instantly there rose in its place an intense eagerness to place in the hands of the avenging General all the available resources of the State—resources which should make him strong enough to push on to ward off from other threatened garrisons, especially from the garrison of the Residency of Lakhnao, a similar calamity. For the moment the Government, the press, the mercantile bodies, public opinion generally, seemed to unite in concentrating their efforts to obtain this wished-for result. Lord Canning had, in the last days of July, sanctioned the raising in Calcutta of a corps of yeomanry cavalry—a corps which, led by a very resolute and able officer, Major J. F. Richardson, was destined to render excellent service. He had, further, in conjunction with the Lieutenant-Governor of Bengal, directed similar enlistments from the unemployed sailors to meet the troubles then threatening in Bengal and Bihár, and he had concluded an arrangement with Jang Bahádur, Prime Minister and virtual ruler of the State of Nipál, for the despatch of a body of Gurkhá troops to the districts of Gorákhpur and Ázamgarh.

So far he had done well. But none of those acts, praise-worthy as they were, touched the crucial point. They did not provide immediate succour to Havelock. Yet at that moment, besides the 53rd, which garrisoned Fort William, there was a wing of the 37th regiment available; the 10th foot garrisoned Dánápur; whilst on the 5th of July, two days before Havelock started from Allahábád on his memorable campaign, the 5th Fusiliers, 800 strong, landed in Calcutta from the Mauritius.

Havelock, we have seen, wanted on the 5th August, according to his own estimate, another thousand men to enable him to reach Lakhnao. Now, on the 5th of July there were 1,200 men available, either at Calcutta, or on their way, steaming towards Allahábád (for the wing of the 37th had been despatched just before) without weakening the garrisons of Calcutta and Dánápur. With a little management that number could have been considerably increased. We left Havelock, in the last chapter, on the 13th August, stranded at Kánhpur for want of such troops. Why, in the terrible crisis which interrupted his victorious career, were the troops which might have been available not promptly despatched to him?

To this question there is an answer, and that answer indicates the difference which arose between the Government and the rest of the European community, and with respect to which the Government adopted a course, timid, shrinking, and politically ruinous. For the sake of a sentiment they risked the temporary loss of the Empire. Indeed, it will be proved that but for the heroic conduct of one man, the late Vincent Eyre, the country between Calcutta and Banáras would have been overrun by the rebels.

The water-line between Calcutta and Allahábád, about 664 miles in length, had one weak middle point at Dánápur and Patná, two places only twelve miles apart. Dánápur was 344 miles from Calcutta, the city of Patná was twelve miles nearer to the capital. At Dánápur there were, as I have already stated, three native regiments, the 7th, 8th, and 40th N. I., one company of European, one of native artillery, and the 10th foot. The position of the two places was a most important one. The province, Western Bihár, of which Patná was the capital, was one of the richest provinces in India. It contained a considerable number of native landowners, men of large estates and ancient lineage. English merchants, too, had invested large sums in the province in the cultivation of indigo, one of its staple exports. It touched on the one side, to the north-west, the revolted districts of Gházípur, Ázamgarh, Juánpur, and Mírzápur; to the north, it touched Nipál; to the east, the division of Eastern Bihár, not only combustible itself, but open to invasion by the sipáhís in Eastern Bengal, then in a state of incipient mutiny.

It will be recognised, then, that it was of paramount importance that the division of Western Bihár, the middle piece between Calcutta and Allahábád, should be preserved from outbreak by a Government anxious to despatch English troops to Allahábád, thence to proceed to reinforce Havelock at Kánhpur.

Up to the period at which I have arrived the province had been preserved from revolt by the energetic measures taken by its Commissioner, Mr

William Tayler. Harassed by the fussy interference of his superior at Calcutta, Mr Frederick Halliday, Mr Tayler had, nevertheless, with resources he had made for himself, put down insurrection in the most inflammable city in India, the headquarters of the intriguing Wahábís, and had preserved, amid great difficulties, complete order in the districts, those of Patná, Gayá, Shahábád, Sáran, Champáran, and Tirhút, which went to make up the division of which he was the pro-consul. His services have never been acknowledged, he has been treated with contumely and insult, but he contributed as much as any man, in that terrible crisis called the Indian Mutiny, to save the Empire.

To the mind of William Tayler there was, towards the end of June, but one possible danger to the province. That danger would be very great if the sipáhís at Dánápur, numbering nearly 3,000 men, were to break out in revolt. If the Government would but order that they should be disarmed all would go well. For that he would answer.

The opinion of Mr Tayler on this point was also the opinion of all intelligent men in Calcutta, that is, of the united merchants and traders, men who had shown their loyalty and devotion by raising the corps of volunteers, of the three arms, of which I have spoken, of the great majority of the members of the services, and of the loyal natives. It was the opinion, in fact, of everyone who was not a secretary to Government, or who hoped, by time-serving and subserviency, to become a secretary to Government. The question had been mooted at an earlier period. The reply, demi-official, of the Government then had been that, with only a sufficient number of European troops to preserve order close to the capital, it did not feel justified in proceeding to a measure which, unless there were sufficient white troops on the spot, might precipitate the evil it was intended to heal. That answer sufficed for the moment. But when the 37th had started, and when preparations were being made to despatch the 5th Fusiliers, in steamers which must pass Patná and Dánápur, it was felt that the time had arrived when the disarming process might be carried out in an effective manner, under circumstances which would render resistance impossible.

These ideas took possession of the English community in Calcutta, and were ventilated by the press. It was believed, at the outset, that the Government would welcome the suggestion as tending to relieve them from a great difficulty. The Government had acknowledged that the weakness of the middle piece constituted at the moment the great difficulty in despatching reinforcements to Havelock. Now that great difficulty could be removed. Great, then, was the surprise when the rumour pervaded the city that the Government had resolved to decline the responsibility which devolves upon all governments—the responsibility of directing the carrying out of a measure which each member of it knew to be essential to the well-being of the Empire.

Great, I say, was the astonishment. Was it for this, men asked one another, that Lord Canning had summoned from Madras Sir Patrick Grant to advise him? Nothing, it was true, had been seen or heard of Sir Patrick Grant since his arrival. It was known that he was occupying comfortable quarters at Government House, and that he was babbling about reorganisation, when the question was the suppression of the Mutiny. But in military matters he was, nominally at least, the chief councillor of the Governor-General, and it was supposed that he, an officer trained with sipáhís, would at least understand the necessity of the position. But rumour further stated that Lord Canning was greatly guided by his advice, and by that of the Lieutenant-Governor of Bengal, Mr Halliday. In the latter no one had any confidence. It was felt, then, that the time had arrived when the leading members of the mercantile community, all of whom, as proprietors of indigo factories, had large interests in Western Bihár, should ask to be allowed to make a personal appeal to Lord Canning. They made a request to this effect on the 17th of July. Lord Canning agreed to receive them on the 20th.

He did receive a deputation from them on that date, listened to their statements, heard from their mouths that the disarming of the native regiments at Dánápur was the one measure necessary to restore public confidence in Bihár; that a favourable opportunity now presented itself for the carrying out of such a measure, inasmuch as the 5th Fusiliers, which had quitted Calcutta by steamer on the 12th, would reach Dánápur about the 22nd; and that then the disarming could be accomplished in two hours. Lord Canning listened to them without interrupting them, then told them very curtly, using the fewest words he could command to express his meaning that he would not comply with their request.

The Government of India had, in fact, previously decided to attempt one of those half-measures which weak and incompetent men cling to in an emergency. Unable to brace themselves to the resolution of directing the disarming of the native regiments, they had, on the 12th of July, by the hand of Sir Patrick Grant, cast the responsibility of disarming or of not disarming on the officer commanding the Dánápur division. That officer, General Lloyd, was to be the sole judge of the advisability or the inadvisability of the measure. 'If,' wrote to him Sir Patrick Grant, on the 12th July, 'when the regiment' (the 5th Fusiliers) 'reaches Dánápur, you see reason to distrust the native troops, and you entertain an opinion that it is desirable to disarm them, you are at liberty to disembark the 5th Fusiliers to assist you in that object.'

The reader will not fail to comprehend the position. The native troops in Bengal and in the North-west Provinces of India had generally mutinied or had been disarmed. At Dánápur, twelve miles from the inflammable city of Patná, the centre of the richest province in India, were three native regiments still carrying their arms. Havelock was at Kánhpur crying for reinforcements. The arrival at Kánhpur of such reinforcements depended on the continued tranquillity of the middle piece of country of which Dánápur and Patná were the centres. The continued tranquillity of that middle piece could only be insured by the prompt disarming of the three native regiments at Dánápur. The public voice, the great mercantile community, besought the Government to issue positive orders for such disarming. The Government absolutely refused, but, as a sop, they threw the responsibility of the action to be taken upon an aged soldier, whose nerves were utterly unequal to the task; who, in fact, emulating the action of his superiors at Calcutta, endeavoured to reconcile the responsibility thrust upon him, with the evident reluctance of the Government that he should exercise it, by devising another half-measure, which brought about the very catastrophe which strong and resolute action would have avoided. Well might Lord Dalhousie write, as he did write, when the news of the catastrophe and its causes reached him: 'Why was it left to General Lloyd, or to General or Mister Anybody, to order measures so obviously necessary to safety?'

For, be it remembered, throughout the period from the outbreak of the mutiny at Mírath and the casting upon the shoulders of General Lloyd of responsibilities which properly belonged to the Government, it had been with the utmost difficulty, and by the display of the rarest qualities of courageous statesmanship, that Mr William Tayler had been able to preserve order at Patná and throughout his division. He had put down an uprising in the city itself, had baffled the machinations of the Wahábí leaders, had instilled fear and discouragement in the ranks of the seditious, and by his splendid example had given confidence to his subordinates. Amongst those who had been acting with him in the districts was a very gallant officer, Major John Holmes, commanding the 12th Irregular Cavalry stationed at Sigaùli, in the Champáran district. Holmes, like most officers serving with the native troops, believed implicitly in the loyalty of his own men, and certainly for some weeks they justified his confidence by their obedience and energy. It is just possible that, if the sipáhís at Dánápur had been quietly disarmed, those troopers would have remained loyal. The result showed that they could not be proof against the successful rising of their brethren at the chief station.

It would serve no good purpose to dwell at length upon the incompetent action which threw the middle piece between Calcutta and Kánhpur into a condition of unparalleled disorder, and delayed the advance of the troops for which the heart of the gallant Havelock was preying upon itself. Under the weight of the responsibility thrust upon him the mind of General Lloyd vacillated like the pendulum of a clock. When, on the 22nd, the main body of the 5th Fusiliers arrived off Dánápur, the pendulum was at the left corner, and he would not order them to disembark. Two days later, when two companies of the 37th reached the station, the pendulum had veered to the right, and he ordered them to land. The day following, the 25th, he resolved not to disarm the sipáhís, but to deprive them of the percussion caps which had been served out to them, and of those in the magazine. By a display of force he succeeded in securing the caps in the magazine. Then, believing he had scored a triumph, he dismissed the European troops, and went comfortably to his luncheon. But when an hour or two later the officers, by his direction, endeavoured to persuade the sipáhís to surrender the caps in their actual possession, the latter broke into open mutiny, and went off towards the river Són, in the direction of Árah. The European troops were at once called out, but there was no one present to give any orders. The General had gone on board of one of the steamers, and in the matter of taking upon themselves the smallest responsibility in his absence the two officers next in command took example from the Government of India. Nothing, or next to nothing, was done. The mutineers got off scot free. It was one of the most painful incidents of those troublous times.

Nor was the calamity confined to Dánápur. The telegraph did its work. The very evening of the day on which these events occurred the troopers of the 12th Irregulars rose in mutiny and murdered their commanding officer and his wife. Similarly, Kunwar Singh, a large landowner, who had considerable estates at Jagdíspur, not far from Árah, and who had had bitter reason to complain of the action of the law courts of Calcutta, intimated to the sipáhís, by some very practical assistance, his sympathy with their movement. It seemed probable that, unless the British should take prompt action, the whole of Western Bihár would be in a blaze.

There were two officials in the province upon whom, at this period, devolved enormous responsibility. The one was ready to take that responsibility, and did take it. The other had completely lost his head. The action of these two officials will now be related. It was the obvious duty of General Lloyd to despatch English troops at once in pursuit of the rebels. He had a sufficient number at his disposal. But the heavy weight of responsibility had made his brain slow, and his arm powerless to strike. He did, indeed, despatch a few riflemen the following day, in a river steamer, to the mouth of the river Són. But there the draught of water was insufficient, and the men returned, having accomplished nothing. Then the General wrote to Mr Tayler to the effect that, far from pursuing the mutineers, he intended to entrench himself at Dánápur, as he feared that, joined by Kunwar Singh, they would return to attack him. Then it was that the nature of William Tayler showed itself. He was a civilian; the other was a soldier. The soldier, sad to recount, his moral faculties overborne, proposed to entrench himself against an enemy who had no thought of attacking him. The civilian, with all his wits about him, his strong faculties never so clear as in the time of danger, deprecated the resolution of the soldier with all the eloquence he could command. He implored him to lose no time in pursuing the rebels, showed that there was yet time to catch them, and that vigour and energy might yet retrieve the disaster.

Tayler's strong exhortations convinced the General. They impressed upon him some of the passionate conviction which animated the daring Commissioner. He despatched then a body of troops, 415 in number, with fifteen officers, commanded by Captain Dunbar, to be conveyed by steamer to a point not far from the spot where the road to Árah strikes the river Són. Thence they would march to the former place, where, it was believed, the sipáhís would be found.

Leaving these men marching, I must return to the sipáhís.

The rebel native soldiers, surprised at being allowed to escape without pursuit, reached the banks of the Són on the early morn of the 26th. For want of boats in which to cross they were delayed there till the evening. Then, having received meanwhile most comforting assurances from Kunwar Singh, they were, thanks to the means provided by that chief, conveyed to the western bank. They then marched to Árah, released the prisoners from the gaol, plundered the treasury, and set forth to hunt for the Europeans. These, however, thanks to the prescience of one of their number, had taken timely precautions to meet their attack.

The story of the leaguer of Árah is a story of foresight, gallantry, perseverance, energy, and devotion unsurpassed in the world's history. The prescient organiser of the successful resistance to the blood-thirsty sipáhís was Mr Vicars Boyle, an engineer connected with the railway. But his companions, Herwald Wake, Colvin, Halls, Combe, Littledale, and the rest, for there were fifteen Englishmen and Eurasians, besides the Deputy Collector, a Muhammadan gentleman named Sayid Azím-úd-dín Khán, fifty Sikhs, inclusive of native officers, a watercarrier and a cook, were all worthy of association with him. They had long regarded the outbreak of the sipáhís at Dánápur as possible, and when it did occur they collected in the house which Mr Vicars Boyle had prepared, provisioned, and to a certain extent fortified. The presence of the Sikhs among them was due, absolutely and entirely, to the prescient care of Mr William Tayler of Patná, a circumstance which was much appreciated at the time, but which, like many other of the noble acts of that gentleman, has been since conveniently forgotten.

The mutinous sipáhís, aided by the levies of Kunwar Singh, crowded to attack the little house on the evening of the 27th. They were met by a stern resistance such as they evidently had not expected. They changed their tactics then, and brought up guns to assist them. They used these on the 28th, and during the day of the 29th. But that night there was a lull, and the garrison was cheered by hearing a musketry fire in the direction from which they expected assistance—the direction of Dánápur.

The musketry fire was indeed the consequence of the proximity of Dunbar's force, but, alas! it was produced mainly by the muskets of the revolted sipáhís. Dunbar, in fact, marching carelessly, and without the precautions essential to a night march in a country occupied by an enemy, had fallen into an ambuscade. He and other officers were killed; the men, surprised, became discouraged, and attempting to retrace their steps to the Són, they were pursued by almost the full force of the rebels. It was a rout as complete as it was disgraceful. Many men were killed and wounded during the retreat. When the survivors reached the Són, they experienced the greatest difficulty in forcing their way to its eastern bank. They at last succeeded; the steamer which had brought them to a certain point was still waiting for them there. On that steamer, in lieu of the 415 men and fifteen officers whom she had carried, full of hope, the previous morning, there were now only fifty men and three officers who had been untouched by the enemy's fire.

The repulse of the force which, at the instance of Mr Tayler, General Lloyd had despatched to relieve Árah added greatly to the despondency of that officer. It would be difficult to exaggerate the gloom, not to say the terror, which fell upon Dánápur. Upon Mr Tayler the effect was very different. It seemed, indeed, impossible to doubt that Árah must fall. If Árah should fall, then the several stations, isolated, each depending on its own resources, must inevitably be overrun. Under these circumstances, Mr Tayler, acting like a skilful general who feels that his detachments would be liable, when separated from one another and unsupported, to be cut up in detail, but would successfully resist the enemy if united, authorised his several subordinate officers at the isolated stations to fall back upon Patná, bringing the contents of their treasuries with them, unless in so doing their personal safety should be endangered. It was a wise and statesmanlike order, and it would have been so accepted by all the world but for the sudden appearance on the scene of a man whose genius and daring suddenly changed disaster into triumph.

Such men are born seldom. The man who accomplished this feat was a major in the artillery, who had served in the first Kábul war, had been kept there a prisoner, who had written a story of the events which led to and followed the disaster to the English, and who had since served in Gwáliár and in Burma. His name was Vincent Eyre. He had but just been recalled from Burma, and had been despatched with a European battery, on board a steamer from Calcutta bound for Allahábád, on the 10th of July.

Eyre had reached Dánápur the evening of the 25th, the day memorable for the successful rising of the three regiments. He had gone on shore and offered his services to the General, but as these were not required, he had proceeded the next day to Baksar, forty-three miles from Árah. There he heard that the mutinied sipáhís were advancing by way of Árah towards Baksar. As this place was the headquarters of the Government stud, and was but thirty miles from Gházípur, Eyre decided to detain the tender of the steamer at Baksar, whilst he should proceed in the latter to Gházípur to ensure the safety of that place. This he did on the 29th; left two guns and his only subaltern to protect Gházípur, took instead twenty-five men of the 78th on to his steamer, and returned that night to Baksar. There he found 154 men of the 5th Fusiliers, who had arrived that afternoon, under the command of Captain L'Estrange. As the information he received conveyed to the mind of Eyre the impression that the rebels had stopped at Árah to besiege our countrymen there, he determined to endeavour to induce L'Estrange to combine with him to march to the relief of that place. He wrote to him to that effect. L'Estrange replied that if Eyre, as senior officer, would send him a written order to that effect, and would take upon himself the entire responsibility, he would obey him. Eyre, who had not graduated in the school of the Calcutta statesmen, issued the order forthwith. He knew, of course, that he was, so to speak, risking his commission, for his orders were to proceed to Allahábád, and the march to Árah would take him nearly fifty miles off his direct road. But to the courageous mind of Eyre the occasion was one in which it was imperative to risk his all—and he risked it.

Eyre's force consisted of forty gunners and three guns, 154 men of the 5th Fusiliers, six officers, including himself, two assistant surgeons, eighteen volunteers, mostly mounted, of whom three were officers, one the Magistrate of Gházípur and one a veterinary surgeon. The twenty-five Highlanders he had borrowed from Gházípur he left at Baksar to take the first opportunity of returning to their station. His total force, it will thus be seen, amounted only to 220 men and three guns. With that he set out, on the 31st of July, to attempt a task which had already, less than forty-eight hours before, though he knew it not, baffled 430 officers and men.

The news which reached him, on the night of the 31st, at his first halting ground of the defeat of Dunbar's party had no effect upon Eyre and his men. They pushed on all the next day without seeing any enemy, and bivouacked for the night at the village of Gujrájganj, some six miles from Árah. After marching a mile the next morning the rebels appeared in great numbers, occupying a wood which Eyre and his men must traverse. He reconnoitred their position, and then attacked them. The rebels had the advantage of numbers, and of position, and they were inspired by their defeat of Dunbar. But Eyre's first attack was so well directed and so sustained that he forced his foe to abandon his position, only however, he discovered to his vexation, to take a far stronger one about a mile in the rear. As this position was strong enough to repel a front attack, Eyre, under cover of the fire of his three guns, made a flank movement to gain the nearest point of the new railway embankment which had been constructed from Árah. The rebels, however, discovered the movement and its object, and commanding as they did the inner chord of the circle, rushed forward to gain it first, at the same time detaching Kunwar Singh's levies to harass the rear of the British. The rebels gained the decisive point first, and stationing themselves behind the trees of a wood which flanked the embankment, opened a severe musketry fire on the British as they approached. Eyre's position was now extremely critical. He must carry that wood, or be lost. Everything depended upon his coolness and self-possession; and, under difficult circumstances, no man ever gave greater evidence of the possession of both these qualities. Calmly surveying the position, he formed his men in skirmishing order, whilst his guns played upon the wood. The damage these effected was not great, as the rebels were well sheltered by the trees. Twice, indeed, they sallied forth to charge the guns, but each time they were repulsed. But they had all the advantage in musketry fire from behind shelter, and at the end of an hour Captain Hastings of the volunteers brought word to Eyre, who, having no subaltern, was obliged to stay with the guns, that the position of the Fusiliers was becoming critical. For such a state of affairs there was but one remedy—recourse to that splendid weapon which, wielded by

British hands, has never failed. The order was given to close up and charge. Promptly was it executed. Led on one flank by L'Estrange, on the other by Hastings, the men of the 5th closed up, and rushing forward with a cheer, cleared the brook which separated them from the wood, and dashed at the enemy. The rebels did not stand to meet the encounter; they gave way in tumultuous disorder. Eyre pushed rapidly on after them, hoping to reach Árah that night, but he was stopped on the way by an impassable torrent. He spent the whole night in improvising a causeway. Over this, in the early morning, he passed his troops and his guns, and an hour later had the gratification of rescuing from their danger the gallant garrison which, for eight days, had successfully defied an enemy fifty times more numerous than themselves.

The rebels, meanwhile, had fled to Jagdispur, the stronghold of Kunwar Singh. Thither Eyre, who was not the man to consider a task completed so long as anything remained to be accomplished, followed them on the 11th of August, and stormed and captured it the following day.

Such was the man, and such was the deed which changed the despair of the British residents of Western Bihár into triumph. Eyre, descending apparently from the clouds, had turned defeat into victory, despair into rejoicings. The Government acted precisely as governments without a backbone will always act. The action of the victorious Eyre was upheld. But his companion in pluck and energy, William Tayler, who had, despite his transcendent services, become obnoxious to the Calcutta clique, was removed from his office and ruined, avowedly because at a critical period, before Eyre had redeemed Dunbar's disaster, and when it seemed certain that the rebels would overrun the province, he had advised concentration at Patná of the resources in men and money of the province. The same Government took the opportunity to reward an officer serving under Mr Tayler, Mr Alonzo Money, for a theatrical display which was really damaging to the interests of the country. This gentleman had left his station for Patná, but had repented and returned to it. Then taking advantage of the arrival of a company of British troops, he marched with them and the contents of the treasury, not to Patná, which was near, and where they were wanted, but to Calcutta, which was more than 300 miles distant, and where they were not wanted—this, too, at a time when Havelock was earnestly crying out for more soldiers.

Eyre left Árah for Allahábád on the 20th of August. The failure of the Government to disarm the three regiments had thus wasted a month at the most critical period of the operations in the vicinity of Kánhpur. But the mischief done to the British cause was not entirely represented by that loss of time. The disturbances in Western Bihár continued. They kept for some time in the province troops who were required in the north-west, nor were they entirely suppressed until a very late period of the following year.

But by this time fresh troops are pouring into Calcutta; a new Commander-in-Chief has arrived to displace Sir Patrick Grant; Sir James Outram, appointed to command the united Dánápur and Kánhpur divisions, is on his way to Allahábád; Captain Peel and Captain Sotheby are forming naval brigades from the crews of the *Shannon* and the *Pearl*; the Residency of Lakhnao is still holding out; Agra, after a calamity, which will have to be recorded, is in a state of siege; the British troops before Dehlí are holding their position on the ridge; Sir John Lawrence is despatching from the Panjáb Nicholson, with a compact force, to join them; Lord Elphinstone is bearing himself bravely at Bombay, Lord Harris in Madras, Sir Bartle Frere in Sind; there have been disturbances in Rájpútáná and in the dominions of Holkar; Mahárájá Sindhiá remains loyal, but his troops are gathering against the English at Kalpí. The situation is on the whole more hopeful than it was in June and July, because it is more defined. The wiser statesmen have recognised that the real enemies of the British are the sipáhís and the populations of the North-western Provinces, of Bundelkhand, of Rohilkhand, and of Oudh. To crush these the recently arrived resources of Great Britain must be directed. But, first of all, it is incumbent to attempt the relief of the Residency of Lakhnao, too long delayed by the action of the Calcutta Government, recorded in this chapter. I must, then, return to Kánhpur.

CHAPTER XVI

The First Relief of the Lakhnao Residency

I have recorded in a previous chapter[1] how the garrison of the Lakhnao Residency had been cheered, on the night of the 25th of July, by the receipt of a letter from Tytler telling them that Havelock was advancing with a force sufficient to bear down all opposition, and that he would arrive in five or six days. The six days passed and no Havelock came. The sound of firing was occasionally heard in the direction of Kánhpur, and this sound tended to confirm the hopes already raised. But they were doomed to be disappointed for the moment. We have seen how Havelock, on the 13th of August, finally recrossed the Ganges.

Three days before that happened the rebels, encouraged doubtless by his retreat from Bashíratganj, made their second grand assault on the position of the Residency. It began about half-past ten in the morning, by the successful springing of a mine, which made a great breach in the defences. Against this they marched in considerable numbers, and with great resolution. But the men of the garrison were on the alert. A heavy musketry fire from the roofs of the adjacent houses was kept on the advancing foe, whilst a stern resistance met their front attack. Eventually they were driven back with enormous loss. A second attack on another point, Sago's house, and a third, on Innes's, Anderson's, and Gubbins's posts, met with a like result. But the attacks had lasted twelve hours. Again the loss of the garrison was small.

Two days later a sortie made by the garrison was repulsed. Six days after that, the 18th, the besiegers made their third grand assault.

The springing of the mine on this occasion, under one of the Sikh squares, was most effective. It made a breach, some twenty feet wide, in the defences. Against this the rebels came with extraordinary enthusiasm.

---

[1] Chapter XIV, page 208.

Again, however, the men of the garrison were ready for them, and again did they drive them back with heavy loss.

Still the rebels persevered. They believed it was but a question of time. They knew to some extent of the sufferings of the garrison; how the necessity to be constantly on the alert must tell upon them. They kept up, then, a fire almost unremitting, varied by sudden rushes on points which they regarded as weak or likely to give way to pressure. In one sense the conviction they held as to the wearied condition of the garrison was too true. Their ranks were rapidly thinning. They had to repair the defences daily, to remove supplies from the buildings which had either fallen in or which succumbed to the enemy's shot, to countermine the rebels' mines, to remove guns, to erect barricades, to bury corpses, to serve out the daily rations, and, with the weak and daily diminishing garrison, to supply fatigue parties of eight or ten men each to do work for which, under ordinary circumstances, ten times that number would not have been considered excessive. The garrison, however, performed all these duties with cheerfulness and resolution. In their ranks there was never a sign of faltering.

Their hopes of relief were becoming less bright. On the 28th of August a letter from Havelock informed them that he had no hope of being able to relieve them for five-and-twenty days. Much might happen in that period. One result of the letter was a diminution of the rations.

Eight days later the rebels made their fourth assault. They attacked two points simultaneously, but in vain. Again were they compelled to turn their backs. On this occasion the loyal sipáhís of the 13th N. I. behaved splendidly.

That these repeated failures dispirited the assailants was shown by the relaxation of their efforts on the morrow of their repulse. They never tried a grand assault after that of the 5th of September, but contented themselves with pouring in an unremitting fire of guns and musketry, with mining, with attempting surprises, and with assailing isolated points. But the labour of the garrison was by no means diminished. The season was the most unhealthy season of the year. Scarcely a day passed but some portion of one or other of the posts crumbled under the enemy's fire. Some idea of the incessant nature of that fire may be gathered from the fact that, on the 8th of September, 280 round-shot, varying in size from a twenty-four to a three-pounder, were gathered from the roof of the brigade mess-house alone.

On the 16th the messenger Angad was again sent out for news. He returned, on the night of the 22nd, with information that help from outside would certainly arrive within a fortnight. The next day a smart cannonade was heard in the direction of Kánhpur. The following morning firing was again heard. That night a messenger who had gone out returned with the information that the relieving force was in the outskirts of the city. The next day it was clear that a tremendous struggle was going on within the city. When, about half-past one, people were noticed leaving the city with bundles on their heads, and when, half-an-hour later, sipáhís and other armed bodies were observed to follow them, it became clear that the end was at hand. The garrison brought every gun and mortar to bear on the retreating foe. At four o'clock the report arose that some English officers, dressed in shooting coats, and some soldiers, wearing blue pantaloons, had been seen in the vicinity of the Motí Mahall. An hour later volleys of musketry, rapidly growing louder, were heard in the city. Soon, the bullets were whistling over the Residency. Five minutes later and the British troops were seen fighting their way through one of the principal streets. Once fairly seen the long pent-up feelings of the garrison found vent in a succession of deafening cheers. Even from the hospital many of the wounded crawled forth to join in that shout of welcome. 'Soon,' continues Captain Wilson, from whose graphic journal I have abridged the account in the text, 'soon all the rear-guard and heavy guns were inside our position; and then ensued a scene which baffles description. For eighty-seven days the Lakhnao garrison had lived in utter ignorance of all that had taken place outside. Wives who had long mourned their husbands as dead were again restored to them. Others, fondly looking forward to glad meetings with those near and dear to them, now for the first time learned that they were alone. On all sides eager inquiries for relations and friends were made. Alas! in too many cases the answer was a painful one.'

But the Residency had been relieved, or, to speak more correctly, had been reinforced. For, after the delirium of joy had given place to sober considerations, it was recognised that the combined troops were not strong enough to escort the non-combatant portion of the garrison through the city, still thronged with armed rebels, and thence to Kánhpur. For that the strengthened garrison must await the arrival of the new Commander-in-Chief, Sir Colin Campbell. His action will be described in due course. Meanwhile, it becomes my duty now to describe how it had become possible for Havelock and Outram to accomplish the splendid feat of arms which had brought joy and consolation to the beleaguered garrison of the Residency.

I left Havelock, just returned to Kánhpur, on the 13th of August. He gave his men a rest on the 14th and 15th, then on the 16th marched against Bithor, at which place nearly 4,000 rebels, mostly revolted sipáhís·

of various regiments, had congregated in his absence. Havelock attacked and defeated them, though only after a very stubborn fight. However, the victory was complete, the position was captured, and two guns were taken. But the British loss was heavy, amounting to between sixty men killed and wounded, and twelve who succumbed to sunstroke.

It was on the day following that Havelock read in the *Calcutta Gazette* the appointment of Outram to the command of Kánhpur. Outram's arrival could not be very distant. This nomination removed Havelock from the position of independent commander to that of a *locum tenens* for his superior officer. In such a case a sense of responsibility must necessarily weigh upon a commander. I have already pointed out that the position at Kánhpur, with a small force, fronted on one side by Oudh in rebellion, in front by provinces in a state of insurrection, to the left rear by the gradually concentrating Gwáliár contingent, was not, in a military sense, defensible except by a large force. It had one merit, it was central. In the eyes of Havelock that fact alone almost compensated for the other disadvantages. He wrote, then, to the Commander-in-Chief to announce that if hopes of speedy reinforcements were held out to him he would continue to hold Kánhpur, otherwise he would be forced to retire on Allahábád. The reply of Sir Colin was of a nature to decide him to remain at Kánhpur.

Since the 3rd of August reinforcements, in small parties, had been gradually arriving at that station. Outram himself came only on the 16th of September. This illustrious man had reached Allahábád on the 2nd of that month, and had despatched thence, on the 5th, to Kánhpur the 5th Fusiliers, Eyre's battery of eighteen-pounders, and had started himself the same evening with the 90th. On the way up Eyre, with 160 infantry and two guns, crushed a body of insurgents who had crossed over from Oudh with the view of cutting Outram's communications. This action completely cleared the road, and enabled Outram to reach Kánhpur with the much-needed reinforcements on the 16th.

His first act illustrated the character of the man. Feeling that, under extraordinary difficulties, Havelock had made a most daring attempt to relieve the garrison of the Lakhnao Residency, and that but for his own arrival that general would have been enabled to renew the attempt under favourable conditions, he resolved that the credit of the relief should still belong to him above all others. He therefore on his arrival issued a divisional order, in which he declared that, 'in gratitude for, and admiration of, the brilliant deed of arms achieved by Brigadier-General Havelock and his galliant troops,' he, Outram, 'will cheerfully waive his rank in favour of that officer on this occasion, and will accompany the force to Lakhnao in his civil capacity, as Chief Commissioner of Oudh, tendering his military services to Brigadier-General Havelock as a volunteer.'

This generous offer was accepted in fitting terms by Havelock.

The force now at Havelock's disposal consisted of 3,179 men of all arms. It was constituted as follows: The first infantry brigade, composed of the Madras Fusiliers, the 5th Fusiliers, the 84th, and two companies of the 64th, was commanded by Neill. The second, composed of the 78th Highlanders, the 90th, and Brasyer's Sikhs, was led by Colonel Hamilton of the 78th, with the rank of Brigadier. The artillery brigade, composed of Maude's battery, Olpherts' battery, and Eyre's battery of eighteen-pounders, was commanded by Major Cooper. Barrow led the cavalry, consisting of 109 volunteers and fifty-nine native horsemen. Crommelin was the Chief Engineer.

With this force, leaving Colonel Wilson of the 64th, with the head-quarters of his regiment and some details of convalescents, in all about 400 men, to hold Kánhpur, Havelock crossed the Ganges, on the 19th, under cover of Eyre's heavy guns. Those guns followed the next day. On the 21st Havelock drove the rebels from Mangalwár, then halting at Unáo for a mouthful of food, pushed on to Bashíratganj, already the scene of three contests, and bivouacked there for the night. It was raining heavily, and not a man but who was wet to the skin. However, the *impedimenta* arrived two hours later, and with it the luxury of dry clothes and a dinner. The rain was still falling as the little force set out at half-past seven the next morning. Marching sixteen miles, it came in sight of the bridge of Banní, a very defensible position had the rebels had the heart to defend it. But badly led, or believing in the greater capabilities of the narrow streets of Lakhnao, they had neither broken down the bridge over the river Sai nor manned the two half-moon batteries which they had constructed on the further side of it. Havelock then crossed the bridge, bivouacked for the night on its further bank, and fired a royal salute to intimate to the defenders of the Residency the near approach of relief.

The 23rd promised to be a day of action. Lakhnao was but sixteen miles distant. The wind no longer bore to the British Camp the customary sound of the booming of heavy guns against the Residency. It was plain that the rebels were concentrating their resources for a stern defence of the city. Havelock gave the men their breakfasts, and then moved forward. It was half-past eight. For some time no enemy was visible. But as the troops approached the Álambagh, some infantry appeared on their flanks, and they soon had evidence that the rebels were prepared to receive them at and near that walled garden. Havelock then halted his men, changed the order of his march from right to left in front, bringing Hamilton's brigade to the left front, their route lying across broken and heavy ground. Eyre's heavy battery then opened on the enemy's batteries, which occupied a tope of trees in front of his centre and left, whilst Olpherts was despatched to the left to cover the movement of the second brigade (Hamilton's) against the right, Barrow's cavalry leading. Overcoming every obstacle, Olpherts' battery took a position on the rebels' right flank and opened fire. The rebels on the left and centre, crushed meanwhile by the play of Eyre's guns, then gave way; but the Álambagh remained, and two guns were firing on the British force from embrasures in its wall. To capture these Neill sent forward a wing of the 5th Fusiliers. The 5th, with their habitual gallantry, stormed the wall. Whilst they were engaged in a fierce fight for the two pieces, Captain Burton of the 78th had forced the main entrance, and rushed to their aid, taking the defenders of the guns in reverse. The Madras Fusiliers followed. The men of the three regiments did their work so well that in ten minutes the Álambagh was cleared of its defenders, and Barrow and Outram and their companions were galloping in pursuit of the fleeing enemy. As they were returning from pursuing the rebels to the Yellow House, near the Chárbágh bridge, a despatch was placed in Outram's hands. It told him that our countrymen had stormed Dehlí. He galloped to Havelock with the news a few minutes later, and Outram, bareheaded, announced the glad tidings to the hurriedly collected soldiers. The ringing shouts with which they received it might almost have been heard in the Residency.

No tents were up, no food was forthcoming, but the day's work had been eminently satisfactory, and the men, exhilarated by their success and by the news, were content to wait until food should arrive. The next day they rested whilst their general made his last arrangements for the advance of the morrow. The rebels kept up a heavy fire all day in their direction, but Havelock had throw.. back his line so as to be beyond its range.

At last the decisive day dawned. The final scheme adopted was to force the Chárbágh bridge, then to follow a winding lane skirting the left bank of the canal, thence to make a sharp turn to the left and push through the fortified palaces and bazaars which covered the ground extending to the very gates of the Residency. It was certain that the Chárbágh bridge and every inch of ground beyond it would be desperately defended. The sick and wounded, the hospital, the baggage, and the food and ammunition reserves would meanwhile be left in the Álambagh, guarded by 300 men, mostly footsore, commanded by Major M'Intyre of the 78th.

At half-past eight o'clock the advance sounded, and the first brigade, with Maude's battery in front, accompanied by Outram, moved off towards the Yellow House, in column of sections, right in front. Soon the rebel fire opened upon them. Maude, however, quickly cleared the way with his guns, and the men pushing on, forced their way to a point near the bridge. There they were halted whilst Outram, with the 5th Fusiliers, should make a detour to the right to clear the Chárbágh garden, with the view of bringing a flanking fire to bear on the strong defences of the bridge.

The position of the rebels, indeed, could scarcely have been stronger. The Chárbágh bridge was defended on its farther side by an earthen rampart about seven feet high, stretching completely across it, but having in the centre an opening through which only one man at a time could pass on foot. On this parapet were mounted six guns, two of them twenty-four-pounders. To the right of the bridge, on the side of the canal by which the British were advancing, were some enclosures occupied by the rebels.

Such was the position. The men behind it were numerous, their guns were loaded, and there was every appearance that it would be desperately defended. On the British side were Maude's two guns in front; to their left, thrown forward, twenty-five men of the Madras Fusiliers, under Lieutenant Arnold, endeavouring to beat down the musketry fire from the tall houses on the other side; behind Maude's guns, close by, covered by a bend of the road and a wall, were the remainder of the Madras Fusiliers, lying down and waiting till Maude's guns should have done their work; to the right, Outram had led the 5th Fusiliers, for the purpose already indicated. These, I need hardly add, were not in sight. In a bay of the wall of the Chárbágh garden stood Neill and his Aidede-Camp, waiting until Outram's flank movement should make itself felt. On the other side of the road, mounted, was young Havelock.

The duel between Maude's guns and those of the rebels had raged for some time. The enemy had all the advantage of fighting under cover, and they had made deadly havoc with Maude's gunners. One after another these had fallen, their places being supplied from the infantry behind them. So great was the pressure that Maude and his Lieutenant, Maitland, were doing the work themselves. At the end of half-an-hour Maude recognised that he was making no impression. Then he called out to young Havelock that he could not fight his guns much longer, and begged him to 'do something.' Havelock rode at once to Neill and suggested that he should charge the bridge. But Neill, feeling himself hampered by the presence of Outram, with his brigade, declared that in his absence he could not take

the responsibility; that Outram must turn up soon. Tytler then attempted to persuade him to give the order, but with the same result.

Meanwhile, nothing had been heard of Outram and the 5th. The position was critical. Maude could not hold on much longer. A charge alone could remedy the position. Recognising this, young Havelock, full of ardour, despairing of overcoming in any other way the obstinacy of Neill, attempted a ruse. Riding to the rear a short distance, he suddenly turned his horse, and galloping back, rode up to Neill and, saluting him, said, as though the order had come from his father, 'You are to carry the bridge, sir.' Neill gave the order, directing Havelock and Tytler to form up the men. At the word Arnold dashed forward with his handful on to the bridge, and made for the barricade. Young Havelock and Tytler were by his side in a moment. Then the hurricane opened. Arnold fell, shot through both thighs. Tytler's horse was killed, and he himself shot through the groin. Of the twenty-eight men who had dashed forward, Havelock and a private named Jakes alone were unwounded. Unable to pass the barricade, Havelock, erect on his horse, waved his sword and called on the main body to come on. Jakes stood by his side, loading and firing as fast as he could. There they stood, the hero officer and the hero private, for fully two minutes exposed to the full fire of the enemy. They stood unharmed. Then suddenly there was a rush, and the Madras Fusiliers dashed forward, cleared the bridge, stormed the barricade, and bayoneted the rebel gunners where they stood. The bridge was gained. The entrance gate into Lakhnao was won.

On the regiments of the second brigade closing up, the whole force crossed by the bridge, and then, in pursuance of the plan indicated, turned sharp to the right along the canal. There was one exception to this movement. The 78th was sent with orders to hold the end of the direct Kánhpur road, cover the advance of the heavy guns, and then to follow the column as its rear-guard. The main body meanwhile, followed the lane along the canal for two miles, then turned northwards near the Dilkushá bridge, when its progress was suddenly checked by a formidable obstacle. Before them, under lee of the Kaisarbágh, was a narrow bridge across a nullah, commanded by guns and musketry fire from that building. The bridge could not hold more than two abreast. However, a rush was made, and the men who crossed opened a fire on the rebels to cover the passage of their comrades. Many men were here struck down, when suddenly the situation was mended by the 78th in a manner presently to be related. Then the crossing was effected, and the men, reuniting, halted under cover of some deserted buildings near the Chatr Manzil.

Darkness was now coming on. Outram, who had found the clearing of the Chárbágh garden more serious than he anticipated, and who had come up after the bridge had been stormed, then proposed that the force should halt where it was—at the Chatr Manzil—to await there the arrival of the rearmost guard, of which they had no tidings, and of those it was escorting. There were many considerations in favour of such a plan, and there was only a sentimental reason against it. But Havelock considered that the importance of joining the beleaguered garrison outweighed every other consideration. So they pushed on through the Khás bazaar, crowded with the enemy. From an archway in this bazaar Neill was shot dead in the act of giving an order to his Aide-de-Camp. Still the British forced their way, despite the continuous musketry fire, until at length they emerged from the bazaar. Then they were gladdened by the sound of cheering from the Residency. The 78th, and others who had pushed their way through other streets, appeared on the scene directly afterwards and joined in the cry. They were not yet, however, within the Residency. The night was dark, and a way had to be made for them before they could enter. At last the defences which had so long bidden defiance to the rebels at the Baillic guard were removed, and there was no obstacle to a joyful union between the relievers and the relieved.

Not all entered that night. Many of the men lay on the ground between the Baillie guard gateway and the Farhatbakhsh palace, and rejoined their comrades early in the morning. It remains now to recount the course of the 78th. That regiment had had a hard time of it. Directed by Havelock to see to the safety of the heavy guns, it had diverged from the main body, and reached a point indicated on the Kánhpur road. There, for a time, the men remained unmolested, when suddenly swarms of natives set upon them. For three hours they resisted every attack; then, the number of the rebels increasing, they stormed a temple, and held it against the infuriated enemy. Vainly did the latter bring up three brass guns. The British soldiers, led on by Webster, Herbert Macpherson, and other gallant officers, charged and captured these, and threw them into the canal. Still the fight went on, and it required another charge before the rebels could be compelled to renounce their hopes of success. The Highlanders then, seeing nothing of the heavy guns, pushed on, with the idea of rejoining their comrades of the main body, but taking a shorter road, through the Hazratganj quarter, they arrived in close vicinity to the Kaisarbágh just as the guns from that building were playing on the Fusiliers in the manner related. The 78th dashed into the battery, and made the road easy by its capture. They then pushed on in an alignment with the rest to the Baillie guard.

But the heavy guns? Their progress had been rendered very difficult by the deep trenches which the rebels had cut across the road. But under the guidance of Lieutenant Moorsom, who knew every inch of the ground, sent by Havelock to direct them, they had deviated from the main road and went by a shorter cut, unopposed, to the Baillie guard. The rearmost guard, however, with two big guns, still remained unaccounted for. To search for and rescue these, Outram, who had assumed command, despatched, on the 26th, a force under Colonel Robert Napier.[2] Napier found them holding the passage in front of the Motí Mahall, and brought them in the following morning. It is sad to have to record that the wounded who had reached that palace were not so fortunate in their attempt to reach the Residency. The volunteer escort mistook the way, and some forty helpless men were done to death, some by the daggers of the rebels, some by the fire wantonly applied to their *dolis*.[3]

The losses sustained in this glorious operation were heavy. The official return puts them at 196 killed and 535 wounded, and there is every reason for believing that that return is accurate. Those losses were incurred in the hope that, as a satisfactory result of them, the defenders of the Residency would be relieved. As it was, they were merely reinforced. At first Outram inclined to the belief that it would be possible to fall back upon Kánhpur. But his better judgment prevailed. Subsequent experience proved most clearly that the women and children could not have been withdrawn by the force under his orders except at a tremendous risk. If it had cost him over 500 men to make his way into the Residency, unencumbered by non-combatants of that stamp, the reader may judge for himself how far he could have succeeded in making the reverse journey under circumstances infinitely more complicated. Eager as was Outram to return to place himself and his troops at the disposal of the Commander-in-Chief, he was surely right, situated as he was, not to attempt it. Circumstances were too strong, even for a man who, throughout his career, had never flinched at either danger or responsibility.

Whilst he remains besieged in the Residency, his troops occupying some of the adjacent palaces, and the Álambágh held by a small detachment, I propose to take a survey of the events which had been passing in that part of the country in which British interests were represented almost solely by the men who occupied the fortress of Agra.

---

[2] The late Lord Napier of Magdala.
[3] A *doli* is an inferior kind of palanquin, used for carrying a wounded man.

CHAPTER XVII

The Leaguer of Agra

In the eighth chapter I have given a brief account of the risings at Fírúzpur, at Áligarh, at Bulandshahr, at Itáwah, at Mainpurí, and of the consequent movements at Agra. I have shown how, in consequence of the rising at Mathurá, on the 30th of May, the Lieutenant-Governor of the North-west, Mr Colvin, had caused the sipáhís of the 44th and 67th N. I. to be disarmed (May 31); how he had directed the raising of volunteers; how, on the 14th of June, the sipáhís of the Gwáliár contingent had mutinied at Gwáliár; and how the English men and women who had survived the massacre consequent upon that mutiny had found refuge at Agra; and, finally, how it was not until the end of June that Mr Colvin had deemed it wise that the Europeans and Eurasians should abandon their houses in the station and take up their abode in the fort of red sandstone built by Akbar in 1565–73. He did not move thither himself till the 4th of June following. I propose now to take up the story, briefly, from that date.

Mr Colvin's order to concentrate the resources in men and supplies of the English at Agra, within the fort, had not been issued a day too soon. Indeed, it is to be regretted that it was not issued earlier, and that, when issued, it was accompanied with restrictions. Mr Raikes, a member of the Civil Service occupying a high position at Agra, records that the order directing the move to the fort forbade the transfer to that place of refuge of 'any property beyond the sort of allowance which a French Customs House officer at Calais or Marseilles passes under the term of a *sac de nuit*.' This extraordinary prohibition, adds the same authority, entailed 'the loss and destruction of books, furniture, archives, records, public and private, and the ruin of hundreds of families.' The victualling of the fort proceeded, however, with great energy.

By the end of June Agra was completely isolated. The entire country between the Jamnah and the Ganges was 'up,' whilst to the west of the former river Bundelkhand was surging with rebels; Rájpútána and Central India had become difficult to hold. Communications with the north, south, west, and east had been severed. In fact, in what direction soever Mr Colvin might turn his glance, the horizon was gloomy in the extreme.

Nor was the position mended by the news which reached him on the 2nd of July. This was to the effect that a strong rebel force had reached Fathpur-Síkrí, twenty-three miles from Agra. To meet these he had within the fort the 3rd European regiment and one battery of European artillery. But he had also native allies upon whom he believed rather fatuously that he could rely. These were a body of 600 Karáulí matchlockmen, commanded by Saifullá Khán, a native official of high character, some levies from Bharatpur, and a detachment of the Kotá contingent. Mr Colvin at once brought the last named within the cantonment, whilst he placed the others at Sháhganj, four miles on the road to Fathpur-Síkrí, to watch the movements of the rebel force at that place.

The following day, the 3rd, Mr Colvin being ill, a council of three gentlemen, Mr Reade, the senior member of the Board of Revenue, Major Macleod of the Engineers, Military Secretary to Mr Colvin, and Brigadier Polwhele, commanding the troops, was appointed to administer affairs. These gentlemen at once took active measures for the public safety. Some of these may sound strange, but they were probably justified under the circumstances. For instance, dreading lest the rebels might enter the station, and let loose upon it a number of hardened criminals, they conveyed the prisoners in the gaol across the Jamnah, and released them. Then they broke down the pontoon bridge communicating with the fort, they brought in all the native Christians, they directed that the Karáulí and Bharatpur levies should be required to give up their guns, two in number, and they directed the officer commanding the Kotá contingent to march against the rebels. These orders sufficed to clear the air. The Bharatpur and Karáulí men, angered by the removal of their guns, removed themselves from the scene. It was the best course for the English they could adopt, for an open enemy is better than a pretended friend. Similarly with the Kotá contingent. No sooner did the men composing it receive the order to advance than they shot down the English sergeant in charge of their military stores, and firing hastily at their European officers, rushed off to join the enemy they had been directed to combat. They did not, happily, effect their full purpose, for whilst a loyal gunner named Mathurá managed unseen to spike their guns, their English doctor, Mathias by name, calm and collected amid dangers, strewed in the sand their powder, ammunition, and case-shot. A party sent out from Agra brought the guns into the fort.

That same evening Mr Colvin entered the fort and resumed authority. The next day, the 5th, the rebels marched in from Fathpur-Síkrí and took up a position at the village of Sassiah, some five miles from the fort. They were reported to consist of 4,000 infantry, 1,500 cavalry, and eleven guns. Brigadier Polwhele, after providing for the defences of the fort, could take into the field against them 568 English infantry, a battery with sixty-nine Englishmen, including officers, and fifty-four native drivers, fifty-five mounted militia, and fifty English volunteers, mostly officers, making a total of 742 Englishmen, besides the officers of the European regiment and the staff. It was a force sufficient, if well handled, to drive the rebel force to Jericho.

Believing that he could so handle it, Polwhele marched from the fort at one o'clock, and proceeded to Sháhganj. There he halted till his reconnoitring parties should come in. These arrived at half-past two with the information that the rebels were still halted at Sassiah. Towards that village Polwhele then moved. When within half-a-mile from it the enemy's left battery opened fire.

There is only one true method of fighting Asiatics. That mode is to move straight on. To play the game of an artillery duello with them, when they have nearly double the number of guns and the advantage of position, is simply madness. The experience of a hundred years would have been reversed if Polwhele, pushing on against the village of Sassiah, had failed to drive the rebels from it. But he did nothing of the sort. Far from profiting from the teachings of history, he tried a plan in which he was bound to be beaten. He halted his infantry, and made them lie down, whilst he engaged in an artillery duello with his six guns against the enemy's eleven. His men were in the open, the rebels were protected by the village of Sassiah. The logical consequences followed. Although the British guns were directed by two of the most gallant and skilled officers the splendid Bengal Artillery ever produced, Captain D'Oyley commanding half the battery on the right, Captain Pearson the other half on the left, the larger calibre of the enemy's guns asserted its superiority. They had, moreover, the exact range. In a short time they succeeded in exploding two tumbrils, and in inflicting considerable damage among the drivers and horses of the British. Vainly did D'Oyley and Pearson send messages to Polwhele to tell him that a persistance in those tactics would exhaust their ammunition without securing for him any corresponding advantage. Polwhele heeded not. Eyre, at Árah, had been in a position somewhat similar, but the moment he had realised that pounding with guns would not win the day against an enemy strongly posted, he had tried the never-failing British charge. But Polwhele would not. Probably, he was hampered by the considerations which hampered Lawrence at Chinhat. The infantry he had with him constituted the sole means at his disposal for the defence of the fort. At all events he persisted in waiting until another tumbril had been exploded by the enemy's fire, and until their cavalry, gathering courage from his inactivity, charged Pearson's half-battery. Cool and collected, Pearson awaited their approach, whilst the company of the Europeans nearest to him rose to their feet, their muskets levelled. A simultaneous fire, well directed, from the guns and the infantry sufficed to ward off the attack, and to send the survivors reeling back to the place whence they had ridden. A similar attempt threatened against D'Oyley's half-battery was defeated by the volunteer horsemen. These, eighteen in number, charged the 200 of the rebels, and though they lost one-third of their number, they forced the rebels to retire.

Two hours and a half had now elapsed. The rebels still occupied their unthreatened position. The English had effected nothing to drive them from it. D'Oyley reported to the Brigadier that his ammunition was all but exhausted. Then, and then only, did the Brigadier issue the order which, given two hours and a half before, could scarcely have failed to achieve success. He ordered the line to advance. The line did advance, and, despite the fire from men stationed in most advantageous positions in Sassiah, the men fought their way into the village. They even captured and spiked one of the enemy's guns. But in advancing to and in taking the village the British losses had been heavy. D'Oyley was mortally wounded.[1] Major Thomas of the Europeans met the same fate. Several men were killed, but at last the village was gained. It required but the support of the guns to complete the victory, but by this time every round had been fired away. In his anxiety for the safety of his men Polwhele had prematurely, and despite of repeated warnings, exhausted the one means by which he could assure success.

For the rebels were not slow to recognise the cause of the silence of the British guns. They at least had ten, and still some, though not an abundance, of ammunition. They at once made a demonstration with the three arms against the village. Polwhele could not defend it with infantry alone, and he ran a great risk of being cut off from the fort. Under those circumstances, he had no other course but to retreat. The retreat was effected in good order; the infantry, though savage with their commander, to whose fatal tactics they rightly attributed the loss of the day, preserving their traditional calmness, and repulsing every attack. Fortunately, before the retreat was concluded, the rebels likewise fell short of gun ammunition.

---

[1] Overcome by the intense pain of the wound, he turned to the man nearest him and said, 'They have done for me now; put a stone over my grave, and say that I died fighting my guns.'

In this fight the British had lost forty-five men killed, and 108 wounded and missing. They had, also, left one gun on the ground, though they recovered it a day or two later. The rebels signalised their triumph by setting fire to every building within their reach. They then returned to Sassiah, took a hasty meal, and set off for Dehlí. Arriving there, on the 8th, they were greeted with a grand salute as 'the victors of Sassiah.'

For the English the blow was severe. Though the rebels had departed, their allies, the rabble and the gaolbirds, finished what they had begun. They ruthlessly plundered the city, the cantonments, and the civil lines, burning the materials they cared not to take away. The following morning the town-crier, by order of the Kotwál, proclaimed the inauguration of the rule of the Mughal.

Of Polwhele's battle it only remains to be said that it should stand out in history as a warning of the manner in which Europeans, or, I would rather say, the British race, should not fight Asiatics. From the date following that on which it was fought began, for the English at Agra, that long and tedious life in the fort, which was terminated only by the arrival of a force, under Greathed, on the 10th of October, made disposable by the fall of Dehlí.

In the interval, September the 9th, Mr Colvin died. He was succeeded temporarily, and until the orders of the Government of India should be known, by the senior Civil servant, Mr E. A. Reade, a man of lofty character—the type of a hard-working, unselfish English gentleman. More than two months later (September 30th), the Government, thinking that the times required a soldier rather than a civilian at the head of affairs, nominated Colonel Hugh Fraser of the Engineers to be their Chief Commissioner for Agra and its dependencies. Colonel Fraser held the office till the 9th of February following.

The slight sketch I have given of the proceedings at Agra, till the fall of Dehlí had released avenging columns to reconquer the North-west, will probably have brought home to the mind of the reader that, to the north and north-west of Allahábád, Dehlí was the central point, the place upon the occupation of which the fate of the towns and districts in those provinces, the fate of Central India, the fate of the Panjáb itself, depended. The whole of the North-west, including Bundelkhand and Rohilkhand, had risen because Dehlí was held by the rebels. The assertion in that Imperial city of the rule of the Mughal was the cause—insurrection all over the country was the consequence. The truth of this axiom was felt more clearly every day by those who were responsible for the maintenance of British authority in the provinces and districts which remained loyal. Equally was it felt by the native princes who adhered to the British connection, by those who had shaken it off, and by the watchers of the atmosphere. If the British should be compelled to abandon their position before Dehlí, it would be scarcely possible to prevent a tremendous conflagration. Most certainly the Panjáb would have risen. In that event, most probably, the districts to the north-west and west of Allahábád would have been completely severed, for a time, from the British.

Dehlí being thus the centre of the situation, the point on the possession of which depended the fate of the surrounding districts, it becomes me, before detailing the result of the struggle before its walls, to take a bird's-eye view of the provinces and districts in which its influence had made itself the most felt. I propose, therefore, to glance at the events which had occurred in the Ságar and Narbadá territories, in Central India, in Rájpútána, in the districts dependent upon Mírath, in Rohilkhand, and, finally, in the Panjáb. before I describe the 'crowning mercy' which was vouchsafed to the British arms in the city which had become the kernel and focus of the revolt.

CHAPTER XVIII

Events in the Ságar and Narbadá Territories, Central India, Rájpútána, the Mírath Districts, Rohilkhand, and the Panjáb

The Ságar and Narbadá territories, immediately south of, and adjoining, the North-west Provinces, comprised, in 1857, the districts of Ságar, Jabalpur, Hoshangábád, Sióní, Damóh, Narsinhpur, Bétul, Chandérí, Jhánsí, Nagód, and Mandlah. When, in 1843, the Gwáliár Darbár commenced those hostilities against the British which culminated in the battle of Máhárájpur, the chiefs and people of those districts, moved partly by their dislike to the foreign system of administration, partly incited by the Gwáliár Darbár, broke into rebellion. On the conclusion of the peace which followed Máhárájpur, the then Governor-General, Lord Ellenborough, made a clean sweep of the officers who had administered the territories, and deputed Colonel Sleeman to inaugurate a better system. Colonel Sleeman, working on eastern ideas, completely succeeded. His successor, Mr Bushby, continued his system with marked success. But after a rule of five or six years Mr Bushby was promoted. Then, in an evil hour, the Ságar and Narbadá territories were placed directly under the Government of the North-west Provinces.

That transfer caused the introduction of the system called after its inventor Mr Thomason. But for the earnest exhortations of the abiest man in the Commission, Major Ternan, that system would have been introduced in all its strictness. Even with some of its most stringent provisions softened down, it worked in a manner to cause great discontent among the chiefs, without satisfying the people.

The mode in which this system worked may be illustrated by the story of the Rájá of Dilhérí, the feudal lord of all the Gond clans. This chief had ever been a loyal supporter of the British connection. For his fidelity in the trying times of 1843 the Government had presented him with a gold medal. Like many of his tribe, he had been rather extravagant in his expenditure, and had incurred debts. These, however, by exercising a strict economy, he had paid off a very short time after the transfer of the Ságar and Narbadá territories to the North-west Government. Now, it was one of the principles of that Government to discourage large landowners. Accordingly, in 1855 just after the Rájá had paid off his debts, Captain Ternan, then in charge of the district in which his estates were situated, received instructions to inform the Rájá that, inasmuch as he had shown himself unfit to hold the title he had inherited, and to manage the estates which had descended to him, he would be deprived of both; that his title would be abolished, and his property distributed among his tenants, he receiving a percentage from the rents. When Ternan, most reluctantly, announced this order to the Rájá, the old man drew from his belt the medal bestowed upon him for his conduct in 1843, and requested him to return it to those who had granted it, as they were now about to disgrace him before his clan and the entire district. With great difficulty Ternan pacified him, but his heart was deeply wounded. Many thought that he would rebel. But, despite the treatment he had received, he was loyal to his British overlord. He sought, indeed, every opportunity of displaying his gratitude to Ternan, who had been censured by the Agra Government for his persistent advocacy of his claims.[1]

The Rájá of Dilhérí was the type of many landowners in the Ságar and Narbadá territories, in fact, throughout the territories subject to the Government of the North-west, who had been ruined by the Thomasonian system. Space does not allow me to give other instances, but in Juánpur, in Ázamgarh, in the delta of the Ganges, in Oudh, in Rohilkhand, they abounded. It was they who roused the country, which offered so stout a resistance to Sir Hugh Rose, between Indúr and Kalpí.

I must pass lightly over the events which happened in the territories of which I am writing. It must suffice to state that three companies of

---

[1] When the Narsinhpur district was in a state of rebellion, the house of Ternan, who had refused to quit it, was surrounded early one morning by a considerable body of matchlockmen. Ternan saw at a glance that they belonged to the Dilhérí clan. He at once summoned the chief, and asked him the reason for such a display. The chief replied: 'You behaved kindly to us, and fought our battle when the title and the estate were confiscated, and you were abused for so doing. Now we hear disturbances are rife, and we come to offer you our services. We will stick by you, as you stuck by us. What do you wish us to do?' Ternan accepted their offer, and the members of the large clan remained loyal, and rendered good service to the British Government throughout the trying events of 1857–58.

the Gwáliár contingent garrisoning Lalitpur mutinied and expelled their European officers on the 13th of June; that a detachment of native infantry sent out from Ságar, under Major Gaussen, rose on the 23rd; that the 3rd Irregulars and the 42nd N. I., stationed at Ságar, broke out on the 1st of July. The last-mentioned mutineers were, however, expelled the day following by the loyal 31st N. I., a regiment loyal to the last. From that moment, and until they were relieved by Sir Hugh Rose, the English men and women, and the loyal sipáhís occupied Ságar, but not one foot of territory beyond it. The districts of Ságar, Chandéri, Jhánsí, Lalitpur. and Jáláun continued until that period to be overrun by rebels. The Rájá of Bánpur, and others of lesser note, boldly asserted their independence.

At Jabalpur, the headquarters of the territories, the 52nd N. I. continued for a long time in the performance of their duty. But in September they too mutinied. They were attacked, however, and completely defeated by a body of Madras troops which had been sent up from Kámthí. They then dispersed, but nevertheless refrained from ravaging the country.

The energetic and far-sighted Ternan, of whom I have already spoken, managed, by means of his good understanding with the natives, to clear the rebels from his district, that of Narsinhpur. The district of Nagód was not so fortunate. The 50th N. I., there located, feigned loyalty for a time, but broke out on the 27th of August, when they coolly dismissed their officers and inaugurated a system of plunder. They, too, formed a part of the rebel force which resisted the progress of Sir Hugh Rose.

It remains now to speak of Jhánsí. The city of Jhánsí was the capital of a dependency which, in the break-up of the Mughal empire which followed the death of Aurangzíb, had been appropriated by one of the Marátha officers serving the Peshwá, and to him confirmed by *sanad*.[2] The territory so appropriated comprised nearly 1,608 square miles, and a population of a quarter of a million. As long as the Peshwá continued to exercise authority in Western India the Marátha officer and his successors administered the territory as vassals of that prince. But on the downfall of the Peshwá, in 1817–18, Jhánsí, with its other territories, was transferred to the British. The ruler, with the title of Subáhdár, accepted the protection of the foreign overlord, and agreed to pay an annual tribute of 74,000 rupees. In return, the British declared his title and position to be hereditary in his family. Fifteen years later, to mark their approval of his rule, they allowed him to assume the title of Rájá. This prince, whose name was Rám Chand Ráo, died without heirs, natural or adopted, in 1835. The Government of

---

[2] *Sanad,* a patent grant or charter issuing from the Government.

India, however, had as we have said, bestowed the hereditary rule upon his family. They therefore appointed his nearest relative, who happened to be his uncle, to succeed him.

This man was a leper, and incapable. After three years of unpopular rule his death left the quasi-royal scat vacant. There was a lengthened inquiry regarding a successor, and then the Government nominated his brother, Bábá Gangadhar Ráo, to succeed him.

It unfortunately happened that this man was also an imbecile. To prevent the country falling into irremediable confusion the Government then carried on the administration by means of British agency. When, in 1843, a financial equilibrium had been restored, the Government was handed over to the Rájá. After a rule, conducted neither wisely nor well for eleven years, this chief died in 1854, the last surviving member of the family to which the Government of India had, in 1818, guaranteed the succession. There remained only his widow, a young, high-spirited, and ambitious lady. But Lord Dalhousie was of opinion that the guarantee did not extend to any person in whose veins the blood of the founder of the dynasty did not run. In spite, then, of the protestations of that lady he declared the state of Jhánsí to have lapsed to the East India Company.

The Rání, like Náná Sáhib, never forgave that which she considered an insult and an outrage. Powerless, she nursed her resentment, until the revolt of Mírath and the seizure of Dehlí gave her the long-wished-for opportunity. She then, in June 1857, gained to her cause the sipáhís stationed at Jhánsí, enticed the English officers and their families to accept her protection, and had them foully murdered. On the 9th of June she caused herself to be proclaimed Rání of Jhánsí.

Bundelkhand, and Réwá or Bághelkhand, include, besides Réwá, the territories of Tehrí or Urchah, Datiá, Chatrpur, Pannah, and Ajaigarh. The area of the combined territories is 22,400 square miles, and the population 3,200,000. More than half of this belongs to Réwá. The Rájá of Réwá was loyal to the British connection in 1857, and having the good fortune to have at his elbow, as his adviser, an officer of marked ability, the late Major Willoughby Osborne, he was able not only to put down mutiny within his territory, but to assist in repressing it outside its borders. The Rájás of Urchah and of Ajaigarh rendered likewise all the assistance in their power to their British overlord. The territories of the Rájás of the other places mentioned were subjected to the invasion and plundering of the rebels, but in their hearts they too were loyal.

Between Chatrpur and the Jamnah lies the district represented by the stations of Náogáng and Bandah, occupied by native regiments, and by several small states ruled by native chiefs. The sipáhís at Náogáng, belonging to the regiments stationed at Jhánsí, mutinied as soon as they had heard of the action of their comrades at that place. The British officers and their wives, forced to flee, were hospitably received by the Rájá of Chatrpur, but had to quit that place, and eventually succeeded in reaching Bandah. The Nuwáb of Bandah received them and other British fugitives kindly. The time arrived, however, when the Nuwáb, unable to contend against the excited passions of his followers, was forced, nominally at least, to cast in his lot with the rebels. The same charge was made against the unfortunate Ráo of Kírwí, a small state in the Bandah district. Though the territories of the chief were overrun by rebels, his sympathies were with his British overlord. He was a minor, and had no more power to repress the insurrection than a child has to knock down a prize-fighter. Yet the time was to come when, because he and others had not repressed the rebels, they were classed and punished as rebels. This was particularly the case with the innocent Ráo of Kírwí.

Speaking generally, it may be said that, in July and during the following months of 1857, the Ságar and Narbadá territories, and the country to the west of the Jamnah generally, Rewah and the town of Ságar excepted, were in the hands of the rebels. It seemed to depend upon the result of the operations before Dehlí as to whether the rebellion would assume a more aggressive form.

To the south-west of Jhánsí lay the territories of Mahárájá Holkar. These territories comprised the important city of Indur, situated on a tributary of the Siprá, with a population of 15,000: the British cantonment of Máu, between thirteen and fourteen miles[3] distant from the Residency at Indur; Mándu, an ancient and famous city, with numerous ruins, once the capital of Dhár, and at a later period the residence of the Muhammadan kings of Málwá; Dipálpur, twenty-seven miles to the north-west of Máu; and Mehidpur, on the right bank of the Siprá, a town garrisoned by a contingent composed of the three arms, officered by British officers.

At Máu there were stationed, in 1857, the 23rd Regiment N. I., a wing of the 1st Native Cavalry, and a field battery of artillery, with European gunners but native drivers. At Mehidpur the troops, with the exception of the officers, were natives.

The acting British Resident, or, as he was styled in official language, the Agent for the Governor-Géneral, was Colonel Henry Marion Durand, one of the ablest and most prescient of the officers serving the Government of

---

[3] A new road has since been made, reducing the distance to ten miles.

India. His career had been one of strange vicissitudes. The unselfishness of his nature had been the cause of his missing chances which seldom recur twice to the same individual.

The events of the 10th of May at Mírath, and the consequences of those events at Dehlí, had produced an unparalleled commotion in the native mind in the territories of Holkar. Durand felt his position to be one of peculiar importance. The maintenance of order in the country north of the Narbadá depended upon one of two contingencies: one was the fall of Dehlí, the other the arrival of reinforcements from Bombay. Now, the road from Bombay to Agra crossed the Narbadá at a point just below Indur, and ran thence through Central India to a point on the Chambal directly to the north of Gwáliár. The maintenance of this road was the prominent feature in the plan of Durand. He resolved, then, to maintain his own position as long as was possible; to sever, as far as he could, all communications between men of the regular army and those of the native contingents; to secure the Narbadá and the important road I have described; and to reassure the native princes[4] under his superintendence.

But events were too strong even for Durand. Dehlí did not fall, and the reinforcements despatched from Bombay, under circumstances presently to be described, halted at Aurangábád. The rumour that Dehlí had fallen greatly aided his efforts to maintain order for a period of fifty-one days after the Mírath outbreak; but, on the 1st of July, he was attacked in the Residency by the native troops of Holkar. The native troops forming the garrison of the Residency either coalesced with the rebels or refused to act against them. No reinforcements, though they had been sent for, came from Máu; and after a brilliant defence of two and a half hours' duration Durand was compelled to evacuate the Residency, with his small European garrison and the eleven women and children under his charge. His first idea was to retreat on Máu, but as his native escort refused to follow him thither, he had no option, eventually, but to retire on Sihor. He and his companions reached that place on the 4th July. Thence he set out, with the briefest possible delay, to urge upon the commander of the Bombay column the necessity of making safe the line of the Narbadá, so as, to use his own words, 'to interpose a barrier between the blazing north and the smouldering south.'

On the night of the day on which Durand had been compelled to evacuate the Residency at Indur the sipáhís at Máu mutinied, killed three of their officers, and made their way to Dehlí. Captain Hungerford,

---

[4] These were Holkar himself, the rulers of the States of Bhopál, Dhár, Dewás, and Barwáni.

who commanded the field-battery, remained in occupation of the fort of Máu, and assumed the duties of the Governor-General's Agent, until the arrival of Durand with the Bombay column enabled the latter to resume his duties.

The Mehidpur contingent remained passively loyal until November. On being attacked then by a rebel force superior in numbers, they displayed mingled cowardice and treachery. Ultimately the majority of them fraternised with the rebels. The station, however, was held for the British up to that period.

With the exception, then, of Bhopál, now to be referred to, and Mehipur, that part of Central India represented by the dominions of Holkar had become hostile to the British from the 1st of July.

Bhopál, indeed, was a brilliant exception. The then reigning Begum, Sikandar Begum, had assumed office, in February 1847, as regent for her daughter. She was a very remarkable woman, possessing great resolution, and a more than ordinary talent for affairs. In six years she had paid off the entire public debt of the State, had abolished the system of farming the revenue, had put a stop to monopolies, had reorganised the police, and had reformed the mint. When she scented the breaking out of the rebellion of 1857, she at once made up her mind to fight for her trusted overlord. As early as April she communicated to the British Agent the contents of a lithographed proclamation, urging the overthrow and destruction of the English, which had been sent her. In June she expelled from her territories a native who was raising men for a purpose he did not care to avow. In July she afforded shelter to Durand and those whom he was escorting. She did all these things under enormous difficulties. Her nearest relations were daily urging upon her an opposite course; her troops mutinied, her nobles murmured. But Sikandar Begum never wavered. She caused the English fugitives to be escorted safely to Hoshangábád, she allayed the excitement in her capital, put down the mutinous contingent with a strong hand, restored, and then maintained, order throughout her dominions. Like Sindhiá, she clearly recognised that the safety of the native princes depended upon the maintenance of the beneficently exercised power of the British overlord.

But Bhopál was the exception. In the other portions of the dominions of Holkar the class whose taste is plunder assumed the upper hand. Their further action depended upon the result of the operations before Dehlí.

Nor, although the Máhárájá Sindhiá was loyal to the core, was it otherwise in the dominions of that potentate. The straggling dominions of Sindhiá contained an area of 19,500 square miles, and comprised the towns of Gwáliár, Nárwár, Bhilsá, Ujjain, Rutlám, and the British cantonment of Nímach.

We have seen how the Gwáliár contingent mutinied on the 14th of June. The contingent represented the feelings of the people over whom the Máhárájá ruled. But he never wavered. Contrasting the British over-lordship with the probable result of the triumph of the sipáhís—and of the Mughal—he recognised that the welfare of himself and his people depended upon the ultimate success of the British arms—and he acted accordingly.

The station of Nímach lies 371 miles to the south-west of Dehlí. The garrison there consisted of the 72nd Regiment N. I., the 7th Regiment of the Gwáliár contingent, and the wing of the 1st Bengal Cavalry. These troops rose in revolt the 3rd of June. The officers and their families escaped to Udaipur. Subsequently Nímach was the scene of many events pertaining more to the history of Rájpútána. The sipáhís ultimately made their way to Dehlí.

To the north-west of the territory which bears the geographical name of Central India lies the province of Rájpútána, one of the most interesting provinces of India. From the time of the departure of the great Lord Welles-ley, 1805, to the close of the Pindárí war, 1818, the princes and people of Rájpútána had suffered from the want of an overlordship which should protect them against a foreign foe. The treatment which they endured at that period was still fresh in the memory, alike of princes and people, when the mutiny of 1857 broke out. From the moment of its commencement, then, the princes of Rájpútána clustered round the waning fragments of the British power, to protect them against an enemy more terrible even than Amír Khán and the Pindárís. It is true that the contingents furnished by Bharatpur and Kotá revolted. Subsequently, too, the mutinied soldiers of Kotá murdered the British Resident, Major Burton, and his two sons. But the Rájá of Bharatpur was a minor, and it has never been proved how far the Máháráo of Kotá was coerced by his soldiers. Certainly the Rájás and Ráos of the other sixteen principalities were entirely loyal, and they proved their loyalty on many a trying occasion.

The station of Nasirábád, in the Ajmír-Mairwárá district of Rájpútána, 150 miles nearer to Dehlí than was Nímach, was garrisoned by the 15th and 30th Regiments N. I., a battery of native artillery, and the 1st Bombay Lancers. The infantry broke into revolt on the 28th of May; the men of the other arms followed suit. Two officers were killed, and two were wounded. The remainder retreated to Biáur, a town in Ajmír-Mairwárá, escorting the women and children.

At a later date, August 22nd, the contingent at Erinpúram, near Mount Ábu, also revolted, and attempted, without much success, to surprise the Europeans, invalided or sick, resting at that sanitarium.

There was one other exception to the general loyalty of the princes, nobles, and people of Rájpútána. That exception was a Thákur or baron of Jodhpur. But that Thákur's grievance was not against the English, but against his liege lord the Rájá. To coerce him, he used the revolted sipáhís—very much, as the result proved—to his own detriment.

But throughout those troublous times the chief figure in Rájpútána was the Governor-General's representative, George St Patrick Lawrence, not the least gifted member of a family which had rendered splendid services to India. So long as George Lawrence remained in Rájpútána it was certain that that province would remain firm and steadfast in its loyalty to its overlord.

It did remain so, despite the risings at Nímach, at Nasirábád, at Erinpúram. Yet, even in loyal Rájpútána, much depended upon the issue of contest before Dehlí. In a population of nine millions there were many needy men who coveted the property of the wealthy. These doubtless looked forward with eagerness to the reports of the victories and defeats, of the sorties and the attacks, which daily inundated the bazaars. And if Dehlí had not fallen, if the English army had failed in its final assault, the encouragement which would have raised the populations elsewhere might not have been without an effect even in Rájpútána.

In Mírath and the adjoining districts to the east the subversion of British authority had not been so complete as might have been expected. In Mírath itself authority had soon been restored. And, thanks to the energy displayed by Mr Dunlop, by Mr Brand Sapte, and others, successful attempts were made to re-establish the British power in the villages near it. In June the energetic Magistrate, Mr Wallace Dunlop, had organised a troop of volunteers, composed of officers without regiments, of members of the Civil Service, and of others who happened to be at Mírath. Major Williams, Captain Charles D'Oyley, and Captain Tyrrhitt occupied the positions of commandant, second in command, and adjutant. Styled, from the colour of the uniform adopted, the Kháki[5] Risálá, this troop, from the end of June to the fall of Dehlí scoured the country, retook villages, punished marauders, and did all that was possible to restore and to maintain tranquillity. The Risálá was often assisted by regular troops, cavalry as well as infantry.

---

[5] Kháki, *i.e.* dust-colour.

The adjoining station of Saháranpur was administered by two men possessing rare capacity and great courage, Mr Robert Spankie and Mr Dundas Robertson. These gentlemen, cast upon their own resources, not only maintained order among a rebellious and stiff-necked people, in very difficult circumstances, but they lent their aid to the adjoining districts. To use the words of the lamented Baird-Smith, Chief Engineer of the force besieging Dehlí, Mr Spankie, aided by his energetic subordinates, 'made law respected throughout the district, saved life and property within and beyond it to almost an incalculable extent.' Major Baird-Smith added: 'The ability to complete the works necessary for the capture of Dehlí, within the short time actually employed, was not more a consequence of the indefatigable exertions of the troops in the trenches than of the constant and laborious preparations systematically carried on for months beforehand. To the latter your' (Spankie's) 'aid was frequent and most important.'

Equally successful were the efforts of Mr H. G. Keene in Dehrá Dún; of Mr R. M. Edwards in Muzaffarnagar. In Bulandshahr the splendid exertions of Mr Brand Sapte restored order temporarily; but that station, Síkandarábád, Málágarh, and Khurjá were so much under the control of the disaffected and turbulent Gujar population that it was not possible to retain them permanently until the fate of Dehlí should be decided. The same remark applies to Áligarh, to Gurgáon, to Hisár, and to the district of Rohtak. The country likewise between Áligarh and Agra, notwithstanding the splendid exertions of the Agra volunteers, and the country between Agra and Dehlí, by way of Mathurá, remained in a state of rebellion during that long period of uncertainty.

In the province of Rohilkhand matters were even worse. From the districts and stations of Bijnáur, of Murádábád, of Badáon, of Barélí, of Sháhjahánpur, the English had been expelled under circumstances of great cruelty, and with much shedding of innocent blood. Then a pensioner of the British Government, Khán Bahádur Khán by name, the descendant and heir of the last ruler of the Rohílahs, proclaimed himself Viceroy of the province, under the King of Dehlí, and despatched the sipáhís he had helped to corrupt, under the orders of Bakht Khán, a Subáhdár of artillery, with the title of Brigadier, to Dehlí. Bakht Khán subsequently became Commander-in-Chief of the rebel forces in the Imperial city. Khán Bahádur Khán governed the province for three months and a half. His rule drove to despair all the honest men in it. The nature of that rule may be gathered from the proverb the inhabitants repeated when describing it after the restoration of British rule. 'Life and property were equally unsafe,' they said; 'the buffalo was to the man who held the bludgeon.'

A glance at the map, then, will show that whilst the province immediately contiguous to Dehlí on the east, the province of Rohilkhand, with a population of over five millions, was absolutely held for the King of Dehlí; whilst the Gujar villages between Mírath and the beleaguered city, and the districts of Rohtak and Hisár to the north of it, were in the possession of the insurgents; whilst Mírath, Saháranpur, and Muzaffarnagar were held with difficulty by the British; whilst the country between Dehlí and Agra had pronounced for the rebels; whilst Central India, and the Ságar and Narbadá territories, were overrun by mutineers; whilst Rájpútána itself alone remained true to its traditionary fidelity; whilst, in a word, whether before Dehlí, or in Mírath and the adjoining stations, or at Ságar and Máu, the British held only the ground occupied by their troops, there was yet a most important province to the north and north-west of the city, containing a numerous and warlike population, which had not yet declared itself. That province was the Panjáb. The question which was uppermost in every man's mind was how long the Panjáb would remain quiescent, Dehlí being unsubdued. To the consideration of the means adopted to answer that question favourably to the British I now invite the attention of the reader.

Sir John Lawrence was at Ráwalpindi when the wires flashed to him the story of the outbreak at Mírath and the seizure of Dehlí. Believing, in common with almost every soldier then in India, that, if promptly assailed by a British force, Dehlí would succumb as readily and as promptly as it had succumbed in the time of Lord Lake, he endeavoured by all the means in his power to impress upon General Anson the urgent necessity of marching upon the rebellious city without the smallest delay. He expressed the most unbounded confidence in the immediate result of such a movement. 'I served for nearly thirteen years in Dehlí,' he wrote, on the 21st of May, when General Anson had expressed his doubts as to the wisdom of attempting, with the means at his disposal, an enterprise against Dehlí, 'and know the people well. My belief is that, with good management on the part of the civil officers, it would open its gates to us on the approach of our troops.' In a subsequent letter he wrote: 'I still think that no real resistance at Dehlí will be attempted; but, of course, we must first get the Mírath force in order, and, in moving against Dehlí, go prepared to fight. My impression is that, on the approach of our troops, the mutineers will either disperse, or the people of the city will rise and open the gates.'

Sir John Lawrence impressed these opinions upon Lord Canning, and in the fourth week of May Lord Canning, under their influence, despatched the most emphatic orders to General Anson to make short work of Dehlí.

That he shared the ideas of Sir John Lawrence as to the easy occupation of that city has been shown in a previous page.[6]

Enough has been written, I imagine, to show clearly that Sir John Lawrence was the author of the plan of campaign the first object of which was the recapture of Dehlí. No blame is due to him for having underrated the difficulties of such an enterprise. Dehlí had become the heart of the rebellion, and it was necessary to strike at the heart. But, the step having been taken in compliance with his urgent solicitations, it became incumbent upon him to employ all the resources of the province he administered to render the success of the enterprise absolutely certain.

To do this required the possession of a moral courage greater than is ordinarily allotted to mortals. The position of Sir John Lawrence in the Panjáb was unique. But eight years had elapsed since the fighting classes of that province, led by some of their most powerful chiefs, had contested its possession with the British, on the fields of Chiliánwálá and Gujarát. Never had the English encountered a foe so determined, so daring, and, despite the unskilfulness of their commanders, so hard to defeat. The English had conquered and had annexed the province. Now, only eight years later, Sir John Lawrence would have to call upon the same fighting classes to aid him in resisting the pretensions of the sipáhís by whose assistance they had been conquered. It was, I repeat, a unique position. Sir John Lawrence had to consider whether he could afford to risk the departure from the province of some of the English regiments which were there for its protection, in order to enable him to despatch to the force besieging Dehlí the assistance without which, as events were soon to make clear, that city could not be taken. He had to recollect that he, too, was encumbered by a large garrison of sipáhís imbued with the leaven of mutiny; that he would have to deal with these; that it would be incumbent upon him to repose a trust nearly absolute in the Sikhs; that, in a word, he would have to risk everything to ensure the success of that march against Dehlí, of which he had been the persistent advocate.

A brave man, morally as well as physically, Sir John Lawrence even courted the ordeal. From the very first he devoted all his energies to the employment of the resources of the Panjáb in the subduing of Dehlí. One of his first acts was to despatch thither the splendid Guide corps, composed entirely of frontier men, and consisting of cavalry and infantry. That corps quitted the frontier on the 13th of May, and, as already related, joined the force before Dehlí the day after Barnard had made good his position on the

---

[6] Page 96.

ridge. His lieutenants at Pashāwar, Herbert Edwards, Neville Chamberlain, and John Nicholson, had, in concert with General Reed, commanding the division, and Sydney Cotton, commanding the brigade, jotted down the heads of a plan for the formation of a moveable column. This scheme was approved by Lawrence, and acted upon somewhat later.

Meanwhile, his lieutenant at Lāhor, Robert Montgomery, had taken the wise precaution of disarming the sipáhís at Mían Mír (May 13th); the general at Pashāwar carried out a similar policy on the 22nd, and generally, by the enlistment of old Sikhs as gunners, and by the timely securing of important places, Sir John made the province, which was to be the base of his operations, as secure as, under the circumstances, it could be made.

That some outbreaks should take place was, in the excited state of the minds of the sipáhís, but natural. These will be related in their proper place.

The first indication of actual outbreak on the part of the sipáhís occurred at Mardán, when the 55th N. I., who had replaced the Guide corps at that station, rose in rebellion rather than surrender their arms, and rushed off towards the hills of Swát. Nicholson pursued them with a few trusty horsemen, caught them on their way, killed 120 of them in fair fight, made 150 prisoners, and forced the remainder to take refuge in the Lund-khur hills. On the 7th of June the native regiments stationed at Jálandhar rose in revolt, and swept on to Lodiáná, on their way to Dehlí. An energetic member of the Civil Service, George Ricketts, in concert with Lieutenant Williams of the Indian army, made a most determined and gallant effort to prevent the passage by them of the Satlaj. But the levies at their disposal were few, and some of these crumbled in their hands. After a fight of two hours' duration the rebels had their way. Williams was shot through the lungs. The rebels, on reaching Lodiáná, roused the population to revolt, released the prisoners, and pushed on to Dehlí. The British troops at Jálandhar pursued them, but with so little energy that, alike at the passage of the Satlaj and at Lodiáná, they were always too late.

Meanwhile, Sir John Lawrence had gradually realised that, in predicting the immediate fall of Dehlí on the appearance before it of the British troops, he had been over-sanguine. As day succeeded day, and the force of the rebels was augmented by the arrival of the mutinied regiments, whilst that of the besiegers decreased by casualties, the outlook assumed very serious proportions. Still more than ever John Lawrence adhered to his resolution at all costs to pierce the heart of the enemy's position. He had had too much experience of the Sikhs not to know that their fidelity depended upon success; that it would be dangerous to prolong indefinitely a situation which already was becoming critical. Impressed with these views, he wrote, on the 9th of June, to Edwardes, suggesting the advisability, under certain circumstances, of relinquishing the British hold on Pasháwar, and withdrawing the British forces across the Indus. Edwardes, Nicholson, and Sydney Cotton replied (June 11) by a joint protest against such a scheme. 'Pasháwar,' wrote Edwardes, 'is the anchor of the Panjáb, and if you take it the whole ship will drift to sea.' Eight days later Edwardes repeated his objections, supporting them with cogent arguments.

But Sir John would not give way. He regarded Dehlí as the decisive point of the scene of action, and argued that the importance of holding Pasháwar must yield to the superior necessity of recapturing Dehlí. 'There was no one thing,' he wrote (June 22nd), 'which tended so much to the ruin of Napoleon, in 1814, as the tenacity with which,[7] after the disaster at Leipsic, he clung to the line of the Elbe, instead of falling back at once to that of the Rhine.' So impressed had he been, almost from the first, of the wisdom of making the sacrifice, under certain circumstances, that he, on June 10th, had written to Lord Canning for permission to carry his plans into effect should the necessity arise.

On the 25th of June he believed that the necessity had almost arisen, and he telegraphed to Edwardes, detailing the bad news that had arrived, and adding, 'if matters get worse, it is my decided opinion that the Pasháwar arrangement should take effect. Our troops before Dehlí must be reinforced, and that largely.' Against this Edwardes, Cotton, and Nicholson strongly protested. The question was set at rest some weeks later by the receipt from Lord Canning of a telegram containing the words: 'Hold on to Pasháwar to the last.'

Before that telegram had arrived events had occurred to show that the position was becoming more and more serious. On the morning of the 7th of July the 14th Regiment N. I. mutinied at Jhelam, and, taking a strong position, repulsed with some loss two attacks made upon it by the English troops. That night the sipáhís evacuated their position and fled. It is supposed that most of them ultimately perished. But the affair was managed in a manner which reflected but little credit on the authorities.

The day following the native troops at Síálkót followed the example of their brethren at Jhelam. The station had been denuded of European troops for the formation of the moveable column. The native regiments were the 46th N. I. and the 9th Cavalry. These men, summoned to Dehlí by the King, were apparently anxious to reach that place, their hands red

---

[7] This should surely read 'before.' Napoleon did fall back on the Rhine after Leipsic.

with the blood of English men and women. They therefore murdered as many of the race as they could find. The survivors took refuge in an old fort, once the stronghold of a Sikh chief, Tej Singh. Then the mutineers, having plundered the treasury, having released the prisoners, and effected all the damage they could, started for Delhí. I shall tell very shortly the fate which befell them on the way.

Meanwhile, the moveable column had been formed, and on the 22nd of June John Nicholson, with the rank of Brigadier-General, had assumed command of it. It augured no small courage on the part of Sir John Lawrence to take a regimental captain from Civil employment, and place him in command over the heads of men his seniors. But the times were critical, and at all costs the best man had to be selected if Dehlí was to be relieved.

The force commanded by Nicholson consisted of the 52nd Light Infantry, Dawes's troop of horse-artillery. Bourchier's field-battery, the 33rd and 35th N. I., and a wing of the 9th native light cavalry. Nicholson joined the force at Jálandhar, and marched straight to Philaúr. Under the walls of the fort of that name he disarmed the two sipáhí regiments, then retraced his steps to Amritsar, a central position commanding Láhor, the Jálandhar Duáb, and the Mánjhá. He was there when news reached him of the mutiny at Jhelam. His first step was to disarm the native regiment, the 59th N. I., located at Amritsar. The next day brought him information that the 58th N. I. and two companies of the 14th, the regiment which had fought at Jhelam, had been disarmed, though in a very clumsy manner, at Ráwalpindí. On the 9th of July he heard of the insurrection at Siálkót, in which the left wing of the regiment, the 9th native cavalry, the right wing of which was with him, had taken a very prominent part. He promptly disarmed that wing; then learning that the Siálkót mutineers were marching on Gúrdáspur, forty miles distant from him, he resolved to intercept them in the course which he felt convinced they would take, *via* Núrpur and Hoshiárpur, to Jálandhar. Quitting Amritsar on the 10th, he made a forced march to Gúrdáspur, reached it the evening of the 11th to find that the rebels were at Núrkót, some fifteen miles from the Rávi, on its northern side. As they would have to cross that river, Nicholson, commanding the inner line, waited until their movement had been pronounced; then learning that they were crossing at Trimmu-ghát, he threw himself upon them, and after a contest so severe that it became necessary to try conclusions with the bayonet, drove them back upon the river, with a loss of between three and four hundred men. Unable, from the intense heat and the exertions to which his men had been exposed, to follow them further, he left a party to guard the ghát, and returned with the bulk of the brigade to Gúrdáspur. The river, meanwhile, had risen, and the rebels, unable to reach the further bank, had taken a position on an island in its centre, whence, by the aid of an old gun they had brought from Síálkót, they hoped to defy all enemies. Nicholson, however, was resolved to give them a lesson. Devoting the three following days to the procuring of boats, watching the rebels carefully during that period, he embarked his infantry, on the morning of the 16th, and landed them at one extremity of the island, whilst he placed his guns so as to cover their advance against the enemy at the further end. These tactics completely succeeded. The rebels were defeated with very heavy loss, many were drowned in attempting to escape, and the few who reached the shore were given up by the villagers.

Nicholson then returned to Lábor, met there Sir John Lawrence, and learned that on his way to and beyond the Satlaj his column would be reinforced by 2,500 men, of whom 400 belonged to the 61st foot, 200 to the 8th foot, 100 to the artillery, and the remainder were Sikhs or Balúchís. On the 24th he received his orders to march for Dehlí, crossed the Bías on the 25th, and pushing forward with all speed, taking up his reinforcements as he marched, reached Bárá, in Sirhind, on the 3rd of August. There he received a despatch from General Wilson, commanding the force besieging Dehlí, telling him that the rebels had established themselves in force on the Najafgarh canal, with the intention of moving on Álípur and his communications to the rear, and requesting him to push forward with all expedition to drive them off. Nicholson did push on, reached Ambálah on the 6th, and thence wrote to Wilson to promise that the column should be at Karnál on the 8th, and would push on thence to Pánípat, where he would rejoin it. Meanwhile, he hurried on in advance to see Wilson. He stayed in camp a few days, took note of all that was going on, then returning, met his column, and marched into camp at the head of it on the 14th of August. There for the moment I must leave him.

CHAPTER XIX

The Siege and Storming of Dehlí

At the close of the ninth chapter we left General Barnard, and the British force under his orders, taking possession, on the 8th of June, of the ridge, whence he was to direct his operations against the rebellious city. He was joined, as I have also pointed out, the day following by the splendid corps of Guides. The experience he had had of the temper of the garrison had been but short, yet it had been sufficient to show him how futile were the anticipations of Lord Canning and Sir John Lawrence that the city would surrender without a struggle.

I propose, before describing the operations of the siege, to set before the reader a bird's-eye view of the relative positions of the combatants.

The city of Dehlí lies on a plain on the right bank of the river Jamnah, and is surrounded on three sides by a lofty stone wall, five and a half miles long. The fourth side, nearly two miles in length, runs parallel to and is covered by the river. On this face, the eastern, it is well protected. To the north-east it was defended by the fort of Salímgarh, the circuit of the high and massive walls of which covered three-quarters of a mile. In this were two gates, called respectively the Calcutta and the North gate. Adjoining the Salímgarh, to the south, was the Citadel or King's palace, built by Sháh Jahán, having walls of red sandstone, very high, and with a circumference of nearly a mile and a half. The entrance to this is from the west, by a gate opening on to the Chandni Chauk, known, in 1857 as the Láhor gate. The other gates were the Kashmír, to the north, near the English church and the Kachahrí or Court of Justice; to the west of this, though facing northward, the Mórí gate; to the proper west, at the angle formed by the north and west faces, the Kábul gate; then, midway between the two angles of the western face, the Láhor gate, forming the entrance to the famous Chandni Chauk, leading through the city to the Citadel; further to the south, just after the wall of defence makes a bend inwards, was the Farásh-kháná gate; at the angle beyond it, the Ajmír gate; then, forming entrances to the southern face, the Turkoman, and beyond it the Dehlí gate; beyond again, facing the river, was the Ráj-ghát gate.

The fort had been strengthened by English engineers and provided with perfect flanking defences. Round the walls, twenty-four feet in height, ran a dry ditch, some twenty-five feet in breadth and somewhat less than twenty in depth, the counterscarp being an earthen slope of very easy descent, much water and weather worn. There was a kind of glacis, but it scarcely merited the name, being but a short slope, seventy or eighty feet in breadth, springing from the crest of the counterscarp, and provided with no special means of obstruction. The place was garrisoned by some 40,000 sipáhís, armed and disciplined by the British. Its walls were mounted with 114 pieces of heavy artillery, capable of being supplied with ammunition from the largest magazine established by the British in the upper provinces. The garrison had, in addition, some sixty pieces of field-artillery, and were well supplied with gunners, drilled and disciplined by the British.

To take this strongly defended city the English general had under his orders some 3000 British soldiers, a battalion of Gurkhás, the corps of Guides, some remnants of native infantry sipáhís, whose fidelity was not assured, and twenty-two field-guns. He had, as we have seen, taken his position on the ridge, an elevation of from fifty to sixty feet above the general level of the city, extending along a line of rather more than two miles, its left resting upon the Jamnah some three or four miles above Dehlí, its right extremity approaching the Kábul gate at a distance of about a thousand yards. The ridge intersected the old cantonment towards its left centre. Following its front towards its right was a road which joined the grand trunk road from Karnál, beyond its extremity, and led down, through a mass of suburban gardens and ancient edifices, to the Kábul gate. Two other roads, also leading from Karnál, diverged through the old cantonment to different gates of the city. The position was open to the rear, and commanded a splendid supply of water from the Najafgarh canal. The English tents, pitched on the left and centre of the ridge, obliquely to the front of attack, were concealed from the view of the enemy by the houses very recently occupied by the officers of the Dehlí brigade, still left standing. The weakest point of the position, that nearest the enemy, was the right. Here a strong body of troops were posted. There was an extensive building known as Hindu Ráo's house. This house had been left empty by its owner, and was promptly occupied. Nearly in the centre of the position was a round tower called the Flagstaff Tower, double storeyed, and offering a good point for observation. Between that tower and Hindu Ráo's house was an old mosque, with good masonry walls, admirably adapted as an outpost. This, too, was occupied. Further along the ridge road, at a distance of some 200 yards from the position on the extreme right, was the Observatory, also capable of being utilised. Beyond Hindu Ráo's house again, to the rear of the position, was the suburb of Sabzímandí, a cluster of houses and walled gardens, which an active enemy might occupy. Beyond this the plain was covered with gardens, groves, houses, and walled enclosures, bordering upon the grand canal. Stretching from the Sabzímandí to the Kábul gate of the city were the villages of Kishanganj, Trevelyanganj, Pahárípur, and Táliwárí, too far off to be occupied in force by the besiegers, and therefore affording a convenient shelter to a daring foe. Somewhat to the south of the Flagstaff, but more to the east, was Metcalfe House, on the Jamnah, with substantial outbuildings, and a mound in its rear. Between that house and the city was an old summer palace of the Mughal sovereigns, called Kudsiyá Bágh, with lofty gateways and spacious courtyards; whilst more remote from the river, and almost in a line with the Kashmír gate of the city, was Ludlow Castle, on the crest of a ridge sloping down towards the city walls, with the dry bed of a drainage canal at its base. Further, on the line of the Jamnah, between the Kudsiyá Bágh and the water-gate of the city, was a spacious house surrounded by trees and shrubs, but so close to the city walls that they seemed almost to overhang it.

Such was the position, or, rather, such were the relative positions. We cannot wonder that, as Barnard surveyed the city and the country between it and his camp, on the morning of the 9th of June, he recognised that he had done rightly not to follow the rebels into the city two days previously. But he knew what was expected from him. He had in his hand the written opinions of Lord Canning and Sir John Lawrence that, with proper action on the part of the British leader, the place must fall. He ordered, then, an assault for the 12th. The scheme had been drawn up by Greathed, Maunsell, and Chesney of the engineers, and by Hodson, afterwards known as 'Hodson of Hodson's Horse,' an officer of great intrepidity. It had been arranged that the troops told off for the attack should assemble between one and two in the morning, and then, under cover of the darkness, should proceed noiselessly to the gates, blow them open, and effect an entrance. At the appointed time and place all the troops were assembled, with the exception of 300 of the 1st Europeans, to be commanded by Brigadier Graves. These never came, and in consequence the enterprise was abandoned. Graves had received no written orders, and as the verbal notice he received would have involved leaving the Flagstaff picket in the hands of natives, he declined to act upon it. It was fortunate he did so, for after events proved that, even had the gates been carried, the force was not nearly strong enough to hold Dehlí. A repulse would possibly have involved the destruction of the besieging force, and the evil consequences of this to British authority in India it is difficult to over-estimate.

On the 14th June General Reed, the senior divisional commander, arrived on the ridge to assume command. For the moment, however, on account of his health, he did not supersede Barnard. That officer continued to direct the operations till his death. In Reed's tent the question of a *coup-de-main* was discussed for several days. The civilian who was consulted, Mr Hervey Greathed, brother of the engineer of the same name, was in favour of adopting a revised plan drawn up by his brother, to be put into execution without delay. But all the senior soldiers, Barnard, Archdale Wilson, and Reed were against it. It is fair to add that they did not object to the plan itself so much as to the moment of executing it. They believed that in the course of fifteen days the force would be so strengthened in numbers as to render it possible to hold all that might be gained. There can be no doubt but that their decision was a wise one.

The decision was arrived at on the 18th, and though Greathed (of the engineers) again subsequently urged a reconsideration, the generals were not to be tempted. In the interval there had been a great deal of fighting. On the 12th the rebels had attacked the British camp in front and rear, and had almost penetrated to its very heart. They were, however, ultimately driven back, and pursued through the grounds of Metcalfe House to the very walls of the city. From that date a strong picket was posted at that house, the communications being maintained from the Flagstaff Tower. The same day attacks made upon Hindu Ráo's house and the Sabzímandí were repulsed with great loss to the rebels. A regiment of irregular cavalry, however, seized the opportunity to go over to them. It was perhaps fortunate, as, under the circumstances in which the British were, it was better to have an open than a secret foe. The day following the rebels made another attack, the 60th Regiment N. I., which had joined them the previous day, taking a leading part in it. They were, however, repulsed. On the 17th the besiegers took the initiative, their attack being led most gallantly by Reid of the Gurkhás, from Hindu Ráo's house, and by Tombs of the horse-artillery, from the camp. The assailants destroyed a battery the rebels were erecting, and drove them back headlong into the city. But the fire from the heavy guns of the rebels prevented a complete following up of the success.

On the 18th, the day on which the decision not to attempt a *coup-de-main* was arrived at, the rebels were reinforced by the mutinied sipáhí brigade from Nasírábád. They brought six guns with them. To celebrate the event, the rebels came out in force, and attacked the British camp in the rear. The contest was most desperate, and the loss on both sides was heavy. Yule of the 9th Lancers was killed; Daly of the Guides and Becher, the Quartermaster-General, were wounded. Night fell upon a drawn battle, the rebels maintaining their position till the early morning. On the 23rd, the anniversary of Plassey, the day foretold as that which would witness the downfall of British rule, they made a supreme effort to verify the prophecy. Fortunately the English had received that day a reinforcement of a company of the 75th foot, four companies of the 2nd Fusiliers, four H. A. guns, and part of a native troop, with some Panjábí infantry and cavalry, in all 850 men. The right bore the brunt of the attack, which was conducted with great courage and a coolness worthy of English troops. Reid and his Gurkhás, however, maintained their position, the 60th Rifles added to the imperishable glory they had previously acquired, and the Guides vied with them in cool courage. But for the steadiness displayed by Reid and the officers and men generally, it would have been impossible to hold the position. They did hold it, however, but it was only as the night fell, and after most desperate fighting, that the rebels fell back.

On the 24th Neville Chamberlain came from the Panjáb to assume the post of Adjutant-General. Reinforcements, too, sufficient to raise the effective strength of the British force to 6,600 men, poured in from the Panjáb. But the rebels likewise had their share of fortune. On the 1st and 2nd of July the Barélí brigade, consisting of four sipáhí regiments of infantry, one of cavalry, a horse-battery, and two post-guns, and commanded by a Subahdár of artillery, Bakht Khán by name, who was almost at once nominated Commander-in-Chief of the rebel forces in the city, marched in. Meanwhile, the arrival of reinforcements within the camp had revived the question of assault. Once more the plans had been arranged, the regiments told off, the date, the 3rd of July, had been fixed, when, suddenly, the information that the rebels contemplated a serious attack on the weakest part of the British position that very day caused its postponement.

To partake in the contemplated assault on the city, the rumour of which had reached him, there had hurried on, from the small detachment he was leading from Rúrkí, a man destined to take a leading part in the eventual storming of the place. This was Baird-Smith of the engineers. Summoned from Rúrkí to take his place as senior officer of his scientific regiment, he arrived, by hard riding, at three o'clock on the morning of the 3rd, to find that the assault had been postponed.

Baird-Smith found that, as far as ordnance was concerned, the British force was in a very unenviable position. The heavy guns consisted of two twenty-four-pounders, nine eighteen-pounders, six eight-inch mortars, and three eight-inch howitzers. The rebels, on the other hand, could bring to bear on any point thirty guns and twelve mortars. What was still worse, the English had in store only sufficient shot for heavy guns for one day, whilst the rebels had the almost inexhaustible supplies of the Dehlí magazine in their midst. To add to the gravity of the position, the day after his arrival in camp, Barnard was seized with cholera. The fell disease carried him off on the 5th. He was a conscientious man and a brave soldier, and his death was universally lamented. General Reed, who had remained in camp since we last saw him there, succeeded to the command.

Before Barnard had been attacked by cholera, Baird-Smith, keenly alive to the difficulty of carrying on a regular siege with resources in guns and material so obviously inadequate, had written to that officer to suggest the advisability of an assault. 'The probabilities of success,' he wrote, 'are far greater than those of failure, and the reasons justifying an assault stronger than those which justified inaction.' Barnard died before the proposal could be considered, and it devolved upon Reed to give the necessary decision. Reed neither rejected nor accepted the plan;[1] but he kept it so long 'in contemplation' that the opportunity passed away.

On the 9th the rebels made another grand attack in force. They despatched the 8th Írregulars, the regiment which had mutinied at Baréli, through the right of the British camp, by the rear, and as their uniform was the same as that of the loyal irregular regiment in the camp, they were allowed to pass unchallenged. The consequences of this mistake were alike deplorable and glorious. They were deplorable in that the cavalry picket at the Mound, half-way between the Ridge and the canal, on discovering their error, turned and fled. Not so the artillery, commanded by James Hills, one of the most gallant and daring soldiers in the world. Hills promptly ordered out his two guns for action. But the rebels were upon him, and he had not time to fire. Then, with the cool courage of a man determined at all cost to stop the foe, he dashed into the midst of the advancing troopers, cutting right and left at them with splendid effect. At last two of them charged him and rolled over his horse. Hills speedily regained his feet, just in time to renew the combat with three troopers—two mounted, the third on foot. The two first he cut down; with the third the conflict was desperate. Hills had been shaken by his fall, and was encumbered by his cloak.

---

[1] Four months afterwards Baird-Smith wrote that he thought then, with the full experience before him of the actual capture, that if an assault had been attempted between the 4th and 14th of July it would have succeeded.

Twice did his pistol miss fire. Then he missed a blow at his opponent's shoulder, and the latter wrested his sword from his tired hand. But Hills was equal to the occasion. Closing with his enemy, he smote him several times with his clenched fist in the face until he fell. Just at the moment Tombs, who had found his way through the enemy, seeing Hills's danger, shot the trooper dead. It was a splendid pistol shot, fired at a distance of thirty paces. To reach that point Tombs had cut his way through the enemy, whose advance Hills had checked, but not completely stopped. The danger to them was not over then. It required the sacrifice of another native trooper to insure perfect safety. But this was only accomplished at the cost to Hills of a sword-cut, which clave his skull to the brain.[2]

By this time the whole British camp was roused, and after a while the rebel troopers were driven back towards Dehlí. A fierce battle had been going on, meanwhile, in the Sabzímandí. This likewise ended in the repulse of the rebels, but not until 233 men had been killed or wounded on the British side.

Five days later there was another hard-fought encounter. This time the rebels attacked Hindu Ráo's house. After a battle which lasted from eight o'clock in the morning till close upon sunset, Neville Chamberlain, with the 75th, Coke's Rifles (Panjábís), and Hodson's Horse, drove back the rebels to the gates of Dehlí. But again was the loss severe, amounting to seventeen men killed and 193 wounded, of whom sixteen were officers, among them Chamberlain, whose left arm was broken. In the week the besiegers had lost, in killed and wounded, twenty-five officers and 400 men.

Meanwhile, Gerald Reed's health had completely broken down. On the 17th, then, he made over command to Archdale Wilson. The day following the rebels made another sortie, but they were repulsed by Colonel Jones of the 60th Rifles. The attack had been made, as often before, on the Sabzímandí. To prevent future attacks in that quarter, the engineers cleared away the houses and walls, which had afforded cover to the rebels, and connected the advanced posts with the main pickets on the Ridge. The effect of this was most salutary. There were no more attacks on the Sabzímandí.

It was the day before this attack, the day, in fact, on which Wilson assumed command, that a report reached the Chief Engineer, Baird-Smith, that the question whether circumstances did not require the raising of the siege, in consideration of the great losses incurred, and the impossibility

---

[2] The wound was not mortal. Hills recovered to render splendid service to his country in India, in China, in Abyssinia, in Afghanistan. He is now Sir James Hills-Johns.

of taking the place without further reinforcements, would be mooted at the next meeting of the General and his staff. Impressed with the absolute necessity of retaining the 'grip we now have on Dehlí,' Baird-Smith took the very earliest opportunity of speaking to Wilson on the subject, and of pointing out the enormous calamities which the raising of the siege would entail. The result of the conversation was to confirm Wilson in his resolution to prosecute the siege, and to render its success certain, by ordering up a siege-train from Fírzúpur.

On the 23rd the enemy made a final attack before the arrival of Nicholson. This time it was directed against Ludlow Castle. The attack was repulsed, but the British, pursuing the rebels too closely to the city walls, suffered very severely.

On the 7th of August Nicholson arrived, as stated in the last chapter, in advance of his troops. On the 12th Showers expelled the rebels from Ludlow Castle, which meanwhile they had managed to occupy. On the 14th Nicholson's column arrived. On the 25th he marched, with a strong force, to attack the rebels, who had moved from Dehlí in great strength to intercept the siege-train. The march took him through marshy ground, intersected with swamps, and lasted a good twelve hours. At length, close upon sunset, the weary soldiers espied the rebels, composed of the Nímach brigade, occupying two villages and a caravansarai, protected by guns and covered by deep water, fordable only in one place. The British, however, waded through the ford, which was breast high, under a fire from the guns at the caravansarai. Against this Nicholson directed his own attack, whilst he sent his other troops against the villages. Addressing his men a few cheering words, he ordered them to lie down. Then the batteries of Tombs and Remmington opened fire. After a few rounds he ordered the men to rise, and he led them through the still marshy ground, they cheering loudly. Needless to say, they carried the position. At the same time the other troops had driven the rebels from the two villages. The sipáhís fought well, but only the Nímach brigade was there, that from Baréli, which had been ordered to support it, not having come up in time. When they found that they were beaten, the sipáhís limbered up their guns and made for the bridge crossing the Najafgarh canal. But Nicholson pursued and caught them, killed about 800 of them, and captured thirteen guns. He then blew up the bridge, and the troops returned next day to Dehlí, taking their spoils with them. Ten days later, the 4th of September, the siege-guns arrived, the remainder of the 60th Rifles on the 6th, and the Jammú contingent, led by Richard Lawrence, one of the four famous brothers, on the 8th.

The arrival of reinforcements had increased the number of troops at the disposal of General Wilson to 8,748 men, of whom 3,317 were British. Barnard had directed the *coup-de-main* of the 12th of June, when his entire force scarcely exceeded half that number. Yet, up to the 20th August, Wilson could with difficulty make up his mind to hazard the assault, which, if successful, would break the back of the Mutiny. On that date he wrote to Baird-Smith a letter, to be subsequently forwarded to the Governor-General, in which he freely stated the reasons on which his hesitation was based, and asked that officer to return the letter, 'with such remarks and emendations as your experience as Chief Engineer suggests.' The answer given by Baird-Smith was empathic, clear, and decided. He gave his voice for prompt and immediate action. True, he argued, the rebels are more numerous than the assailants; true that their position is formidable, their resources are unlimited, their defences strong. But in war something must be risked. In his opinion, the risk of a repulse, in an attack well contrived and well organised, was less than the risk of further delay. The Panjáb, he argued, on the authority of Sir John Lawrence, denuded of its European troops, was quivering in the balance. To wait for reinforcements would involve inaction, at a time when action alone, in all human probability, could secure the continued acquiescence of the Sikhs. And if the Sikhs were to rise the danger would extend to the very camp in which Wilson commanded.

These reasons, clear, pointed, logical, decided Wilson. Though he still believed that the results of the proposed operations would 'be thrown on a hazard of a die,' he was willing, on the advice of the Chief Engineer, to try that hazard. For the decision to assault the rebellious city Baird-Smith, then, was responsible. He at once, in conjunction with his second in command, Alexander Taylor, drew up the plan of assault.

To understand the plan the Chief Engineer worked out it is necessary that I should lay before the reader a short and concise description of the defences to be assailed. I cannot do this better than in the very words of Baird-Smith.

'The eastern face,' he wrote, 'rests on the Jamnah, and during the season of the year when our operations were carried on the stream may be described as washing the base of the walls. All access to a besieger on the river front is therefore impracticable. The defences here consists of an irregular wall, with occasional bastions and towers, and about one-half the river face is occupied by the palace of the King of Dehlí and its outwork, the old Mughal fort of Salímgarh. The river may be described as the chord of a rough arc formed by the remaining defences of the place. These consist of a succession of bastioned fronts, the connection being very long, and the outworks limited to one crown work at the Ajmír gate, and martello towers, mounting a single gun, at such points as require additional flanking fire to that given by the bastion themselves. The bastions are small, generally mounting three guns in each face, two in each flank, and one in the embrasure at the salient. They are provided with masonry parapets, about twelve feet in thickness, and have a relief of about sixteen feet above the plane of site. The curtain consists of a simple masonry wall or rampart, sixteen feet in height, eleven feet thick at top, and fourteen or fifteen at bottom. The main wall carries a parapet, loopholed for musketry, eight feet in height and eight feet in thickness. The whole of the land front is covered by a berme of variable width, ranging from sixteen to thirty feet, and having a scarp wall eight feet high. Exterior to this was a dry ditch, of about twenty-five feet in width, and from sixteen to twenty in depth. The counter-scarp is simply an earthen slope, easy to descend. The glacis is a very short one, extending only fifty or sixty yards from the counter-scarp. Using general terms, it covers from the besiegers' view from one-half to one-third of the walls of the place.'

Such being the defences, the plan of assault traced out may be thus stated.

It was necessary that the attack should be directed against the northern face—the face represented by the Morí, Kashmír, and Water bastions, and the curtain wall connecting them. Fortunately the carelessness of the rebels allowed the besiegers to concentrate on the curtain wall a fire sufficient to crush that of the defence, and thus to effect breaches through which the infantry could be launched. The plan of the Chief Engineer, then, was to crush the fire of the Morí bastion. That fire silenced, the advance on the British left, which was covered by the river, would be secure, and there the assault would be delivered. The evening of the 7th was fixed for the commencement of the tracing of the assailing batteries.

That day Wilson issued a stirring order to the troops, telling them that the hour was at hand when, as he trusted, they would be rewarded for their past exertions by the capture of the city. That evening the engineers began their work. For No. 1 battery a site had been selected below the Ridge, in the open plain, within 700 yards of the Morí bastion. This battery was divided into two sections, the right one to be commanded by Major Brind, a real hero of the siege, intended to silence the Morí bastion; the left one by Major Kaye, designed to keep down the fire from the Kashmír bastion until the order for the delivering of the assault should be given.

The engineers worked with so much energy at these sections that, on the morning of the 8th, whilst still unfinished, and mounting but one gun, the enemy discovered Brind's section, and opened upon it a fire so concentrated and so incessant that to venture from its protection was to invite almost certain death. A little later the rebels tried to improve the opportunity by despatching a body of infantry and cavalry from the Láhor gate. This diversion really favoured the English. For, whilst it lasted, the men in the new battery worked with such a will that they succeeded in completing five platforms. As each platform was completed the gun mounted on it opened against the enemy. It is needless to add that the sortie, which had thus given badly-wanted time to the defenders, was beaten back with loss. The first section of No. 1 battery had no sooner been completed than its fire, well directed by the energetic Brind, rendered the Morí bastion harmless. Nor had the gallant Kaye done his work with less zeal. The fire directed from the left section had done good work against the Kashmír bastion, when, at noon of the 10th, the half-battery caught fire from the constant discharge of the guns. For a moment or two it seemed that the hard work of the three previous days would be thrown away, for the rebels at once directed on the burning battery every gun they could command.

But from such a catastrophe the battery was saved by the gallantry of Lieutenant Lockhart, on duty on the spot, with two companies of the 2nd Gurkhás. As soon as he saw the fire, Lockhart, apprehending its fatal consequences, suggested to Kaye whether it might not be possible to save it by working from the outside, and on the top of the parapet. Kaye replied that something might be done if a party were to take sandbags to the top, cut them, and smother the fire with the sand. But the attempt, under the concentrated fire of the rebels, involved almost certain death. Lockhart nobly thought that the occasion was one to justify the risk. Calling for volunteers, he jumped on the parapet, followed by six or seven Gurkhás, and set himself to the task. The enemy's fire immediately redoubled. Two of the Gurkhás were shot dead. Lockhart rolled over the parapet, with a shot through his jaw, but the survivors persevered, and by incredible exertions succeeded in extinguishing the fire.

Meanwhile No. 2 battery had been traced, also on the evening of the 7th, in front of Ludlow Castle, 500 yards from the Kashmír gate. This, too, was divided into two sections, at a distance from each other of 200 yards. They were both directed against the Kashmír bastion, and intended to silence its fire, to knock away the parapet to the right and the left that gave cover to its defenders, and to open a breach for the stormers. Before dawn of the 11th it had been completed and armed, and was then unmasked. Major Campbell commanded the left section, the right was first entrusted to Major Kaye, transferred to it from the ignited left section of No 1; but on that officer being wounded, on the 11th, it was placed in the capable hands of Major Edwin Johnson.

The third battery required in its construction a large amount of skill and daring. It was traced, under the directions of Captain Medley of the engineers, within 160 yards of the Water bastion. This battery was finished and armed by the night of the 11th.

A fourth battery, commanded by the gallant Tombs for four heavy mortars, was traced in the Kudsiyá Bágh. It was completed on the 11th, ready to open fire when its fire might be required.

The rebels had been neither blind nor indifferent to the active movements in the camp of the besiegers. Recognising at last that the meditated attack would be directed against their left, they adopted measures which, if carried out sooner, would have added enormously to the difficulties of the attack, if, indeed, they had not rendered it impossible. They at once set to work to mount heavy guns along the curtain between the bastions on the northern face. In other convenient nooks they mounted light guns. Taking advantage, too, of the broken ground, they made in one night an advanced trench parallel to the left attack, and 350 yards from it, covering their entire front. This trench they lined with infantry.

A tremendous fire from both sides continued from the opening of the new batteries till the afternoon of the 13th, the damage done to assailants and defenders being tremendous. Never was there displayed in the British army greater energy, more splendid determination. Men fearlessly exposed themselves to repair damages. Each man felt that on his own personal exertions the issue greatly depended. At length, on the afternoon of the 13th, Wilson and Baird-Smith came to the conclusion that two sufficient breaches had been made. Wilson directed, accordingly, that they should be examined.

This dangerous duty was performed by four young engineer officers— Medley and Lang for the Kashmír bastion, Greathed and Home for the Water. The two first named reached the edge of the ditch undiscovered, descended into it, and although they saw the enemy was on the alert, carefully examined the breach. They returned, pursued by a volley, to report it practicable. A similar report reached Baird-Smith from Greathed and Home. He therefore advised Wilson not to delay a single day, but to assault the coming morning. Wilson, agreeing with him, issued forthwith the necessary orders.

The order of the attack was as follows: Nicholson, with 300 men of the 75th, under Lieutenant-Colonel Herbert; 250 men of the 1st Fusiliers, under Major Jacob; 450 men of the 2nd Panjáb Infantry, under Captain

Green, was to storm the breach near the Kashmír bastion, and escalade the face of the bastion. The engineers attached to this column were Medley, Lang, and Bingham.

At the same time Brigadier William Jones of the 61st, commanding the second column, composed of 250 men of the 8th foot, under Lieutenant-Colonel Greathed; 250 men of the 2nd Fusiliers, under Captain Boyd; 350 men of the 4th Sikh Infantry, under Captain Rothney, was to storm the breach in the Water bastion. The engineers with this column were Greathed, Hovenden, and Pemberton.

Similarly, Colonel Campbell of the 52nd Light Infantry, commanding the third column, composed of 250 men of the 52nd, under Major Vigors; 250 Gurkhás of the Kumáon battalion, under Captain Ramsay; 500 men of the 1st Panjáb Infantry, under Lieutenant Nicholson, was to assault by the Kashmír gate after it should have been blown open. The engineers were Home, Salkeld, and Tandy.

Major Reid of the Sirmúr battalion commanded the fourth column, composed of the Sirmúr battalion (2nd Gurkhás), the Guide corps, such of the pickets, European and native, as could be spared from Hindu Ráo's house, and 1,200 men of the Kashmír (Jammú) contingent, led by Captain Richard Lawrence, was to attack the suburb of Kishanganj, and enter by the Láhor gate. The engineers attached to this column were Maunsell and Tennant.

The fifth, or reserve column, was commanded by Lieutenant-Colonel Longfield of the 8th foot. It consisted of 250 men of the 61st, under Lieutenant-Colonel Deacon; 450 men of the 4th Panjáb Infantry, under Captain Wilde; 300 men, Balúch battalion, under Lieutenant-Colonel Farquhar; 300 men of the Jhínd auxiliary force, under Lieutenant-Colonel Dunsford. To these were subsequently added 200 men of the 60th Rifles, under Lieutenant-Colonel John Jones of that regiment. This column was to support the first column. Its engineers were Ward and Thackeray.

In a work which professes to give merely a compendium of the story of the great Indian Mutiny space will not allow me to follow the several columns step by step. I must content myself with giving a summary of the tremendous conflict that followed. At three o'clock in the morning the columns of assault were drawn up. There was not a man amongst those who composed them who did not feel that upon the exertions of himself and his comrades depended the fate of India. There was a slight but inevitable delay; then, as day was dawning the columns advanced, and quietly took up the positions assigned them until signal to advance should be given. Meanwhile, an explosion party, consisting of Lieutenants Home and Salkeld, Sergeants Smith and Carmichael, Corporal Burgess, Bugler Hawthorne, and eight native sappers, covered by 100 men of the 60th Rifles, sped their way to the front to attach kegs of powder to, and blow up, the Kashmír gate. The bugle-sound from this point was to be the signal of success, and for the advance of the third column.

Nicholson, after one glance to see that the first and second columns were in position, gave the order just after daybreak to advance. The first column moved steadily forward at a walk, until it reached the further edge of the jungle; then the engineers and storming party rushed to the breach near the Kashmír bastion, and in a few seconds gained the crest of the glacis. Upon them there the whole fire of the rebels seemed to be concentrated. So fierce was it that for ten minutes it was impossible to let down the ladders. At last they let down two, and down these the officers led their men. Once in the ditch, to mount the escarp and scramble up the breach was the work of a few seconds. There the rebels, who had been so bold up to that point, did not await them. They could not stand the hand-to-hand encounter, but fell back on the second line. The breach at this point was won.

Simultaneously the second column, its engineers in front, pressed forward towards the breach in the Water bastion, whilst the storming party, carrying the ladders, moved to the appointed spot, and though exposed to a tremendous fire, which made great execution in their ranks, let down their ladders and carried the breach; their supports, by mistake, rushed to the counter-scarp of the curtain, slid into the ditch, climbed the breach, and won the rampart. The mistake was a fortunate one, for although the actual storming party had been reduced by the fire concentrated upon it in its advance to twenty-five, the supports entering into a vital point of the defences, where an attack had not been anticipated, paralysed the rebels. Jones promptly seized the situation to clear the ramparts as far as the Kábul gate, on the summit of which he planted the column flag, carried that day by Private Andrew Laughnan of the 61st.[3]

Meanwhile, the forlorn hope, composed of the two officers and their following, whose names are given in a preceding page, had advanced straight on to the Kashmír gate, in the face of a very heavy fire. Arrived in front of it, Home and Salkeld, and their followers, each carrying a bag containing twenty-five pounds of gun-powder, crossed the ditch by a barrier gate, which they fortunately found open, to the foot of the great double gate. The enemy seemed completely paralysed by the audacity of

---

[3] This flag was subsequently, the 1st of January 1877, presented by Sir William Jones to Her Majesty.

the proceeding, and for a moment suspended their fire. Home and Salkeld used the opportunity to attach the bags to the gateway, then to fall back as fast as they could. The bags were laid when the rebels, recovering their senses, reopened their deadly fire. Home had time to jump into the ditch unhurt. Salkeld was not so fortunate. He had laid his bags, when he was shot through the arm and leg, and fell back disabled on the bridge. He handed the port-fire to Burgess, bidding him to light the fusee. Burgess, in trying to obey, was shot dead. Carmichael then seized the port-fire, lighted the fusee, and fell back mortally wounded. Then Smith, thinking Carmichael had failed, rushed forward to seize the port-fire, but noticing the fusee burning, threw himself into the ditch.[4] The next moment a tremendous explosion shattered the massive gate. Home then told the bugler, Hawthorne, to sound the advance. The bugle-call, repeated three times, was not heard in the din. But the gallant commander of the third column, Campbell, noticing the explosion, at once ordered the advance of the column. It dashed forward, crossed the bridge, and entered the city just as the first and second columns had won the breaches. Campbell at once pressed on to the main-guard, cleared the Water bastion, forced his way through the Kashmír gate bazaar, reached the gate opening on the Chandni Chauk, forced it, and pressed on till a sudden turn brought him within sight of the great mosque, the Jamí Masjíd, its arches and gates bricked up, and impossible to be forced without powder bags or guns. He waited in front of it for half-an-hour, in the expectation of the successful advance of the other columns. But as there were no signs of such approach, he fell back on the Begam Bágh, a large enclosure. There I must leave him to relate the progress of the fourth column.

An unfortunate incident, a failure on the part of the department concerned to carry out the General's instructions, interfered greatly with the success of the fourth column. It was formed up, composed as already detailed, at 4.30 A.M., in front of the Sabzímandí picket. But the four H. A. guns which had been ordered to accompany it had not arrived. When at last they did come they brought with them only sufficient gunners to man one gun. Reid was waiting until gunners could be procured when he heard the explosion at the Kashmír gate. He discovered immediately afterwards that 500 of the Jammú troops, despatched two hours earlier for

---

[4] Of the six British engaged in this deed of valour two were killed, Burgess and Carmichael. Salkeld died a few days later. Home was killed, during the same month, at the assault of Málagarh. Smith and Hawthorne alone survived. They both received the Victoria Cross. Home and Salkeld were also recommended for it, but they did not survive to get it.

the purpose of effecting a diversion by occupying the Idgar, had become engaged. No time was to be lost, so he pushed on without any guns at all.

On this point it must suffice to state that the assault failed. Reid, who was greatly embarrassed by the want of guns, facing, as he had to face, the unbroken wall of Kishanganj, eighteen feet high, lined with guns and marksmen, had gained the canal bridge with the head of his column, and was meditating a diversion to draw off the attention of the rebels from the main attack when a musket ball, coming from a slanting direction, struck him on the head, and knocked him into the ditch, insensible. How long he remained so he never knew. Those about him thought he had been killed. When he returned to his senses, he found himself on the back of one of his Gurkhás. He was very weak, but he had still strength enough to send for Captain Lawrence, and to direct him to take command, and to support the right. The delay, however, had been very injurious, and the disorder was increased by the fact that Captain Muter, seeing Reid fall, and regarding Lawrence in the light of a political officer, had assumed command of the portion of the column with which he was serving. By the time that Lawrence had asserted his authority success had become impossible. He withdrew his men, therefore, leisurely and in good order, on the batteries behind Hindu Ráo's house. The attack on the Idgar, made by the Jammú troops alone, was still more unfortunate. They were not only repulsed, but lost four guns.

The repulse of the fourth column added greatly to the difficulties of the other three. To these I must return.

I left the first and second columns victorious inside the breach. Nicholson at once massed his men on the square of the main-guard, and turning to the right, pushed on along the foot of the walls towards the Láhor gate, whence a galling fire was being kept up on his men. Beyond the Kábul gate, which, as we have seen, had been occupied by the second column, he hoped to feel the support of the fourth column. But, as just related, the attack of that column had failed, and it was this failure which rendered his advance difficult and dangerous.

To reach the Láhor gate Nicholson had to push on under the fire of the Burn bastion, then to force his way through a long lane, every building in which was manned by sharpshooters—the further end of it commanded by two brass guns, one about 160 yards from its opening, pointed in the direction of the advance, the other about 100 yards in rear of and commanding it. Behind both was a bullet-proof screen, whilst projecting, as it were, from the wall was the bastion commanding the Láhor gate, armed with heavy pieces, and capable of holding a thousand men.

In his advance Nicholson had been exposed to a continuous fire, but he had a position at the Kábul gate which was strong enough for him to maintain until the movements of the other columns should facilitate his advance. But Nicholson, though urged to halt there, was so fully impressed with the necessity of taking the fullest advantage of the so far successful assault that he resolved at all costs to push on to the Láhor gate. He felt this the more because he was convinced that the repulse of the fourth column had renewed the hopes of an enemy peculiarly liable to be affected by success or its opposite. He directed, then, his men to storm the narrow lane of which I have spoken.

Gallantly did his men respond. With a rush not to be withstood they cleared the space up to the first brass gun, and captured it. Then they dashed on the second. But within ten yards of this they were assailed by a fire of grape and musketry, by volleys of stones and round-shot, thrown by hand, so severe that they recoiled under the terrible and ceaseless shower. Not quite all, indeed. Lieutenant Butler, who many a time on the field of battle earned the Victoria Cross, which could be bestowed only once, penetrated beyond the second gun, up to the bullet-proof screen. How he escaped with his life was a miracle, but he rejoined his men.

The men had recoiled only to form again, and once more rush for-ward. Again did they capture the first gun, which this time Greville (1st Fusiliers) spiked, and again did they dash at the second. Never has there been a greater display of heroism, of contempt for death. The leader of the assault, Jacobs, of the 1st Fusiliers, was mortally wounded. Wemyss, Greville, Caulfield, Speke (the brother of the African traveller), Woodcock, Butler, all attached to the same regiment, were in turn struck down. The men, greatly discouraged by the fall of their officers, were falling back a second time, when an inspiring voice called upon them to follow where their general led. It was the clear-sounding voice of Nicholson, But the broken order could not be restored in a moment, and before a sufficient number of men could respond to the inspiring cry, a bullet pierced the body of the illustrious leader.

The wound was mortal, and Nicholson knew it to be so. But neither the pain he suffered, nor the consciousness of approaching death, could quench the ardour of his gallant spirit. He still called upon his men to go on. But he was asking that which had now become impossible. He had no guns, and already eight officers and fifty men had fallen in the attempt. There was nothing for it but to retire on the Kábul gate. This was done, and Jones assumed the command of the two columns.

We have left the third column in front of the Jamí Masjíd, without artillery to beat down its defences. Campbell maintained this position for an hour and a half, exposed to a heavy fire of grape, musketry, and canister. The failure of the attack of the fourth column was fatal to a longer maintenance of that position. The Láhor gate being in the hands of the rebels, he was liable to be cut off. He fell back, then, in a soldierly manner, on the Begam Bágh, resolved to hold it till he could communicate with headquarters. An hour and a half later, however, learning that the fourth column had failed, and that the first and second had been unable to advance beyond the Kábul gate, he fell back on the church, and disposed his men for the night in it and in the houses in the vicinity.

Scott's field-battery which had entered the city by the Kashmír gate, had during all this time rendered splendid service to the several columns, but at a large expenditure of life.

Meanwhile, the failure of the fourth column had become known to the English leaders outside the city, and Wilson had directed Hope Grant to move down, with 200 of the 9th Lancers and 400 Sikh cavalry, to cover the Sabzímandí defences and Hindu Ráo's house, laid open to attack. At the same time Tombs's battery, under Grant's order, opened fire on the advancing rebels. Insofar as related to the checking of the rebels' advance these measures were successful, but Tombs's fire provoked a reply from the heavy guns on the Burn bastion, and this fire, at a distance of 500 yards, made terrible openings in the ranks of the cavalry. Six officers and forty-two men were struck down. Rosser of the Carabineers fell with a bullet through his forehead: Nine officers of the Lancers had their horses shot under them. But for two long hours they stood to receive fire. They felt that by drawing upon themselves the attention of the rebels they were serving the common cause. In vain did the battery of the gallant Bourchier come up to aid them with its fire. The blazing from the Burn bastion still continued. Nor did they move until information came that the stormers had established their positions for the night. They then fell back on Ludlow Castle, conscious that they had not only prevented the disastrous results which the defeat of the fourth column might have entailed, but that they had occupied the rebels' attention with very considerable advantage to the main operations. The reserve column, meanwhile, led by Longfield, had followed the third column through the Kashmír gate, and cleared the college gardens. One portion of the column had occupied those gardens, the other held the Water bastion, the Kashmír gate, Skinner's house, and another large building.

Thus ended the first day's operations. The result may thus be briefly **summarised.** The entire space inside the city, from the Water bastion to the Kábul gate, was held by the first, second, third, and fifth columns. The fourth column, outside the city, held the batteries behind Hindu Ráo's house. It was clear, then, that within the city a solid base had been obtained for further development. But the cost had been enormous. In the day's fight the assailants had lost sixty-six officers and 1,104 men in killed and wounded. Four out of the five assaulting columns were within the walls, but the position they held was extended, and their right flank was very open to attack. The rebels were still strong in numbers, in guns, and in position. They, too, had had success as well as reverses, and they had no need to abandon hope of ultimate victory.

To the British general the result of the day's work was discouraging. The plan which had been so urgently pressed upon him had failed to secure success; his columns had been stopped and driven back; instead of the whole city, his troops held simply a short line of rampart. Very doubtful as to whether it was not his duty to withdraw to the ridge, he asked Baird-Smith if he thought he could hold what had been taken. The reply of Baird-Smith was decisive: 'We must do so.' Neville Chamberlain also wrote in the same sense to the General. The opinions of these two strong men sufficed to decide Wilson.

The 15th was employed by the troops within the city in securing the positions gained, in preparing the means to shell the city, in the restoration of order, and in putting a stop to indiscriminate drinking and plundering. The rebels, strange to say, interfered but slightly with this programme. The result showed how thoroughly Baird-Smith and Chamberlain had mastered the nature of Asiatics. The stationary position of the British cowed them. A retreat would have roused them to energetic action.

The 16th gave further evidence of the marked effect on their spirits of the British lodgment. In the early morning of that day they evacuated Kishanganj, whence, on the 14th, they had repulsed the fourth column. The British then stormed the great magazine, the scene of the heroic action of Willoughby and his comrades on the 11th of May. It was found to be full of guns, howitzers, and ammunition. Vainly did the rebels, during the afternoon, make a desperate attempt to recover it. They were repulsed with loss.

If the progress made was, in the desponding language of General Wilson, 'dreadfully slow work,' it was sure. Bit by bit the important positions in the city were wrested from the rebels. On the 17th and 18th the bank, Major Abbott's house, and the house of Khán Muhammad Khan, were occupied, and the besiegers' posts were brought close to the Chandni Chauk and the palace. On the evening of the 18th the position occupied by the besiegers was as follows: Their front was marked by the line of the canal, on the banks of which light guns were posted at the main junction of the streets, and sandbag batteries erected. The right and left, indicated respectively by the Kábul gate and the magazine, communicated by a line of posts. The rear was secure against attack. It had been attempted, during that day to extend the right, in the manner contemplated by the gallant Nicholson, to the Láhor gate, but the attack, directed by Greathed of the 8th, had failed.

It had become absolutely necessary to take that gate, now twice attempted. The Burn bastion, which commanded it, was no longer supported, as on the 14th, by rebels in Kishanganj and Tálíwárí. The General then authorised Alexander Taylor of the Engineers to work his way, on the morning of the 19th, to the Burn bastion. Whilst Taylor, with a party of men, was engaged in this somewhat slow process, Brigadier William Jones held himself in readiness to proceed, with 500 men from the 8th, 75th, and Sikh regiments, to attack the Láhor gate. This time success crowned the joint efforts. Taylor worked his way through the buildings to the summit of a house commanding the bastion. Then Jones advanced, and finding it abandoned, took up his post there for the night. Early the following morning he launched his troops from it, and carried the Láhor gate with a rush, then the Garstin bastion. After that success, dividing his force, he detached one portion up the Chandni Chauk to capture the Jamí Masjíd, the other to gain the Ajmír gate. Major Brind arrived opportunely with reinforcements to command in the carrying out of the first of these operations. He entered the mosque without difficulty. Simultaneously Jones occupied the Ajmír gate.

Brind, when he had carried the Jamí Masjíd, had noticed, with the eye of a true soldier, that the one thing wanting to assure complete success was to storm the palace at once. He sent for and obtained permission to attempt it. His success was complete. The famous fort-palace of Sháh Jahán was not even defended. The gates were blown in, and British troops entered. The Salímgarh had been previously seized by the brilliant forethought of a young lieutenant named Aikman. The same afternoon Wilson took up his quarters in the Imperial palace.

Dehlí was now virtually won. But there still remained in the vicinity, even in the city itself, thousands of armed rebels, ready to take advantage of the slightest slackness on the part of the victors. So large had been the casualties that Wilson had fit for service but little over 3,000 men. From these the guards of the several posts had to be provided. The King of Dehlí was still at large, a rallying point to the disaffected. It seemed to the General essential that a determined effort should be made to capture his person.

The King and his principal advisers had been painfully affected by the success which had depressed General Wilson. The lodgment effected at so much cost, on the 14th, which had caused Wilson to doubt the advisability of proceeding further, had produced in the mind of the King and his surroundings the conviction that, unless the British should retire, the game of the revolters was up. Fortunately he had no Baird-Smith at his elbow to whisper to him how the small hours of the night might be advantageously employed. And although he felt that as long as the Láhor gate, the magazine, and the fort should hold out there was still hope, yet the success of the British on the 14th, partial though it was, had taken all the fight out of the rebels. The men who, whilst the British were on the ridge, had been so daring in sortie, so unremitting in attack, had been completely demoralised by the display made by the British on the 14th. The reader will notice how lacking in force and energy were the blows they struck after the British troops had displayed their enormous superiority in hand-to-hand fighting on that day. The fact that the lodgment effected on the ramparts on the first day of the assault had cowed them, accounts for the remarkable ease with which the British were able to push forward on the 15th, 16th, 17th, 18th, and 19th.

When at last, on the 19th, the Burn bastion had been captured, the Commander-in-Chief, the old artillery Subahdár, Bakht Khán, represented to the King that his only way of safety lay in flight; he begged him to accompany the sipáhí army, which still remained intact, and with it to renew the war in the open country. That was the course which the descendant of Bábar, had he been young, would have undoubtedly followed. But the King was old—other influences were at work—and the King was persuaded to reject the bold counsels of his general and to accept those of his Queen and courtiers. He allowed the sipáhí army to depart, whilst he took refuge at the tomb of Humáyún, three miles and a half south from the city, prepared to submit to the conqueror.

Information of this retreat was conveyed to an officer who throughout the siege had made himself conspicuous for his love of adventure and daring, Hodson, of Hodson's Horse. Hodson asked and obtained the General's permission to bring in the old man, on the condition that his life should be spared. Hodson performed his task with tact and discretion. That night, the 20th, the King slept a prisoner in the Begam's palace.

But there were still his sons, the princes, to whom rumour had ascribed an active participation in all the bloody deeds which had characterised the early days of the rebellion. Hodson learned the day following that two of these, and a grandson, lay concealed in Humáyún's tomb, or in the vicinity. Again did he ask and obtain permission to bring them in. This time there was no stipulation for their lives. Hodson rode out with a hundred armed troopers, found them, persuaded them to surrender, disarmed their numerous following, placed the arms on carts, the princes on a native akka (or gig), and led the long cavalcade in the direction of the Láhor gate. They had safely accomplished five-sixths of the journey to that gate when Hodson, on the pretext that the unarmed[5] crowd was pressing too closely on his troopers, halted the carts, made the three princes descend, stripped them, and shot them with his own hand. It was a most unnecessary act of bloodshed, for it would have been as easy to bring in the princes as it had been easy to bring in the King.

Whilst these events were occurring outside the walls, Wilson had, commissioned Brind to clear the city of the murderers and incendiaries who, to the number of many thousands, still lurked within it. Brind accomplished this task with the completeness which was necessary.

On the 21st the restoration of regular rule was announced in the appointment of Colonel Burn to be Governor of the city. The day following John Nicholson died from the effects of the wounds he had received on the 14th. He had lingered in agony for eight days; but, as fortunate as Wolfe, he had lived long enough to witness the complete success of the plans to the attempting and accomplishing of which he had so much contributed. He died with the reputation of being the most successful administrator, the greatest soldier, and the most perfect master of men in India. The reputation was, I believe, deserved. He was of the age which a great master, whom in face he resembled, the late Lord Beaconsfield, has called 'that fatal thirty-seven.'[6]

'In the history of sieges,' I wrote in a work published at the time,[7] and which correctly recorded all the impressions of the hour, 'that of Dehlí will ever take a prominent place. Its strength, its resources, and the prestige

---

[5] The crowd had been disarmed at the tomb. Hodson was not the man to allow armed men to collect with impunity.

[6] Arguing that 'genius, when young, is divine,' the author of *Coningsby* proceeds to illustrate his argument by quoting the names of Alexander the Great, Don John of Austria, Gaston de Foix, Condé, Gustavus Adolphus, Duke Bernhard of Weimar, Banner, Cortez, Maurice of Saxony, Nelson, Clive, John de Medici, Luther, Ignatius Loyala, John Wesley, and Pascal. 'Pascal,' he continues, 'wrote a great work at sixteen, and died at thirty-seven.' Then, 'Ah! that fatal thirty-seven, which reminds me of Byron.' He shows, further, how Raphael died at thirty-seven, and, still supporting his argument that 'genius, when young, is divine,' brings forward the names of Richelieu, Bolingbroke, Pitt, Grotius, and Acquaviva. To this long list Nicholson, the greatest by far of all the Panjáb school, might most properly be added.

[7] *The Red Pamphlet*, published in 1857.

attached to it in the native mind, combined to render formidable that citadel of Hindustán. Reasonably might the *Northern Bee* or the *Invalide Russe* question our ability to suppress this rebellion if they drew their conclusions from the numerical strength of the little band that first sat down before Dehlí. But the spirit that animated that handful of soldiers was not simply the emulative bravery of the military proletarian. The cries of helpless women and children, ruthlessly butchered, had gone home to the heart of every individual soldier, and made this cause his own. There was not an Englishman in those ranks, from first to last, who would have consented to turn his back on Dehlí without having assisted in meting out to those bloody rebels the retributive justice awarded them by his own conscience, his country, and his God. It was this spirit that buoyed them up through all the hardships of the siege; that enabled them, for four long months of dreary rain and deadly heat, to face disease, privation, and death without a murmur.'

The siege was indeed calculated to bring out all the great qualities which distinguish the British soldier. Vying with him, alike in his endurance of hardships, his contempt of death, his eagerness for enterprise, were the Gurkhás of the Himaláyas, the frontier men of the Guides, the hardy Balúchís, the daring Sikhs, the resolute Patháns. Nor will English-speaking races soon forget the names of those gallant officers who contributed so much to the success of the undertaking. There were many besides those I am now mentioning. But a careful and impartial examination of correspondence, public and private, has especially brought before me, amongst the most deserving, the names of Baird-Smith, of Nicholson, of Barnard, of Neville Chamberlain, of Charles Reid, of James Brind, of Frederick Roberts, of Hope Grant, of John Jones, of Edwin Johnson, of Alec Taylor, of Tait, of Lockhart, of Turnbull, of Seaton, of Hodson, of Dighton Probyn, of Daly, of Tombs, of Renny, of Jacob, of John Coke, of Speke, of Greville, of Watson, of Medley, of James Hills, of Quintin Battye, of Rosser, of Aikman, of Salkeld, of Home. There are many others, for the list is a long one.

These men have now broken the back of the rebellion. We shall see them display equal energy in the task which supervenes on the morrow of victory—the following of it up.

CHAPTER XX

From Dehlí to Agra and Kánhpur— Sir Colin Campbell at Kánhpur

No sooner had the capture of Dehlí been thoroughly assured than Wilson despatched a corps of 2,790 men, under the command of Colonel Edward Greathed of the 8th foot, to open the country between Dehlí and Agra, and to join Sir Colin Campbell at Kánhpur or its vicinity.

Greathed set out on the morning of the 24th of September, crossed the Hindan, and marched, by way of Dadri and Sikandarábád, on Bulandshahr, punishing on his way the inhabitants proved to have committed atrocities, reassuring those who had remained loyal. He arrived before Bulandshahr on the 28th, attacked and completely defeated a rebel force which attempted to cover that town, then pushing on, occupied it and Málagarh. In destroying the fortifications of the latter he had the misfortune to lose, by an accident, Lieutenant Home of the Engineers, one of the survivors of the gallant men who had blown up the Kashmír gate on the 14th. Thence, still pushing on, Greathed reached Khúrjá, a considerable town. Here the passions of the troops were roused to extreme fury by the sight of the skeleton, pronounced by the medical officers to be the skeleton of a European female, stuck up on the roadside exposed to public gaze, the head severed from the body. They were for taking instant vengeance on the inhabitants. But, in deference to the remonstrances of the civil officer accompanying the force, who represented the impolicy of destroying a place of considerable importance, and which paid a large revenue to the State, Greathed spared Khúrjá,

From Khúrjá Greathed marched on Álígarh, defeated there a body of the rebels who had so long dominated the district, and marching in the direction of Agra, reached Bijaigarh on the 9th of October. There he received the most pressing solicitations from the authorities at Agra to hasten to their relief. A formidable body of rebels, he was told, was threatening the sandstone fort, 'and his credit would be at stake if Agra were attacked and he so near.' Greathed was but forty-eight miles from Agra. He accordingly despatched that night the cavalry and horse-artillery, with instructions to hurry on by forced marches. Four hours later he followed with the infantry, mounting his men on elephants, carts, and camels to get over the ground the more quickly. Whilst he is thus hurrying on I propose to ask the reader to take a bird's-eye glance at Agra.

Of the condition of Agra after the defeat of Polwhele and the death of Mr Colvin I have written in a previous chapter.[1] Ever since that time, whilst the life within the fort had been dull and monotonous, the country around had been occupied and reoccupied by roving bands of rebels. The mutineers from Máu and other parts of Central India, though detained for a time at Gwáliár, thanks to the loyalty of Máhárájá Sindhiá, had broken loose from his hold early in September, and marched on to Dholpur. Thence they had gradually spread detachments over the districts of Khairágarh, Fathpur-Síkrí, Irádatnagar, and Fathábád. The news of the doubtful success, as it seemed, of the British in the storming of Dehlí, on the 14th, had not discouraged them. The success of the British on the following days had even had the effect of releasing from Dehlí a considerable body of men who hoped to renew their tactics elsewhere. A number of these had reached Mathurá, on the 26th, and joined there by a large body of mutinied sipáhís, effected a day or two later a junction with the rebels from Central India. These were the men whose threatening attitude was now causing consternation in Agra, though so indifferently was the Intelligence department managed that no one within the fort knew exactly where they were.

Meanwhile, Greathed, pushing on with speed, crossed the bridge of boats under the walls of the fort at sunrise on the morning of the 10th. Inquiring as to the position of the rebels, he was told by the authorities within the fort that 'the insurgent force from Dholpur was beyond the Kárí Nadí, ten miles from cantonments, across which they would find difficulty in passing.'[2] The same authorities wished Greathed to encamp in a 'series of gardens overgrown by brushwood, where their guns would not have had a range of fifty yards, and where the cavalry could not possibly act.'[3] But Greathed was too good a soldier to accede to such a proposition. He insisted on encamping on the parade ground, a magnificent grassy plain, with not an obstacle within three or four hundred yards of it, and at that distance only some high crops. There the camp was pitched, the

---

[1] Chapter xvii., page 252.

[2] Major Norman, who adds: 'This information was given in positive terms.'

[3] Bourchier's *Eight Months' Campaign,* a book which everyone should read.

horses were picketed, and the men proceeded to divest themselves of their accoutrements, preparatory to taking their well-earned breakfasts. Between the camp and the fort a lively communication was opened, and conscious of security, the authorities took few if any precautions regarding the characters they admitted.

But the rebels, instead of being, as the Agra authorities believed, 'beyond the Kárí Nádí, ten miles from cantonments,' were in the cantonment itself, hidden from the sight of the troops by the long crops which bounded the view of Greathed's force. Taking advantage of the security into which the men of that force had been lulled, and of the facilities permitted to strangers of every degree to go in and out of the camp, four of them, dressed as conjurors, came strolling up to the advanced guard of the 9th Lancers. The sergeant in charge of the post ordered them off, whereupon one of them drew his *talwár* and cut him down, and another who rushed to his rescue. Eventually these four men were despatched by the troopers, but before the occurrence had become known to everyone in the camp round-shot, from the leafy screen in its front, came pouring in. The alarm sounded, but there was scarcely need for it. The soldiers of Dehlí, accustomed to sudden attacks, turned out with all possible speed. But though they used every despatch,[4] before they were ready, the rebel cavalry, springing from no one knew where, appeared as if by magic on the scene. They had charged the still motionless artillery, and had sabred the gunners of one gun, when a squadron of the 9th Lancers, which had formed up very rapidly, dashed on them and drove them back in disorder. The charge cost the squadron dear, for French, who led it, was killed; Jones, his subaltern, was dangerously wounded, and several men were killed or wounded. But it gave the respite that was wanted, and allowed Greathed, who had hurried from the fort, to deploy his line and to despatch Watson, with a portion of his cavalry, to turn the left flank of the rebels, whilst he should advance from the centre. He was joined, as he advanced, by a battery of artillery, which Pearson had manned, experimentally, with men of Eurasian extraction, and which on this occasion rendered excellent service. The prompt advance of the force, the celerity with which it had been transformed from a heterogeneous mass of individuals sleeping or lounging into a living machine, upset the calculations of the rebels, and the British cavalry, gallantly led by Ouvry, Probyn, Watson, and the guns, splendidly managed by Bourchier, Turner, and Pearson, completed the confusion which this celerity had produced.

---

[4] For a lifelike description of this surprise, and the events connected with it, everyone should read Bourchier's *Eight Months' Campaign*.

They fell back in disorder, pursued in front by the infantry, which had been joined by the 3rd Europeans from the fort—under Colonel Cotton, who, by virtue of his seniority to Greathed, took the command—and on the flanks by the cavalry and artillery. The infantry followed them as far as their camp, which was found standing midway between Agrá and the Kárí Nadí, and there halted, dead tired; but the pursuit was continued as far as that stream by the two other arms. Only once did the rebels attempt to make a stand, but then a few rounds of grape sent them flying. They were unable to carry a single gun across the stream. For seven miles the road was one continued line of carts, guns, ammunition waggons, camels, and baggage of every description. The whole of this fell into the hands of the victors. Much that was useless they destroyed; but they brought back into camp thirteen pieces of ordnance and vast quantities of ammunition. No victory could have been more rapid or decisive. It was a splendid performance, especially if one takes into consideration the circumstances under which the battle was engaged. Bourchier's nine-pounder battery had marched thirty miles without a halt before the action began. From first to last Greathed's cavalry and artillery had marched over sixty-four miles, the infantry fifty-four, in less than thirty-six hours, to be then surprised in camp, to beat off the surprisers, and to follow them up ten miles. It was a great performance—well marched, well fought, and well followed up. The force did not return to its encamping ground till seven o'clock in the evening.

The victory secured the restoration round Agra of law and order. The return of law and order, again, was illustrated by a change in the command, contrived and carried out in a very mysterious manner. Greathed had not given satisfaction either to the Agra authorities or to the representative of a very powerful military clique in his camp. Under their joint influence the Secretary to the Agra Government wrote to Dehlí to request that Hope Grant of the 9th Lancers might be sent down to assume command. Hope Grant was sent, and travelling rapidly, joined the column at Firuzábád, the third march from Agra on the Kánhpur road, and with it reached Kánhpur on the 26th October. At Kánhpur Grant found that Sir Colin Campbell had made arrangements to increase the column to the divisional strength of about 5,000 men. On the 30th Hope Grant crossed the Ganges into Oudh, and in consequence of orders received from Sir Colin, encamped his force in a plain beyond the Banní bridge, within a few miles of the Alambágh, to await there further instructions.

Whilst Hope Grant was marching into Oudh, other columns, despatched from Dehlí, were doing excellent work in the districts contiguous to that city. In all of these the authority of the Mughal had been recognised, and sharp actions were requistite to prove to the revolted populations that the power of that family had ceased for ever. Whilst Van Cortlandt, an excellent officer, with native levies, cleared the ground to the north-west of the city, Showers, with a mixed column, marched to the west and south-west, forced the chief of Ballabgarh to submit, and took in succession Ríwárí, Jajhar, and Kanáurí. He returned to Dehlí, on the 19th of October, with three rebel chiefs as prisoners, and much booty, specie of the value of £80,000, seventy guns, and a large quantity of ammunition.

Scarcely had Showers returned when the mutinied troops of the Jodhpur legion, fresh from a victory over the soldiers of the loyal Rájá of Jaipur, invaded the territories he had but just overrun, and occupied Ríwárí. Against them Gerrard, an officer of conspicuous merit, was despatched with a strong column.[5] Gerrard, marching from Dehlí, the 10th of November, reoccupied Ríwárí on the 13th, and pushed on to Narnúl, which the rebels had occupied in considerable force. So strong, indeed, was their position there that, had they had the patience to await attack, Gerrard would have found that all his work had been cut out for him. But, either from sheer incapacity or from utter recklessness, no sooner had it been reported to him that the British were in sight than the rebel leader advanced to meet him in the plain. The cavalry fight which followed was most desperately contested; the Guides, led by Kennedy, and the Carabineers by Wardlaw, fighting splendidly against considerable odds. The rebels, too, fought well, but eventually they gave way. On the left the Multání horse, new levies, had at first displayed considerable reluctance to join in the fray. Roused at length by the example of their officers, and by the success achieved by the Carabineers and the Guides, they joined in the combat, and took their proper place in the front. Meanwhile, the infantry and the artillery had been following up the advantage gained by the defeat of the rebel horse. The enemy was now in full flight. At this crisis Gerrard, riding in front, conspicuous on his white Arab charger, was mortally wounded by a mus-ketball. In the momentary confusion which followed, the rebels, rallying, made a despera e effort to restore the fortunes of the day. In vain, however. The Fusiliers charged and drove them into flight, and completed their expulsion from the fort of Narnúl. Caulfield, who had succeeded to the command, followed up his advantage. He, however, a few days later, was relieved by Seaton, and, under orders from headquarters, that officer led

---

[5] The 1st Fusiliers, the 7th Panjáb Infantry, Cookworthy's troop of horse-artillery, Gillespie's heavy battery, the Carabineers, the cavalry of the Guides, the Multání horse.

back the force to Dehlí, preparatory to taking part in the measures which Sir Colin Campbell was devising for the recovery of Oudh, Fathgarh, and Rohilkhand.

Sir Colin Campbell had arrived in Calcutta on the 13th of August. Already at that period, although Dehlí had not fallen, the position for an advance from Kánhpur, though far from perfect, had, thanks to the splendid efforts of Neill, Frederick Gubbins, William Taylor, Vincent Eyre, Havelock, and Outram, materially improved. There was, however, still much to be accomplished. The line of 600 miles, the security of which had been prominently put forward by Mr Secretary Beadon in the early days of the Mutiny, was not only insecure, but was being daily broken. The evil had been intensified for a time by the refusal of the Government to disarm the native regiments at Dánápur, and by the consequences of that refusal. Then, too, the division of Chutiá Nagpur, a mountainous territory lying between Southern Bihár, Western Bengal, Orísá, and the Central Provinces was surging with revolters, and these were constantly traversing the grand trunk road, impeding communications, and rendering travelling dangerous. However, none of these difficulties daunted Sir Colin. His aim was to despatch troops, and to proceed himself, to Kánhpur, thence to march to relieve Outram and Havelock. Under the pressure of his requisitions the Government organised a bullock-train for the despatch of troops to Allahábád, whilst he sent out strong parties to patrol the road. The opportune arrival of the British troops intended for China, but which the patriotism of Lord Elgin had placed at the disposal of the Government of India, enabled Sir Colin to utilise the means thus prepared for their despatch. Then the *Shannon* and the *Pearl* arrived, and Captain William Peel, of glorious memory, proceeded to organise his famous brigade from the crew of the former, whilst Captain Sotheby did the same from the crew of the *Pearl*. Troops arrived from England in October. On the 27th of that month Sir Colin, having completed all his arrangements for the prompt despatch of regiments as they might arrive, set out for Allahábád. Narrowly escaping capture on his way from a body of rebels who had broken the famous line, he arrived there the evening of the 1st of November.

He found matters in good progress. The Naval brigade had left Allahábád for Kánhpur in two detachments, on the 23rd and 28th October. The 53rd and drafts for other regiments had accompanied the second detachment, the whole commanded by Colonel Powell of the 53rd. Sir Colin, having organised a party, under Longden of the 10th, for the clearing of the Ázamgarh district, set out for Kánhpur on the 2nd, and arrived there on the 3rd. He found the position there, in a military point of view, dangerous. Oudh was still teeming with rebels, whilst to the south-west of him, within a distance of forty-five miles, the trained soldiers of the Gwáliár contingent were threatening his communications. The road which he had but just traversed, between Allahábád and Kánhpur, was liable to invasion from Oudh, and was far from safe. Only two days before he had proceeded along it Powell and Peel had a very sharp encounter with the rebels at Kajwá, twenty-four miles from Fathpur, in which, though it terminated in a victory, Powell had been killed, and ninety-five men killed and wounded. The problem Sir Colin had to consider was whether, with the road communicating with Allahábád liable to invasion, and his left rear seriously threatened, he could venture to engage in an operation which would occupy many days, and the duration of which any untoward accident might prolong. The rebels were well served by spies, and Sir Colin well knew the opportunities which his invasion of Oudh with the bulk of his force would open to men possessing soldierly instincts. In war, however, it is always necessary to risk something. The rescue of the garrison of the Residency seemed to Sir Colin's mind the most pressing necessity. He resolved, then, to attempt it with as little delay as possible.

We have seen how he had ordered Hope Grant, with a portion of the Dehlí force, to await further instructions in the plain beyond the Banní bridge. There he formed the *poiet d'appui* of the invading army, upon which all carts and supplies were to concentrate. Thither, too, he had despatched all his available troops. Arranging to leave behind him at Kánhpur about 500 European troops, under Windham of Crimean fame, and some Sikhs, and giving authority to Windham to detain a brigade of Madras sipáhís, under Carthew, expected the next day, Sir Colin and his staff quitted Kánhpur on the 9th, and joined Hope Grant beyond the Banní bridge the same afternoon.

CHAPTER XXI

The Second Relief of the Lakhnao Residency—Windham and the Gwáliár Contingent

Before describing the proceedings of Sir Colin Campbell and his force it will be well to cast a glance at the occupants of the Residency, increased in numbers since the 25th of September by the arrival of the troops so gallantly led by Outram and Havelock.

These troops had, as I have said, scarcely entered the defences when it was universally realised that their advent had constituted not a relief but a reinforcement; that means of transport for the ladies and children, the sick and wounded, were wanting; that an enormous addition had been made to the hospital list; and that, even had transport been available, the combined force was not strong enough to escort them to Kánhpur. Compelled thus, perforce, to remain, Outram devoted all his endeavours to the providing of accommodation for the increased force. With this view he caused to be occupied the palaces along the line of river, the Táráwálá Kothí, the Chatar Manzil, and the Farhatbakhsh. These he consigned to the newly arrived troops, under the command of Havelock, whilst the old troops continued to occupy their former posts. The care of the important post of the Álambágh he consigned to Major McIntyre of the 78th, with 250 men fit for duty, and others who, although sick at the time, speedily became convalescent. The orders to McIntyre were to hold the place as long as he could, and only in case of absolute necessity to fall back upon Kánhpur.

The six weeks that followed have not incorrectly been termed a blockade. No longer did the rebels make those desperate assaults from posts which dominated the defences. The attacks rather came now from the defenders. They came in the shape of sorties, of countermining, of extending their borders. To write a history of the sorties would require a volume. It must suffice here to state that they were frequent and successful. It is true that an attempt made on the 3rd of October, and one or two following days, to open communications with the Álambágh, by way of the intermediate houses, was relinquished. But even this attempt resulted in a certain advantage to the garrison. Boring through a number of houses, they seized a large mosque just beyond them, and made of it a permanent outpost. This was held successfully, and with great advantage, until Sir Colin arrived. By these and similar means the limits of the British position became gradually extended. Extension meant relief to the old garrison from all molestation on its east, north-east, and south-east faces; that is, from the Kánhpur road to the commencement of the river front. Meanwhile, the defences of the original Residency were repaired, and new batteries were constructed. No longer was heard that incessant musketry fire from a distance not exceeding the width of the Strand. From the posts occupied in a vicinity so close the rebels had been driven so far that their musketry fire could no longer effect mischief within the entrenchment. But they did not even then feel baffled. Withdrawing to a convenient distance, they so planted their guns that the balls might be sure to clear the outer defences and lodge within the entrenchment. To annoy still further the garrison they constantly shifted their point of fire. They knew not, apparently, the deadly result to the garrison of this mode of attack, for they displayed no continuity in the working of it.

On the 9th of October the garrison was cheered by the news of the complete success obtained at Dehlí, and of the successful march of Greathed's column as far as Bulandshahr. Then it was that, realising that Sir Colin Campbell's march to his relief had now become a question of three or four weeks, Outram set to work to devise a plan to communicate with him as he should approach. Already he had forwarded to the Álambágh a despatch for Sir Colin, containing plans of the city and the approaches to it, and his own idea as to the best mode of effecting a junction. But though written despatches might tell much, something more, something in the shape of personal communication with Sir Colin, by an intelligent man who knew every point of the position of the blockaded garrison, seemed to Outram to be almost essential. But how to secure to Sir Colin such personal communication? It could be accomplished only by one of the garrison, and by that one having recourse to disguise. But for a European to disguise himself, and to attempt to penetrate in that disguise the hostile masses which surrounded the blockaded position, which guarded every avenue, and carefully watched every approach, was apparently to court certain and ignominious death. No one could be asked to incur such a risk. Indeed, it would have required, on the part of Outram, a conviction that the chances of success were at least equal to those of failure to allow him to accept the offer of a volunteer.

The anxiety of Outram for some such personal communication was greater when he learned that Sir Colin was on the point of joining the force between the Álambágh and the Banní bridge, and there can be no doubt that his anxiety on this head became generally known. Amongst others it reached the ears of one Thomas Henry Kavanagh, a clerk in one of the civil offices. Kavanagh at once communicated to Outram his readiness to assume the *rôle*. To all appearance there were few men less qualified than Kavanagh to escape detection. For he was a fair man, much taller than the general run of the natives of Oudh, and his red hair glittered like gold. On the other hand, he possessed a courage that nothing could daunt, a perfect knowledge of the native *patois*, and a will of iron. No one loved a brave man more than Outram. The offer made by Kavanagh was an offer after his own heart. But, humane beyond the ordinary run of men, he hesitated to expose a fellow-creature to almost certain death. Whatever doubts he may have entertained on this head were, however, dissipated after his first interview with Kavanagh. In him he recognised a man whose innate pluck and iron resolution would carry him through all dangers. He accepted, therefore, his offer, and bade him prepare for his enterprise.

Kavanagh then had his hair and his skin stained with lamp-black; the hair he also cut short. Then, donning the dress of a *Badmásh*—a native 'swashbuckler,' a type very common in those days—he set out, on the evening of the 9th of November, accompanied by a native spy of proved fidelity, Kanáují Lál by name.

Mr Kavanagh subsequently published an account[1] of his journey, which may yet be read with deep interest. It was not without its alarms. He did not reach the Álam-bágh that night, but, on the morning of the 10th, he fell in with a party of the Panjáb cavalry, and this party conducted him to Sir Colin, who, as we have seen, had reached the plain beyond Banní bridge the previous evening.[1]

Sir Colin Campbell had, on his arrival, despatched Adrian Hope of the 93rd, with a large convoy of provisions, to the Álambágh. The sick and wounded he had despatched in carts to Kánhpur. On the 10th he halted to confer with Kavanagh, and to complete his arrangements. On the 11th his engineer park arrived, and he issued orders for an advance the following day. At sunrise on the 12th the troops marched. Sir Colin's plan,

---

[1] *How I Won the Victoria Cross*, Ward & Lock. After a somewhat chequered career, Kavanagh died in St Thomas's Hospital in 1883.

based mainly on that which Outram had sent him, was to move on the Álambágh, to store there all the *impedimenta*; then, drawing to himself the detachments still in the rear, to make, with a wide sweep, a flank march to the right on the Dilkushá park and the Martiniére; then to force the canal close to its junction with the Gúmtí; then, covered by that river, to advance on the Sikandarábágh. This point once secured, he would detach a portion of the force to seize the barracks to the north of Hazratganj, and plant there batteries to play on the Kaisarbágh. During that time he would move, with the main body, on the Sháh Najaf and Motí Mahall, and forcing these, would effect a junction with Outram. That officer would support this operation by opening a heavy fire on all the intermediate positions held by the rebels. Forcing these, he would then move out, with all his sick and wounded, women and children, and effect a junction with Sir Colin.

The first day's march had the object of placing the force solidly in communication with the Álambágh, the garrison of which, still commanded by the gallant McIntyre, had been gradually increased to 930 Englishmen, a few Sikhs, and eight guns. This having been effected at the cost of one or two successful skirmishes with the rebels, Sir Colin proceeded to arrange for his decisive advance on the morrow. First, he despatched Hope to seize the fort of Jalálábád, to the right rear of the Álambágh. He then stacked within the Álambágh all the camp equipage not required for the hard work in prospect. His last reinforcements arriving that evening, he placed the 75th, which had suffered much, and the strength of which had been reduced to something under 300, within the Álambágh, to relieve the men till then located there. He gave them, also, a few Sikhs from Brasyer's regiment and some guns. Counting up his men, he found that, after deducting those sent back with sick and wounded and the garrison of the Álambágh, he had fit for service about 4,700 men. These he divided into six brigades. There were the Naval brigade, commanded by William Peel; the Artillery brigade, comprising the batteries of Blunt, Remmington, Travers, Bridge, and Bourchier, commanded by Brigadier Crawford; the Cavalry brigade, led by Brigadier Little, and comprising two squadrons of the 9th Lancers, one each of the 1st, 2nd, and 5th Panjáb Cavalry, and Hodson's Horse; the 3rd Infantry brigade, commanded by Greathed, and composed of the remnant of the 8th, of a battalion formed of detachments of the three regiments shut up in the Residency, and the 2nd Panjáb N. I.; the 4th, led by Adrian Hope, and consisting of the 93rd, a wing of the 53rd, the 4th Panjáb Infantry, and a battalion also formed from men proceeding to join the regiments to be relieved; the 5th, led by Russell, and comprising the 23rd Fusiliers and a portion of the 82nd. Hope Grant, with the rank of Brigadier-General, directed the operations, under the supervision of the Commander-in-Chief.

The following morning the troops, having breakfasted, set out at nine o'clock, and after some skirmishing carried the Dilkushá. Not halting there, they pressed on to the Martinière and carried that also. Sir Colin proceeded to secure the position thus gained by placing in the gardens of the Martinière Hope's brigade and Remmington's troop. Russell he placed on the left, in front of the Dilkushá, whilst he directed Little, with the cavalry, to occupy a line drawn from the canal on his right to a wall of the Dilkushá park on his left. With him he posted likewise Bourchier's battery. Somewhat later in the day, Russell, under his orders, occupied, with some companies, two villages on the canal covering the left of the advance.

But the rebels had no intention to allow the British general to remain in peaceful occupation of his line of attack. No sooner had they realised the exact nature of his dispositions than they massed their troops towards their centre, with the intention of making a grand assault. Little, noticing the gathering, sent an officer, Grant, to reconnoitre. On receiving Grant's report he despatched to the front the gallant Bourchier, supporting him with his cavalry. It was seen that the rebels had lined the opposite bank of the canal, and had only been prevented from making their forward movement by the timely occupation by Russell of the two villages above referred to. Bourchier's guns quickly sent back their skirmishers, and his fire reaching their supporting masses, these in their turn also fell back. A second attempt, made about five o'clock, on the Martinière was baffled by the vigilance of Adrian Hope and the successful practice of Remmington's guns. Here, again, Bourchier's battery and Peel's guns rendered splendid service, literally 'crushing,' by their flank fire, the rebels out of their position.

The troops bivouacked for the night in the places they had gained. The next day, the 15th, was devoted to preparations, though it was not altogether free from desultory skirmishing. In the evening Sir Colin signalled to Outram, by a code previously arranged, that he would advance on the morrow.

Accordingly, early on the morning of the 16th, a strong body of cavalry, with Blunt's horse-artillery and a company of the 53rd, forming the advance guard, marched from the right, crossed the canal, then dry, followed for about a mile the bank of the Gúmtí, then, turning sharply to the

left, reached a road running parallel to the Sikandarábágh. Sir Colin had
so completely deceived the enemy as to his line of advance that this movement, followed though the advance guard was by the main body of the
infantry, was absolutely unopposed, until the advance, making the sharp
turn mentioned, entered the parallel road. Then a tremendous fire from
enclosures near the road, and from the Sikandarábágh, opened on their
flank. Their position was very dangerous, for they were literally broadside
to the enemy's fire. The danger was apparent to every man of the advance.
It served, however, only to quicken the resolve to baffle the rebels. The
first to utilise the impulse was the gallant Blunt. Noticing that there was
a plateau whence he could assail the Sikandarábágh on the further side of
the road, hemmed in by its banks, apparently impossible for artillery to
mount, he turned his horses' faces to the right bank, galloped up it, gained
the open space on the plateau, and, unlimbering, opened his guns on the
Sikandarábágh. It was one of the smartest services ever rendered in war. It
at once changed the position.

For, whilst Blunt was drawing on himself the fire of the rebels by his
daring act, the infantry of Hope's brigade had come up with a rush and
cleared the enclosures bordering the lane and a large building near them.
There remained only the Sikandarábágh itself. Against the massive walls
of this building the light guns of Blunt's battery, and the heavier metal
of those of Travers, who had joined him, were doing their best to effect
a breach. No sooner was this breach believed to be practicable than there
ensued one of the most wonderful scenes witnessed in that war. Suddenly
and simultaneously there dashed towards it the men of the wing of the 93rd
and the Sikhs, running for it at full speed. A Sikh of the 4th Rifles reached
it first, but he was shot dead as he jumped through. A young officer of the
93rd, Richard Cooper by name, was more fortunate. Flying, so to speak,
through the hole, he landed unscathed. He was closely followed by Ewart
of the same regiment, by John I. Lumsden, attached to it as interpreter,
by three privates of the same regiment, and by eight or nine men, Sikhs
and Highlanders. Burroughs of the 93rd had also effected an entrance,
for he was in the enclosure before Ewart, but he was almost immediately
wounded. The enclosure in which these officers and men found themselves
was 150 yards square, with towers at the angles, a square building in the
centre, and was held by 2,000 armed men. It seemed impossible that one
of the assailants should escape alive.

But what will not the sons of this little island do when the occasion
demands it? It must suffice here to say that they rushed forward and

maintained a not unequal contest till reinforcements poured in through the gate. Lumsden was killed, Cooper received a slash across his forehead at the moment that he laid his antagonist dead at his feet. Ewart, attacked by numbers, preserved his splendid presence of mind and slew many. He was still holding his own against enormous odds when the front gate was burst open and reinforcements dashed in. Then the struggle increased in intensity. It was a fight for life or death between the rebels and the masters against whom they had risen. For, it must not be forgotten, the defenders were all sipáhís who had rebelled. Nor did the struggle cease so long as one man of the 2,000 remained alive.

Whilst this bloody scene was being enacted at the Sikandarábágh a detachment of the same brigade had captured the large building known as the Barracks, Captain Stewart of the 93rd greatly distinguishing himself. Then Sir Colin made preparations to storm the Sháh Najaf, a massively built mosque in the direct road to the Residency, situated in a garden surrounded by very strong loopholed walls.

It was at the Sháh Najaf that the rebels had counted to stop the British advance. They almost succeeded. For three hours the front attack made no way. Worse still, the road along which the force had advanced became so jammed that retreat by it was impossible. All this time the troops were exposed to a deadly fire of heavy guns and musketry. From other points, too, heavy guns were brought to play upon the baffled soldiers of England. A shot from one of these blew up one of Peel's tumbrils. The men were falling fast. Even the bright face of William Peel became overclouded. Sir Colin sat on his white horse, exposed to the full fire of the enemy, his gaze bent on the Sháh Najaf, upon whose solid walls not even the heaviest guns could make an impression. As a last resource he collected the 93rd about him, and told them that the Sháh Najaf must be taken, that he had not intended to employ them again that day, but that as the guns could not open a way they must make one. In carrying out this necessary work he would go with them himself.

But neither the dashing gunners of Middleton's battery, the daring of the Highlanders and the Sikhs, the persistent fire of the heavy guns of Peel, could effect the desired end. The Sháh Najaf baffled them all. The shades of evening were falling fast. Success seemed impossible. Then Adrian Hope, collecting about him some fifty men, stole silently and cautiously through the jungle to a portion of the wall on which, before the assault, a sergeant of his regiment had thought he had detected a sign of weakness. On reaching it unperceived, Hope found there a narrow fissure. Up this a single man was with difficulty pushed. He helped up others. More men were sent for. Then those who had entered moved forward. The surprise to the rebels as these men advanced was so thorough that they made no resistance, but evacuated the place. The fight was then over. Adrian Hope's victorious stormers had but to open the main gate to their comrades outside.

The British force halted there for the night. The occupation of the Sháh Najaf had rendered success on the morrow certain. In the capture of that place they had accomplished an action declared by their leader to be 'almost unexampled in war.' The same praise might be given to the wonderful storming of the Sikandarábágh. It is impossible to discriminate narrowly when almost every man was deserving. But it may at least be affirmed that the conduct of Cooper, Ewart, Lumsden, and the privates Dunley, Mackay, and Grant at the Sikandarábágh; of Stewart at the Barracks; of Sergeant Paton, who first pointed out to Adrian Hope the weak point in the wall of the Sháh Najaf; of Adrian Hope himself; of Blunt, who made possible the attack on the Sikandarábágh; of William Peel, of Travers, of Middleton, of Bourchier, of the two Alisons, of Anson, and of many others, for the list is a very long one, gave ample proof that the race which, from the basis of a little island in the Atlantic, had made the greatest empire the world has seen had not degenerated.

The next morning the force, thoroughly refreshed by sleep, advanced to complete its work. To reach the Residency the troops had yet to carry the mess-house and the Motí Mahall, and to do this whilst the guns of rebels posted in the Tárá Kothí and the Kaisarbágh were playing on their left flank. To secure his left, then, Sir Colin detached the 5th Brigade, under Russell, to seize Banks's house and four bungalows close to the Barracks, and to convert them i..to military posts. By this process his left rear would be secured, and his retirement with the *impedimenta* from the Residency made safe. He then proceeded to cannonade the mess-house.

No sooner had the musketry fire of the enemy been completely silenced than the order to storm was given. This feat of arms was most gallantly achieved by Captain Hopkins of the 53rd—one of the bravest men that ever lived, a man who literally revelled in danger—who carried the place with a rush. He had just reached the entrance when Roberts, now the Commander-in-Chief in India, handed him a Union Jack, and requested him to hoist it on one of the turrets. Hopkins, assisted by one of his men, did this twice in succession. Twice was the Jack shot down. Hopkins was about to hoist it the third time when he received an order from Sir Colin to desist. The flag was attracting too earnestly the attention of the enemy. In an equally gallant manner Captain Garnet Wolseley had carried the houses to the right of the mess-house, and pushing on his enterprise, had stormed the Motí Mahall. It was a great feat.

An open space, nearly half a mile in width, still intervened between the assailants and the advanced posts of Outram and Havelock. On this space the fire of the guns from the Kaisarbágh played with unintermitting fury. To cross it was to run a great risk. But in those days risks when an object was to be gained were not considered. Outram, Havelock, Napier,[2] Vincent Eyre, young Havelock, Dodgson, Sitwell, Russell, and Kavanagh attempted it. They did not all pass the ordeal unscathed; Napier, young Havelock, Sitwell, and Russell were struck down. The others reached the Motí Mahall uninjured. Then, to use the language of Sir Colin, 'the relief of the garrison had been accomplished.'

The conversation between the Commander-in-Chief and his visitors was short. When it was finished, again had the visitors to traverse the terrible space. Sir Henry Havelock, leaning on Dodgson, could, from the weak state of his health, walk but slowly, but amid the continuous storm of bullets the two returned unscathed. It was Havelock to whom Outram had consigned the task of working out towards the relieving force so as to give it a hand as soon as the mess-house and Motí Mahall should be carried; and right well had the gallant veteran performed the task allotted to him.

It remained now to Sir Colin to devise a plan for the withdrawal of the women and children. It was no easy task even after he had by his advance made a way for the movement. It seemed to him, at first, absolutely necessary to silence the fire of the Kaisarbágh. The plan he adopted was the following.

I have told how, on the first day of the advance, he had directed Russell to occupy Banks's bungalow and the bungalows adjoining. This had been done. But to complete the communications it was necessary also to seize a building known as the Hospital, between the bungalows and the Barracks, already taken. In attempting to take this Russell was wounded, Biddulph was killed, and Hale, who succeeded, though he took the Hospital, was unable to maintain himself there. Whilst this attack was progressing, the

---

[2] The late Lord Napier of Magdala. Sitwell was A.D.C. to Outram; Russell, a very gallant officer of the Engineers. Dodgson was, and happily is, one of the bravest and most retiring men that ever lived. No one has suffered so much from the innate modesty of his nature. Young Havelock is the present Sir Henry Havelock-Allan.

rebels, gathering heart, attacked the pickets between the Barracks and the Sikandarábágh in considerable force. They were repulsed after some hard fighting, in which Remmington and his troop covered themselves with glory.

The line of retirement by Banks's house proving difficult and dangerous, Sir Colin reconnoitred the ground between the positions actually held by the British and the canal, and finally resolved to move by that. He carried out the operation on the 20th and four following days. Turning the fire of William Peel's heavy guns on the Kaisarbágh, so as to lead the rebels to expect an assault, he moved the women and children from the place in which they had been so long defended, and on the evening of the 22nd had them safely landed in the Dilkushá. Hale, who commanded the rear-guard, joined him there on the 23rd. On the 24th, whilst he was halting, though not resting there, the gallant Havelock passed away. He had indeed fought a good fight, and he had died as he had lived, in the performance of his duty. On the 26th the noblest of his comrades followed his remains to his grave in the Álambágh.

That place had been reached on the 25th. There Sir Colin made a fresh distribution of his force, leaving Outram, with rather less than 4,000 men, at the Álambágh, threatening the still rebellious Lakhnao, whilst he should return to look after Windham at Kánhpur. About that place he was very anxious, for he had no news, and the reports received were to the effect that heavy firing had been heard in that direction. On the 27th, then, at eleven o'clock in the morning, Sir Colin started for Kánhpur. He slept at Banní, and really alarmed, started early the next morning on his forward march towards the Ganges. On his way he received despatches which showed him that the place was in great peril. At Mangalwár he halted his troops, fired three salvoes to announce his approach, and galloped forward, with his staff, in mingled fear and hope as to the state of the bridge of boats. To his joy he saw, by the pale evening light, that it was intact. Vast sheets of flames, arising from burning buildings showed to him as clearly that the rebels must have beaten Windham and occupied Kánhpur. How it had all happened I must tell whilst I leave my readers watching Sir Colin and his staff crossing the bridge, on the late evening of the 28th, to find out the reason, and to remedy the catastrophe.

Windham had been left with about 500 Europeans and a few Sikhs, a number that would be largely augmented, to occupy and improve the entrenchment erected by Havelock on the river, and to watch the movements of the Gwáliár rebels then threatening from Kalpí, fortyfive miles distant. Between the 9th and the 15th Windham received reinforcements in the shape of Carthew's brigade of Madras sipáhís, largely reduced in numbers; and, between that date and the 26th, of drafts from several European regiments, and half a native regiment of Carthew's brigade. Anxious regarding the movements of the Gwáliár rebels, commanded, he believed, by Tantiá Topí, he took up, on the 17th, with his augmented force, a position, at the junction of the Kalpí and Dehlí roads, covering Kánhpur, and whence he could closely watch the movements of the rebels. He occupied that position up to the 20th. He had heard then of the successful capture of the Sikandarábágh and the Sháh Najaf. But, on the 22nd, having in the interval received no further news, he was disquieted by the rumour that the police guard left at the Banní bridge had been surprised and defeated. Sensible of the all-importance that Sir Colin's communications with Kánhpur should be maintained intact, he despatched, on the 23rd, a wing of a sipáhí regiment, with two guns, to re-occupy the bridge at Banní. Had he contented himself with doing that, and with maintaining his watchful position, it is possible that the catastrophe which followed might have been avoided.

But Windham, brave as a lion, was anxious to do something. He accordingly transmitted to Sir Colin a plan he had devised of meeting the advance of the Gwáliár rebels by a system of 'aggressive defence,' by which he might destroy them in detail. Receiving no reply to that proposal, he resolved to carry it out. Early on the 24th, then, he marched six miles down the Kalpí road, and took a position so decidedly threatening to the rebels that, regarding it as a challenge, they took up the glove, and resolved to try to beat Windham at his own game.

Of the action which followed, fought on the 26th, 27th, and 28th, it must suffice to state that, whilst the early advantage lay with Windham, the astute leader opposed to him quickly perceived that the very success of his enemy might, with the numerical superiority he possessed, be used against him. Windham, though he had succeeded, had been compelled, by the nature of the ground, to fall back for the night to a position he considered he could hold until Sir Colin should arrive. It was a weak position, however, and Tantiá Topí saw that it offered many advantages to a superior force which should attack it. Having that superior force, he attacked him then the following morning, and after a contest, in which there were many changes of fortune, and the display of much soldierly ability on the part of Brigadier Carthew, drove Windham back into Kánhpur. Not content with that, he renewed the attack the following day, seized the station of Kánhpur, fired the bungalows, burned the clothing prepared for the relieved garrison of Lakhnao, and the stores for the British army, and forced Windham to take refuge within the entrenchment. This was the position of affairs at Kánhpur when Sir Colin Campbell crossed the Ganges on the evening of the 28th of November.[3]

---

[3] In my larger history (Kaye's and Malleson's *History of the Indian Mutiny*, cabinet edition, vol. iv., pages 159–81) I have given a detailed account of this famous action, of which Cardew was the real hero. I cannot quit the subject of the final relief of the Residency without mentioning the names of those gallant men whose exertions so greatly contributed to its defence before their reinforcement by Havelock and Outram. They were, according to the report of the commander of the garrison, Colonel Inglis, Lieutenant James, of the Commissariat, of whom it was written: 'It is not too much to say that the garrison owe their lives to the exertions and firmness of this officer'; Captain Wilson, the D.A. Adjutant-General, 'ever to be found where shot was flying thickest'; Lieutenants Hardinge, Barwell, and Birch; Mr, now Sir George, Couper; Mr Capper; Mr Martin; Colonel Master; Major Apthorp; Captain Gould Weston; Captains Sanders, Boileau, and Germon; Lieutenants Loughnan, Aitken, Anderson, Graydon, Longmore, and Mr Schilling, commanding posts; Lieutenants Anderson, Hutchinson, and Innes, of the Engineers; Lieutenants Thomas, M'Farlane, and Bonham, of the Artillery, and Captain Evans, employed with that arm; Major Lowe, commanding the 32nd; Captain Bassano; and Lieutenants Lawrence, Edmonstone, Foster, Harmar, Cork, Clery, Brown, and Charlton of that regiment; of other regiments, Captain O'Brien, Kemble, Edgell, Dinning; Lieutenants Sewell, Worsley, Warner, Ward, Graham, Mecham, and Keir. In the Medical Department, Superintending-Surgeon Scott; Surgeons Brydon, Ogilvie, and Campbell; Assistant-Surgeons Fayrer, Bird, Partridge, Greenhow, and Darby; and Apothecary Thompson. In other departments, Captain Carnegie; the Rev. Messrs Harris and Polehampton; Mr M'Crae, Mr Cameron, and Mr Marshall.

CHAPTER XXII

Sir Colin Campbell Recovers the Duáb

As soon as Sir Colin Campbell had mastered the extent of Windham's disaster he recrossed the Ganges to Mangalwár, then pushing forward with his convoy of women and children, well covered by his troops, baffled an attempt of the rebels to destroy the bridge of boats, and re-entered Kánhpur. His convoy he encamped, on November 30, on the further side of the canal, near the mouldering remains and riddled walls of the position Wheeler had held so long, and then turned to look at the position occupied by the rebels.

It was a strong one. Numbering 25,000 men, of whom rather less than one-half were trained sipáhís, they rested their centre on the town, separated from the British force by the Ganges canal, and interspersed with bungalows, high walls, and cover of various kinds. Their right stretched out behind the canal into the plain, and was covered in front by lime-kilns and mounds of brick. Over the canal they had thrown a bridge, but the extreme right flank was uncovered. Their left rested on the Ganges. They were very resolute, and very confident.

Before attacking them Sir Colin spent two days in making preparations for the despatch of his large convoy of women and children, of sick and wounded, to Allahábád. He sent them off on the night of the 3rd, then, waiting until they had placed some miles between themselves and Kánhpur, he carefully examined the rebels' position, and concluded that, strong as it was on the left and in the centre, it might be possible to turn the right and roll them up. He had with him, inclusive of recently arrived troops, about 5,000 infantry, 600 cavalry, and thirty-five guns. The infantry of this force he divided into four brigades. The third, commanded by Greathed, counted the 8th, the 64th, and the 2nd Panjáb Infantry. The fourth, under Adrian Hope, contained the 53rd, the 42nd, the 93rd, and the 4th Panjáb Rifles. The fifth, under Inglis, counted the 23rd, the 32nd, and the 82nd. The sixth, led by Walpole, was formed of the 2nd and 3rd Battalions

Rifle Brigade, and a part of the 38th. The cavalry, commanded by Little, consisted of the 9th Lancers, and details of the 1st, 2nd, and 5th Panjáb Cavalry and Hodson's Horse. The artillery counted Peel's Naval brigade, the troops of Blunt and Remmington, the batteries of Bourchier, of Middleton, of Smith, of Longden, and of Bridge, under the chief command of Dupuis. To Windham was consigned the charge of the entrenchment.

With this force Sir Colin attacked the rebels on the morning of the 6th of December. After an artillery fire, which lasted two hours, he directed Greathed to make a false attack on the centre whilst Walpole, Hope, and Inglis should turn the right. Walpole thereupon crossed the canal, and attracted the fire of the rebels, whilst Adrian Hope, supported by Inglis, took a long sweep to the left, and then, wheeling round, charged the unprotected flanks of the rebels' right. In this movement the 4th Panjáb Rifles and the 53rd covered themselves with glory. They drove the rebels from mound to mound despite a resistance resolute and often fierce. At length they reached the bridge which the rebels had thrown over the canal. This the enemy had well cared for. Upon it they had concentrated so strong an artillery fire that it seemed almost impossible to force the way across. But the gallant men, who had pushed the rebels before them up to that point, were not to be daunted by appearances. They rushed at the bridge with a stern determination to carry it. The rebels seemed equally resolved to prevent them. For a moment the struggle seemed doubtful, when a rumbling sound was heard, and William Peel and his sailors, dragging a heavy twenty-four-pounder, came up with a run, planted the gun on the bridge, and opened fire. The effect was decisive. Whilst it roused the assailants to the highest enthusiasm, it completely cowed the rebels. With loud shouts Highlanders, Sikhs, and 53rd men rushed past the gun, dashed at the rebels, and drove them before them in wild disorder. The Gwáliár camp was now almost within their grasp. But before they could reach it the gallant Bourchier, always in the front, passed them at a gallop, and, unlimbering, opened fire. A few minutes later the assailants repassed the guns, and the Gwáliár camp was their own.

The victory was now gained. The Gwáliár portion of the rebel force made, in wild flight, for the Kalpí road. In that direction they were pursued by Sir Colin in person to the fourteenth milestone. They had lost their camp, their stores, their magazines, a great part of their material, and their prestige.

The remainder of the rebels, composed for the most part of the armed retainers of revolted princes, had fallen back on the Bithor road. The pursuit of these Sir Colin had entrusted to the chief of his staff, General

Mansfield. Mansfield advanced to a position from which he might have forced the surrender of the whole of the rebel force as it passed him. But Mansfield was shortsighted, and he cared not to trust to the sight of others. Consequently, to the intense indignation of his men, he allowed the rebels to defile close to him, unpunished and unpursued, taking with them their guns. What Sir Colin said to the chief of his staff may not be known. But he despatched, on the 9th, a force under Sir Hope Grant to remedy his tremendous mistake. Hope Grant marched in pursuit of them, discovered their line of retreat by the articles which the heavy roads had compelled them to abandon, caught them on the banks of the river just as they were about to escape across it into Oudh, and completely defeated them, taking all their guns. He pushed on further to Bithor, found it evacuated, and, as far as it was possible, destroyed it.

Thus did Sir Colin avenge the defeat sustained by Windham. He was anxious to push on at once to recover the Duáb, but he had to wait a fortnight for the arrival of carriage. It reached him on the 23rd. Meanwhile, learning that Seaton was advancing from Áligarh with a portion of the Dehlí force, he detached Walpole's brigade to occupy Itáwah and Mainpúrí. Seaton, about the same time, defeated the rebels between Gangárí and Kásganj, and had pushed on to Patiálí, where they were reported to be in force. Here he attacked, and inflicted upon them a defeat which crushed the life out of many and the heart out of all. Advancing rapidly towards Mainpúrí, he defeated on the way a rebel Rájá, and by means of a very daring expedition made by Hodson and M'Dowell opened communications with Sir Colin, then with his force at Mirán-kí-sarái (December 30). Four days later Seaton effected a junction with Walpole.

Meanwhile, the necessary carriage having arrived, Sir Colin had marched from Kánhpur, the 24th December. He had reached, we have seen, Mirán-kí-sarái on the 30th. On the 2nd of January he forced a passage across the bridge over the Kálí Nadí, in face of a very strong opposition, and drove the survivors of the rebels into Rohilkhand. The next day he occupied the fort of the rebel Nuwáb of Fathgarh, a man who had almost equalled Náná Sáhib in his cruelties towards Englishmen, and who was now a fugitive. There, the following day, the junction of Walpole and Seaton's divisions raised his force to more than 10,000 men. Sir Colin was anxious now to push on at once to the recovery of Rohilkhand. But Lord Canning, who, now unfettered by the mischievous Calcutta councillors who had misled him, was at Allahábád, strongly insisted, and rightly insisted, that the reconquest of Oudh demanded the earliest consideration. Sir Colin gave way, and made immediately preparations for carrying into effect the determination of the Governor-General. Manœuvring so as to induce in Rohilkhand the belief that he intended to invade that province, he directed Seaton to hold Fathgarh and the Duáb, Walpole to make a demonstration against Rohilkhand, whilst, on the sandy plain between Unáo and Banní in Oudh, he massed infantry, cavalry, engineers, artillery commissariat waggons, and camp followers. By the 23rd of February he had collected there seventeen battalions of infantry, fifteen of which were British; twenty-eight squadrons of cavalry, including four English regiments; fifty-four light and eighty heavy guns and mortars. There we must leave them waiting for the order to advance whilst we examine the events which had occurred in the interval in Eastern Bengal, in Eastern Bihár, and, finally, in the Banáras districts, and in Eastern Oudh. The operations in these latter served as adjuncts to the great movement Sir Colin was contemplating against Lakhnao.

CHAPTER XXIII

Eastern Bengal, Eastern Bihár, Ázamgarh, Allahábád, and Eastern Oudh

When Sir Colin Campbell had started for Allahábád and Kánhpur to carry out, in the North-west Provinces, those great military measures which I have described in the three chapters immediately preceding, he was well aware that he had left behind him many districts smouldering with revolt, others in which rebellion was raising its head, and which would require sharp measures of repression. With these I propose now briefly to deal.

In Eastern Bihár, presided over by a gentleman of marked energy of character, Mr George Yule, there had been, up to the time of the revolt of the native garrison of Dánápur, no outbreak on the part of the two sipáhí regiments located there—one, the 63rd, at Barhámpur, the other, the 32nd, at Bánsí. Some men of the 5th Irregular Cavalry, stationed at Rohní, had indeed made a dastardly attempt to murder their officers, but their commandant, Major Macdonald, had frustrated their attempt, and had displayed an energy and a promptness of action which had completely dominated the restless spirits of the disaffected. Mr Yule, ever watchful, had, with the aid of a small party of Europeans, maintained order in his division. But when Western Bihár, sympathising with the revolted sipáhís of Dánápur, rose he deemed it wise to secure the important posts of Bhágalpur and Mungér, posts necessary to assure the free navigation of the Ganges. These places secured, he could hear with comparative indifference of the rising of the 5th Irregulars, on the 14th of August, more especially as the men of that regiment failed to induce either of the two native regiments in his division to join them. His position, however, was full of peril, for those regiments were not to be depended upon,[1] and he was exposed to

---

[1] Two companies of the 32nd mutinied a fortnight later, and all but captured Sir Colin Campbell as he was journeying up country.

the inroad of mutineers from Chutiá Nágpur on the one side and from Eastern Bengal on the other.

Chutiá Nágpur a mountainous district lying between Southern Bihár, Western Bengal, Orísa, and the Central Provinces, and inhabited by aboriginal tribes, possessed four principal military stations, Hazáríbágh, Ránchí, Chaibásá, and Parúliá. The troops stationed there were a detachment of the 8th N.I. and the local Rámgarh battalion, composed of horse, foot, and artillery. The Commissioner was Captain Dalton, a man of energy and ability.

Regarding this district it is merely necessary to record that its difficulties commenced when the native troops of Dánápur were allowed to rise in revolt. From that time to the very close of the rebellion it remained a festering sore in the heart of the country, the mutineers harassing the neighbouring district, and interrupting communications along the grand trunk road. Major English of the 53rd, despatched by Sir Colin Campbell to deal with them, inflicted a great defeat on their main body at Chatrá, on the 2nd of October, and thus temporarily relieved the grand trunk road. When English was compelled to march north-westwards, Rattray, with his Sikhs, replaced him, and maintained in the most salient posts a rough kind of order. But the danger was not wholly averted until the repression of Kunwar Singh and his brothers, after the fall of Lakhnao, pacified Western Bihár.

In Eastern Bengal there had been, first, manifestations, then outbreaks, quite sufficient to cause considerable alarm. On the 18th of November the sipáhís stationed at Chitragáon, and which belonged to the regiment which had made itself conspicuous for its disloyalty at Barrackpur, the 34th N.I., mutinied, released the prisoners from the gaol, and quitted the station, carrying with them the contents of the treasury, and three elephants. They made for Hill Tiparah, avoiding British territory, hoping thus to reach their homes. Four days later the authorities at Dháká attempted to disarm the sipáhís stationed there, numbering 350 men. The attempt failed, for the sipáhís resisted, and although in the contest which followed they were beaten, yet, as at Dánápur, the majority got off with their muskets, and started for Jalpaigúrí, where was located the headquarters of their regiment, the 73rd.

The Government of India had been alive to the importance of taking measures to provide against the consequences of an outbreak in Eastern Bengal. The natural run of successful revolters would, they knew, be for the important stations at Púrniá, Dinájpur, and Rangpur. To avert the danger from these, which may be described as the gates of Bengal and

Eastern Bihár, Mr Halliday had obtained the sanction of the Government of India to enlist bodies of sailors, then lying idle in Calcutta, to serve as garrisons in those and other places. The precaution was not taken an hour too soon. But it was taken in time, and by means of it, and of the gallant and loyal conduct of the Silhat Light Infantry, led by Byng—who was killed—and after him by Sherer, the rebels from Chitragáon were intercepted and destroyed.

Those from Dháká were, in a certain sense, more fortunate. Baffled by Mr Halliday's precautions in their original intentions, they apparently resolved to make for Jalpaigúrí, to effect there a junction with the main body of their regiment, the 73rd. That regiment had been kept from outbreak by two circumstances; the first, that they were located in an isolated station, cut off from their comrades, and they had but a dim perception of what was passing in the world beyond them: and, secondly, by the splendid firmness of their commanding officer, Colonel George Sherer, who, on the first symptoms of mutiny had seized the ringleaders, brought them to a court-martial, and, in pursuance of the sentence recorded, had had them blown away from guns, despite the order of the cowed authorities in Calcutta that he should release them. The execution of those three rebels had saved many hundreds of lives, and had helped to maintain order. But not even the haughty bearing of Sherer would have kept his men to their allegiance had their mutinied comrades reached Jalpaigúrí. It became, then, a great object to prevent them, and this task was entrusted to the capable hands of George Yule.

With a company of the 5th Fusiliers, a few local levies, and the officers of the district at his disposal, Yule marched to meet and baffle the Dháká mutineers. Joined by the Yeomanry Cavalry, to be presently referred to, he prevented them from entering Purniá, barred to them the road to Jalpaigúrí, and, finally, compelled them to cross the frontier into Nipál. Thence, after suffering many hardships, they made their way into Oudh, only to fall there by the bullet and the sword.

In Western Bihár, and in the districts belonging to the commissioner-ship of Banáras, those of Juánpur, Ázamgarh, and Gorákhpur, abutting on Eastern Oudh, the danger had been more pronounced and more serious.

The removal of Mr William Tayler from the administration of the affairs of Western Bihár had given a marked *impetus* to the rebellion. The feeble men who succeeded him, Mr Samuells and Mr Alonzo Money, were as shuttlecocks in the hands of Kunwar Singh and his partisans. The diffi-culties of the situation were, too, considerably aggravated by the action of the landowners of Ázamgarh and Gorákhpur, and by the exposure of the districts of Chaprá, Champáran, and Muzaffarpur, to the incursions of rebels from Oudh. The arrival of the 5th Irregulars, and, a little later, of the two mutinied companies of the 32nd N. I., from Eastern Bihár, still further increased the difficulties of the situation. Vainly did Rattray, with his Sikhs, pressed by Alonzo Money, attempt to bar the way to the 5th. He was compelled to fall back on Gayá. The victors, but for the prompt action of Skipwith Tayler, the son of the far-seeing man whom personal spite had removed from the scene of his triumphs, would have massacred all the residents at that station. After that there was a slight change of fortune, and Rattray avenged his defeat, by the 5th, by annihilating a body of rebels at Akbarpur (October 7), and by compelling the retreat of the two companies of the 32nd at Danchuá (November 6).

The Government of India had, in the meantime, accepted the offer of the able ruler of Nipál, Jang Bahádur, to despatch, to co-operate with their own troops in the Ázamgarh districts and in Eastern Oudh, a division of Gurkhás, led by their own officers. The Government had also raised a regiment of cavalry, styled the Yeomanry Cavalry, composed for the most part of European adventurers, and commanded by Major J. F. Richardson, a very gallant officer of the regular army. They had, further, directed Brigadier Rowcroft to co-operate, with a force under his command, on the eastern frontier of Oudh, and they had ordered to him Richardson and his yeomanry corps, fresh from aiding Yule in his pursuit of the Dháká mutineers. The Naval brigade of Captain Sotheby had likewise been directed to join Rowcroft.

The Nipál troops, to the number of 3,000, had entered the Gorákhpur division at the very end of July, had disarmed the sipáhís stationed at Gorákhpur on the 1st of August, had occupied Ázamgarh on the 13th, Juánpur on the 15th of the same month. Joined there by three officers deputed for that purpose by the British Government, by the lion-hearted Venables, and by the highspirited Judge of Gorákhpur, William Wynyard, they had surprised and defeated the rebels at Mandurí, and had followed up their victory by occupying Mubárakpur and Atráoliá. They beat them again at Kudyá on the 19th of October, and at Chandá on the 30th. Just after the last-named action they were joined by a small European force, composed of 320 men of the 10th foot, two guns, and 170 men of the 17th Madras N. I., the whole commanded by Longden of the 10th. Three days later the Oudh rebels again crossed the border, but again were they driven back. By this time the conclusion had forced itself on the Government that successfully to combat the rebellion in those mutinous districts more troops were required, and they arranged with Jang Bahádur for the co-operation of a further body of 9,000 picked Gurkhás, to be commanded by Jang Bahádur in person, but to which a British officer, Colonel Mac-Gregor, should be attached as Brigadier-General. They arranged, likewise, to increase Longden's force, and to place it under General Franks, C.B., an officer of tried merit. Whilst these two bodies, united, should clear the ground to the north of Banáras and to the east of Oudh, and then march on Lakhnao, to co-operate with Sir Colin Campbell in the operations against that city, which we have seen him contemplating, the force above referred to, under Rowcroft, should move from Tirhút along the Gandak towards Gorákhpur, and remain in observation on the frontier. It is necessary first, whilst the others are assembling, to deal with Rowcroft's force.

That force, composed of thirty men of the Royal Marines, 130 of the Sotheby's Naval brigade, 350 Nipál troops, fifty of the police battalion, and four twelve-pound howitzers, was, in December, at Mirwá, forty-nine miles from Chaprá. Seven miles distant from him, at Sobanpur, was a force of 1,200 regular sipáhís, supported by 4,000 armed adventurers. These Rowcroft attacked on the 26th, defeated, followed up to Mijáulí, and drove across the Gandak. Thence, in obedience to orders, Rowcroft marched to Burhat-ghát, on the Gográ, to await there further instructions. On the approach of Jang Bahádur with his army (December 23 to January 5) he was directed to ascend the Gográ, to co-operate with the Nipál leader, who had signalised his advance by defeating the rebels at Gorákhpur. Rowcroft reached Barárí, in close vicinity to Jang Bahádur's camp, on the 19th January, and was joined by a brigade of Nipál troops the day following. The next day, to assure the passage of the river by the main body of the Gurkhás, he drove the rebels from Phúlpur. Joined then by the Yeomanry Cavalry, he proceeded to enter upon the second part of his instructions, to keep open the communications whilst Jang Bahádur should march on Lakhnao.

The task was no light one, for the surrounding districts were surging with revolters. Rowcroft and his comrades, however, displayed a skill and energy not to be surpassed in the carrying out of their duties. Captain Sotheby, on the 18th February, captured the strong fort of Chándípur. On the 28th Rowcroft defeated the rebels at Gorákhpur. The force then crossed the Oudh frontier and occupied Amorhá. There it repulsed with great loss an attack made upon it by a greatly superior body of rebels. In this battle the Yeomanry Cavalry greatly distinguished themselves. There I must leave Rowcroft, waiting for reinforcements which had been promised, whilst I record the movements of the Governor-General, and the final clearing of the districts round Allahábád Fathpur, and Kánhpur, which preceded the advance of Sir Colin Campbell into Oudh.

In the third week of January 1858 Lord Canning quitted Calcutta for Allahábád, to assume there the administration of the Central Provinces. Freed from the pernicious influence of his Calcutta councillors, Lord Canning displayed at Allahábád a vigour, a wisdom, and an energy in marked contrast to the narrow policy which had characterised his action when he had deferred to advice thrust upon him by the councillors he had inherited from his predecessor. He reached Allahábád the 9th of February, and at once made his presence felt. The districts to the west and south of that place and Kánhpur had been to a great extent cleared of the rebel bands which had infested them by the united efforts of Carthew, of Barker, and of Campbell. Early in March moveable patrols were appointed, under the direction of Lieutenant-Colonel Christie, still more completely to clear the district. By degrees the country to the west and north-west of Allahábád was quieted. But the districts to the east of it, the turbulent districts of Ázamgarh and Juánpur, remained a danger to Lord Canning for some time after he had moved his headquarters to Allahábád. How that danger was averted by the skill and gallantry of Lord Mark Kerr I shall tell in another chapter.

I left Jang Bahádur crossing the Gográ, at Phúlpur, on the 21st of February. He marched forward on the 25th, and pushing on, reached the vicinity of Lakhnao, ready to co-operate with Sir Colin Campbell, on the 10th of March. There, for the present, I shall leave him. Franks's force, which, as I have stated, was an amplification of Longden's, had been organised by the end of December. After temporarily clearing the Ázamgarh district, it moved forward, hampered by the want of cavalry, on the 21st of January. At Sikandrá Franks came in sight of a large rebel force. It was the day on which it had been arranged that his cavalry should join him, the 22nd. He waited for them till the evening, when, to his delight, they came up, accompanied by four H. A. guns. There was no more hesitation. Early the next morning Franks attacked the rebels, and defeated them. Obliged then, in obedience to orders, to send back his cavalry to Allahábád, Franks moved to Singrámáo, and waiting there until the arrival of Rowcroft at Gorákhpur should enable Jang Bahádur to advance, set out the same day, the 19th of February, in the direction of Súltánpur. He reached Chandá the same day, and inflicted, in front of it, a severe defeat on the rebels. Occupying Chandá, he pushed on to Rámpúrá, halted there for two hours, then moving to Hamírpur, defeated another body of rebels, marching to the assistance of those disposed of at Chandá. Pushing on thence, he occupied the strong fortress of Budháyun in the face of the rebels, and completely defeated them in the hardfought battle of Súltánpur[2] (February 23). The Láhd Light Horse joined him that evening, and the Jálandhar Cavalry the following morning. Franks pushed on rapidly after the battle. On the 1st of March Aikman, who commanded the Jálandhar Cavalry, heard of the presence three miles off the road of a rebel chief who had long been 'wanted.' Aikman dashed after him, caught him, killed more than a hundred of his men, and drove the remainder into the Gúmtí, capturing two guns. It was the resolute courage of Aikman that did it all, and for his daring and persistence he was awarded the Victoria Cross.

On the 4th Franks had reached Améthí, within eight miles of Lakhnao. Hence he proceeded to attack the fort of Daurárá, two miles off the road. But, in striking contrast to his usual tactics, he made the attack in a slovenly manner, and was repulsed. It was unfortunate for him, for it was believed he was to have held the command in the storming of Lakhnao, which Sir Colin, after the repulse, conferred upon Outram.

The assaulting army, numbering 20,000 men and 180 guns, is now collected round the doomed city. In the next chapter I shall have to relate how Sir Colin Campbell employed it.

---

[2] In this battle Macleod Innes of the Engineers gained the Victoria Cross by a deed of splendid daring.

CHAPTER XXIV

The Storming of Lakhnao

The army concentrated by Sir Colin Campbell before Lakhnao consisted of the troops which, as I have told, he had massed in the plains between Unáo and Banní, of the Nipál troops, of Franks's division, and of the men he had left in the Álambágh under the command of Outram. Of the three first I have written in the three chapters immediately preceding. It remains now to say a word regarding the last.

Outram had been left, on the 26th of November, with between three and four thousand[1] men of all arms, twenty-five guns and howitzers, and ten mortars, to occupy a position which should remind the Lakhnao rebels of the presence of British troops. He did not locate all these in the Álambágh, but occupying that royal garden—a square of about 500 yards—with a sufficient number, he ranged the remainder in the open about half-a-mile behind it. He thus occupied a position across the Kánhpur road, touching the fort of Jalálábád with his right. Where this position was not naturally covered by swamps he placed batteries, dug trenches, and planted abattis to protect it.

The rebels in Lakhnao had been so severely handled by Sir Colin in his relief of the Residency that for some time they made no attempt to disturb Outram. But as time passed the memory of the losses they then sustained faded, and on the 22nd December they made a skilfully conceived attempt to sever Outram's communications with Banní. But the British general was well served by his spies, and catching the rebels whilst marching to execute their plan, he inflicted upon them a very severe defeat.

About a fortnight later Outram despatched to Kánhpur a convoy of empty carts, guarded by 530 men and four guns. The rebels soon obtained information of this movement, and believing that the force resting on the Álambágh had been severely crippled, they determined to make a supreme effort to destroy Outram. Accordingly, on the 12th, they issued

---

[1] The number was close upon 4,000, but of these about 500 had been sent to guard the Banní bridge.

from Lakhnao to the number of 30,000. They massed this body opposite to the extreme left of Outram's position, then gradually extended it so as to face his front and left. To the front attack Outram opposed two brigades, the one consisting of 733 English troops, the other of 713, whilst he directed the ever-daring Olpherts to take four guns, and, supported by the men of the military train, to dash at the overlapping right of the rebels. Olpherts fell on them just as they were developing their overlapping movement, and not only compelled them to renounce it, but to fall back in confusion. The two brigades operating against the centre were equally successful. They not only drove back the rebels, but foiled an insidious movement which their leader was planning against the right of the British position. By four o'clock the rebels were in full flight. Their losses were heavy.

But the famous Maulaví, one of the chief authors of the rebellion, was in Lakhnao, and the Maulaví had sworn that he would capture the convoy despatched with empty carts to Kánhpur, but now returning with the carts laden. Accordingly, on the night of the 14th, he quitted Lakhnao with a considerable force, in very light marching order, turned the British camp, and occupied a position whence he could fall upon the convoy as it marched. Fortune seemed to favour him, for a violent dust-storm concealed his presence from the leader of the covering party, who, moreover, had no warning of his presence. But the careful watchfulness of Outram foiled him. Noting how the weather favoured an attack, he despatched Olpherts, with two guns and a detachment of infantry, supported by others troops, to aid in bringing in the convoy. Olpherts cleared the ground of the Maulaví and his troops, and the convoy reached the camp in safety. On the 16th another attack made by the rebels was repulsed with loss. From that date till the 15th of February they made no sign.

Then, directed by the Maulaví, they made an attack in force, only to be repulsed. They followed it up by a second the following day, with a like result. On the 21st they made a third, and on the 25th a fourth and very serious one. In all they were completely beaten. The last defeat apparently convinced them that it was hopeless to attempt to dislodge Outram.

Thus did that illustrious man, aided by his capable officers, by Berkeley, his chief of the staff, by Vincent Eyre, by Olpherts, by Maude, by Dodgson, by Macbean, by Moorsom, by Gould Weston, by Chamier, by Hargood by Barrow, by Wale, and by that excellent officer of the Engineers, Nicholson, by Brasyer, and by many others, for the list is a long one, maintain, with a comparatively small force, the position assigned to him by the

Commander-in-Chief. Towards the end of February his force had been increased, but it never equalled 5,000 men. It was computed, on the other hand, that the rebels had at their disposal no fewer than 120,000 men. Of these 27,550 were trained sipáhís, and 7,100 trained cavalry soldiers. Of the remainder, 5,400 were new levies, 5150 were Najíbs, or men drilled and armed in the native fashion, 800 belonged to the camel corps they had organised, whilst the armed followers of the talukdárs numbered 20,000. Such was the force which guarded the city the storming of which by Sir Colin Campbell I shall now briefly describe.

The city of Lakhnao stretches, in an irregular form, on the right bank of the Gúmtí for a length from east to west of nearly five miles. The extreme width of it on the western side is a mile and a half. The eastern side diminishes to the width of rather less than a mile. Two bridges, one of iron, the other of masonry, span the Gúmtí, whilst a canal of deep and rugged section, enclosing the city on the east and south sides, bears away to the south-west, leaving the approach there open, but intersected by ravines. Towards the north-east, where the canal joins the Gúmtí, its banks are naturally shelving and easy.

The strong positions held by the rebels within the city were the Kaisarbágh, a palace about 400 yards square, containing several ranges of buildings. It had been completed only in 1850, and was not originally fortified. The rebels, however, had greatly strengthened it. To the east of the Observatory, overlooking the river, were the Farhatbakhsh palace and the palaces adjoining, the Residency, the ruins of the Machchí Bhawan, the great Imámbárah, the Jamániabágh, the Shésh Mahall, Alí Nakí's house, extending to the west along the banks of the river, the Musábágh, a mile and a half beyond it, the little Imámbárah, and a range of palaces stretching from the Kaisarbágh to the canal. Beyond the canal, on the east of the city, was the Martiniére. Overlooking this and the eastern suburbs, on the brow of a table-land, stood the Dilkushá.

The rebels, profiting by their experience of the British action in the previous November, had greatly strengthened the line by which Sir Colin had then advanced. They had, too, formed three lines of defence. The first rested on Hazratganj, at the point where the three roads into Lakhnao converge. The right of the second line rested on the little Imámbárah, thence, embracing the mess-house, it joined the river bank near the Motí Mahall. The third covered the Kaisarbágh. These defences were protected by a hundred guns. All the main streets were likewise protected by bastions and barricades, and every building of importance, besides being loopholed, had an outer work protecting the entrance to it.

Whilst thus protecting the city on three sides, the rebels had neglected the northern side. Sir Colin detected this error, and resolved, in his plan of attack, to take full advantage of it.

Whilst, then, he determined to cross the Gúmtí with his main force, and to march by the Hazratganj on the Kaisarbágh, he would employ a strong division, under Outram, to turn those defences. He could not, with the force at his disposal, completely hem in the city, but he hoped that, as he pushed on the main body in the line indicated, Outram would be able to move round the angle on one side, whilst Jang Bahádur and the force at the Álambágh would close up round the corresponding angle on the other.

Having resolved on this plan, he advanced, with his main body, on the Dilkushá park and captured it. Whilst he erected batteries there to keep down the rebels' fire, he continued to bring up his troops. By the 4th he had assembled there the whole of the siege-train, and had the bulk of his force, Franks's division and the Nepálese excepted, thoroughly in hand. That force now occupied a line which touched on the right the Gúmtí, at the village of Bibiápur, then, intersecting the Dilkushá, stopped at a point nearly two miles from Jalálábád. The interval was occupied by Hodson's Horse, 1,600 strong. Outram still continued to occupy his former position. On the 5th Franks and the Nepálese arrived.

During the night of the 4th Sir Colin had directed the throwing of two bridges over the Gúmtí near Bibiápur. One of these was completed by the morning of the 5th, and across it a picket had been sent to cover the completion of the remaining works. These were finished by midnight on the 5th. Sir Colin then sent Outram and his division across the river. He was very anxious for the success of the movement he had consigned to that officer, for he had resolved not to stir a step until Outram, charged to turn the rebels' position and to take them in reverse, should have marched beyond, and thus have turned the first line of defence.

Outram crossed and marched up the Gúmtí for about a mile. The river makes a sharp bend at that point; so Outram left the sinuosities of the river, and marched straight on in the direction of the city. He encamped that evening about four miles from it, facing it, his left resting on the Faizábád road, about half a mile in advance of the village of Chinhat.

The following day and the 8th were spent in skirmishing, but on the 9th Outram made his spring. Preluding it with a heavy fire from the batteries he had constructed, he sent Walpole to attack the rebels' left, whilst he led his own left column across the Kokrail stream. Waiting there till Walpole had completed the task allotted to him, he then stormed the Chakar Kóthí, the key of the rebels' position, and thus turned and rendered useless to them the strong line of entrenchments they had thrown up on the right bank of the Gúmtí. In the attack on the Chakar Kóthí, Anderson of the Sikhs and St George of the 1st Fusiliers greatly distinguished themselves, whilst, in opening communications with Adrian Hope's brigade on the opposite bank, young Butler of the 1st Fusiliers performed a deed of cool intrepidity which won for him the Victoria Cross. The result of the day's operations was that Outram occupied the left bank of the Gúmtí as far as the Bádsháhbágh. His position took the rebels completely in reverse.

Sir Colin had waited the three days, the 6th, 7th; and 8th, whilst Outram was making his preparations; but, on the 9th, he too advanced, carried the Martiniére, and moved Adrian Hope's brigade from the vicinity of Banks's house to a point whence, some six hundred yards from the river, it could communicate, as thanks to the gallantry of Butler it did communicate, with Outram on the opposite bank. Sir Colin completed the operation the next day by storming Banks's house. The two army corps were then in complete communication.

During the night of the 10th Outram erected batteries to cover his projected movement of the following day; then, when that day dawned, he carried all the positions leading to the iron bridge—the bridge leading to the Residency—and established batteries close to it. In this operation he lost two most gallant officers, Thynne of the Rifle Brigade, and Moorsom of the Quartermaster-General's department. He continued to carry out the operations entrusted to him on the 12th, 13th, 14th, and 15th. He established himself, that is to say, in a position which enabled him, during those days, to rake and attack, by artillery fire in flank and rear, the positions which Sir Colin was assailing in front. It is impossible to overestimate the value of the assistance which Outram thus rendered to the main attack.

Meanwhile, Sir Colin, having stormed Banks's house on the 10th, occupied without opposition the Sikandarábágh on the 11th, and, owing to the happy audacity of three engineer officers, Medley, Lang, and Carnegy, took possession, also without fighting, of the Kadam Rasúl, and of that Sháh Najaf which had almost foiled him during his advance in November. But the Begum Kothí promised to offer a fierce resistance. It belched forth fire and flame, and it was so strong as to seem capable of repelling a direct attack. Lugard, however, who commanded the force in front of it, resolved to attempt one. The troops he employed were those companions in glory, the 93rd Highlanders and the 4th Panjáb Rifles, led by that model of a soldier the chivalrous Adrian Hope. The assault, made at four o'clock in the afternoon, though opposed with a fury and discipline almost equal to that of the assailants, was successful. But, to use the language of Sir Colin, 'it was the sternest struggle which occurred during the siege.' Six hundred corpses testified to the unerring force of the British and Sikh bayonet.

The capture of the Begum Kothí gave to the Chief Engineer, Brigadier Napier, the opportunity of pushing his approaches, by means of sappers and of heavy guns, through the enclosures, to the mess-house, the little Imámbárah and to the Kaisarbágh. The 12th, then, was chiefly an engineers' day. Some changes, however, were made in the disposition of the troops; Franks's division relieved that of Lugard as the leading division, and the Nepálese troops were brought into line. They were placed on the extreme left, so as to hold the line of the canal beyond Banks's house. The 13th was, likewise, an engineers' day. On that day the Nepálese were moved across the canal against the suburb to the left of Banks's house, so as to attract the attention of the rebels to that quarter. By the evening the engineers' work was completed. All the great buildings to the left, up to the little Imámbárah, had been sapped through, and by nine o'clock the next morning the heavy guns had effected a breach in its walls. Franks was then directed to storm it. He carried out the operation with brilliant success.

The storm of the little Imámbárah had whetted the martial instincts of the men. Following up the rebels as they evacuated it, they forced their way into a palace which commanded three of the bastions of the Kaisarbágh. Thence they brought to bear on the rebels below them so heavy a fire that one by one they deserted their guns. Their flight left the second line of defence virtually at the mercy of the British. It was turned. A daring advance alone was necessary to gain it. The rebels, recognising this, had no thought but to save themselves. They ran then for security into the buildings between the little Imámbárah and the Kaisarbágh. But the 90th and Brasyer's Sikhs, who were in the front line of stormers, had equally recognised the advantages of their position. Led by young Havelock and Brasyer, they forced their way, cheering, under a terrible fire, into a courtyard adjoining the Kaisarbágh, driving the rebels before them. At this conjuncture young Havelock, seeing with a soldier's eye the extent of the possibilities before him, ran back to the detachment of the 10th in support and ordered it to the front. Annesley, who commanded it, led it forward with alacrity, nor did his men halt till, driving the rebels before them, they had penetrated to the Chíní bazaar, to the rear of the Tárá Kothí and the mess-house, thus turning the rebels' third line. The rebels, congregated in the Tárá Kothí and mess-house, numbering about 6,000, realising their position, evacuated those buildings, and made as though they would re-enter the city through an opening in the further gateway of the Chíní bazaar, and thus cut off the Sikhs and the 90th. But Havelock, with great presence of mind, advanced with some Sikhs to the support of Brasyer, and seizing two adjoining bastions, turned the six guns found upon them with so much effect against the rebels that their attempt was checked, and they abandoned it. By this time the fourth note sent by young Havelock[2] had reached Franks, and that gallant officer pushed forward every available man in support of the advance. The results already achieved far surpassed in importance those which had been contemplated for the day, and the question arose whether the advantage should be pursued. After a brief consultation Franks and Napier decided in favour of pushing on. Some necessary rearrangement of troops followed. Then, whilst those on the right advanced and occupied in succession, with but little resistance, the Motí Mahall, the Chatar Manzil, and the Tárá Kothí, Franks sent his men through the court of Saadat Ali's Mosque into the Kaisarbágh itself. The resistance there was fierce, but of short duration. The stormers were wound to a pitch which made them irresistible. They stormed, one after another, the courts and the summer-houses which made up the interior of the palace, and drove the rebels headlong into the garden. There those who failed to escape—and they were the majority—soon found the rest from which there is no awakening.

I will not attempt to describe the plundering which followed the capture of this newest of the palaces of the Kings of Oudh. Rather would I dwell on the great military result thereby obtained. In the morning of that 14th of March the British line had stretched from the Sháh Najaf to Hazratganj. That evening it ran from the Chatar Manzil to the Residency side of the Kaisarbágh. Two strong defensive lines of works, including the Citadel, on which the second line rested, defended by nearly 40,000 men, had been stormed. All honour to the men who planned and carried out so magnificent a work: to Havelock and Brasyer, to Franks and Napier, to Annesley, to the men of the 10th and 90th, and to the Sikhs. All honour, also, to those who gave their lives in the noble enterprise.

The rebels would have been completely destroyed, and the whole of Lakhnao would have lain, helpless, the next morning at the feet of Sir Colin Campbell if, whilst Franks and Napier were storming the Kaisarbágh, Outram had crossed by the iron bridge and cut off those who escaped from the several places as they were stormed. That this did not happen was no fault of Outram. He recognised the advantage to be gained, and applied during the day for permission to execute such a manœuvre. The reply was

---

[2] The 'young Havelock' alluded to in the text is the present Sir Henry Havelock-Allan, son of the general who first relieved the Residency.

the most extraordinary ever received by a general in the field. It consisted of a short note from Mansfield, chief of the staff, telling him he might cross by the iron bridge, but that 'he was not to do so if he thought he would lose a single man.' Such a proviso was a prohibition, for not only were guns posted to defend the bridge, but the bridge was commanded by a mosque and several loopholed houses. The loss, then, would have greatly exceeded that of one man. That the proviso was dictated by a very shortsighted policy can be realised by the slightest reflection. The ultimate pursuit of the rebels who escaped because Outram did not cross caused an infinitely greater loss of men to the British army than the storming of the bridge and the taking of the rebels in rear would have occasioned.

On the right bank of the Gúmtí Sir Colin devoted the 15th to the consolidating of the position he had gained. On the left bank, sensible, too late, of the error he had allowed to be committed by the despatch to Outram of the absurd order on which I have commented, he despatched Hope Grant, with his cavalry, and Campbell, with his infantry brigade and 1,500 cavalry, to pursue the rebels on the Sítápur and Sandílá roads respectively. But the rebels had taken neither of these roads; the pursuit, therefore, was fruitless. It was not till the 16th that Sir Colin directed Outram to cross the Gúmtí, near the Sikandarábágh, and to join him, with Douglas's brigade, at the Kaisarbágh, leaving Walpole, with Horsford's brigade, to watch the iron and stone bridges. Outram crossed as directed, was joined by the 20th and Brasyer's Sikhs, and was then ordered by Sir Colin in person to push on through the Residency, take the iron bridge in reverse, and then, advancing a mile further, storm the Machchí Bhawan and the great Imámbárah. Outram carried both places without much opposition; but before he had accomplished his task the rebels, with the design of retreating on Faizábád, had made a strong attack on Walpole's pickets. They had been unable to force these—probably they never seriously intended to do so— but they held them in check whilst the bulk of their comrades made good their retreat on to the Faizábád road. I need not point out how impossible retreat by that road would have been had Sir Colin permitted Outram to cross on the 14th.

The rebels attempted the same day another diversion, by suddenly attacking the Álambágh, but Franklyn, who commanded, Vincent Eyre, with his heavy guns, Robertson, with the military train, and Olpherts completely foiled them.

Whilst the operations I have described had been carried out in the advance, Jang Bahádur and the Nepálese had, on the 14th and 15th, moved up the canal and taken in reverse the positions which, for three months, the rebels had occupied in front of the Álambágh. Jang Bahádur performed this task with ability and success. One after another the positions held by the rebels, from the Chárbágh up to the Residency, on that side, fell into his hands.

On the 17th Outram, pursuing his onward course, occupied without resistance the Huséní Mosque and the Daulat Kháná. In the afternoon he caused to be occupied a block of buildings known as Sharif-ud-daula's house. The rebels evacuated it hastily, but an accidental explosion, caused by the careless unpacking of gunpowder found there, caused the deaths of two officers and some thirty men. On the 18th he proceeded to clear the streets in front of the position he had secured, when he received Sir Colin's orders to drive the rebels from the Músábágh. Whilst he should march against that place, Campbell of the Bays was to take 1,500 cavalry, and a due proportion of guns, and be ready to pounce upon the rebels as Outram should drive them from the Músábágh. The Nepálese were likewise so placed as to cut off their retreat in the other direction.

Outram, as usual, did his part thoroughly. He captured Alí Nakí's house and the Músábágh. The rebels fled from the last-named place by the road which Campbell should have guarded. But Campbell was not to be seen. He had engaged a part of his force in a small operation which had given Hagart, Slade, Bankes, and Wilkin, all of the 7th Hussars, an opportunity of displaying courage of no ordinary character, followed though their splendid deed was by the severely wounding of the second and the death of the third; but as to the main object of his mission he did nothing. It was officially stated that he had lost his way.[3] The rebels, consequently, escaped.

Not all, however. Outram was there to repair to a certain extent Campbell's error. Noticing that the rebels were preparing to escape from the Músábágh, he had despatched to cut them off the 9th Lancers, followed by some infantry and field-artillery. These killed about 100 of them, and captured all their guns.

This was the concluding act of the storming of Lakhnao. The day following was issued Lord Canning's proclamation confiscating the entire proprietary right in the soil of Oudh, save in the case of six comparatively inferior chiefs. To rebel landowners who should at once surrender immunity from death and imprisonment was promised, provided that they could show that they were guiltless of unprovoked bloodshed. To those who had protected British fugitives special consideration was promised. The principles embodied in the proclamation were just, and when the

---

[3] Hope Grant (*Incidents of the Sepoy War*) is very, but not unjustly, severe on Campbell.

time came they were acted upon with such consideration as to secure the loyalty which had been alienated by the enforcement of the stern code which had immediately followed the annexation; but at the moment the effect was to embitter the hearts of those against whom the proclamation was directed.

It having been ascertained that the famous Maulaví was still in Lakhnao, and that from Shádatganj, in the heart of the city, he still bade defiance to the conqueror, Lugard was sent, on the 21st, with the 93rd and 4th Panjáb Rifles, to attack him. He and his followers were effectively dislodged, and were pursued by Campbell, this time on the spot. But the Maulaví escaped. Two days later Hope Grant, sent after the rebels who had fled by the Faizábád road, caught a considerable number of them at Kúrsí, cut up many, and captured thirteen guns.

Lakhnao had fallen, but the province of which Lakhnao was the capital still remained to be subdued. How this was accomplished, how Rohilkhand was recovered, and how the rebels were driven from Ázamgarh into Western Bihár, and there annihilated, I shall show in the next chapter.

CHAPTER XXV

Ázamgarh—Reconquest of Rohilkhand, of Oudh, of the Ázamgarh and Western Bihár Districts

Whilst Sir Colin Campbell was putting the last finishing stroke to his operations against Lakhnao there occurred an event in the Ázamgarh district which taxed very severely the resources immediately available to Lord Canning. On the 27th of March an express informed the Governor-General that, on the 22nd, Kunwar Singh, the famous chieftain of Western Bihár, had surprised the British force, under Colonel Milman, near Atráoliá, twenty-five miles from Ázamgarh, had forced it to fall back on the last-named place, and was there besieging it. It was too true. Milman, whose force consisted of 206 men of the 37th foot and of 60 Madras Cavalry, had been caught napping; had fallen back, first on Koilsá, then on Ázamgarh; had received there reinforcements in the shape of 46 men of the Madras Rifles (natives) and 280 men of his own regiment, the 37th foot, under Colonel Dames, who, as senior officer, then assumed command. On the 27th Dames had attempted a sortie, and had been beaten back.

The situation was a difficult one for Lord Canning, for Ázamgarh was not very distant from Allahábád, where he was and if Kunwar Singh were to compel the surrender of the force behind the walls of Ázamgarh the conflagration might reach even Banáras. Realising to the fullest extent the possibilities which Kunwar Singh might utilise, whilst Oudh still remained unsubdued, Lord Canning took prompt and efficient measures to nip the evil in the bud. There happened to be at Allahábád a wing of the 13th L.I., commanded by a most gallant soldier, Lord Mark Kerr. Lord Canning sent for Lord Mark, explained to him the situation, and authorised him to take the measures he might consider necessary to deal with it. That night Lord Mark started, with his wing, 391 strong, for Banáras, picked up there a troop—fifty-five men and two officers—of the Queen's Bays, seventeen gunners and one officer, with two six-pounder guns and two $5\frac{1}{2}$-inch mortars, and set out for Ázamgarh the night of the 2nd of April. His entire force consisted of twenty-two officers and 444 men. On the evening of the 5th he had reached Sarsána, eight miles from Ázamgarh. Kunwar Singh had notice of his arrival there, and prepared an ambush for him, to entrap him whilst he should be pushing on in the early grey of the next morning. Lord Mark did so push on, and became entangled in the ambush, but by a display of combined coolness and courage, very remarkable under the circumstances, largely outnumbered as he was, not only extricated his men, but inflicted upon the rebels a crushing defeat, and relieved Ázamgarh. It was one of the most brilliant achievements of the war.

The Commander-in-Chief had received news of Milman's disaster on the 28th of March. Realising, as Lord Canning had realised, its full significance, he despatched at once General Lugard, with three English regiments, 700 Sikh sabres, and eighteen guns, to march, by way of Atráoliá, to Ázamgarh, there to deal with Kunwar Singh. To Lugard's operations I shall refer presently. Meanwhile, I propose to take up the story of the measures decided upon for the pacification of Rohilkhand and of Oudh.

For the reconquest of Oudh Sir Colin detailed one army corps, under Hope Grant, to march to Bárí, twenty-nine miles from Lakhnao, to expel thence the rebels collected there under the Maulaví, to march eastward thence to Muhammadábád, and, following the course of the Gogra, to reconnoitre Bitaulí, thence to cover the return to their own country of the Nipál troops, under Jang Bahádur. Whilst Hope Grant should be moving in that direction, Walpole, with a moveable column, was to march up the Ganges, await near Fathgarh the arrival of Sir Colin, who would draw to himself as he advanced other columns converging to the same point.

Hope Grant carried out his instructions to the letter. He defeated the Maulaví at Bárí, found Bitaulí evacuated, saw Jang Bahádur on his way to the frontier, and then returned to protect the road between Kánhpur and Lakhnao, seriously threatened at Unáo. Walpole was less successful. Obstinate, self-willed, and an indifferent soldier, he led his column against the fort of Ruyiá, two miles from the Ganges, and fifty-one west by north from Lakhnao, attacked it on its only unassailable face, and after losing several men, and the most gifted soldier in the British army, the accomplished Adrian Hope, allowed the defenders to escape from the face which he himself should have assailed. He moved on thence, expelled the rebels from Sirsá, and was joined on the Rohilkhand side of Fathgarh, on the 27th of April, by Sir Colin.

Seaton, who had been left at Fathgarh, noticing that the rebels had collected in consideable force in front of him, had issued from that place on the 6th April, and had inflicted on them a crushing defeat at Kankar, between Aliganj and Bángáun. By this victory he secured the gates of Duáb against an enemy issuing from either of the menaced provinces. Whilst he was keeping that door closed, Penny, with another column, was moving down from Bulandshahr. Penny met Sir Colin at Fathgarh, on 24th April, then crossed the Ganges and marched on Usehat. Finding that place deserted, and being told that his march to Budáun would not be opposed; Penny started on a night march for that place. But the rebels lay in ambush for him and surprised him, and although his column defeated them, he was slain. Colonel Jones of the Carabineers succeeded him, and under his orders the column marched to join Sir Colin at Míránpur Katrá on the 3rd of May.

Whilst these columns, united under Sir Colin, should invade Rohilkhand from its eastern side, it had been arranged that a brigade, under Colonel Coke, should enter it from Rúrkí. Coke had arrived at Rúrkí the 22nd of February, but so disorganised was the country that April was approaching before he could complete his commissariat arrangements. When he was ready, Sir Colin made the command a divisional one, and sent Colonel John Jones to lead it. The change, however, did not affect the order of the proceedings, for the good understanding between Coke and his superior in rank remained perfect to the end.

The division crossed the Ganges at Hardwár on the 17th of April, defeated the rebels at Bhogníwálá (17th), and at Naghíná (21st), and reached the vicinity of Murádábád on the 26th of April. Entering that place, Coke was able to seize the persons of several notorious rebels, and then pushed on to take part in the operations which Sir Colin was directing against Barélí.

Sir Colin, joined on the 27th of April by Walpole, had entered Sháhjahánpur the 30th. He had hoped to find there the Maulaví and Náná Sáhib, but both had fled he knew not whither. Leaving there a small detachment, under Colonel Hale, he moved then on Miránpur Katrá, picked up there, as I have told, the brigade but recently commanded by Penny, and marched on Barélí. There Khán Bahádur Khán still tyrannised. It seemed as though he had resolved to strike a blow for the permanence of his sway.

It was seven o'clock on the morning of the 5th of May when Sir Colin led his troops to attack the rebel chieftain. In his first line he had the

Highland brigade, composed of the 93rd, 42nd, and 79th, supported by that excellent Sikh regiment the 4th Panjáb Rifles, and the Balúch battalion, with a heavy field-battery in the centre, and horse-artillery and cavalry on both flanks. The second line, composed of the 78th, seven companies of the 64th, and four of the 82nd, and the 2nd and 22nd Panjáb Infantry, protected the baggage and the siege-train. The enormous superiority of the rebels in cavalry required such a precaution.

It was apparently the object of the rebels to entice the British to the position they had selected as the best for their purposes, for they abandoned their first line as Sir Colin advanced, and fell back on the old cantonment of Barélí, covering their movement with their cavalry and guns. Sir Colin, inclined to húmour them, anxious only to bring them to action, crossed the Nattiá rivulet, and was advancing beyond it, when the Gházís, men who devoted their lives for their religion, made a desperate onslaught on a village which the 4th Panjábis had but just entered. With the *élan* of their rush they swept the surprised Sikhs out of the village, and then dashed against the 42nd, hastening to their support. Sir Colin happened to be on the spot. He had just time to call out, 'Stand firm, 42nd; bayonet them as they come on!' when the Gházís were upon them. But vain was their rush against that wall of old soldiers! They killed some indeed, but not a single man of the Gházís survived. Some of them, however, had got round the 42nd, and inflicted some damage. But they, too, met the fate of their comrades. The first line then advanced, and for about a mile and a half swept all before it. Just then the information reached Sir Colin that the rebel cavalry had attacked his baggage, but had been repulsed. He halted to enable the second line, with the baggage and heavy guns to close up, sending only the 79th and 93rd to seize the suburbs in their front. This attempt led to fresh fighting with the Gházís, which, however, ended as had the previous attacks. In a very important particular the halt made by Sir Colin, desirable as it was in many respects, was unfortunate, as it enabled the rebel chief to withdraw, with his troops, from the town. It would even have been better had the attack been delayed for a single day; for on the following morning, as Sir Colin entered the evacuated town on the one side, the division commanded by Jones and Coke entered it on the other. Khán Báhádar Khán eventually escaped into Nipál.

Meanwhile, the Maulaví, who had evacuated Sháhjahánpur on the approach of Sir Colin, had no sooner learnt that the British general was approaching Barélí, than he turned back from Muhamdí, and resolved to surprise Hale at Sháhjahánpur. It is more than probable that, had he marched without a halt, he would have succeeded. But when within four miles of the place he stopped to rest his men. This halt gave to a loyal villager the opportunity to hasten to apprise Hale of his approach, and that officer had time to take measures to meet his enemy. Giving up the town, he fell back on the gaol. The Maulaví, who had eight guns, followed him to that place, invested it and from the 3rd to the morning of the 11th of May kept up against it an all but incessant cannonade.

Information of the position of Hale reached Sir Colin on the 7th. He at once despatched John Jones, with the 60th Rifles, the 79th, a wing of the 82nd, the 22nd Panjáb Infantry, two squadrons of the Carabineers, the Multání horse, and guns in proportion, to dispose, if he could, of the most persistent of all the rebels. Jones started on the 8th, reached the vicinity of Sháhjahánpur the 11th, drove the rebel outposts before him, and effected a junction with Hale. But the Maulaví was too strong in cavalry to permit of his being attacked with any chance of success. Jones halted, then, until he should receive from Sir Colin troops of the arm of which he stood in need. The Maulaví, meanwhile, occupied the open plain, whither rebels who had been elsewhere baffled flocked to him from all sides. Matters continued so till the morning of the 15th, when the Maulaví, whose following had greatly increased, attacked Jones. The fight lasted all day without his having been able to make the smallest impression on the serried ranks of the British. Sir Colin, meanwhile, deeming the campaign at an end, had distributed his forces. He was himself on his way to Fathgarh, with a small body of troops, when he received Jones's message. Sending then for the remainder of the 9th Lancers, he turned his course towards Sháhjahánpur, and effected a junction there with Jones on the 18th.

Even then he was too weak in cavalry to force the rebels to a decisive battle. A skirmish, however, brought on a partial action near the village of Panhat. It resulted in the repulse of the rebels, and in nothing more. But the Maulaví, realising that he could make no impression on the British infantry, fell back into Oudh, to await there better fortune. Sir Colin then distributed the troops, and closed the summer campaign. He had reconquered Rohilkhand, but a great part of Oudh still remained defiant.

A fortunate chance rid him, a few days later, of his most dangerous and persistent enemy. No sooner had the Maulaví realised that Sir Colin had put his troops in summer quarters than, with a small following, he attempted on the 5th of June to effect a forcible entrance into the town of Powain. The Rájá, a supporter of the British, had refused him entry, and when the Maulaví, seated on his elephant, pressed forward to force the gate, the Rájá's brother seized a gun and shot him dead. Thus ignominiously, by the hands of one of his own countrymen, terminated the life of one of the principal fomentors of the Mutiny, and its ablest and most persistent supporter.

It will be recollected that when Sir Colin, after the capture of Lakhnao, distributed his forces for the pursuit of the rebels, he despatched a strong column, under General Lugard, to Ázamgarh to dispose there of Kunwar Singh. To the proceedings of that general and of his successors I must now ask the reader's attention.

Lugard left Lakhnao on the 29th of March, and made straight for Juánpur. When approaching that place he learned that the rebels had collected a few miles off to the number of 3,000. He reached Tígrá on the afternoon of the 11th of April, after a march of sixteen miles, attacked the rebels the same evening, and defeated them, with the loss of eighty killed, and two guns. The victors lost but one killed and six wounded; but the killed man was the gallant Charles Havelock, nephew of the renowned General. Lugard then marched for Ázamgarh, still invested by Kunwar Singh with 13,000 men. That wily chieftain was resolved not to stake the issue of the campaign on a single battle. Whilst ranging his troops, therefore, so as apparently to guard the Tons, he really left there a widely spread out screen, whilst with the main body he hastily retreated towards the Ganges. Lugard forced (April 15) the passage of the Tons, but the 'screen' left by Kunwar Singh had made so resolute a defence that the main body had gained some twelve miles before they were overtaken. They were mostly old sipáhís, and on this occasion they did credit to the training they had received. Forming up, on the approach of the British, like veterans, they repulsed, whilst still retreating, every attack, and finally forced the pursuers to cease their efforts. The latter had to mourn the death this day, from wounds received in the fight, of the illustrious Venables, the famous indigo planter, who, with his comrade Dunn, had almost single-handed held his district when it had been abandoned by those to whose care it had been committed. On this day Middleton of the 29th foot greatly distinguished himself by the rescue from crowds of the rebels of young Hamilton of the 3rd Sikhs, who lay seriously wounded, and who ultimately died of his wounds.

Lugard, on entering Ázamgarh, had found for the moment sufficient occupation cut out for him in the district. He therefore committed the pursuit of Kunwar Singh to Brigadier Douglas. But before Douglas could make much way the rebel chief had reached the village of Naghai, where, in a strong position, he awaited his pursuer. Douglas attacked him there on the 17th, but though he forced the position, it was only to find himself baffled. Kunwar Singh had defended it long enough to secure two lines of retreat to his troops. By these his divided army fell back, misleading the pursuers, and re-uniting when the pursuit ceased. On the 20th, however, Douglas succeeded in catching the rebels whilst halted at Sikandarpur, almost, indeed, in surprising them. But again they disappeared by several paths, to re-unite again at some fixed spot. Not only did they so re-unite, but, succeeding in putting on a false scent the officer who had been charged to pounce upon them should they attempt to cross the Ganges, they actually crossed that river, and reached Jagdispur unmolested. There Kunwar Singh received a large addition to his force. His first overt act was to completely defeat, with considerable loss, a party of·troops led against him by Captain Le Grand of the 35th foot (April 23). Again did Western Bihár seem at the mercy of the rebels. Expresses were sent across the river urging Douglas to come to the rescue. Douglas at once crossed into Sháhábád, but, before he could act, the veteran chief, who had been driven by his wrongs into rebellion, and who had more than repaid the British for the insults he deemed they had showered upon him, was no more. Kunwar Singh died three days after he had defeated Le Grand.

From that date till the pacification at the close of the year the contest in Western Bihár assumed all the character of a guerilla warfare. The rebels were surrounded, they were beaten, they were pursued, only again to reappear. From the end of April to the end of November they kept the district in continuous turmoil. To the genius of the present Sir Henry Havelock-Allan, then Captain Havelock, it was due finally that they were expelled. That officer devised a system of mounted infantry who should give them no rest. In three actions, fought on the 19th, 20th, and 21st of October, he killed 500 of them, and drove 4400 across the Kaimur hills. In those hills, on the 24th of November, Douglas surprised these, killed many of them, and took all their arms and ammunition. Before the close of the year he could boast that the districts he had been sent to pacify had been completely cleared. But it had taken a long time, and had cost many lives.

CHAPTER XXVI

Western and Central India

Amongst the few matters on which the British had reason to congratulate themselves when the Mutiny broke out there stood out prominently the fact that the administration of the Western Presidency was in the hands of a man so capable, so brave, so resolute, and so unselfish as was Lord Elphinstone. From the very hour the news of the rising of the 10th of May, at Mírath, reached him he displayed a power equal to every emergency. He arranged to despatch to Calcutta the 64th and 78th regiments, then on their way from Persia; he telegraphed to Mr Frere, Commissioner of Sind, to send the 1st Bombay Fusiliers from Karáchí to the Panjáb; he urged General Ashburnham to proceed to Calcutta to place at the disposal of Lord Canning the troops proceeding to China; he chartered steamers, he wrote for troops to Mauritius and to the Cape, he entrusted the care of Bombay to the wise supervision of Mr Forjett, and he formed a moveable column with the object of saving the line of the Narbadá and of relieving Central India.

In his own Presidency Lord Elphinstone had need for the exercise of the greatest prudence combined with the greatest decision. The nobles and landowners of the districts known as the Southern Maráthá country, comprising the territories of Belgáon, Jamkhandí, Kolápur, Míráj, Múdhal, Dhárwár, Sanglí, and Satárah had been alienated by the action of the Inám Commission—a commission instituted to search out titles to property obtained during the decadence of the Mughal Empire. In these districts Lord Elphinstone was represented by a very able member of the Civil Service, Mr George Berkeley Seton-Karr, a gentleman whose sympathies were greatly with the class who had suffered from the Imperial legislation, and whose influence over them enabled him to repress for a time their excited feelings. His task was a difficult one, for treason was stalking abroad, and the sipáhís of the regiments in the Marátha country, mostly Oudh men, were displaying symptoms akin to those which had been so largely manifested in the Bengal Presidency. But, considering the means at his disposal, he did wonders. In June he arrested an emissary from the rebels in the North-western Provinces. Having, in July, obtained from the Governor enlarged powers, he prevented an outbreak in Belgáon, and despatched from that station the two companies of the 29th N.I., whose presence there might have been fatal. Finding, then, that the conspiracy had its ramifications all over the province, he gradually disarmed the districts under his charge, and succeeded, amid a thousand difficulties, in maintaining law and order. But, even so late as April 1858, he recognised that the fire was still smouldering, and was forced to apply for increased powers. Instead of granting to the official who had conducted the affairs of a difficult province with marked success the powers he asked for, the Bombay Government, whilst maintaining him in his civil duties as administrator, relieved him of his political functions, and bestowed these upon a gentleman who had been a member of the detested Inám Commission, Mr Charles Manson. Almost immediately followed the rebellion of the Chief of Nargúnd, the murder of Manson, the despatch to the districts of troops, under Colonel George Malcolm and Brigadier Le-Grand Jacob, and finally the suppression of the rebellion in the August following.

In Bombay itself the danger had been no slight one. Fortunately, the arrangements for the maintenance of internal order had been entrusted to the competent hands of Mr Charles Forjett, Superintendent of Police. That most able and energetic officer detected the conspiring of the sipáhís stationed there; brought it home to some of the sipáhí officers, theretofore incredulous, that his suspicions had been well founded; prevented by his daring courage, an outbreak when it was on the point of explosion, and literally saved the island. That this is no exaggerated statement is proved by the terms of address made to Mr Forjett by the native mercantile community of Bombay when, on his retirement, they presented him with a testimonial. 'They presented it,' they wrote, 'in token of strong gratitude for one whose almost despotic powers and zealous energy had so quelled the explosive forces of native society that they seemed to have become permanently subdued.' Lord Elphinstone likewise recorded a minute expressive of his deep sense of the services rendered by this able, energetic, and honest servant of the Government.

I have stated that among the earlier acts of Lord Elphinstone was the despatch in the direction of Central India, of a column composed of the troops then available. This column marched from Puná on the 8th of June, under the command of Major-General Woodburn, whose orders were to proceed to Máu. Woodburn reached Aurangábád the 23rd of June, disarmed there a cavalry regiment of the Haidarábad contingent which had mutinied, but lost much precious time by halting to try the prisoners he had taken. Fortunately sickness compelled him to resign his command. His successor, Colonel C. S. Stuart of the Bombay army, a very capable officer, quitted Aurangábád the 12th of July, and reached Asírgarh the 22nd. There Stuart was met by Colonel Durand, who had hurried westward to meet his column. From Asírgarh Stuart marched to Máu, and then proceeded to recover Gújrí, to protect Mandlésar, to bombard and capture the fort of Dhár, to disperse the rebels who had advanced from Nímach, to crush rebellion in Málwá, and to re-enter Indur in triumph (14th December). On the 17th Sir Hugh Rose arrived to take the command of the force which was to reconquer Central India.

Sir Hugh Rose was eminently qualified for the task committed to him. He was a diplomat as well as a soldier; and in Syria, at Constantinople, and in the Crimea he had displayed a firmness, an energy, a resolution which marked him as a man who required only the opportunity to distinguish himself. He found himself now in command of two brigades. The first, composed of a squadron of the 14th Light Dragoons, a troop of the 3rd Bombay Cavalry (native), two cavalry regiments of the Haidarábád contingent, two companies of the 86th foot—joined a little later by the remaining companies,—the 25th Bombay N. I., an infantry regiment of the Haidarábád contingent, three light field-batteries, and some sappers, was commanded by Brigadier Stuart. The second, consisting of the headquarters of the 14th Light Dragoons, the headquarters of the 3rd Bombay Cavalry, a regiment of cavalry of the Haidarábád contingent, the 3rd Bombay Europeans, the 24th Bombay N. I., an infantry regiment of the Haidarábád contingent, a proportion of field-artillery, and a siege-train, was commanded by Brigadier Steuart of the 14th Light Dragoons. Troops from Bhopál, to the number of 800, formed also part of the force.

Sir Hugh marched with the second brigade from Sihor, on the 16th of January, for Ráhatgarh; the first, which set out from Máu on the 10th, marching in a parallel line to it in the direction of Gunah. Sir Hugh invested Ráhatgarh on the 24th, took possession of the town on the 26th, defeated the rebel Rájá of Bánpur, who had advanced to relieve the fortress on the 27th, and found the place evacuated on the morning of the 28th. Having discovered, two days later, that the same rebel Rájá was posted, with his forces, near the village of Barodíá, fifteen miles distant, he marched against and completely defeated him. He then pushed on Ságar, which had been held, isolated in the heart of a rebel country, mainly through the loyalty of the 31st Regiment N. I., faithful amid the faithless, for more than six months; reached it on the 3rd of February; marched on the 9th, after pacifying the surrounding country, against the strong fortress of Garhákotá, twenty-five miles distant, compelled the rebels to evacuate it, pursued, and cut them up. Waiting there until he should hear that a column which, under the orders of Brigadier Whitlock, should have quitted Jabalpur, and gathering in meanwhile supplies for his campaign, he marched, on the 26th of February, for Jhánsí. On his way he inflicted a very severe defeat on the rebels at Madanpur, despite a most determined resistance. This defeat so daunted them that they evacuated, without resistance, the formidable pass of Malthón, the forts of Narhat, Suráhí, Maráurá, Bánpur, and Tal-Bahat, and abandoned the line of the Bíná and the Betwá, retaining only, on the left bank of the latter, the fortress of Chanderí.

Meanwhile, Brigadier Stuart, with the first brigade, had, as we have seen, quitted Máu on the 10th of January, and marched upon Gunah, the road to which had been cleared in a most gallant and effective manner by a detachment of the Haidarábád contingent, directed by Captains Orr and Keatinge. The fort of Chandérí, mentioned in the preceding paragraph, lies about seventy miles to the east of Gunah. The town and the fort have alike been famous since the time of Akbar. Against it Stuart marched from Gunah, and, on the 5th of March, reached Khukwásá, six miles from it, that distance being represented by a dense jungle. This jungle Stuart forced not without resistance—though a resistance neither so fierce nor so effective as the nature of the ground made possible—and encamped to the west of the fort. The next few days he spent in clearing the surrounding country and in placing his guns in position. On the 13th his batteries opened fire, and on the 16th effected a breach in the defences. On that date the bulk of the 86th was still twenty-eight miles from him. Stuart sent to the commanding officer an express informing him of the situation. The express reached the 86th just as they had completed a march of thirteen miles. Nevertheless, they at once set out again, and, marching quickly, reached Stuart by ten o'clock on the 16th. Early the next morning Stuart stormed the fort of Chandérí, with the loss of twenty-nine men, two of whom were officers. He then pressed on to join Sir Hugh Rose before Jhánsí.

Sir Hugh had reached Chanchanpur, fourteen miles from Jhánsí, when he received a despatch from the Commander-in-Chief directing him to march against the fort of Charkhárí, some eighty miles from the spot where he stood. The Agent to the Governor-General, Sir Robert Hamilton, who accompanied Sir Hugh, received from Lord Canning a despatch couched in similar terms. To obey would be to commit an act of folly scarcely conceivable, for Jhánsí was the objective point of the campaign—the seat of the rebellion—the strong-hold of one of the authors of the Mutiny—and Jhánsí was within fourteen miles. To leave the objective point, when so close to it, in order to attack a distant fortress against which it was probable Whitlock was then marching, would be an act so devoid of commonsense that Sir Robert Hamilton courageously resolved to give Sir Hugh the means by which he could evade obedience to the order, positive though it was. He wrote, accordingly, to Lord Canning, stating that he had taken upon himself the entire responsibility of directing, as Governor-General's Agent, Sir Hugh Rose to proceed with his operations against Jhánsí.

Fortified by this order, Sir Hugh set out for and reached Jhánsí on the 21st. The strength of the fortress struck him as remarkable. Standing on an elevated rock, built of massive masonry, with guns peeping from every elevation, it commanded the country far and near. The city, from the centre of three sides of which the rock rises, the rock forming the fourth side, sheer and unassailable, was four and a half miles in circumference. It was surrounded by a massive wall, from six to eight feet thick, varying in height from eighteen to thirty feet, having numerous flanking bastions armed as batteries, and was garrisoned by 11,000 men, commanded by a woman who possessed all the instincts, all the courage, all the resolution of a warrior of the type so well known in consular Rome.

Satisfied by a reconnaissance that it would be necessary to take the city before thinking of the fortress, Sir Hugh, joined the same night and on the 24th by his first brigade, invested it on the night of the 22nd. For the seventeen days which followed the defensive works rained without intermission shot and shell on the besieging force. It was evident that the Ráni had infused some of her lofty spirit into her compatriots. Women and children were seen assisting in the repair of the havoc made in the defences by the fire of the besiegers, and in carrying food and water to the soldiers on duty. It seemed a contest between the two races, under conditions unusually favourable to the besieged.

By the 29th a breach in the outer wall had been effected, though it was barely practicable. On the evening of the 31st information reached Sir Hugh that an army was advancing from the north, led by Tántiá Topí, to the relief of the fortress.

Since his defeat by Sir Colin Campbell at Kánhpur, in the preceding December, Tántiá Topí had fallen back on Kalpí, had issued thence some time in February, with 900 followers, to besiege Charkhárí, had captured it, and, his force increased by the junction of five or six regiments of the

Gwáliár contingent and some local levies to 22,000 men and twenty-eight guns, was now responding to a request sent him by the Rání of Jhánsí to march to her relief.

The situation in which the advance of Tántiá placed Sir Hugh Rose, critical as it was, was a situation with which that bold and resolute leader was peculiarly qualified to grapple. He met it with the hand of a master. Recognising that to interrupt the siege operations would give the rebels a confidence sufficient to impel them to resolutions more perilous to himself than any which boldness would be likely to cause, he resolved still to press the siege, whilst, with the troops not on actual duty, amounting to 1,500 men, of whom only one-third were Europeans, he would march to intercept Tántiá Topí. This plan he carried out. At four o'clock the following morning (April 1) Tántiá advanced towards the point where the 1,500 men of Sir Hugh's force lay ready for action. When the rebels came within striking distance Sir Hugh opened fire, then simultaneously attacking their right and left, doubled both up on the centre, and then sent his infantry to charge it. These three blows, delivered with the most perfect precision, so surprised the rebels that their first line broke and fled. There still remained the second line, covered by a belt of jungle, and led by Tántiá in person. Recognising his danger, and anxious to save his second line and guns, Tántiá fired the jungle and retreated. The men with him were the men of the Gwáliár contingent, and these, drilled in olden days by British officers, were true to the teaching they had received. So orderly and well-conducted was their retreat that they succeeded in carrying their guns and some of the fugitives of the first line across the Betwá. But the British cavalry and horse-artillery, splendidly led, were not to be baffled. Dashing at a gallop through the burning jungle, they followed Tántiá for several miles, nor did they cease until they had captured every one of his twenty-eight guns.

The garrison at Jhánsí was proportionately depressed by the failure of Tántiá Topí to relieve them, and Sir Hugh resolved to take advantage of their depression to storm at the earliest possible date. This was the second day after his victory over Tántiá. At three o'clock in the morning of the 3rd of April the stormers marched on the positions assigned to them. The left attack, divided into two columns, the right led by Colonel Lowth, the right by Major Stuart, both of the 86th, and having in its ranks Brockman, Darby, and Jerome of the same regiment, succeeded, after a desperate fight, in storming the wall and seizing the positions assigned to them. The right attack, the left column of which was led by Colonel Liddell, the left by Captain Robinson, both of the 2nd Europeans, had tremendous difficulties to overcome. The rampart they had to escalade was very high, and their scaling ladders were too short. Thanks, however, to the splendid gallantry of three officers of the engineers, Dick, Meiklejohn, and Bonus, and of Fox of the Madras Sappers, they succeeded in gaining a footing there. Just then Brockman, from the left attack, made a timely charge on the flank and rear of the defenders. Their persistence immediately diminished, and the right attack made good its hold. The stormers now marched on the palace, gained it after a stubborn resistance, and drove the rebels helter-skelter from the town. There they were set upon by the 24th Bombay N. I. and dispersed. But desultory fighting continued all night. The Ráni took advantage of the darkness and disorder to ride with a small following for Kalpí, where she arrived safely. Early the next morning Sir Hugh occupied Jhánsí. Its capture had cost him 343 killed and wounded, of whom thirty-six were officers. The rebels' loss he put down roughly at 5,000.

Leaving a small but sufficient garrison in Jhánsí, Sir Hugh marched on the 25th of April for Kalpí, a place whence throughout the Mutiny the rebels had sallied to harass and destroy. On the 5th of May he stormed Kunch, defeating the rebels in its vicinity, but, owing to the heat of the day, he could not prevent their seizing the Kalpí road and marching along it. He sent, however, his cavalry in pursuit, and these, gallantly led by Prettijohn of the 14th Light Dragoons, pursued the enemy for miles. Pushing on, he established himself at Guláulí, near Kalpí, on the 15th.

Sir Hugh had been strengthened, on 5th, by the addition of the 71st Highlanders, and at Guláulí he came in touch with Colonel G. V. Maxwell, commanding a column composed of the 88th, the Camel Corps, and some Sikhs, on the left bank of the Jamnah. The rebels, too, had been considerably strengthened, and their position at Kalpí being very formidable, intersected by labyrinths of ravines, impossible for artillery and cavalry, their confidence had returned. The natural advantages of their position they had improved by throwing up intrenchments at all the salient points.

Sir Hugh spent the five days following his arrival at Guláulí in establishing his batteries, in effecting a junction with Maxwell, and in constant skirmishes with the rebels. On the 21st his batteries opened fire, and on the 22nd he delivered his attack. The battle that ensued was one of the fiercest and most hotly contested of that terrible war. At one phase of it the rebels, strongest on the decisive point, gained an actual advantage. The thin red line began to waver. The rebels, animated by a confidence they had never felt before, pressed on with loud yells, the British falling back towards the field-guns and the mortar battery. Then Brigadier C. S. Stuart, dismounting, placed himself by the guns, and bade the gunners defend them with their lives. Just at the moment, when the British were well-nigh exhausted, 150 men of the Camel Corps came up and turned the tide. At the moment the rebels had advanced within twenty yards of the battery and of the outpost tents, the latter full of men struck down by the sun. Another quarter of an hour and there would have been a massacre. But the timely arrival of the Camel Corps saved the day, converted defeat into victory, and enabled Sir Hugh Rose to close with glory the first part of his dashing Central Indian campaign.

For the defeat he inflicted on the rebels was decisive. They dispersed in all directions, broken and dispirited. In five months Sir Hugh had, under many difficulties, traversed Central India, crossed deep rivers, stormed strong fortresses, defeated the rebels in the field, and re-established British authority in an important region of India. It was impossible to have done this better than Sir Hugh Rose did it. As a campaign his was faultless.

Meanwhile, the column under Whitlock had moved, on the 17th of February, from Jabalpur towards Bundelkhand. The movements of this officer were as slow as those of Sir Hugh had been rapid. On the 19th of April, however, he appeared before Bandah, and defeated the troops which the Nuwáb of that place had collected. From Bandah he intended to march to Kalpí, every step in the road having been cleared for him by Sir Hugh. But on his way thither he received instructions to turn from his course and march against Kírwí, the Ráo of which, an irresponsible minor, a ward of the British, was charged with having rebelled. The little Ráo, who had no idea of rebellion, displayed his confidence in his overlord by riding out to Whitlock's camp to welcome him. Whitlock then occupied Kírwí without the semblance of opposition, and declared all the enormous treasures it contained to be spoils of the victors. In this contention he was supported by the Government of India, and the spoil was subsequently divided. But to the ordinary reader the decision will always remain a puzzle.

Sir Hugh Rose, after his five months' campaign, had the right to hope that he might be allowed some rest, and he had applied for leave on medical certificate, accompanying his application with the formal resignation of his command. But, on the 1st of June, there occurred, close to Gwáliár, an event which upset all his calculations. The news of it reached him on the 4th. It was to the effect that Tántiá Topí and the Rání of Jhánsí, re-collecting their scattered followers, had marched on Morár; that Sindhiá, marching to meet him at the head of 6,000 infantry, 1,500 cavalry, and his own bodyguard, 600 strong, had had the mortification to be deserted by his troops, and had fled, without drawing rein, to Agra. Sir Hugh had previously despatched a party, under Colonel Robertson, on the track of the rebels he had defeated at Kalpí.[1] On the 1st that officer had notified to him that Tántiá and his followers had taken the road to Gwáliár. Sir Hugh had at once sent forward the remainder of Brigadier Stuart's brigade. On the 5th he started himself, with a small force, to overtake Stuart.

Sir Hugh overtook Stuart at Indúrkí on the 12th, and, pushing on, reached Bahádurpur, five miles to the east of Morár, on the 16th. There he was joined by General Robert Napier and by a portion of the Haidarábád contingent. The following morning he attacked and completely defeated the rebels posted at Morár. General Smith's brigade of the Rájpútáná field force, which had been ordered to proceed to Gwáliár, attacked them the following morning on the hilly ground between Kotah-kí-sarai and Gwáliár, and after a severe contest forced them to retreat. In this action the famous Rání of Jhánsí was killed, fighting boldly to the last. The rebels, however, though beaten, were still numerous, and the position taken up by Smith for the night left him exposed to the attack of their united force. Sir Hugh then resolved to finish with them. Accordingly, leaving Napier, with one column, at Morár, Sir Hugh, on the 18th, opened communications with Smith, and cutting off the rebels from Gwáliár, sent, on the 19th, Stuart to attack their left, whilst Raines should amuse them on the right. The action which followed was completely successful. In it Brockman of the 86th again greatly distinguished himself. One consequence of it was the capture of the city of Gwáliár the same evening. The fort still defied the victors; but by an extraordinary act of daring on the part of two British officers, Rose and Waller, with a small following, this apparently impregnable place fell into their hands in the grey dawn of the 20th.

When, on the 19th, Sir Hugh had recognised that his attack on the rebels was succeeding, he had sent a despatch to Napier to pursue and follow them up as far and as closely as was possible. Napier set out at nine o'clock on the morning of the 20th, and the following morning came up with the enemy, about 12,000 strong, posted at the village of Jaurá-Alípur. He at once attacked and defeated them, taking from them twenty-five guns and all their ammunition, tents, carts, and baggage. This victory was, for the time, their death-blow. Apparently it finished the campaign.

His work accomplished by the restoration of Sindhiá, Sir Hugh Rose resigned his command, and proceeded, covered with laurels, to Bombay,

---

[1] During this expedition Major Gall, of the 14th Light Dragoons, an officer whose leading had been conspicuous throughout the campaign, was despatched with Brockman and two companies of the 86th to seize the guns in the palace and fort of Jalaun. This service Major Gall performed with his usual skill and daring.

to assume there the office of Commander-in-Chief of that Presidency. He was replaced in command of the Central India force by Robert Napier. This officer was soon to find that the security which had seemingly followed the victory of Jaurá-Alípur was but temporary.

Tántiá Topí, escaping from that field, had fled in a north-westerly direction. Finding, however, that his escape would be difficult, he had turned and made for Jaipur. There were ranged round the area in which he would be likely to move Napier's force at, and in the vicinity of, Gwáliár itself, a smaller force at Jhánsí, another at Síprí, a fourth at Gunah, a fifth at Nasirábád, and a sixth at Bharatpur. There were other forces round the outer ring of this girdle. It seemed, therefore, that the chances of escape for Tántiá were small indeed.

Yet so extraordinary was the vitality of this remarkable man that for more than nine months he kept all the troops I have mentioned, and many others, in a state of perpetual movement against him. On the 28th of June 1858, he and his small following were baffled by Brigadier Roberts in his attempt to gain Jaipur. Two days later Holmes foiled him in an attempted raid on Tonk; on the 7th of August, Roberts caught and defeated him near Sanganír. This action was a type of all the actions fought by Tántiá. It was his wont to occupy a strong position covered by skirmishers. These skirmishers held the position long enough to ensure the retreat of the main body. On this occasion Tántiá escaped; fought Roberts again, on the 14th, on the Banás, and again escaped. As he fled towards the Chambal the pursuit was taken up by Parkes, who, however, was misled by false information. Tántiá then moved on Jhalrá-Patan, of which he took possession. Levying there a heavy contribution, he made as though he would march on Indur, but finding two British columns at Nalkérah, he moved on Rájgarh. Thence, on the approach of Michel, who had succeeded Roberts, he fled into the jungles, was followed, caught, and defeated by Michel, again fled, and for a moment disappeared from view. Napier, meanwhile, had had troubles of his own to contend with. Mán Singh, Rájá of Narwar, had rebelled against Sindhiá, and Napier had do spatched Smith to coerce him. Smith not being strong enough, Napier had followed, had compelled the evacuation of Narwar, and had despatched Robertson in pursuit of the rebels. Robertson had caught and defeated a division of them, commanded by Ajít Singh, on the Parbatí river (September 4), and had then returned to Gunah. Some of the fugitives succeeded in joining Tántiá.

That chief, after a rest of eight days at Sironj, to which place he had made his way through the jungles, had marched against Iságarh, taken thence the supplies he wanted, and had attempted the strong place of Chandérí. The Maráthá chief who held the fortress for Sindhiá was deaf alike to his promises and his threats, so Tántiá made for Migráulí. There he was encountered by Michel, completely defeated, and lost his guns. Then he fled to join Ráo Sáhib, nephew of Náná Sáhib, at Lalitpur. The two chiefs met only to separate. Then Ráo Sáhib was caught and beaten by Michel. The two chiefs met once again and resolved to cross the Narbadá. They conducted this operation with great skill, and though Tántiá's right wing was annihilated by Michel at Kurai, he escaped across the river, and caused an alarm which spread even to Bombay. There, pursued by a column under Sutherland, he crossed and recrossed the river, and was caught and attacked at Kargun, only to escape with the loss of the guns, with which he had been mysteriously re-supplied. He then took the bold step of marching on Barodah, arrived within fifty miles of it, when finding the pursuit too hot, he turned, recrossed the Narbadá, and reached Chota Udaipur. There Parkes caught him and beat him. Tántiá then fled to the Banswárá jungles. There his position was desperate, for the cordon around him was complete. But, bold as he was able, he broke out to march on Udaipur. Finding Rocke with a force in the way, he returned to the jungles; suddenly emerging thence, he baffled Rocke, and took his way toward Mandesar. Caught at Zírápur, he fled to Baród; was pursued thither by Somerset there and beaten; then, when his fortunes were desperate, was met by the rebel chief Mán Singh, and another famous rebel, Prince Firsúzháh, recently completely defeated by Napier Ranod.

Mán Singh did not stay with Tántiá, and the case of the latter, completely surrounded, again seemed hopeless. Attempting to creep out in a north-westerly direction, he was surprised by Showers at Dewásá, and again (January 21) by Holmes at Sikar. The surprise was so complete that the rebel force broke up, and Tántiá, 'tired of running away,' took refuge with Mán Singh in the Parón jungles. There an attempt was made by the British authorities to persuade Mán Singh to make his submission. Mán Singh not only submitted, but was induced by hopes of personal advantage to betray the hiding-place of his old comrade. At midnight, on the 7th of April, Tántiá was surprised there as he slept, taken into Síprí, brought to a court-martial, charged with having waged war against the British Government, condemned, and sentenced to be hanged. The sentence was carried out on the 18th of April.

Tántiá Topí was a marvellous guerilla warrior. In pursuit of him,

Brigadier Parke had marched, consecutively, 240 miles in nine days; Brigadier Somerset, 230 in nine days, and, again, seventy miles in forty-eight hours; Colonel Holmes, through a sandy desert, fifty-four miles in little over twenty-four hours; Brigadier Honner, 145 miles in four days. Yet, he slipped through them all—through enemies watching every issue of the jungles in which he lay concealed, only to fall at last through the treachery of a trusted friend. His capture, and the surrender of Mán Singh, finished the war in Central India. Thenceforth his name only survived.

CHAPTER XXVII

The Last Embers of the Revolt

In Haidarábád, throughout the Mutiny, the loyalty of the Nizam and of his able minister, Salar Jung, had been the surest guarantees of peace. In the early days of July 1857, the turbulence of the foreign troops in the service of the Nizam had caused an attack upon the Residency. But the able representative of British authority in that territory, Major Cuthbert Davidson, warned by Salar Jung, had time to make preparations which terminated not only in the discomfiture of the rebels, but in the capture and punishment of the leaders. Of the necessity of disarming one of the cavalry regiments at Aurangábád I have spoken in its place. But the aberration of the mutineers was but temporary. The men returned to their duty, and rendered, with their comrades in the contingent of the three arms, excellent service to the State. A little later, the Rájá of Shorápur, a Hindu tributary of the Nizam, broke out into treacherous revolt. But Major Davidson, acting in concert with Lord Elphinstone, called up from the Southern Maráthá country the column serving under Colonel Malcolm, whilst the Governor of Madras, Lord Harris, despatched to the spot a force under Major Hughes. The troops of the Haidarábád contingent, under Captain Wyndham, proceeded likewise to aid in the coercion of the deluded prince. The latter, after a vain attempt to lure Wyndham to his destruction, surrendered himself as a prisoner. There can be little doubt but that his mind was affected, for he committed suicide when it was announced to him that, after four years of detention, he would be allowed to resume his position.[1]

Meanwhile, Sir Hope Grant, under orders from Sir Colin Campbell, had proceeded in carrying out his plan for the pacification of Oudh. I last quitted him near Lakhnao, on the 16th of May. From that date to the end of August he continued his operations, beating the rebels in every encounter, and finally halting at Súltánpur. There he thought it wise to

---

[1] Of this episode Colonel Meadows Taylor has written a most interesting account: *Story of My Life*.

suspend operations till the close of the rainy season. He resumed them in the middle of October.

Meanwhile, there had been some fighting in Rohilkhand. At Philibhít it became known that the rebels were concentrated in force at Nuriah. Thence they were dislodged by a force commanded by Captain Sam Browne, under circumstances of great gallantry, which gained for that officer the coveted cross. In the turbulent district of Ázamgarh, too, the rebels had again raised their heads. They were, however, cleared from the district by a force under Brigadier Berkeley, who, pushing his success, recovered Eastern Oudh as far as Súltánpur, where he touched Hope Grant's force. Rowcroft, meanwhile, with his own troops and the sailors of the *Pearl* brigade, had defeated the rebels at Amorhá and Harhá; Eveleigh had punished them between Husénganj and Mohan; Dawson had captured Sandélá. The British forces rested during two months of the rainy season, but that period was employed by sending Sikhs in steamers up the Ganges to clear the banks of that river.

In October operations were resumed. The rebels began by attacking Sandélá. They were held in check by Dawson until, first, Major Maynard, then Brigadier Barker, arrived and inflicted upon them a crushing defeat. In the same month Eveleigh defeated them at Miánganj, and Seaton near Sháhjahánpur, whilst the Rájá of Powain repulsed an attack made upon his fortified town. Sir Colin Campbell, now become Lord Clyde, then resolved to clear the entire province of rebels by acting by columns in all its districts simultaneously. Whilst one column, drawn from Rohilkhand, should clear the north-west of Oudh, and, sweeping all before it, should establish itself at Sítápur, four columns should clear the Baiswárá country, another column should guard the Duáb, another the Kánhpur road, whilst smaller columns, radiating from Lakhnao, Nuwábganj, Daryábád, and Faizábád should clear the districts around them.

This plan was acted upon with complete success. On the 3rd of November, Wetherall, marching to join Hope Grant, stormed Rámpur Kasiá. Hope Grant, joining him there, moved against Améthí on one side, whilst Lord Clyde attacked it on another. The place surrendered on the 8th. The strong fort of Shankarpur was evacuated by Béní Mádhu, a noted rebel, on the night of the 10th, and occupied the next day. Eveleigh, following Béní Mádhu, caught him two days later at Dundiá Khérá, and defeated him, taking three of his guns. On the 24th that rebel was again encountered, this time by Lord Clyde, and completely defeated. In the meanwhile the strong places in Eastern Oudh had fallen in succession, and by the end of November that part of the province was completely subdued. Nor had the columns sweeping the north-western districts been less successful.

Troup had cleared the ground as far as Sítápur; Gordon, Carmichael, and Horsford had done the same in the districts south of the Gogra, whilst Hope Grant, catching the rebels beaten by Rowcroft at Tulsipur, had swept them into Nipál. Then Lord Clyde, moving on Sikrórá, and in touch with Grant on the one side and Rowcroft covering Gorákhpur on the other, drove the Begum and Náná Sáhib before him from Bondí and Báhráitch, cleared the country between Nanpárá and the Gogra, then marching on Bánkí, close to the Nipál frontier, surprised and defeated the rebels, and swept the survivors into Nipál. Jang Bahádur, loyal to the core, informed the rebels who crossed that they must not look to him for protection. He even permitted British troops to come over and disarm any considerable body of rebels who might have sought refuge there.

Lord Clyde, rightly regarding the pacification of Oudh as completed, quitted the province, leaving it to Hope Grant to carry out such operations as might be necessary. What little remained to be done was then done thoroughly. Whilst Colonel Walker crushed, at Bangáon, the more hardened rebels, the survivors of the regiments which had perpetrated the Kánhpur massacre, Grant himself pursued the terrified remnant across the hills into Nipál. Dislodgment alone was necessary, for they had neither arms, nor money, nor food. Contenting himself with locating troops to prevent their return, Grant reported (May 1859) that Oudh was at last at peace. Thanks to the generous policy pursued by Lord Canning, in confiscating that he might restore with a clear title, Oudh has ever since remained a bulwark of British supremacy.

The pacification of Oudh was the closing act of the drama the curtain of which had been raised in 1857. In the interval Sir John Lawrence had, with characteristic energy, put down an attempted rising in the Gughaira district, turbulent even in the time of Akbar; his brother, George Lawrence, had dispersed the few malcontents in Rájpútáná; the rebels had been crushed, though after a tedious and desultory warfare, in the Chutiá Nágpur districts; whilst Western Bihar had, as related, been pacified by the dispersion of the last adherents of the family of Kunwar Singh. When Sir Hope Grant finally cleared Oudh of the last remnants of the rebels,[2] in May 1859, then, and then only, could it be said that the Mutiny had been absolutely stamped out.

---

[2] It is believed that amongst these was Náná Sáhib. It was always a matter of regret that this man's fate was never certainly known. Many reports regarding him were circulated afterwards: that he had died in Nipál; later, that he had been seen in Gwáliár. But the uncertainty regarding his fate has remained to this day.

CHAPTER XXVIII

Conclusion

On the 27th of January 1858, the King of Dehli had been brought to trial in the Privy Council chamber of his palace, charged with making war against the British Government, with abetting rebellion, with proclaiming himself as reigning sovereign of India, with causing, or being accessory to, the deaths of forty-nine people of British blood or British descent; and with having subsequently abetted others in murdering Europeans and others. After a patient trial, extending over forty days, the King was declared to be guilty of the main points of the charges, and sentenced to be transported for life. Ultimately, he was sent to Pegu, where he ended his days in peace.

Meanwhile, in England, it had been found necessary, as usual, to find a scapegoat for the disasters which had fallen upon India. With a singular agreement of opinion the scapegoat was declared to be the Company which had won for England that splendid appanage. In consequence it was decreed to transfer the administration of India from the Company to the Crown. An Act carrying out this transfer was signed by the Queen on the 2nd of August 1858.

Her Majesty thought it right, as soon as possible after the transfer had been thus effected, to issue to her Indian subjects a proclamation declaratory of the principles under which she intended thenceforth to administer their country. To the native princes of India she announced then, in that proclamation, that all treaties in force with them would be accepted and scrupulously maintained; that she would respect their rights, their dignity, and their honour as her own; that she would sanction no encroachments on the rights of any one of them; that the same obligations of duty which bound her to her other subjects would bind her also to them. To the natives of India generally Her Majesty promised not only complete toleration in matters of religion, but admission to office, without question of religion, to all such persons as might be qualified for the same by their education, ability, and integrity. The Queen declared, further, that she would direct that, in administering the law, due attention should be paid to the ancient rights, usages, and customs of India; that clemency should be extended to all offenders (in the matter of the Mutiny) save to those who had been or should be convicted of having taken part in the murder of British subjects; that full consideration should be given to men who had thrown off their allegiance, or who had been moved to action by a too credulous acceptance of the false reports circulated by designing men; that to all others who would submit before the 1st of January 1859 unconditional pardon should be granted.

This proclamation virtually conceded the right the denial of which had so greatly unsettled the minds of native princes, the right of adoption. It was hailed everywhere as a binding charter. In the large centres of India natives of every religion and creed, Hindus, Muhammadans, and Parsís, met in numbers to draw up loyal addresses expressive of their deep sense of the beneficent feelings which had prompted the proclamation, of their gratitude for its contents, and of their loyalty to the person of the illustrious lady to whose direct rule they had been transferred.

Published on the 1st of November 1858, this proclamation immediately followed the complete collapse of the Mutiny. Practically, there remained only the capture of Tántiá Topí and the expulsion of the remnant of the rebels from Oudh. How these ends were accomplished I have told in the two chapters immediately preceding. In both these cases the conclusion was foregone. It was but a question of a brief time. The rebels in Central India and in Oudh, as well as those few still remaining in Western Bihár and in Chutiá Nagpur, represented the dying embers of a fire which had been extinguished. It now remains for me to sum up in a few words the moral of the Mutiny, the lessons which it taught us, and its warnings.

But before I proceed to this summing up, I am anxious to say a word or two to disabuse the minds of those who may have been influenced by rumours current at the period as to the nature of the retaliation dealt out to the rebels by the British soldiers in the hour of their triumph. I have examined all those rumours—I have searched out the details attending the storming of Dehli, of Lakhnao, and of Jhánsí—and I can emphatically declare that, not only was the retaliation not excessive, it did not exceed the bounds necessary to ensure the safety of the conquerors. Unfortunately war is war. It is the meeting in contact of two bodies of men exasperated against each other, alike convinced that victory can only be gained by the destruction of the opponent. Under such circumstances it is impossible to give quarter. The granting of quarter would mean, as was proved over and over and over again, the placing in the hands of an enemy the power to take life treacherously. It was well understood, then, by both sides at the storming of the cities I have mentioned, that no quarter would be granted. It was a necessity of war. But beyond the deaths he inflicted in fair fight, the British soldier perpetrated no unnecessary slaughter. He merited to the full the character given to his predecessor in the Peninsular War by Sir William Napier. He proved by his conduct that, 'whilst no physical military qualification was wanting, the fount of honour was still full and fresh within him.'

'It has been said that, in certain cases, a new kind of death was invented for convicted rebels, and that the punishment of blowing away from guns was intended to deprive the victim of those rites, the want of which doomed him, according to his view, to eternal perdition. Again, I assert that there is absolutely no foundation for this statement. The punishment itself was no new one in India. It was authorised by courts-martial, the members of which were native officers. Its infliction did not necessarily deprive the victim of all hope of happiness in a future life. The fact, moreover, that the Government of India, jealously careful never to interfere with the religious beliefs of the natives, sanctioned it, is quite sufficient to dispel the notion I have mentioned. The blowing away of criminals from guns was a punishment which was resorted to only when it was necessary to strike a terror which should act as a deterrent. It was in this sense that Colonel Sherer had recourse to it at Jalpaigúrí; and it is indisputable, that he thus saved thousands of lives, and, possibly, staved off a great catastrophe.

Whilst on the question of punishments, I am desirous to disprove an assertion so often repeated that it has been accepted as true—that the term 'Clemency Canning' was invented in Calcutta by the men who opposed the policy of the Government of India. The term 'Clemency Canning' had its origin in a phrase, 'the Clemency of Canning,' applied by the *Times* newspaper of October 17, 1857, to a circular issued by the Government of India, dated the 31st July of that year, and intended to restrain, prematurely, as the *Times* considered, the hands of its officers. The phrase was not intended to denounce clemency in the abstract, but the offer of clemency to men who believed they were triumphing, who had still possession of the North-west Provinces, and of Oudh. In that sense, and in no other, was it applied. The argument of those who, alike in India and in England, denounced the circular may be expressed in these words: 'Put down the Mutiny first, that you may exercise clemency afterwards.'

I proceed now to deal with the two questions I have indicated in a preceding page—The lessons which the Mutiny has taught us, and its warnings.

The gradual conquest of India by a company of merchants inhabiting a small island in the Atlantic has ever been regarded as one of the most marvellous achievements of which history makes mention. The dream of Dupleix was realised by the very islanders who prevented its fulfilment by his countrymen. But great, marvellous even, as was that achievement, it sinks into insignificance when compared with the reconquest, with small means, of that magnificent empire in 1857–58. In 1857, the English garrison in India was surprised. There were not a dozen men in the country who, on the 1st of May of that year, believed that a catastrophe was impending which would shake British rule to its foundations. The explosion which took place at Mírath ten days later was followed, within five weeks, by similar explosions all over the North-west Provinces and in Oudh, not only on the part of the sipáhís, but likewise on the part of the people. The rebel sipáhís were strong in the possession of many fortified places, of a numerous artillery, of several arsenals and magazines. In trained soldiers they preponderated over the island garrison in the proportion of at least five to one. They inaugurated their revolt by successes which appealed to the imagination of an impulsive people. At Dehlí, at Kánhpur, at Jhánsí, in many parts of Oudh, and in the districts around Agra, they proved to them the possibility of expelling the foreign master. Then, too, the majority of the population in those districts, landowners and cultivators alike, displayed a marked sympathy with the revolted sipáhís. For the English, in those first five weeks, the situation was bristling with danger. A false move might have temporarily lost India. In a strictly military sense they were too few in numbers, and too scattered, to attempt an offensive defence. It is to their glory that, disregarding the strictly scientific view, they did attempt it. The men who administered British India recognised at a glance that a merely passive defence would ruin them. They displayed, then, the truest forecast when they insisted that the resources still available in the North-west and in the Panjáb should be employed in an offensive movement against Dehlí. That offensive movement saved them. Though Dehlí offered a resistance spreading over four months, yet the penning within her walls of the main army of the rebels gave to the surprised English the time necessary to improvise resources, to receive reinforcements, to straighten matters in other portions of the empire.

The secret of the success of the British in the stupendous conflict which was ushered in by the Mutiny at Mírath and the surprise of Dehlí, lay in the fact that they never, even in the darkest hour, despaired. When the news of the massacre of Kánhpur reached Calcutta, early in July, and the chattering Bengális, who would have fainted at the sight of a sword drawn in anger, were discussing which man amongst them was the fittest to be

Chancellor of the Exchequer under the King of Dehlí,[1] there was not an Englishman in that city who did not feel the most absolute confidence that the cruel deed would be avenged. There was not one cry of despair—not one voice to declare that the star of Great Britain was about to set. In the deepest distress there was confidence that the sons of Britain would triumph. The same spirit was apparent in every corner of India where dwelt an English man or an English woman. It lived in the camp before Dehlí, it was strong in the Residency of Lakhnao, it prevailed in every isolated station where the few Europeans were in hourly dangers of attack from rebels who gave no quarter. Nowhere did one of them shrink from the seemingly unequal struggle. As occasion demanded, they held out, they persevered, they pressed forward, and, with enormous odds against them, they wore down their enemies, and they won. The spirit which had sustained Great Britain in her long contest against Napoleon was a living force in India in 1857–58, and produced similiar results.

How did they accomplish the impossible? The answer must spring at once to the lips of those who have witnessed the action of our country-men in every part of the world. The energy and resolution which gave the Britain which Cæsar had conquered to the Anglian race; which almost immediately brought that Britain to a preponderant position in Europe; which, on the discovery of a new world, sent forth its sons to conquer and to colonise; which, in the course of a brief time, gained North America, the islands of the Pacific, and Australasia; which, entering only as third on the field, expelled its European rivals from India; that energy and that res-olution, far from giving evidence of deterioration in 1857, never appeared more conspicuously. It was a question of race. This race of ours has been gifted by Providence with the qualities of manliness, of endurance, of a resolution which never flags. It has been its destiny to conquer and to maintain. It never willingly lets go. Its presence in England is a justifi-cation of its action all over the world. Wherever it has conquered, it has planted principles of order, of justice, of good government. And the Prov-idence which inspired the race to plant these great principles, endowed it with the qualities necessary to maintain them wherever they had been planted. Those principles stood them in good stead in 1857. It was the sense of the justice of England which, in the most terrible crisis of her history in India, brought her the support of the Sikhs, conquered but eight years before; of the princes and people of Rájpútána, rescued from oppression but twenty-nine years before; of that Sindhiá, whose great

---

[1] I can personally testify to this fact.

ancestor was England's deadliest enemy; of the Nizam, our ally since the time of Clive; of Maisur, restored by Marquess Wellesley to its ancient ruler; of Nipál, our nearest independent neighbour. But for the consequences of that sense of the justice of England, we might have been temporarily over-whelmed. Supported by it, the race did the rest. It showed itself equal to difficulties which, I believe, no other created race would have successfully encountered.

So much for the moral of the story. Mistakes doubtless were made, especially in certain details at the outset of the rebellion. Some injustices were committed, mainly by the men who made the mistakes. But, taking it as a whole, there is no epoch in the history of Great Britain in which the men and women of these islands shone with greater lustre than throughout this period of 1857–59. From the moment he quitted the pernicious air of Calcutta Lord Canning stood in the van, the far-seeing, courageous, resolute Englishman. Lords Elphinstone and Harris, at Bombay and Madras, were in all respects worthy of their chief. The three Lawrences in the Panjáb, at Lakhnao, and in Rájpútána, upheld the glory of that sister island irrevocably united to Great Britain. Scotland con-tributed Sir Colin Campbell, Sir Robert Napier, Adrian Hope, Lums-den, killed at the Sikándarabágh, Charles MacGregor, and hosts of kindred warriors. Frere in Sind, William Tayler at Patná, Wynyard at Gorákhpur, Spankie and Dunlop in the Mírath districts, showed what great things Englishmen, untrained to arms, left to their own resources, could accomplish. Their action prevailed all over India. There was scarcely one exception to it. To name every man and his achievements would require a volume exceeding in bulk the present record.

So much, I repeat, for the moral of the Mutiny. One word now regarding its lessons and its warnings. The determining cause of the Mutiny of 1857 was the attempt to force Western ideas upon an Eastern people. This was especially the case in the North-western Provinces, where the introduction of the Thomasonian system unsettled the minds of noble and peasant. It was the case in Oudh, where the same system suddenly superseded the congenial rule of the ex-King. Nowhere else in India was the rebellion more rampant and more persistent than in those provinces. Three hundred years previously the great Akbar had attempted to interfere with the village system, but, after a short experience, he had recoiled. He recognised in good time that custom is nowhere so strong as in India, and that interference with that system would uproot customs as dear as their lives to the children of the soil. The English, rushing in where Akbar had feared to tread, met their reward in a general uprising. It is scarcely too much to assert that in the provinces I have mentioned the hand of almost every man was against us.

More than thirty years have elapsed since the Mutiny was crushed, and again we witness a persistent attempt to force Western ideas upon an Eastern people. The demands made by the new-fangled congresses for the introduction into India of representative institutions is a demand coming from the noisy and unwarlike races which hope to profit by the general corruption which such a system would engender. To the manly races of India, to the forty millions of Muhammadans, to the Sikhs of the Panjáb, to the war-like tribes on the frontier, to the Rohílás of Rohilkhand, to the Rájputs and Játs of Rájpútáná and Central India, such a system is utterly abhorrent. It is advocated by the adventurers and crochet-mongers of the two peoples. Started by the noisy Bengális, a race which, under Muhammadan rule, was content to crouch and serve, it is encouraged by a class in this country, ignorant for the most part of the real people of India, whilst professing to be in their absolute confidence. The agitation would be worthy of contempt but for the element of danger which it contains. I would impress upon the rulers of India the necessity, whilst there is yet time, of profiting by the experience of the Mutiny. I would implore them to decline to yield to an agitation which is not countenanced by the real people of India. I entreat them to realise that the Western system of representation is hateful to the Eastern races which inhabit the continent of India; that it is foreign to their traditions, their habits, their modes of thought. The people of India are content with the system which Akbar founded, and on the principles of which the English have hitherto mainly governed. Our Western institutions, not an absolute success in Europe, are based upon principles with which they have no sympathy. The millions of Hindustan desire a master who will carry out the principles of the Queen's proclamation of 1858. Sovereigns and nobles, merchants and traders, landlords and tenants prefer the tried, even-handed justice of their European overlord to a justice which would be the outcome of popular elections. India is inhabited not by one race alone, but by many races. Those races are subdivided into many castes, completely separated from each other in the inner social life. If the higher castes are the more influential, the lower are the more numerous. The attempt to give representation to mere numbers would then, before long, provoke religious jealousies and antipathies which would inevitably find a solution in blood. A rising caused by such an innovation on prevailing customs would be infinitely more dangerous than the Mutiny of 1857. Concession to noisy agitation on the part of the ruling power would place the lives, the fortunes, the interests of the loyal classes of India at the mercy of the noisiest, most corrupt and most despised race in India. Against such concession—the inevitable forerunner of another rising—and equally against fussy interference with the Hindu marriagelaw—I, intimately associated on the most friendly terms, for thirty-five years, with the manlier races of India, make here, on their behalf, my earnest protest.